Company's Coming

Ground Beef Recipes

S0-AQL-450

Jean Paré

ORIGINAL SERIES

Ground Beef
Recipes

Jean Paré

www.companyscoming.com
visit our website

Divider Photo

1. Caribbean Beef Salad, page 120
2. Chili Gumbo, page 75
3. Spinach-Stuffed Meatloaf, page 98

Props courtesy of:
Danesco Inc.
Pier 1 Imports

We gratefully acknowledge the following suppliers for their generous support of our Test and Photography Kitchens:

Broil King Barbecues
Corelle®
Hamilton Beach® Canada
Lagostina®
Proctor Silex® Canada
Tupperware®

Cooking tonight?

A selection of
feature recipes
is only a
click away—
absolutely *FREE!*

Visit us at
www.companyscoming.com

Table of Contents

Appetizers

Burgers

Casseroles

Chilies &
Sauces

Meatballs

Foreword 6

Ground Beef Hints & Tips 8

Ground Beef Safety 9

Testing for Doneness 9

Appetizers 10

Burgers & Patties 20

Casseroles & One-Dish Meals 34

Chilies & Sauces 66

Meatballs 79

Meatloaves 93

Sandwiches

Soups
&Salads

Stovetop

Sandwiches, Wraps & More 102

Soups & Salads 118

Stovetop Dishes. 134

Measurement Tables 150

Recipe Index 151

Recipe Notes 159

Foreword

If we peek into the freezer of a typical family home, we're sure to find a pound of ground. Whether it's hamburgers or meat sauce, shepherd's pie or cabbage rolls, we just can't get enough. We even sing about it—surely that poor meatball in "On Top of Spaghetti" deserves a better end!

Convenient, economical and versatile, ground beef is a menu mainstay. Think back to Mom's special Monday-night meatloaf or Uncle Harry's famous, eye-watering chili. And a young person moving away from home will often stuff at least one good skillet-supper recipe inside that box of hand-me-down dishes.

Ground Beef Recipes celebrates the versatility of this popular ingredient, and offers fresh ideas to tempt your friends and family. From Cheeseburger Pie and Salsa Porcupines to Roquefort Beef Tarts and Blue Moon Dumplings, the recipes include kid-pleasers as well as elegant company fare. And with dishes such as Sloppy Joe Tacos and Tandoori Chili, there's a range of tastes from the familiar to the exotic.

Fans of slow cookers will find two delicious ideas on these pages. On busy days, our Bolognese Sauce and Porcupine Stew will make coming home a pleasure when these inviting meals are waiting.

Many of the recipes featured here can be frozen. Make a double batch of our Tasty Meatballs, freeze the extras on a cookie sheet until firm, and pop them into a resealable freezer bag. Do this with our patties too! And remember that you can scramble-fry large quantities of ground beef and freeze in amounts suitable for recipes.

Any of the oven-cooked casseroles, chilies, meat sauces, meatloaves and dairy-free soups can also be frozen. Wrap each item securely or place in airtight containers. Use freezer-to-oven dishes to get supper on the table in no time.

Our tips for proper handling, storage and cooking of ground beef will help you take advantage of this delicious meal option. Explore the new kitchen-tested flavours we developed for *Ground Beef Recipes* and discover your favourites!

Jean Paré

Nutrition Information Guidelines

Each recipe is analyzed using the most current version of the Canadian Nutrient File from Health Canada, which is based on the United States Department of Agriculture (USDA) Nutrient Database.

- If more than one ingredient is listed (such as "hard margarine or butter"), or if a range is given (1 – 2 tsp., 5 – 10 mL), only the first ingredient or first amount is analyzed.
- For meat, poultry and fish, the serving size per person is based on the recommended 4 oz. (113 g) uncooked weight (without bone), whichis 2 – 3 oz. (57 – 85 g) cooked weight (without bone)— approximately the size of a deck of playing cards.
- Milk used is 1% M.F. (milk fat), unless otherwise stated.
- Cooking oil used is canola oil, unless otherwise stated.
- Ingredients indicating "sprinkle," "optional," or "for garnish" are not included in the nutrition information.

Margaret Ng, B.Sc. (Hon.), M.A.
Registered Dietitian

Ground Beef Hints & Tips

Labelling

Canadian government standards regulate the labelling of ground beef, which is packaged according to fat content:

Extra-Lean:	no more than 10% fat
Lean:	no more than 17% fat
Medium:	no more than 23% fat
Regular:	no more than 30% fat

American regulatory standards require a lean/fat description on the label. The leanest choice is 95% lean/5% fat.

A Healthy, Economical Choice

Our test kitchen used lean and extra-lean ground beef for *Ground Beef Recipes*. But if there's a sale on regular or medium ground, don't limit your options! You can cut the fat content by draining cooked ground beef.

Those with specific dietary needs can further reduce total fat by placing drained, scramble-fried ground beef in a colander and rinsing with hot water.

Depending on your personal tastes and grocery budget, you may prefer to use regular or medium ground beef for some recipes, and lean or extra-lean for others. Generally, all types of ground beef can be used interchangeably; however, for best results:

• Use lean and extra-lean ground beef for fillings and meatloaves, where drippings are difficult to drain.

• Regular and medium ground beef can be used for burgers and meatballs, where fat will drip away during cooking, or for scramble-frying to use in chilies, soups and sauces, where fat is drained before adding other ingredients.

Cooking Tips

No matter which type of ground beef you use, the following tips will ensure that your dishes always taste their best:

• Gently mix ground beef with other ingredients until combined. Overmixing results in dense, heavy burgers and meatloaves.

• Shape patties and meatballs in uniform sizes for even cooking.

• To prevent the loss of juices that keep patties moist, turn them over only once, halfway through cooking time, and avoid pressing them with a spatula.

Cooking Methods for Patties

Recipes in this book use a variety of cooking methods for ground beef patties. These methods are interchangeable. If you have a favourite way to cook your patties, use it! Just follow the cooking times in the recipe, and remember to test for doneness, as indicated on page 9.

• To use a gas barbecue, preheat to medium. Place patties on greased grill.

• To use an electric grill, preheat for 5 minutes. Place patties on greased grill.

• To broil, place patties on a greased broiler pan on centre rack in oven.

• To pan-fry, heat 2 tsp. (10 mL) cooking oil in a large frying pan on medium.

Ground Beef Safety

Because the surface area of ground beef is greater than that of whole cuts, ground beef is more susceptible to harmful bacteria when handled or exposed to work surfaces. From the moment you place ground beef in your shopping cart, follow these food safety rules:

- Separate ground beef from fresh produce in your shopping cart and grocery bags, and keep it cool when transporting it home. Refrigerate or freeze ground beef within two hours of purchase.

- Store fresh (not previously frozen) uncooked ground beef in the refrigerator at 40°F (4°C) for up to 24 hours or in the freezer at 0°F (-18°C) for up to three months from the "packaged on" date.

- Ground beef labelled "previously frozen" should not be refrozen. Store in the refrigerator and use within 24 hours of purchase, or cook completely before refreezing. Fully cooked ground beef may be stored in the refrigerator for up to two days or in the freezer for at least three months.

- Always thaw frozen ground beef on a plate in the refrigerator, and never at room temperature. The plate will prevent drippings from contaminating fresh produce and other foods. Ground beef may be thawed in the microwave when it is cooked immediately afterward, or cooked from frozen when scramble-frying.

Testing for Doneness

- Ground beef is fully cooked when it reaches 160°F (71°C). Even when a patty, meatball or meatloaf is no longer pink inside, it may not be completely cooked. Test and be sure with a good-quality, digital meat thermometer that provides an exact temperature reading, and not just a doneness range. (The no-longer-pink indicator works for scramble-frying because all surfaces of the ground beef are cooked.)

- Remove meatloaves, meatballs and patties from heat before testing. Insert the thermometer into a loaf's centre layer of beef, or into the centre of the thickest part of the patty or meatball. Do not insert into stuffings or fillings. Check more than one item for doneness as hot and cold spots in your oven or barbecue may cause food to cook unevenly.

Glorious Ground Beef

Ground beef provides 12 essential nutrients, including zinc, niacin and B vitamins, and is an excellent source of protein.

Pastry Pinwheels

Mildly spiced, rich pastry swirls around beef and bubbling cheese. Sharp cheese is used for best flavour.

All-purpose flour	1 1/2 cups	375 mL
Paprika	1/2 tsp.	2 mL
Cayenne pepper	1/4 tsp.	1 mL
Salt	1/4 tsp.	1 mL
Cold hard margarine (or butter), cut up	1/2 cup	125 mL
Ice water	3 tbsp.	50 mL
Large egg	1	1
Fine dry bread crumbs	2 tbsp.	30 mL
Dried basil	1/4 tsp.	1 mL
Dried oregano	1/8 tsp.	0.5 mL
Dried thyme	1/8 tsp.	0.5 mL
Extra-lean ground beef	1/2 lb.	225 g
Grated sharp Cheddar cheese	1/2 cup	125 mL

Combine first 4 ingredients in medium bowl. Cut in margarine until mixture resembles coarse crumbs. Slowly add water, stirring with fork until mixture starts to come together. Do not overmix. Turn out pastry onto work surface. Shape into slightly flattened disc. Wrap with plastic wrap. Chill for 30 minutes.

Combine next 5 ingredients in large bowl.

Add ground beef and cheese. Mix well. Roll out pastry between 2 sheets of waxed paper to 8 x 16 inch (20 x 40 cm) rectangle (see Note). Discard top sheet of waxed paper. Press beef mixture evenly on top of pastry, leaving 1/2 inch (12 mm) edge on both long sides. Roll up tightly from 1 long side, jelly-roll style, using waxed paper as guide. Press seam against roll to seal. Cut into 1/2 inch (12 mm) slices. Arrange, cut-side up, about 1 inch (2.5 cm) apart on parchment paper-lined baking sheet. Bake in 400°F (205°C) oven for about 20 minutes until pastry is golden, and internal temperature of beef reaches 160°F (71°C). Makes 32 pinwheels.

1 pinwheel: 78 Calories; 4.9 g Total Fat (2.7 g Mono, 0.4 g Poly, 1.5 g Sat); 13 mg Cholesterol; 5 g Carbohydrate; trace Fibre; 3 g Protein; 75 mg Sodium

Pictured on page 17.

Note: To keep the bottom sheet of waxed paper from moving while rolling out the pastry, dampen the work surface underneath.

Cheeseburger Puffs

Kids and adults alike will love these bite-size, cheesy puffs.
Serve with barbecue or honey mustard sauce for dipping.

Cooking oil	1 tsp.	5 mL
Lean ground beef	1/2 lb.	225 g
All-purpose flour	1/2 cup	125 mL
Garlic powder	1/4 tsp.	1 mL
Onion powder	1/4 tsp.	1 mL
Salt	1/8 tsp.	0.5 mL
Water	1/2 cup	125 mL
Hard margarine (or butter), cut up	1/4 cup	60 mL
Large eggs	2	2
Grated medium Cheddar cheese	1/2 cup	125 mL
Finely chopped green onion	2 tbsp.	30 mL
Pepper	1/4 tsp.	1 mL

Heat cooking oil in medium frying pan on medium. Add ground beef. Scramble-fry for about 10 minutes until no longer pink. Drain. Set aside.

Combine next 4 ingredients in small cup.

Heat and stir water and margarine in heavy medium saucepan on high until boiling and margarine is melted. Reduce heat to medium. Add flour mixture all at once. Stir vigorously for about 1 minute until mixture pulls away from side of saucepan to form soft dough. Remove from heat. Let stand for 5 minutes.

Add eggs 1 at a time to dough, beating after each addition until well combined. Dough will be thick and glossy.

Add beef and remaining 3 ingredients. Mix well. Drop, using about 1 tbsp. (15 mL) for each, about 2 inches (5 cm) apart onto greased baking sheets. Bake in 425°F (220°C) oven for 15 to 17 minutes until golden. Let stand on baking sheets for 5 minutes before removing to wire racks to cool. Makes about 36 puffs.

1 puff: 41 Calories; 2.9 g Total Fat (1.5 g Mono, 0.3 g Poly, 0.9 g Sat); 17 mg Cholesterol; 2 g Carbohydrate; 0 g Fibre; 2 g Protein; 41 mg Sodium

Roquefort Beef Tarts

Tender pastry holds a mellow blue cheese and beef filling—perfect with a glass of red wine.

Cooking oil	1 tsp.	5 mL
Lean ground beef	1/2 lb.	225 g
Crumbled Roquefort cheese	3/4 cup	175 mL
Finely chopped green onion	2/3 cup	150 mL
Large eggs	3	3
Milk	1/3 cup	75 mL
Sour cream	1/3 cup	75 mL
Salt	1/8 tsp.	0.5 mL
Pepper	1/8 tsp.	0.5 mL
Frozen mini tart shells, thawed	36	36

Heat cooking oil in medium frying pan on medium. Add ground beef. Scramble-fry for about 10 minutes until no longer pink. Remove from heat. Drain.

Add cheese and onion. Stir. Set aside.

Beat next 5 ingredients with whisk in medium bowl until well combined.

Arrange tart shells on 2 ungreased baking sheets. Spoon beef mixture into shells. Pour egg mixture over top until full. Bake on separate racks in 375°F (190°C) oven for about 25 minutes, switching position of baking sheets at halftime, until pastry is golden and egg mixture is set. Makes 36 tarts.

1 tart: 81 Calories; 5.4 g Total Fat (2.3 g Mono, 0.6 g Poly, 2.2 g Sat); 25 mg Cholesterol; 5 g Carbohydrate; 0 g Fibre; 3 g Protein; 136 mg Sodium

Pictured on page 17.

Appetizers

Nachos With Avocado Salsa

Great nibblies for a party or for a halftime snack during the big game.
Add a bowl of sour cream to the tray before serving.

AVOCADO SALSA		
Large tomatoes, seeds removed, finely chopped	2	2
Ripe medium avocado, finely chopped	1	1
Finely chopped red onion	1/4 cup	60 mL
Lemon juice	1 tbsp.	15 mL
Garlic clove, minced (or 1/4 tsp., 1 mL, powder)	1	1
Salt	1/4 tsp.	1 mL
Cooking oil	1 tsp.	5 mL
Lean ground beef	1 lb.	454 g
Can of red kidney beans, rinsed and drained	19 oz.	540 mL
Medium salsa	1 1/2 cups	375 mL
Chopped red pepper	1 cup	250 mL
Bag of tortilla chips	11 1/4 oz.	320 g
Grated medium Cheddar cheese	1 1/2 cups	375 mL

Avocado Salsa: Combine first 6 ingredients in medium bowl. Makes about 2 cups (500 mL) salsa.

Heat cooking oil in large frying pan on medium. Add ground beef. Scramble-fry for about 10 minutes until no longer pink. Drain.

Add next 3 ingredients. Stir. Cook for about 10 minutes, stirring often, until red pepper is tender-crisp.

Arrange tortilla chips close together on ungreased baking sheet. Scatter beef mixture over top. Sprinkle with cheese. Broil on centre rack in oven for about 2 minutes until cheese is melted. Serve with Avocado Salsa. Serves 10 to 12.

1 serving: 392 Calories; 22 g Total Fat (10.5 g Mono, 2.2 g Poly, 7.4 g Sat); 42 mg Cholesterol; 33 g Carbohydrate; 6 g Fibre; 18 g Protein; 529 mg Sodium

Beefy Potato Cups

A bit fussy to make, but a delight for meat-and-potato lovers.
These may be prepared in the morning and chilled.
Pop them in the oven just before guests arrive.

Baby potatoes	12	12
Water		
Ice water		
Bacon slice, diced	1	1
Lean ground beef	1/4 lb.	113 g
Finely chopped onion	1/3 cup	75 mL
Grated medium Cheddar cheese	1/4 cup	60 mL
Sour cream	2 tbsp.	30 mL
Mayonnaise	1 tbsp.	15 mL
Steak sauce	1 tbsp.	15 mL
Chopped fresh chives (or 3/4 tsp., 4 mL, dried)	1 tbsp.	15 mL
Pepper, just a pinch		
Grated medium Cheddar cheese	1/3 cup	75 mL
Chopped fresh chives, for garnish		

Cook potatoes in water in large saucepan until tender-crisp. Drain. Immediately plunge into large bowl of ice water. Let stand for about 5 minutes until cold. Drain. Cut each potato in half lengthwise. Trim thin slice from bottom of each half. Using small spoon, scoop out potato flesh from halves, leaving 1/4 inch (6 mm) thick shells. Finely chop potato flesh. Reserve 1/2 cup (125 mL). Keep any remaining potato flesh for another use.

Cook bacon in small frying pan on medium until almost crisp.

Add ground beef and onion. Scramble-fry for about 10 minutes until beef is no longer pink. Drain.

Add reserved potato flesh and next 6 ingredients. Stir. Arrange potato shells on greased baking sheet. Fill with beef mixture.

(continued on next page)

Appetizers

Sprinkle with second amount of cheese. Bake in 350°F (175°C) oven for about 10 minutes until beef mixture is heated through and cheese is melted. Remove to large serving platter.

Garnish with chives. Makes 24 potato cups.

1 potato cup: 42 Calories; 2.2 g Total Fat (0.8 g Mono, 0.2 g Poly, 1 g Sat); 6 mg Cholesterol; 4 g Carbohydrate; trace Fibre; 2 g Protein; 39 mg Sodium

Pictured on page 17.

Artichoke Beef Dip

Ooey, gooey, cheesy dip for crackers, bread or veggie sticks.

Cooking oil	1 tsp.	5 mL
Lean ground beef	1/2 lb.	225 g
Garlic clove, minced (or 1/4 tsp., 1 mL, powder)	1	1
Chili powder	1/2 tsp.	2 mL
Ground coriander	1/4 tsp.	1 mL
Can of artichoke hearts, drained and chopped	14 oz.	398 mL
Mayonnaise	1 cup	250 mL
Sour cream	1 cup	250 mL
Grated Monterey Jack With Jalapeño cheese	1/2 cup	125 mL
Grated Parmesan cheese	1/2 cup	125 mL
Thinly sliced green onion	1 tbsp.	15 mL

Heat cooking oil in medium frying pan on medium. Add next 4 ingredients. Scramble-fry for about 10 minutes until ground beef is no longer pink. Drain. Transfer to large bowl.

Add next 5 ingredients. Stir. Spread evenly in greased 1 quart (1 L) casserole. Bake, uncovered, in 350°F (175°C) oven for about 30 minutes until heated through.

Sprinkle with onion. Makes about 4 cups (1 L).

1/4 cup (60 mL): 190 Calories; 17.5 g Total Fat (8.4 g Mono, 4.2 g Poly, 4.3 g Sat); 28 mg Cholesterol; 3 g Carbohydrate; 1 g Fibre; 6 g Protein; 216 mg Sodium

Homemade Snack Sausage

A firm, lean roll that will remind you of summer sausage.
Great garlic flavour. Serve with cheese and crackers.

Water	2 tbsp.	30 mL
Curing salt (not coarse salt)	2 tbsp.	30 mL
Liquid smoke	2 tsp.	10 mL
Onion powder	1 tsp.	5 mL
Dry mustard	1/2 tsp.	2 mL
Garlic powder	1/2 tsp.	2 mL
Pepper	1/2 tsp.	2 mL
Lean ground beef	1 lb.	454 g
Lean ground pork	1 lb.	454 g

Combine first 7 ingredients in large bowl.

Add ground beef and pork. Mix well. Divide into 2 equal portions. Roll each portion into 2 inch (5 cm) diameter log. Wrap each log tightly with heavy-duty foil. Chill for 24 hours. Using fork, poke holes in foil on top and bottom of logs. Set on broiler pan or on wire rack set on baking sheet with sides. Bake in 300°F (150°C) oven for 2 hours. Let stand in foil until cooled. Chill. Each roll cuts into 32 slices, for a total of 64 slices.

1 slice: 26 Calories; 1.6 g Total Fat (0.7 g Mono, 0.1 g Poly, 0.6 g Sat); 8 mg Cholesterol; 0 g Carbohydrate; 0 g Fibre; 3 g Protein; 227 mg Sodium

Pictured on page 17.

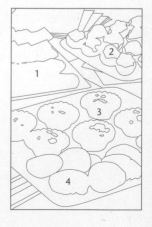

1. Homemade Snack Sausage, above
2. Beefy Potato Cups, page 14
3. Roquefort Beef Tarts, page 12
4. Pastry Pinwheels, page 10

Props courtesy of: Danesco Inc.

Blue Moon Dumplings

You'll want to serve these crispy, deep-fried dumplings more than once in a blue moon! Blue cheese and basil add delicious flavour to the beef filling.

Large egg	1	1
Crumbled blue cheese	1/3 cup	75 mL
Chopped fresh basil (or 3/4 tsp., 4 mL, dried)	1 tbsp.	15 mL
Pepper	1/4 tsp.	1 mL
Extra-lean ground beef	1/2 lb.	225 g
Round dumpling wrappers	30	30
Large egg, fork-beaten	1	1
Cooking oil, for deep-frying		

Combine first 4 ingredients in medium bowl.

Add ground beef. Mix well.

Spoon about 2 tsp. (10 mL) beef mixture onto centre of 1 wrapper. Brush 1/2 of edge with second egg. Fold wrapper over beef mixture. Pinch edges to seal. Place on waxed paper-lined baking sheet. Cover with damp tea towel to prevent drying. Repeat to make 30 dumplings.

Deep-fry dumplings in small batches in hot (375°F, 190°C) cooking oil for about 2 minutes until wrapper is golden, and internal temperature of beef reaches 160°F (71°C). Remove to paper towels to drain. Makes 30 dumplings.

1 dumpling: 68 Calories; 4 g Total Fat (2 g Mono, 0.8 g Poly, 0.9 g Sat); 27 mg Cholesterol; 5 g Carbohydrate; trace Fibre; 3 g Protein; 76 mg Sodium

1. Giant Biscuit Burger, page 24
2. Presto Pesto Burgers, page 21
3. Teriyaki Burgers, page 22

Props courtesy of: Pfaltzgraff Canada
Tupperware®
Wiltshire®

Gouda Burgers

Horseradish adds delicious flavour to these cheesy burgers.

Large egg	1	1
White (or brown) bread slice, processed into crumbs	1	1
Finely chopped onion	1/2 cup	125 mL
Prepared horseradish	1 tbsp.	15 mL
Worcestershire sauce	1 tbsp.	15 mL
Salt	1/4 tsp.	1 mL
Pepper	1/8 tsp.	0.5 mL
Lean ground beef	1 lb.	454 g
Smoked Gouda cheese slices	4	4
HORSERADISH MAYONNAISE		
Mayonnaise	1/4 cup	60 mL
Dijon mustard (with whole seeds) or prepared mustard	1 tbsp.	15 mL
Chopped fresh chives (or 3/4 tsp., 4 mL, dried)	1 tbsp.	15 mL
Prepared horseradish	1 tbsp.	15 mL
Multi-grain rolls, split and toasted	4	4
Honey ham slices, halved	2	2
Tomato slices	8	8

Combine first 7 ingredients in large bowl.

Add ground beef. Mix well. Divide into 4 equal portions. Shape into patties to fit rolls. Place on greased broiler pan or on greased wire rack set on greased baking sheet with sides. (For other cooking methods, see page 8.) Broil on centre rack in oven for 5 to 7 minutes per side until fully cooked, and internal temperature of beef reaches 160°F (71°C).

Top patties with cheese slices. Broil for another 3 to 4 minutes until cheese is melted.

Horseradish Mayonnaise: Combine first 4 ingredients in small bowl. Makes about 6 tbsp. (100 mL).

Spread each roll with Horseradish Mayonnaise. Serve patties, topped with ham and tomato slices, in rolls. Makes 4 burgers.

1 burger: 592 Calories; 35.6 g Total Fat (15.6 g Mono, 5.5 g Poly, 11.9 g Sat); 164 mg Cholesterol; 29 g Carbohydrate; 3 g Fibre; 39 g Protein; 1151 mg Sodium

Presto Pesto Burgers

Work magic in the kitchen with these tantalizing burgers.
The aroma of basil and garlic makes them especially appealing.

Large egg	1	1
White (or brown) bread slice, processed into crumbs	1	1
Finely chopped onion	1/2 cup	125 mL
Grated Parmesan cheese	1/4 cup	60 mL
Basil pesto	2 tbsp.	30 mL
Garlic clove, minced (or 1/4 tsp., 1 mL, powder)	1	1
Lean ground beef	1 lb.	454 g
BASIL MAYONNAISE		
Mayonnaise	1/4 cup	60 mL
Basil pesto	2 tbsp.	30 mL
Onion (or hamburger) buns, split and toasted	4	4
Roasted red peppers, drained, blotted dry, cut into strips	1 1/4 cups	300 mL
Shaved Parmesan cheese	1/2 cup	125 mL
Chopped fresh basil (optional)	2 tbsp.	30 mL

Combine first 6 ingredients in large bowl.

Add ground beef. Mix well. Divide into 4 equal portions. Shape into 5 inch (12.5 cm) diameter patties. Preheat gas barbecue to medium. (For other cooking methods, see page 8.) Cook patties on greased grill for 5 to 7 minutes per side until fully cooked, and internal temperature of beef reaches 160°F (71°C). Transfer to large plate. Cover to keep warm.

Basil Mayonnaise: Combine mayonnaise and pesto in small bowl. Makes about 6 tbsp. (100 mL).

Spread each bun with Basil Mayonnaise. Serve patties, topped with remaining 4 ingredients, in buns. Makes 4 burgers.

1 burger: 593 Calories; 35.9 g Total Fat (16.9 g Mono, 6.5 g Poly, 10 g Sat); 135 mg Cholesterol; 31 g Carbohydrate; 2 g Fibre; 35 g Protein; 796 mg Sodium

Pictured on page 18.

Teriyaki Burgers

Classic

The grilled pineapple slices made this recipe an instant hit when it first appeared in The Beef Book.

Reserved pineapple juice	1/4 cup	60 mL
Steak sauce	3 tbsp.	50 mL
Soy sauce	2 tbsp.	30 mL
Finely grated, peeled gingerroot	1 1/2 tsp.	7 mL
(or 1/4 tsp., 1 mL, ground ginger)		
Sesame seeds, toasted (see Tip,	1 1/2 tsp.	7 mL
page 129)		
Lean ground beef	1 lb.	454 g
Chopped fresh bean sprouts	1 cup	250 mL
Green onions, thinly sliced	2	2
Canned pineapple slices, drained and	4	4
juice reserved		
Hamburger buns, split	4	4

Combine first 5 ingredients in small bowl. Measure 1/4 cup (60 mL) into medium bowl. Set aside remaining pineapple juice mixture as basting sauce.

Add next 3 ingredients to pineapple juice mixture in medium bowl. Mix well. Divide into 4 equal portions. Shape into 1/2 inch (12 mm) thick patties. Preheat gas barbecue to medium. (For other cooking methods, see page 8.) Cook patties on greased grill for 5 to 7 minutes per side, brushing with basting sauce, until fully cooked, and internal temperature of beef reaches 160°F (71°C). Transfer to large plate. Cover to keep warm.

Blot pineapple slices with paper towels. Cook on greased grill for 2 to 3 minutes per side until heated through.

Serve patties, topped with pineapple slices, in buns. Makes 4 burgers.

1 burger: 361 Calories; 12.8 g Total Fat (5.6 g Mono, 1.1 g Poly, 4.4 g Sat); 57 mg Cholesterol; 35 g Carbohydrate; 2 g Fibre; 26 g Protein; 987 mg Sodium

Pictured on page 18.

Green Chili Burgers

Lime and Chinese five-spice powder give these burgers a subtle Asian flavour.
Top with hoisin or plum sauce and garnish with fresh bean sprouts or suey choy.

Large egg	1	1
Fine dry bread crumbs	1/2 cup	125 mL
Can of diced green chilies	4 oz.	113 g
Sour cream	2 tbsp.	30 mL
Grated lime zest	1 tsp.	5 mL
Lime juice	1 tsp.	5 mL
Chinese five-spice powder	1/2 tsp.	2 mL
Salt	1/2 tsp.	2 mL
Garlic powder	1/4 tsp.	1 mL
Lean ground beef	1 lb.	454 g
Sesame hamburger buns, split	6	6

Combine first 9 ingredients in large bowl.

Add ground beef. Mix well. Divide into 6 equal portions. Shape into 4 inch (10 cm) diameter patties. Preheat gas barbecue to medium. (For other cooking methods, see page 8.) Cook patties on greased grill for 5 to 7 minutes per side until fully cooked, and internal temperature of beef reaches 160°F (71°C).

Serve patties in buns. Makes 6 burgers.

1 burger: 302 Calories; 10.7 g Total Fat (4.6 g Mono, 0.9 g Poly, 3.9 g Sat); 76 mg Cholesterol; 30 g Carbohydrate; 2 g Fibre; 20 g Protein; 573 mg Sodium

Paré Pointer
Vampires are such a pain in the neck.

Giant Biscuit Burger

This plate-sized novelty burger will impress the kids. A hearty sandwich for the guys on game night, too. You can use the dough to make smaller biscuits to serve with meatloaf or meatballs.

GIANT BISCUIT

All-purpose flour	2 cups	500 mL
Baking powder	4 tsp.	20 mL
Granulated sugar	2 tsp.	10 mL
Salt	1/2 tsp.	2 mL
Milk	3/4 cup	175 mL
Cooking oil	1/4 cup	60 mL
Fine dry bread crumbs	1/2 cup	125 mL
Italian dressing	1/3 cup	75 mL
Seasoned salt	1 tsp.	5 mL
Parsley flakes	1 tsp.	5 mL
Lean ground beef	1 lb.	454 g
Mayonnaise	1/4 cup	60 mL
Sweet pickle relish	1/4 cup	60 mL
Large tomato slices	6 – 8	6 – 8
Thinly sliced onion	1/4 cup	60 mL
Grated medium Cheddar cheese	1/2 cup	125 mL
Green leaf lettuce leaves	3	3

Giant Biscuit: Combine first 4 ingredients in large bowl. Make a well in centre.

Add milk and cooking oil to well. Stir until just moistened. Turn out dough onto lightly floured surface. Knead 8 to 10 times. Roll or pat out to 8 inch (20 cm) diameter circle. Place on greased baking sheet. Bake in 425°F (220°C) oven for about 15 minutes until golden. Cool. Makes 1 biscuit.

Combine next 4 ingredients in medium bowl.

Add ground beef. Mix well. Roll into ball. Place on ungreased 12 inch (30 cm) pizza pan or on baking sheet with sides. Pat out to 9 inch (22 cm) diameter patty. Bake for about 15 minutes until fully cooked, and internal temperature of beef reaches 160°F (71°C). Transfer to large plate. Cover to keep warm.

(continued on next page)

Burgers & Patties

Cut biscuit in half horizontally. Spread mayonnaise on top half. Spread relish on bottom half.

Layer tomato slices, onion and cheese, in order given, on top of relish. Carefully slide patty onto cheese. Top with lettuce. Cover with top half of biscuit. Cuts into 8 wedges.

1 wedge: 499 Calories; 29 g Total Fat (14.7 g Mono, 7.2 g Poly, 5.4 g Sat); 48 mg Cholesterol; 42 g Carbohydrate; 3 g Fibre; 18 g Protein; 908 mg Sodium

Pictured on page 18.

Borscht Burgers

Baba would be proud! Tasty patties with a Ukrainian influence.
Excellent topped with Horseradish Mayonnaise, page 20.

Large egg	1	1
Milk (or water)	2/3 cup	150 mL
Crushed buttery crackers	1/2 cup	125 mL
Finely chopped onion	1/2 cup	125 mL
Potato flakes	1/3 cup	75 mL
Grated fresh beets	1/3 cup	75 mL
Dill weed	1/2 tsp.	2 mL
Salt	1 tsp.	5 mL
Pepper	1/4 tsp.	1 mL
Lean ground beef	1 lb.	454 g
Cooking oil	2 tsp.	10 mL
Hamburger buns, split	6	6

Combine first 9 ingredients in large bowl.

Add ground beef. Mix well. Divide into 6 equal portions. Shape into 4 inch (10 cm) diameter patties.

Heat cooking oil in large frying pan on medium. (For other cooking methods, see page 8.) Add patties. Cook for 5 to 7 minutes per side until fully cooked, and internal temperature of beef reaches 160°F (71°C).

Serve patties in buns. Makes 6 burgers.

1 burger: 333 Calories; 13.3 g Total Fat (6 g Mono, 1.9 g Poly, 4 g Sat); 75 mg Cholesterol; 32 g Carbohydrate; 2 g Fibre; 20 g Protein; 773 mg Sodium

Jalapeño Popper Burgers

Cheese-filled, breaded and deep-fried jalapeño peppers are known as "poppers."
Now you can enjoy spicy popper flavour in a burger stuffing!

Crushed seasoned croutons	1/2 cup	125 mL
Block of cream cheese, softened	4 oz.	125 g
Sliced pickled jalapeño peppers, chopped	2 – 3 tsp.	10 – 15 mL
Ground cumin	1/4 tsp.	1 mL
Garlic powder	1/4 tsp.	1 mL
Seasoned croutons	1/4 cup	60 mL
Crushed seasoned croutons	1/3 cup	75 mL
Finely chopped onion	1/4 cup	60 mL
Worcestershire sauce	1 tsp.	5 mL
Chili powder	1/4 tsp.	1 mL
Lean ground beef	1 lb.	454 g
Salsa	1/4 cup	60 mL
Pickled jalapeño pepper slices	12 – 16	12 – 16
Hamburger buns, split	4	4

Put first amount of crushed croutons into small shallow dish.

Beat next 4 ingredients in small bowl. Add whole croutons. Stir. Divide into 4 equal portions. Shape into 3 to 4 inch (7.5 to 10 cm) diameter patties. Press both sides of each cheese patty into crushed croutons until coated. Set aside.

Combine next 4 ingredients in large bowl.

Add ground beef. Mix well. Divide into 8 equal portions. Shape into 5 inch (12.5 cm) diameter patties. Place each cheese patty between 2 beef patties. Pinch edges to seal. Arrange on greased broiler pan or on greased baking sheet with sides. (For other cooking methods, see page 8.) Broil on centre rack in oven for 5 to 7 minutes per side until fully cooked, and internal temperature of beef reaches 160°F (71°C).

Serve patties, topped with salsa and jalapeño pepper slices, in buns. Makes 4 burgers.

1 burger: 544 Calories; 27.8 g Total Fat (11 g Mono, 1.9 g Poly, 12.5 g Sat); 92 mg Cholesterol; 43 g Carbohydrate; 3 g Fibre; 30 g Protein; 804 mg Sodium

Chipotle Jerk Burgers

Don't be intimidated by the long list of ingredients—they all work together to create the delicious "jerk" flavour of these smoky burgers.

Thinly sliced green onion	1/2 cup	125 mL
Fine dry bread crumbs	1/3 cup	75 mL
Chipotle chili pepper in adobo sauce, chopped (see Tip, page 74)	1	1
Frozen concentrated orange juice, thawed	2 tbsp.	30 mL
Soy sauce	2 tbsp.	30 mL
Finely grated, peeled gingerroot (or 3/4 tsp., 4 mL, ground ginger)	1 tbsp.	15 mL
Brown sugar, packed	1 tbsp.	15 mL
Garlic clove, minced (or 1/4 tsp., 1 mL, powder	1	1
Dried crushed chilies	1/2 tsp.	2 mL
Dried thyme	1/2 tsp.	2 mL
Ground allspice	1/2 tsp.	2 mL
Ground cinnamon	1/4 tsp.	1 mL
Ground cloves	1/4 tsp.	1 mL
Salt	1/4 tsp.	1 mL
Lean ground beef	1 lb.	454 g
ORANGE MAYONNAISE		
Mayonnaise	1/2 cup	125 mL
Frozen concentrated orange juice, thawed	1 1/2 tbsp.	25 mL
Hamburger buns, split	4	4

Combine first 14 ingredients in large bowl.

Add ground beef. Mix well. Divide into 4 equal portions. Shape into 4 inch (10 cm) diameter patties. Preheat gas barbecue to medium. (For other cooking methods, see page 8.) Cook patties on greased grill for 5 to 7 minutes per side until fully cooked, and internal temperature of beef reaches 160°F (71°C).

Orange Mayonnaise: Combine mayonnaise and concentrated orange juice in small bowl. Makes about 1/2 cup (125 mL).

Spread each bun with Orange Mayonnaise. Serve patties in buns. Makes 4 burgers.

1 burger: 601 Calories; 36 g Total Fat (18.5 g Mono, 8.7 g Poly, 6.7 g Sat); 74 mg Cholesterol; 41 g Carbohydrate; 2 g Fibre; 27 g Protein; 1210 mg Sodium

Mango Pepper Patties

A colourful and delicious way to dress up ground beef patties.
Be sure to select red peppers that are large enough to make nice rings.

MANGO SALSA		
Large red peppers, halved crosswise	2	2
Diced ripe mango	1 cup	250 mL
Thinly sliced green onion	1/4 cup	60 mL
Apple cider vinegar	1 tbsp.	15 mL
Granulated sugar	1 tbsp.	15 mL
Cooking oil	2 tsp.	10 mL
Salt	1/8 tsp.	0.5 mL
Pepper, just a pinch		
Large egg	1	1
Graham cracker crumbs	1/2 cup	125 mL
Finely chopped onion	1/2 cup	125 mL
Chili paste (sambal oelek)	1 tbsp.	15 mL
Salt	1/4 tsp.	1 mL
Lean ground beef	1 lb.	454 g

Mango Salsa: Cut one 1 1/2 inch (3.8 cm) ring from each red pepper half, for a total of 4 rings. Set aside. Finely chop remaining red pepper. Put into medium bowl.

Add next 7 ingredients. Stir. Makes about 2 1/4 cups (550 mL) salsa.

Combine next 5 ingredients in large bowl.

Add ground beef. Mix well. Divide into 4 equal portions. Put 1 portion inside each red pepper ring. Flatten into patties to fill rings. Preheat gas barbecue to medium. (For other cooking methods, see page 8.) Cook patties on greased grill for about 10 minutes per side until fully cooked, and internal temperature of beef reaches 160°F (71°C). Serve with Mango Salsa. Serves 4.

1 serving: 338 Calories; 14.8 g Total Fat (6.7 g Mono, 1.5 g Poly, 4.7 g Sat); 111 mg Cholesterol; 28 g Carbohydrate; 3 g Fibre; 24 g Protein; 372 mg Sodium

Pictured on page 36.

Burgers & Patties

Mushroom Burgers

Mmm, mushrooms! These tasty, moist burgers
are loaded with them, inside and out.

Large egg	1	1
Chopped fresh white mushrooms	1/2 cup	125 mL
Fine dry bread crumbs	1/2 cup	125 mL
Grated part-skim mozzarella cheese	1/4 cup	60 mL
Tomato sauce	1/4 cup	60 mL
Dried oregano	1 tsp.	5 mL
Lean ground beef	1 lb.	454 g
Cooking oil	1 tsp.	5 mL
Sliced fresh white mushrooms	1 1/2 cups	375 mL
Lemon juice	2 tsp.	10 mL
Salt	1/4 tsp.	1 mL
Pepper	1/4 tsp.	1 mL
Hamburger buns, split	4	4

Combine first 6 ingredients in large bowl.

Add ground beef. Mix well. Divide into 4 equal portions. Shape into 4 to 5 inch (10 to 12.5 cm) diameter patties. Preheat gas barbecue to medium. (For other cooking methods, see page 8.) Cook patties on greased grill for 5 to 7 minutes per side until fully cooked, and internal temperature of beef reaches 160°F (71°C). Transfer to large plate. Cover to keep warm.

Heat cooking oil in medium frying pan on medium-high. Add second amount of mushrooms. Heat and stir for about 2 minutes until mushrooms start to brown. Reduce heat to medium.

Add next 3 ingredients. Cook for about 5 minutes, stirring often, until mushrooms are browned and liquid is evaporated.

Serve patties, topped with mushrooms, in buns. Makes 4 burgers.

1 burger: 428 Calories; 17.7 g Total Fat (7.8 g Mono, 2 g Poly, 5.9 g Sat); 115 mg Cholesterol; 36 g Carbohydrate; 3 g Fibre; 30 g Protein; 722 mg Sodium

Grilled Tournedos

A patty that's puttin' on the ritz! Wrapped with bacon, capped with mushrooms and served on toast rounds, it's ready for a special occasion.

Texas bread slices	8	8
Large egg, fork-beaten	1	1
Steak sauce	2 tbsp.	30 mL
Dijon mustard (with whole seeds)	2 tbsp.	30 mL
Salt	1/8 tsp.	0.5 mL
Pepper	1/8 tsp.	0.5 mL
Lean ground beef	1 lb.	454 g
Precooked bacon slices	8	8
Hard margarine (or butter)	1 tbsp.	15 mL
Large fresh whole white mushrooms, stems removed	8	8
Dry sherry	2 tbsp.	30 mL
Balsamic vinegar	1 tsp.	5 mL
Hard margarine (or butter), softened	3 tbsp.	50 mL
Chopped fresh parsley (or 1/2 tsp., 2 mL, flakes)	2 tsp.	10 mL
Chopped fresh thyme leaves (or 1/4 tsp., 1 mL, dried)	1 tsp.	5 mL
Pepper, sprinkle		

Using 3 inch (7.5 cm) round cookie cutter, cut out circle from centre of each bread slice. Set bread rounds aside. Process remaining bread into crumbs in blender or food processor. Measure 1/2 cup (125 mL) crumbs into large bowl (see Note).

Add next 5 ingredients. Stir.

Add ground beef. Mix well. Divide into 8 equal portions. Shape into 1 1/4 inch (3 cm) thick patties.

Wrap 1 bacon slice around side of each patty. Secure with wooden picks. Preheat gas barbecue to medium. (For other cooking methods, see page 8.) Cook patties on greased grill for 8 to 10 minutes per side until fully cooked, and internal temperature of beef reaches 160°F (71°C). Transfer to large plate. Cover to keep warm.

(continued on next page)

Burgers & Patties

Melt first amount of margarine in medium frying pan on medium. Add mushrooms. Cook for about 5 minutes, stirring often, until softened.

Add sherry and vinegar. Heat and stir until liquid is evaporated. Remove from heat.

Combine remaining 4 ingredients in small bowl. Spread 1 side of each bread round with margarine mixture. Cook on greased grill, margarine-side down, for about 2 minutes until golden. Turn bread over. Toast opposite side. Serve tournedos, topped with mushrooms, on toast rounds. Serves 4.

1 serving: 665 Calories; 33.2 g Total Fat (17 g Mono, 3.6 g Poly, 9.7 g Sat); 122 mg Cholesterol; 54 g Carbohydrate; 3 g Fibre; 35 g Protein; 1242 mg Sodium

Pictured on page 36.

Note: Freeze the remaining crumbs in an airtight container to use in meatloaf or meatball recipes.

Hickory Patties

Not all patties need to be tucked into a bun! These have a delightfully smoky flavour, making them an excellent choice to serve with potato or macaroni salad, roasted potatoes or baked beans.

Large egg	1	1
Fine dry bread crumbs	1/2 cup	125 mL
Chopped onion	1/4 cup	60 mL
Hickory barbecue sauce	1/4 cup	60 mL
Beef bouillon powder	1 tsp.	5 mL
Pepper	1/8 tsp.	0.5 mL
Lean ground beef	1 lb.	454 g
Cooking oil	2 tsp.	10 mL

Combine first 6 ingredients in medium bowl.

Add ground beef. Mix well. Divide into 4 equal portions. Shape into 4 inch (10 cm) diameter patties.

Heat cooking oil in large frying pan on medium. (For other cooking methods, see page 8.) Add patties. Cook for 5 to 7 minutes per side until fully cooked, and internal temperature of beef reaches 160°F (71°C). Makes 4 patties.

1 patty: 359 Calories; 21.8 g Total Fat (9.7 g Mono, 1.9 g Poly, 7.6 g Sat); 118 mg Cholesterol; 14 g Carbohydrate; 2 g Fibre; 25 g Protein; 498 mg Sodium

Pineapple Salsa Patties

Refreshing fruit salsa is a tasty side for these
sesame-studded patties with a terrific teriyaki taste!

PINEAPPLE GINGER SALSA

Pineapple tidbits, drained	1 cup	250 mL
Diced tomato	1/4 cup	60 mL
Sliced green onion	1/4 cup	60 mL
Chopped fresh cilantro or parsley	1 tbsp.	15 mL
Finely chopped pickled ginger slices, drained	1 tbsp.	15 mL
Apple cider vinegar	1 tbsp.	15 mL
Lime juice	1 tbsp.	15 mL
Brown sugar, packed	2 tsp.	10 mL
Grated lime zest	1 tsp.	5 mL
Ground cumin	1/2 tsp.	2 mL
Dried crushed chilies	1/2 tsp.	2 mL
Large egg	1	1
Crushed sesame rice crackers	1 cup	250 mL
Sliced green onion	3 tbsp.	50 mL
Thick teriyaki basting sauce	2 tbsp.	30 mL
Finely chopped pickled ginger slices, drained	1 tbsp.	15 mL
Garlic clove, minced (or 1/4 tsp., 1 mL, powder)	1	1
Lean ground beef	1 lb.	454 g

Pineapple Ginger Salsa: Combine first 11 ingredients in medium bowl. Cover. Chill for at least 1 hour to blend flavours. Makes about 2 cups (500 mL) salsa.

Combine next 6 ingredients in large bowl.

Add ground beef. Mix well. Divide into 4 equal portions. Shape into 1/2 inch (12 mm) thick oval patties. Preheat gas barbecue to medium. (For other cooking methods, see page 8.) Cook patties on greased grill for about 8 minutes per side until fully cooked, and internal temperature of beef reaches 160°F (71°C). Serve with Pineapple Ginger Salsa. Serves 4.

1 serving: 414 Calories; 23.5 g Total Fat (7.9 g Mono, 3.4 g Poly, 9.6 g Sat); 111 mg Cholesterol; 24 g Carbohydrate; 1 g Fibre; 29 g Protein; 682 mg Sodium

Hot Shot Burgers

*Spiced just right! Complement these juicy burgers with
a dollop of guacamole, or add your favourite condiments.*

Large egg	1	1
White (or brown) bread slice, processed into crumbs	1	1
Finely chopped onion	1/4 cup	60 mL
Chili powder	2 tbsp.	30 mL
White vinegar	1 1/2 tbsp.	25 mL
Worcestershire sauce	1 tsp/	5 mL
Ground oregano	1/2 – 1 tsp.	2 – 5 mL
Salt	1/2 tsp.	2 mL
Pepper	1/2 tsp.	2 mL
Garlic powder	1/4 tsp.	1 mL
Lean ground beef	1 lb.	454 g
Cooking oil	2 tsp.	10 mL
Hamburger buns, split	4	4

Combine first 10 ingredients in medium bowl.

Add ground beef. Mix well. Divide into 4 equal portions. Shape into 4 inch (10 cm) diameter patties.

Heat cooking oil in large frying pan on medium. (For other cooking methods, see page 8.) Add patties. Cook for 5 to 7 minutes per side until fully cooked, and internal temperature of beef reaches 160°F (71°C).

Serve patties in buns. Makes 4 burgers.

1 burger: 372 Calories; 16.4 g Total Fat (7.3 g Mono, 1.7 g Poly, 5 g Sat); 111 mg Cholesterol; 29 g Carbohydrate; 2 g Fibre; 27 g Protein; 699 mg Sodium

Beef And Vegetable Pie

Rich pastry encloses a filling of creamy beef and vegetables.

Cooking oil	2 tsp.	10 mL
Lean ground beef	1 lb.	454 g
Frozen mixed vegetables	2 cups	500 mL
Can of condensed cream of mushroom soup	10 oz.	284 mL
Beef bouillon powder	1 tsp.	5 mL
Onion powder	1/2 tsp.	2 mL
Pepper	1/4 tsp.	1 mL
Pastry for 2 crust 9 inch (22 cm) pie, your own or a mix		

Heat cooking oil in large frying pan on medium. Add ground beef. Scramble-fry for about 10 minutes until no longer pink. Drain. Transfer to medium bowl. Cool. Add next 5 ingredients. Stir.

Divide pastry into 2 portions, making 1 portion slightly larger than the other. Shape each portion into slightly flattened disc. Roll out larger portion on lightly floured surface to about 1/8 inch (3 mm) thickness. Line 9 inch (22 cm) pie plate. Spoon beef mixture into shell. Roll out smaller portion on lightly floured surface to about 1/8 inch (3 mm) thickness. Dampen edge of shell with water. Cover beef mixture with pastry. Trim and crimp decorative edge to seal. Cut 2 or 3 small vents in top to allow steam to escape. Bake on bottom rack in 400°F (205°C) oven for 15 minutes. Reduce heat to 350°F (175°C). Bake for another 35 to 40 minutes until golden. Let stand on wire rack for 10 minutes before serving. Cuts into 6 wedges.

1 wedge: 436 Calories; 25.6 g Total Fat (11 g Mono, 4.2 g Poly, 8.1 g Sat); 40 mg Cholesterol; 33 g Carbohydrate; 2 g Fibre; 18 g Protein; 830 mg Sodium

Pictured on page 35.

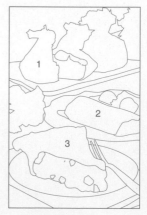

1. Surf 'N' Turf Bundles, page 44
2. Beef And Cheese Rolls, page 42
3. Beef And Vegetable Pie, above

Props courtesy of: Casa Bugatti
Cherison Enterprises Inc.
The Bay

Lazy Cabbage Roll Casserole

All the flavour, without the fuss! This recipe, from
One-Dish Meals, *is perfect for busy cooks who want a taste of tradition.*

Bacon slices, diced	4	4
Lean ground beef	1 1/2 lbs.	680 g
Chopped onion	1 cup	250 mL
Tomato juice	1 1/4 cups	300 mL
Can of condensed tomato soup	10 oz.	284 mL
Salt	1/2 tsp.	2 mL
Pepper	1/4 tsp.	1 mL
Coarsely shredded cabbage, lightly packed	8 cups	2 L
Long grain white rice	1/3 cup	75 mL

Cook bacon in large frying pan on medium until crisp. Transfer with slotted spoon to paper towels to drain. Set aside.

Heat 2 tsp. (10 mL) drippings in same pan on medium. Add ground beef and onion. Scramble-fry for about 10 minutes until beef is no longer pink. Drain. Add next 4 ingredients. Stir. Remove from heat.

Spread cabbage evenly in ungreased 9 x 13 inch (22 x 33 cm) pan. Press down lightly. Sprinkle rice over cabbage. Scatter bacon over rice. Spread beef mixture on top. Cover with foil. Bake in 350°F (175°C) oven for about 1 1/2 hours until rice is tender and liquid is absorbed. Serves 6.

1 serving: 316 Calories; 13 g Total Fat (5.5 g Mono, 1.2 g Poly, 4.8 g Sat); 60 mg Cholesterol; 25 g Carbohydrate; 3 g Fibre; 25 g Protein; 885 mg Sodium

1. Grilled Tournedos, page 30
2. Tuscan Stuffed Tomatoes, page 56
3. Mango Pepper Patties, page 28

Props courtesy of: Danesco Inc.

Creamy Zucchini Wedges

An omelet-like base makes this a great choice for brunch.

Grated zucchini (with peel)	5 cups	1.25 L
Salt	1 tbsp.	15 mL
Grated part-skim mozzarella cheese	3/4 cup	175 mL
Grated sharp Cheddar cheese	1/2 cup	125 mL
Large eggs, fork-beaten	3	3
Cooking oil	2 tsp.	10 mL
Lean ground beef	1 lb.	454 g
Chopped onion	1/2 cup	125 mL
Curry powder	1 tsp.	5 mL
Ground cumin	1/2 tsp.	2 mL
Block of cream cheese, cut up	8 oz.	250 g
Orange juice	3 tbsp.	50 mL
Grated orange zest	1 tsp.	5 mL
Pepper	1/4 tsp.	1 mL
Red medium pepper, cut into 1/4 inch (6 mm) rings	1	1
Grated Parmesan cheese	1/3 cup	75 mL

Put zucchini into large bowl. Sprinkle with salt. Stir. Let stand for 1 hour. Drain. Rinse with cold water. Drain. Gently squeeze out excess water. Return to same bowl.

Add next 3 ingredients. Mix well. Spread evenly in greased 12 inch (30 cm) deep dish pizza pan. Bake in 400°F (205°C) oven for about 20 minutes until set and golden.

Heat cooking oil in large frying pan on medium. Add next 4 ingredients. Scramble-fry for about 10 minutes until ground beef is no longer pink. Remove from heat. Drain.

Add next 4 ingredients. Stir until cream cheese is melted. Spread on top of zucchini crust.

Top with red pepper rings and Parmesan cheese. Bake for 10 to 15 minutes until golden. Cuts into 8 wedges.

1 wedge: 339 Calories; 24.5 g Total Fat (8.2 g Mono, 1.4 g Poly, 13 g Sat); 162 mg Cholesterol; 7 g Carbohydrate; 2 g Fibre; 23 g Protein; 768 mg Sodium

Pictured on page 107.

Saffron Meatball Casserole

Saffron is a little pricey, but its exotic flavour makes this dish a real treat.
Orange zest adds a pleasant taste and aroma.

Large egg	1	1
Finely chopped onion	1/2 cup	125 mL
Crushed buttery crackers	1/2 cup	125 mL
Ground allspice	1 tsp.	5 mL
Salt	1/4 tsp.	1 mL
Cayenne pepper, just a pinch		
Lean ground beef	1 lb.	454 g
Cooking oil	1 tsp.	5 mL
Basmati rice	1 cup	250 mL
Prepared chicken broth	1 1/2 cups	375 mL
Orange juice	1/2 cup	125 mL
Finely chopped green onion	1/4 cup	60 mL
Liquid honey	2 tbsp.	30 mL
Grated orange zest	2 tsp.	10 mL
Saffron threads, crushed (or turmeric)	1/8 tsp.	0.5 mL
Salt	1/8 tsp.	0.5 mL

Combine first 6 ingredients in large bowl.

Add ground beef. Mix well. Roll into 1 1/2 inch (3.8 cm) balls. Arrange on greased baking sheet with sides. Bake in 375°F (190°C) oven for about 20 minutes until fully cooked, and internal temperature of beef reaches 160°F (71°C). Transfer to paper towels to drain. Set aside.

Heat cooking oil in large frying pan on medium. Add rice. Heat and stir for 1 minute.

Add remaining 7 ingredients. Stir. Bring to a boil. Transfer to greased 2 quart (2 L) shallow baking dish. Arrange meatballs in single layer on top of rice mixture. Bake, covered, in 350°F (175°C) oven for about 30 minutes until rice is tender and liquid is absorbed. Serves 4.

1 serving: 510 Calories; 15.7 g Total Fat (6.8 g Mono, 2 g Poly, 5 g Sat); 112 mg Cholesterol; 62 g Carbohydrate; 1 g Fibre; 29 g Protein; 692 mg Sodium

Pictured on page 89.

Phyllo Lasagne

An elegant and impressive dish featuring a fusion of Greek and Italian flavours. Definitely worth the effort!

Cooking oil	2 tsp.	10 mL
Lean ground beef	1 lb.	454 g
Chopped onion	1/2 cup	125 mL
Dried thyme	1 1/2 tsp.	7 mL
Chopped portobello mushrooms	2 cups	500 mL
Cooking oil	1 tsp.	5 mL
Chopped onion	1/2 cup	125 mL
Garlic clove, minced (or 1/4 tsp., 1 mL, powder)	1	1
Cans of artichoke hearts (14 oz., 398 mL, each), drained and chopped	2	2
Roasted red peppers, drained, blotted dry, diced	1/2 cup	125 mL
Dried oregano	1 1/2 tsp.	7 mL
Large eggs	2	2
Grated Asiago cheese	1 cup	250 mL
Goat (chèvre) cheese, softened and cut up	8 oz.	225 g
Sour cream	1/4 cup	60 mL
Pepper	1/2 tsp.	2 mL
Finely chopped walnuts	1/3 cup	75 mL
Fine dry bread crumbs	1/3 cup	75 mL
Frozen phyllo pastry sheets, thawed according to package directions	16	16
Hard margarine (or butter), melted	3/4 cup	175 mL

Heat first amount of cooking oil in large frying pan on medium. Add ground beef, first amount of onion and thyme. Scramble-fry for about 10 minutes until beef is no longer pink. Drain.

Add mushrooms. Cook for 3 to 4 minutes, stirring often, until liquid is evaporated. Transfer to large bowl. Set aside.

Heat second amount of cooking oil in same pan. Add second amount of onion and garlic. Heat and stir for 2 minutes.

(continued on next page)

Add next 3 ingredients. Cook for about 5 minutes, stirring often, until onion is softened. Remove from heat.

Combine next 5 ingredients in medium bowl. Set aside.

Stir walnuts and bread crumbs in small bowl.

Work with pastry sheets 1 at a time. Keep remaining sheets covered with damp tea towel to prevent drying. Lay 1 sheet on work surface. Brush with margarine. Fold in half crosswise. Place in greased 9 × 13 inch (22 × 33 cm) pan. Brush with margarine. Repeat, layering 4 more pastry sheets on top.

To assemble, layer ingredients on top as follows:

1. 1/3 walnut mixture

2. Beef mixture

3. 3 pastry sheets, prepared as above

4. 1/3 walnut mixture

5. Artichoke mixture

6. 3 pastry sheets, prepared as above

7. 1/3 walnut mixture

8. Cheese mixture

9. 5 pastry sheets, prepared as above

Score top layers of pastry by making 2 parallel cuts about 3 inches (7.5 cm) apart across the length of the pan. Cut at an angle across lengthwise cuts to make diamond shapes. Bake, uncovered, in 350°F (175°C) oven for about 45 minutes until crisp and golden. Serves 8.

1 serving: 653 Calories; 44.9 g Total Fat (20 g Mono, 6.5 g Poly, 15.5 g Sat); 122 mg Cholesterol; 36 g Carbohydrate; 3 g Fibre; 29 g Protein; 737 mg Sodium

Pictured on page 108.

Paré Pointer

By rehearsing his sermon, is a minister practising what he preaches?

Beef And Cheese Rolls

Cheesy beef wrapped in golden pastry. Serve these delicious rolls with a side salad for lunch or dinner.

Cooking oil	2 tsp.	10 mL
Extra-lean ground beef	1 lb.	454 g
Finely chopped onion	1/2 cup	125 mL
Garlic cloves, minced (or 1/2 tsp., 2 mL, powder)	2	2
Pepper	1/4 tsp.	1 mL
Grated havarti cheese	3 cups	750 mL
Crumbled feta cheese	1 cup	250 mL
Dill weed	2 – 3 tsp.	10 – 15 mL
Paprika	1 1/2 tsp.	7 mL
Frozen phyllo pastry sheets, thawed according to package directions	6	6
Hard margarine (or butter), melted	1/4 cup	60 mL
Fine dry bread crumbs	1/4 cup	60 mL
Paprika (optional)	1/2 tsp.	2 mL

Heat cooking oil in large frying pan on medium. Add next 4 ingredients. Scramble-fry for about 10 minutes until ground beef is no longer pink. Drain.

Add next 4 ingredients. Heat and stir until cheese starts to melt. Transfer to large bowl. Let stand until cool enough to handle. On large sheet of waxed paper, roll 1/2 of beef mixture into 16 inch (40 cm) long log. Repeat with remaining beef mixture.

Work with pastry sheets 1 at a time. Keep remaining sheets covered with damp tea towel to prevent drying. Lay 1 sheet lengthwise on work surface. Brush with margarine. Place second sheet on top, aligning edges evenly. Brush with margarine. Place third sheet on top, aligning edges evenly. Sprinkle 1 tbsp. (15 mL) bread crumbs along 1 long side of pastry near edge. Holding waxed paper, carefully place 1 log on top of bread crumbs. Discard waxed paper. Sprinkle 1 tbsp. (15 mL) bread crumbs on top of log. Roll up to enclose. Brush with margarine. Repeat to make second roll. Cut each roll into 4 pieces, for a total of 8 pieces. Arrange, cut-side up, on greased baking sheet with sides.

(continued on next page)

Sprinkle with second amount of paprika. Bake in 375°F (190°C) oven for about 25 minutes until pastry is golden. Serves 4.

1 serving: 421 Calories; 29.2 g Total Fat (11.2 g Mono, 2.2 g Poly, 14 g Sat); 92 mg Cholesterol; 13 g Carbohydrate; trace Fibre; 26 g Protein; 767 mg Sodium

Pictured on page 35.

Beef Corncake

A cheesy crust tops this cornbread-style casserole.

Cooking oil	2 tsp.	10 mL
Lean ground beef	1 lb.	454 g
All-purpose flour	1 cup	250 mL
Yellow cornmeal	1 cup	250 mL
Baking powder	1 tsp.	5 mL
Baking soda	1 tsp.	5 mL
Salt	1 tsp.	5 mL
Large egg	1	1
Cooking oil	1/4 cup	60 mL
Granulated sugar	1 tbsp.	15 mL
Can of cream-style corn	14 oz.	398 mL
Thinly sliced onion	1 1/2 cups	375 mL
Milk	1 cup	250 mL
Seasoned salt, sprinkle		
Grated medium Cheddar cheese	2 cups	500 mL

Heat first amount of cooking oil in large frying pan on medium. Add ground beef. Scramble-fry for about 10 minutes until no longer pink. Remove from heat. Drain. Set aside.

Combine next 5 ingredients in large bowl. Make a well in centre.

Beat next 3 ingredients in medium bowl.

Add beef and next 4 ingredients. Stir. Add to well in cornmeal mixture. Stir until just moistened. Spread evenly in greased 9 x 13 inch (22 x 33 cm) pan.

Sprinkle with cheese. Bake, uncovered, in 350°F (175°C) oven for 45 to 55 minutes until wooden pick inserted in centre comes out clean. Cuts into 8 pieces.

1 piece: 488 Calories; 24.9 g Total Fat (10.4 g Mono, 3.4 g Poly, 9.3 g Sat); 88 mg Cholesterol; 43 g Carbohydrate; 3 g Fibre; 24 g Protein; 897 mg Sodium

Surf 'N' Turf Bundles

Beautiful bundles with the combined flavours of shrimp and beef.

Cooking oil	2 tsp.	10 mL
Lean ground beef	1 lb.	454 g
Chopped fresh white mushrooms	1 cup	250 mL
Finely chopped onion	1/2 cup	125 mL
Can of condensed cream of mushroom soup	10 oz.	284 mL
Fine dry bread crumbs	1 cup	250 mL
Sour cream	1/2 cup	125 mL
Chopped fresh tarragon leaves (or 3/4 tsp., 4 mL, dried)	1 tbsp.	15 mL
Pepper, just a pinch		
Frozen phyllo pastry sheets, thawed according to package directions	12	12
Hard margarine (or butter), melted	1/2 cup	125 mL
Frozen uncooked extra-large shrimp (peeled and deveined), thawed	1 lb.	454 g
Chopped fresh chives (or 3/4 tsp., 4 mL, dried)	1 tbsp.	15 mL

Heat cooking oil in large frying pan on medium. Add ground beef, mushrooms and onion. Scramble-fry for about 10 minutes until beef is no longer pink. Remove from heat. Drain.

Add next 5 ingredients. Stir. Set aside.

Work with pastry sheets 1 at a time. Keep remaining sheets covered with damp tea towel to prevent drying. Lay 1 sheet lengthwise on work surface. Brush with margarine. Place second sheet on top, aligning edges evenly. Brush with margarine. Make 2 crosswise cuts, dividing pastry into 3 equal strips (Diagram 1). Place left and right pastry strips diagonally on centre strip to form an X (Diagram 2).

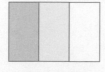
Diagram 1

Diagram 2

Diagram 3

(continued on next page)

Spoon about 1/2 cup (125 mL) beef mixture onto centre of X. Place 2 or 3 shrimp on top. Sprinkle 1/2 tsp. (2 mL) chives over shrimp. Gather ends of pastry strips and press together at top of filling to enclose, allowing corners to flare outward (Diagram 3). Repeat with remaining ingredients. Place on greased baking sheet with sides. Bake in 350°F (175°C) oven for 20 to 30 minutes until pastry is golden. Makes 6 bundles.

1 bundle: 612 Calories; 34.9 g Total Fat (16.7 g Mono, 6.2 g Poly, 9.4 g Sat); 134 mg Cholesterol; 41 g Carbohydrate; 1 g Fibre; 32 g Protein; 1065 mg Sodium

Pictured on page 35.

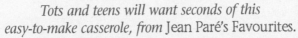

Tater Tot Casserole

Tots and teens will want seconds of this easy-to-make casserole, from Jean Paré's Favourites.

Cooking oil	2 tsp.	10 mL
Lean ground beef	1 1/2 lbs.	680 g
Can of condensed cream of celery soup	10 oz.	284 mL
Salt	1 tsp.	5 mL
Pepper	1/4 tsp.	1 mL
Frozen potato tots (gems or puffs)	4 cups	1 L
Water	1/3 cup	75 mL

Heat cooking oil in large frying pan on medium. Add ground beef. Scramble-fry for about 10 minutes until no longer pink. Remove from heat. Drain.

Add 1/2 of soup, salt and pepper. Stir. Spread evenly in ungreased 9 x 9 inch (22 x 22 cm) pan.

Arrange potato tots in single layer on top of beef mixture.

Combine remaining soup and water in small bowl. Drizzle over potato tots. Bake, uncovered, in 350°F (175°C) oven for about 1 hour until potato tots are golden. Serves 6.

1 serving: 378 Calories; 21 g Total Fat (8.7 g Mono, 2.3 g Poly, 8 g Sat); 62 mg Cholesterol; 25 g Carbohydrate; 3 g Fibre; 23 g Protein; 1353 mg Sodium

Variation: Add 2 cups (500 mL) frozen mixed vegetables to beef mixture before spreading in pan. Now you have a full meal!

Leek-Crowned Beef Pie

Before it's cut, this main dish pie looks like a quiche. A rich leek and cheese layer rests atop a savoury beef and sausage combination.

Hard margarine (or butter)	1 tbsp.	15 mL
Medium leeks (white part only), thinly sliced	2	2
Large eggs, fork-beaten	3	3
Homogenized milk	1/2 cup	125 mL
Grated Parmesan cheese	1/4 cup	60 mL
Salt, just a pinch		
Pepper, just a pinch		
Cooking oil	2 tsp.	10 mL
Lean ground beef	1/2 lb.	225 g
Italian sausages, casings removed, chopped	1/2 lb.	225 g
Chopped onion	1 cup	250 mL
Garlic cloves, minced (or 1/2 tsp., 2 mL, powder)	2	2
Can of condensed cream of mushroom soup	10 oz.	284 mL
Dried basil	1/2 tsp.	2 mL
Dried oregano	1/2 tsp.	2 mL
Pastry for 9 inch (22 cm) deep dish pie shell, your own or a mix		

Melt margarine in large frying pan on medium. Add leek. Cook for about 5 minutes, stirring often, until softened. Transfer to medium bowl.

Add next 5 ingredients. Stir. Set aside.

Heat cooking oil in same pan on medium. Add ground beef and sausage. Scramble-fry for about 10 minutes until no longer pink. Transfer with slotted spoon to separate medium bowl. Set aside.

Heat 1 tsp. (5 mL) drippings in same pan on medium. Add onion and garlic. Cook for 5 to 10 minutes, stirring often, until onion is softened.

Add beef mixture and next 3 ingredients. Heat and stir for 1 minute. Cool slightly.

(continued on next page)

Roll out pastry on lightly floured surface to about 1/8 inch (3 mm) thickness. Line 9 inch (22 cm) deep dish pie plate. Trim pastry, leaving 1/2 inch (12 mm) overhang. Roll under and crimp decorative edge. Spread beef mixture evenly in shell. Pour leek mixture over top. Bake on bottom rack in 400°F (205°C) oven for 15 minutes. Reduce heat to 350°F (175°C). Bake for another 35 to 40 minutes until knife inserted in centre comes out clean. Cuts into 6 wedges.

1 wedge: 420 Calories; 27.3 g Total Fat (11.5 g Mono, 4.5 g Poly, 9 g Sat); 149 mg Cholesterol; 25 g Carbohydrate; 2 g Fibre; 19 g Protein; 877 mg Sodium

Pictured on page 53 and on back cover.

 Hot peppers get their fiery heat from the capsaicin contained in their seeds and ribs. Removing the seeds and ribs will reduce the heat. When handling hot peppers, wear rubber gloves and avoid touching your eyes. Remember to wash your hands well afterwards.

Paré Pointer
Why is traffic slowest during rush hour?

Shepherd's Pie

You'll hook them for sure with this steaming shepherd's pie! First published in Lunches, *it's still a hit!*

Cooking oil	2 tsp.	10 mL
Lean ground beef	1 1/2 lbs.	680 g
Chopped onion	1 cup	250 mL
All-purpose flour	1 tbsp.	15 mL
Salt	1 1/2 tsp.	7 mL
Pepper	1/4 tsp.	1 mL
Milk	1/3 cup	75 mL
Cooked peas	1 cup	250 mL
Cooked sliced carrot	1 cup	250 mL
Ketchup	1 tbsp.	15 mL
Worcestershire sauce	1 tsp.	5 mL
Prepared horseradish	1 tsp.	5 mL
Potatoes, peeled, cut up	1 1/2 lbs.	680 g
Water		
Milk	3 – 4 tbsp.	50 – 60 mL
Hard margarine (or butter)	1 tbsp.	15 mL
Seasoned salt	1/2 tsp.	2 mL
Hard margarine (or butter), melted	2 tbsp.	30 mL
Paprika, sprinkle		

Heat cooking oil in large frying pan on medium. Add ground beef and onion. Scramble-fry for about 10 minutes until beef is no longer pink. Drain.

Add flour, salt and pepper. Stir well. Slowly add first amount of milk, stirring constantly. Heat and stir for about 2 minutes until boiling and thickened. Add next 5 ingredients. Stir. Spread evenly in greased 8 x 8 inch (20 x 20 cm) pan. Set aside.

Cook potato in water in large saucepan until tender. Drain. Add second amount of milk, first amount of margarine and seasoned salt. Mash. Spread on top of beef mixture.

Brush mashed potatoes with second amount of margarine. Using fork, score wave pattern on top. Sprinkle with paprika. Bake, uncovered, in 350°F (175°C) oven for about 30 minutes until heated through and mashed potatoes are golden. Serves 6.

1 serving: 369 Calories; 17.6 g Total Fat (9 g Mono, 1.5 g Poly, 5.3 g Sat); 58 mg Cholesterol; 28 g Carbohydrate; 4 g Fibre; 25 g Protein; 918 mg Sodium

Greek Salad Pizza

Colourful, Greek-style toppings on a knife-and-fork pizza. Serve with lemon wedges to squeeze over top for an extra splash of flavour.

Cooking oil	1 tsp.	5 mL
Lean ground beef	1/2 lb.	225 g
Chopped onion	1/2 cup	125 mL
Garlic clove, minced (or 1/4 tsp., 1 mL, powder)	1	1
Box of frozen chopped spinach, thawed and squeezed dry	10 oz.	300 g
Dried oregano	1 tsp.	5 mL
Prebaked pizza crust (12 inch, 30 cm, diameter)	1	1
Pizza sauce	1/4 cup	60 mL
Grated part-skim mozzarella cheese	1 cup	250 mL
Can of sliced ripe olives, drained	4 1/2 oz.	125 mL
Crumbled feta cheese	1 cup	250 mL
Chopped tomato	1 cup	250 mL
Chopped fresh mint leaves (optional)	1 tbsp.	15 mL

Heat cooking oil in medium frying pan on medium. Add ground beef, onion and garlic. Scramble-fry for about 10 minutes until beef is no longer pink. Drain.

Add spinach and oregano. Heat and stir for 2 minutes.

Place pizza crust on ungreased baking sheet. Spread pizza sauce on crust. Scatter beef mixture over sauce.

Sprinkle with mozzarella cheese. Bake in 450°F (230°C) oven for about 10 minutes until crust is golden and cheese is melted and starting to brown.

Scatter remaining 4 ingredients, in order given, over top. Cuts into 8 wedges.

1 wedge: 258 Calories; 12 g Total Fat (3.7 g Mono, 0.7 g Poly, 5.7 g Sat); 42 mg Cholesterol; 22 g Carbohydrate; 2 g Fibre; 16 g Protein; 590 mg Sodium

Pictured on page 108.

Picadillo Pie

Picadillo (pee-kah-DEE-yoh) is a meat hash often made with ground beef.
The inclusion of fruit makes it distinct. Picadillo is traditionally used as
a filling in various dishes—here it forms the base of a tasty casserole.

Cooking oil	2 tsp.	10 mL
Lean ground beef	1 1/2 lbs.	680 g
Chopped fresh white mushrooms	1 cup	250 mL
Chopped onion	1 cup	250 mL
Garlic cloves, minced (or 1/2 tsp., 2 mL, powder)	2	2
Chili powder	2 tsp.	10 mL
Ground cumin	1 tsp.	5 mL
Dried oregano	1 tsp.	5 mL
Can of diced tomatoes (with juice)	28 oz.	796 mL
Sliced pimiento-stuffed olives	3/4 cup	175 mL
Chopped dried apricot	1/2 cup	125 mL
Dark raisins	1/2 cup	125 mL
Sweet potatoes (or yams), peeled, cut up	2 lbs.	900 g
Potatoes, peeled, cut up	1 lb.	454 g
Water		
Hard margarine (or butter)	3 tbsp.	50 mL
Yellow cornmeal	3 tbsp.	50 mL
Large egg, fork-beaten	1	1
Dried oregano	1/2 tsp.	2 mL
Salt	1/4 tsp.	1 mL
Pepper	1/4 tsp.	1 mL

Heat cooking oil in large frying pan on medium. Add ground beef.
Scramble-fry for about 10 minutes until no longer pink. Drain.

Add next 6 ingredients. Cook for about 5 to 10 minutes, stirring
occasionally, until onion is softened and liquid is evaporated.

Add next 4 ingredients. Stir. Bring to a boil. Spread evenly in greased
3 quart (3 L) shallow baking dish. Set aside.

Cook sweet potato and potato in water in large saucepan until
tender. Drain.

(continued on next page)

Add remaining 6 ingredients. Mash. Spread on top of beef mixture. Using fork, score decorative pattern on potato mixture. Bake, uncovered, in 375°F (190°C) oven for about 40 minutes until potato mixture is firm. Cuts into 8 pieces.

1 piece: 417 Calories; 16.2 g Total Fat (8.4 g Mono, 1.6 g Poly, 4.4 g Sat); 69 mg Cholesterol; 50 g Carbohydrate; 6 g Fibre; 21 g Protein; 714 mg Sodium

Pictured on page 54.

Baked Spinach Portobellos

Basil and assertive, salty cheeses make these a delightful treat.

Bacon slices, diced	4	4
Lean ground beef	1/2 lb.	225 g
Chopped onion	1/2 cup	125 mL
Garlic clove, minced (or 1/4 tsp., 1 mL, powder)	1	1
Box of frozen chopped spinach, thawed and squeezed dry	10 oz.	300 g
Chopped fresh basil (or 3/4 tsp., 4 mL, dried)	1 tbsp.	15 mL
Ground nutmeg	1/4 tsp.	1 mL
Goat (chévre) cheese, cut up	4 oz.	113 g
Crumbled feta cheese	3/4 cup	175 mL
Portobello mushrooms (about 4 inch, 10 cm, diameter)	6	6

Cook bacon in large frying pan on medium until almost crisp. Add ground beef, onion and garlic. Scramble-fry for about 10 minutes until beef is no longer pink. Drain.

Add spinach, basil and nutmeg. Heat and stir for about 2 minutes until spinach is heated through and basil is fragrant. Add goat and feta cheeses. Stir. Remove from heat.

Remove stems from mushrooms. Using small spoon, remove gills from mushroom caps. Spoon beef mixture into mushrooms. Arrange in ungreased 9 x 13 inch (22 x 33 cm) pan. Cover with foil. Bake in 375°F (190°C) oven for about 30 minutes until mushrooms are softened. Remove foil. Bake for another 10 minutes until top of beef mixture is firm and slightly crisp. Makes 6 stuffed mushrooms.

1 stuffed mushroom: 234 Calories; 14.3 g Total Fat (4.2 g Mono, 0.9 g Poly, 7.9 g Sat); 52 mg Cholesterol; 11 g Carbohydrate; 3 g Fibre; 18 g Protein; 406 mg Sodium

Hot Tamale Two-Step

Warm things up with our spicy twist on the tamale pie.

Cooking oil	2 tsp.	10 mL
Lean ground beef	1 lb.	454 g
Chili powder	1 tbsp.	15 mL
Seasoned salt	2 tsp.	10 mL
Garlic powder	1/2 tsp.	2 mL
Onion powder	1/2 tsp.	2 mL
Large eggs	2	2
Milk	2 cups	500 mL
Frozen kernel corn	2 cups	500 mL
Can of diced tomatoes (with juice)	14 oz.	398 mL
Yellow cornmeal	1 cup	250 mL
Can of sliced jalapeño peppers, drained	4 oz.	114 mL
Grated sharp Cheddar cheese	1 cup	250 mL
Can of sliced ripe olives, drained	4 1/2 oz.	125 mL

Heat cooking oil in large frying pan on medium. Add ground beef. Scramble-fry for about 10 minutes until no longer pink. Drain. Add next 4 ingredients. Heat and stir for about 1 minute until fragrant. Remove from heat.

Combine next 6 ingredients in large bowl. Add beef mixture. Stir well. Spread evenly in greased 2 quart (2 L) casserole. Bake, uncovered, in 375°F (175°C) oven for about 1 hour until firm.

Sprinkle with cheese and olives. Bake for another 5 to 10 minutes until cheese is melted. Serves 6.

1 serving: 442 Calories; 19.2 g Total Fat (7.4 g Mono, 1.7 g Poly, 8.2 g Sat); 134 mg Cholesterol; 41 g Carbohydrate; 4 g Fibre; 28 g Protein; 811 mg Sodium

Pictured on page 54.

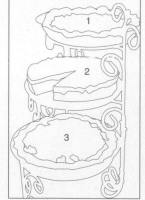

1. Leek-Crowned Beef Pie, page 46
2. Ricotta Swiss Wedges, page 97
3. Cheeseburger Pie, page 58

Props courtesy of: Casa Bugatti
Cherison Enterprises Inc.
Pyrex® Bakeware

Beefy Burrito Bake

Tangy cheese makes these stuffed tortillas especially tempting.

Cooking oil	2 tsp.	10 mL
Lean ground beef	1 lb.	454 g
Sliced fresh white mushrooms	1 1/2 cups	375 mL
Chopped onion	1/2 cup	125 mL
Low-sodium prepared beef broth	1 1/4 cups	300 mL
Envelope of reduced sodium taco seasoning mix	1 1/4 oz.	35 g
Flour tortillas (9 inch, 22 cm, diameter)	8	8
Skim evaporated milk	1 cup	250 mL
Pasteurized cheese loaf, cubed	9 oz.	250 g

Heat cooking oil in large frying pan on medium. Add ground beef, mushrooms and onion. Scramble-fry for about 10 minutes until beef is no longer pink. Drain. Add broth and taco seasoning. Stir. Bring to a boil. Reduce heat to medium-low. Simmer, uncovered, for about 10 minutes until thickened.

Spoon about 1/4 cup (60 mL) beef mixture along centre of each tortilla. Fold sides over filling. Roll up from bottom to enclose. Arrange, seam-side down, on greased baking sheet with sides. Bake in 350°F (175°C) oven for about 15 minutes until heated through.

Heat and stir evaporated milk and cheese in medium saucepan on medium for about 10 minutes until cheese is melted. Spoon over burritos. Serves 8.

1 serving: 398 Calories; 19.2 g Total Fat (6.8 g Mono, 2 g Poly, 8.7 g Sat); 59 mg Cholesterol; 32 g Carbohydrate; 2 g Fibre; 24 g Protein; 1193 mg Sodium

1. Picadillo Pie, page 50
2. Hot Tamale Two-Step, page 52
3. Fiesta Strata, page 65

Props courtesy of: Anchor Hocking Canada
Danesco Inc.
Out of the Fire Studio
Pyrex® Bakeware

Tuscan Stuffed Tomatoes

*You can almost feel the warmth of the Tuscan sun when you
feast your eyes on these golden-topped, stuffed tomatoes.
Add a salad and a glass of wine—Buon Appetito!*

Large tomatoes	8	8
Salt, sprinkle		
Cooking oil	1 tsp.	5 mL
Lean ground beef	1 lb.	454 g
Finely chopped green onion	1/2 cup	125 mL
Garlic clove, minced (or 1/4 tsp., 1 mL, powder)	1	1
Salt	1/4 tsp.	1 mL
Pepper	1/8 tsp.	0.5 mL
Cooked orzo (about 1/2 cup, 125 mL, uncooked)	1 cup	250 mL
Chopped fresh parsley (or 1 tbsp., 15 mL, flakes)	1/4 cup	60 mL
Coarsely chopped pine nuts, toasted (see Tip, page 129)	3 tbsp.	50 mL
Dried oregano	1 tbsp.	15 mL
Dried crushed chilies	1/2 tsp.	2 mL
Salt	1/2 tsp.	2 mL
Crumbled feta cheese	1/2 cup	125 mL
Grated Parmesan cheese	1/4 cup	60 mL
Grated Parmesan cheese	1/4 cup	60 mL
Chopped green onion	1/4 cup	60 mL
Kalamata olives, pitted (see Note)	8	8

Trim 1/4 inch (6 mm) slice from bottom of each tomato. Using small spoon,
scoop out pulp from each tomato, reserving 1 cup (250 mL). Sprinkle inside
of each with salt. Place cut-side down, on 2 large microwave-safe plates.
Microwave each plate on high (100%) for about 1 minute until tomatoes
are slightly softened. Set aside.

Heat cooking oil in large frying pan on medium. Add next 5 ingredients.
Scramble-fry for about 10 minutes until ground beef is no longer pink. Drain.

(continued on next page)

Add reserved tomato pulp and next 6 ingredients. Stir. Cook for 5 minutes, stirring occasionally.

Add feta cheese and first amount of Parmesan cheese. Stir. Remove from heat. Arrange tomatoes on greased baking sheet with sides. Fill with beef mixture.

Sprinkle with second amounts of Parmesan cheese and onion. Top with olives. Broil on centre rack in oven for 8 to 10 minutes until Parmesan cheese is golden. Makes 8 stuffed tomatoes.

1 stuffed tomato: 268 Calories; 12.7 g Total Fat (4.6 g Mono, 1.6 g Poly, 5.2 g Sat); 44 mg Cholesterol; 21 g Carbohydrate; 3 g Fibre; 19 g Protein; 539 mg Sodium

Pictured on page 36.

Note: To pit an olive, place it on a cutting board and press the olive with the flat side of a wide knife until you feel the olive give. The flesh will split, making it easy to remove the pit. Alternatively, use a sharp knife to split the olive from top to bottom, cutting through the flesh to the pit.

Paré Pointer

The turtles crossed the road to get to the shell station.

Cheeseburger Pie

The whole family will love this hearty meal. You can also
cut the dough into biscuits to serve with soup or chili.

Cooking oil	2 tsp.	10 mL
Lean ground beef	1 lb.	454 g
Chopped onion	1/2 cup	125 mL
Ketchup	2 tbsp.	30 mL
Salt	3/4 tsp.	4 mL
Pepper	1/4 tsp.	1 mL
BISCUIT CRUST		
All-purpose flour	2 cups	500 mL
Baking powder	1 tbsp.	15 mL
Granulated sugar	2 tsp.	10 mL
Salt	1/2 tsp.	2 mL
Milk	2/3 cup	150 mL
Cooking oil	1/3 cup	75 mL
Can of diced tomatoes, drained	14 oz.	398 mL
Granulated sugar	1/2 tsp.	2 mL
Grated medium Cheddar cheese	1 cup	250 mL

Heat cooking oil in large frying pan on medium. Add ground beef and onion. Scramble-fry for about 10 minutes until beef is no longer pink. Drain.

Add next 3 ingredients. Stir. Cool.

Biscuit Crust: Combine first 4 ingredients in large bowl. Make a well in centre.

Add milk and cooking oil to well. Stir until just moistened. Roll into ball. Press into bottom and up side of greased 9 inch (22 cm) pie plate. Spread beef mixture evenly in crust.

Combine tomatoes and second amount of sugar in small bowl. Spoon over beef mixture. Sprinkle with cheese. Bake in 350°F (175°C) oven for about 45 minutes until crust is golden and cheese is melted. Cuts into 6 wedges.

1 wedge: 525 Calories; 28.1 g Total Fat (13.2 g Mono, 4.9 g Poly, 8 g Sat); 61 mg Cholesterol;
43 g Carbohydrate; 2 g Fibre; 25 g Protein; 1017 mg Sodium

Pictured on page 53 and on back cover.

Hash Brown Pizza

The enticing aroma of this recipe, from
Jean Paré's Favourites, will call everyone to
the kitchen for dinner so you don't have to.

Large egg	1	1
Can of condensed Cheddar cheese soup	10 oz.	284 mL
Pepper	1/2 tsp.	2 mL
Bag of frozen hash brown potatoes, thawed	2 1/4 lbs.	1 kg
Cooking oil	2 tsp.	10 mL
Lean ground beef	1 lb.	454 g
Finely chopped onion	2 tbsp.	30 mL
All-purpose flour	2 tbsp.	30 mL
Can of condensed tomato soup	10 oz.	284 mL
Granulated sugar	2 tsp.	10 mL
Garlic powder	1/4 tsp.	1 mL
Salt	1/2 tsp.	2 mL
Pepper	1/8 tsp.	0.5 mL
Grated medium Cheddar cheese	2 cups	500 mL

Combine first 3 ingredients in large bowl. Add hash brown potatoes. Stir well. Spread evenly in greased 12 inch (30 cm) pizza pan, pressing with back of spoon to form rim around edge. Bake in 450°F (230°C) oven for 20 to 25 minutes until firm.

Heat cooking oil in large frying pan on medium. Add ground beef and onion. Scramble-fry for about 10 minutes until beef is no longer pink. Drain.

Add flour. Stir well. Add next 5 ingredients. Heat and stir for about 5 minutes until boiling and thickened. Remove from heat.

Sprinkle 1/2 of cheese over potato crust. Spread beef mixture on top of cheese. Sprinkle with remaining cheese. Bake for 4 to 5 minutes until cheese is melted and bubbling. Cuts into 8 wedges.

1 wedge: 414 Calories; 21.1 g Total Fat (6.9 g Mono, 1.6 g Poly, 10.8 g Sat); 96 mg Cholesterol;
34 g Carbohydrate; 3 g Fibre; 23 g Protein; 948 mg Sodium

Beef Barley Cabbage Rolls

Cabbage roll fans are sure to be impressed with these large, hearty rolls!
Wholesome barley makes these just a little different.

Large head of green cabbage	1	1
Boiling water		
Low-sodium prepared beef broth	3 cups	750 mL
Pearl barley	1 cup	250 mL
Bacon slices, cooked crisp and crumbled	8	8
Medium onion, finely chopped	1	1
Large carrot, finely chopped	1	1
Large celery rib, finely chopped	1	1
Chopped fresh thyme leaves	2 tsp.	10 mL
(or 1/2 tsp., 2 mL, dried)		
Salt	1/4 tsp.	1 mL
Pepper	1/8 tsp.	0.5 mL
Ground cloves	1/8 tsp.	0.5 mL
Lean ground beef	2 lbs.	900 g
Tomato juice	1 1/4 cups	300 mL
Low-sodium prepared beef broth	1 cup	250 mL
Low-sodium prepared beef broth,	1 2/3 cups	400 mL
approximately		
Hard margarine (or butter)	1 1/2 tbsp.	25 mL
All-purpose flour	3 tbsp.	50 mL
Drops of liquid gravy browner (optional)	1 – 2	1 – 2

Remove core from cabbage. Trim about 1/2 inch (12 mm) slice from bottom. Place, cut-side down, in Dutch oven. Cover with boiling water. Cover Dutch oven with foil. Heat on medium-low for about 30 minutes, using tongs to remove leaves to tea towel as they start to soften and loosen. Blot dry. Cut 'V' shape along tough ribs of leaves to remove. Cut larger leaves into 2 equal pieces. Set aside.

Measure first amount of broth into large saucepan. Bring to a boil on high. Add barley. Stir. Return to a boil. Reduce heat to medium-low. Simmer, covered, for about 20 minutes, stirring occasionally, until tender and broth is absorbed. Cool.

(continued on next page)

Combine next 8 ingredients in large bowl.

Add barley and ground beef. Mix well. Spoon about 1/2 cup (125 mL) beef mixture onto centre of 1 cabbage leaf. Fold sides over filling. Roll up tightly from bottom to enclose. Repeat with remaining cabbage leaves and beef mixture. Arrange cabbage rolls tightly together, seam-side down, in single layer in greased large roasting pan. Layer any extra cabbage leaves on top of rolls.

Combine tomato juice and second amount of broth in small bowl. Pour over cabbage rolls. Bake, covered, in 350°F (175°C) oven for about 2 hours until cabbage is softened. Carefully spoon liquid from roasting pan into 4 cup (1 L) heatproof liquid measure. Cover cabbage rolls to keep warm.

Add enough of third amount of broth to liquid measure to equal 3 cups (750 mL) liquid.

Melt margarine in medium saucepan on medium. Add flour. Heat and stir for about 2 minutes until golden. Slowly add broth mixture, stirring constantly. Bring to a boil. Reduce heat to medium-low. Simmer, uncovered, for about 20 minutes, stirring often, until thickened.

Add gravy browner. Stir. Pour over cabbage rolls. Serves 8.

1 serving: 460 Calories; 23.1 g Total Fat (10.4 g Mono, 1.6 g Poly, 8.5 g Sat); 69 mg Cholesterol; 34 g Carbohydrate; 5 g Fibre; 30 g Protein; 933 mg Sodium

Meaty Lasagne

A classic lasagne at first glance, but with a
touch of fennel for a subtle, tasty difference.

Cooking oil	2 tsp.	10 mL
Lean ground beef	2 lbs.	900 g
Tomato pasta sauce	3 cups	750 mL
Finely chopped onion	2 tbsp.	30 mL
Worcestershire sauce	1 tsp.	5 mL
Dried oregano	1 tsp.	5 mL
Fennel seed	1/2 tsp.	2 mL
Pepper	1/4 tsp.	1 mL
Large eggs	2	2
Ricotta cheese	3 cups	750 mL
Grated Parmesan cheese	1/3 cup	75 mL
Ground nutmeg	1/8 tsp.	0.5 mL
Lasagna noodles	12	12
Grated part-skim mozzarella cheese	3 cups	750 mL
Grated Parmesan cheese	1/2 cup	125 mL

Heat cooking oil in large deep frying pan or Dutch oven on medium. Add ground beef. Scramble-fry for about 10 minutes until no longer pink. Drain.

Add next 6 ingredients. Stir. Bring to a boil. Reduce heat to medium-low. Simmer, covered, for 25 minutes, stirring occasionally. Remove from heat. Set aside.

Combine next 4 ingredients in medium bowl. Set aside.

Cook noodles in boiling salted water in large uncovered pot or Dutch oven for 12 to 15 minutes, stirring occasionally, until tender but firm. Drain. Rinse with cold water. Drain well.

(continued on next page)

To assemble, layer ingredients in greased 9 × 13 inch (22 × 33 cm) pan as follows:

1. 4 lasagna noodles, slightly overlapping to fit pan

2. 1/3 ricotta cheese mixture

3. 1/3 meat sauce

4. 4 lasagna noodles, slightly overlapping

5. 1/3 ricotta cheese mixture

6. 1/3 meat sauce

7. 4 lasagna noodles, slightly overlapping

8. 1/3 ricotta cheese mixture

9. 1/3 meat sauce

Sprinkle with mozzarella cheese and second amount of Parmesan cheese. Bake, uncovered, in 350°F (175°C) oven for about 45 minutes until heated through and cheese is melted and golden. Serves 12.

1 serving: 503 Calories; 26.9 g Total Fat (9.5 g Mono, 2 g Poly, 13.3 g Sat); 130 mg Cholesterol; 28 g Carbohydrate; 1 g Fibre; 36 g Protein; 695 mg Sodium

Paré Pointer

It's hard to find something you've lost—except for those few pounds.

Porcupine Stew

In this tasty slow-cooker recipe, old-fashioned meatballs bristle with rice.

Medium onion, cut into 8 wedges	1	1
Coarsely chopped carrot	4 cups	1 L
Red baby potatoes, larger ones cut in half	1 lb.	454 g
Dill weed	1 tsp.	5 mL
Pepper, sprinkle		
Large egg	1	1
Long grain white rice	1/2 cup	125 mL
Finely chopped onion	1/3 cup	75 mL
Fine dry bread crumbs	1/4 cup	60 mL
Garlic cloves, minced (or 1/2 tsp., 2 mL, powder)	2	2
Worcestershire sauce	2 tsp.	10 mL
Seasoned salt	1/2 tsp.	2 mL
Pepper	1/4 tsp.	1 mL
Lean ground beef	1 1/2 lbs.	680 g
Cooking oil	2 tsp.	10 mL
Can of condensed tomato soup	10 oz.	284 mL
Prepared beef broth	1 cup	250 mL
Water	1/2 cup	125 mL

Layer onion wedges, carrot and potatoes, in order given, in 4 to 5 quart (4 to 5 L) slow cooker. Sprinkle with dill weed and first amount of pepper.

Combine next 8 ingredients in large bowl.

Add ground beef. Mix well. Divide into 12 equal portions. Roll into balls.

Heat cooking oil in large frying pan on medium. Add meatballs. Cook for about 10 minutes, turning often, until fully cooked and internal temperature of beef reaches 160°F (71°C). Arrange meatballs in single layer on top of potatoes.

Combine remaining 3 ingredients in small bowl. Pour over meatballs. Cover. Cook on Low for 8 to 10 hours or on High for 4 to 5 hours. Remove meatballs and vegetables with slotted spoon to separate large serving bowls. Top with sauce from slow cooker, or serve on the side. Serves 6.

(continued on next page)

1 serving: 505 Calories; 21 g Total Fat (9 g Mono, 1.9 g Poly, 7.5 g Sat); 100 mg Cholesterol; 50 g Carbohydrate; 6 g Fibre; 29 g Protein; 813 mg Sodium

Pictured on page 144.

Fiesta Strata

This make-ahead Tex-Mex dish needs to be chilled overnight before baking. Serve with salad and salsa, and let the fiesta begin!

Cooking oil	2 tsp.	10 mL
Lean ground beef	1 lb.	454 g
Chopped onion	1/2 cup	125 mL
Roasted red peppers, drained, blotted dry, cut into strips	1/2 cup	125 mL
Can of diced green chilies	4 oz.	113 g
Chili powder	1/2 tsp.	2 mL
Flour tortillas (9 inch, 22 cm, diameter)	6	6
Large eggs	4	4
Milk	2 cups	500 mL
Ground cumin	1/4 tsp.	1 mL
Grated Monterey Jack cheese	1 1/2 cups	375 mL

Heat cooking oil in large frying pan on medium. Add ground beef and onion. Scramble-fry for about 10 minutes until beef is no longer pink. Drain.

Add next 3 ingredients. Heat and stir for 2 to 3 minutes until fragrant. Remove from heat.

Place 1 tortilla in greased 3 quart (3 L) round casserole. Fold edge if necessary to fit into casserole. Spread about 1/2 cup (125 mL) beef mixture on top. Repeat, layering remaining tortillas and beef mixture, ending with a tortilla.

Beat next 3 ingredients with whisk in medium bowl. Pour over top.

Sprinkle with cheese. Cover. Chill overnight to allow flavours to blend and tortillas to absorb liquid. Bake, uncovered, in 350°F (175°C) oven for about 1 1/4 hours until puffed and golden. Cuts into 8 wedges.

1 wedge: 360 Calories; 18.3 g Total Fat (6.8 g Mono, 2 g Poly, 7.8 g Sat); 159 mg Cholesterol; 24 g Carbohydrate; 2 g Fibre; 24 g Protein; 366 mg Sodium

Pictured on page 54.

Sloppy Ginos

Italian-style sloppy joes. This zesty chili is served on focaccia bread instead of buns. A hearty knife-and-fork sandwich.

Cooking oil	2 tsp.	10 mL
Lean ground beef	1/2 lb.	225 g
Italian sausages, casings removed, chopped	1/2 lb.	225 g
Chopped onion	1/2 cup	125 mL
Garlic clove, minced (or 1/4 tsp., 1 mL, powder)	1	1
Diced green pepper	1/4 cup	60 mL
Diced red pepper	1/4 cup	60 mL
Italian seasoning	1/2 tsp.	2 mL
Fennel seed	1/4 tsp.	1 mL
Dried crushed chilies	1/4 tsp.	1 mL
Can of tomato sauce	14 oz.	398 mL
Herb focaccia bread (10 inch, 25 cm, diameter)	1	1

Heat cooking oil in large frying pan on medium. Add next 4 ingredients. Scramble-fry for about 10 minutes until ground beef and sausage are no longer pink. Drain.

Add next 5 ingredients. Stir. Cook for about 5 minutes, stirring occasionally, until green and red peppers are tender.

Add tomato sauce. Heat and stir for about 1 minute until heated through.

Cut bread into 6 wedges. Place on ungreased baking sheet. Broil on top rack in oven for about 2 minutes until golden. Remove to dinner plates. Top with beef mixture. Serves 6.

1 serving: 339 Calories; 12.7 g Total Fat (6.1 g Mono, 2.2 g Poly, 3.2 g Sat); 33 mg Cholesterol; 40 g Carbohydrate; 3 g Fibre; 16 g Protein; 1012 mg Sodium

Paré Pointer

We were given a mouth that closes and ears that do not—there's a message here.

Meat Sauce

This versatile sauce, from The Beef Book, *is just the thing over spaghetti or in a lasagne. The chili heat can be adjusted, depending on personal preference.*

Cooking oil	2 tsp.	10 mL
Lean ground beef	1 lb.	454 g
Medium onions, chopped	2	2
Celery ribs, chopped	2	2
Green medium pepper, chopped	1	1
Garlic clove, minced (or 1/4 tsp., 1 mL, powder)	1	1
Can of diced tomatoes (with juice)	28 oz.	796 mL
Can of crushed tomatoes	14 oz.	398 mL
Water	1/3 cup	75 mL
Chopped fresh parsley (or 2 1/2 tsp., 12 mL, flakes)	3 tbsp.	50 mL
Chopped fresh basil (or 3/4 tsp., 4 mL, dried)	1 tbsp.	15 mL
Bay leaf	1	1
Dried oregano	1 tsp.	5 mL
Dried crushed chilies	1 tsp.	5 mL
Granulated sugar	1/2 tsp.	2 mL
Salt	1/2 tsp.	2 mL
Pepper, sprinkle		

Heat cooking oil in large saucepan on medium. Add next 5 ingredients. Scramble-fry for about 10 minutes until ground beef is no longer pink. Drain.

Add remaining 11 ingredients. Stir. Bring to a boil. Reduce heat to medium-low. Simmer, uncovered, for about 45 minutes, stirring occasionally, until vegetables are softened and sauce is thickened. Discard bay leaf. Serves 6.

1 serving: 196 Calories; 8.5 g Total Fat (3.8 g Mono, 1 g Poly, 2.7 g Sat); 39 mg Cholesterol; 15 g Carbohydrate; 3 g Fibre; 16 g Protein; 574 mg Sodium

Tandoori Chili

Excellent flavour and fiery heat in a complex
spice combination. Serve with pappadums.

Cooking oil	2 tsp.	10 mL
Lean ground beef	1 lb.	454 g
Chopped onion	1 cup	250 mL
Finely grated, peeled gingerroot	1 tbsp.	15 mL
(or 3/4 tsp., 4 mL, ground ginger)		
Garlic clove, minced (or 1/4 tsp., 1 mL,	1	1
powder)		
Paprika	3 tbsp.	50 mL
Dried crushed chilies	2 tsp.	10 mL
Ground cumin	1 1/2 tsp.	7 mL
Ground cardamom	1/2 tsp.	2 mL
Ground coriander	1/2 tsp.	2 mL
Salt	1/2 tsp.	2 mL
Pepper	1/2 tsp.	2 mL
Ground cloves	1/4 tsp.	1 mL
Ground cinnamon	1/4 tsp.	1 mL
Can of chickpeas (garbanzo beans),	19 oz.	540 mL
rinsed and drained		
Can of diced tomatoes (with juice)	14 oz.	398 mL
Water	1 cup	250 mL
Can of tomato sauce	7 1/2 oz.	213 mL
Plain yogurt	1 cup	250 mL

Heat cooking oil in large frying pan or Dutch oven on medium. Add next 4 ingredients. Scramble-fry for about 10 minutes until ground beef is no longer pink. Drain.

Add next 9 ingredients. Heat and stir for about 1 minute until fragrant.

Add next 4 ingredients. Stir. Bring to a boil. Reduce heat to medium-low. Simmer, uncovered, for about 20 minutes, stirring occasionally, until slightly thickened.

Add yogurt. Heat and stir for about 10 minutes until heated through. Serves 6.

1 serving: 274 Calories; 10.7 g Total Fat (4.3 g Mono, 1.6 g Poly, 3.3 g Sat); 40 mg Cholesterol; 25 g Carbohydrate; 4 g Fibre; 21 g Protein; 706 mg Sodium

Pictured on page 72.

Rosy Beef Sauce

A creamy sauce brimming with vegetables. Perfect with penne.

Cooking oil	2 tsp.	10 mL
Lean ground beef	1 lb.	454 g
Chopped onion	2 1/2 cups	625 mL
Chopped zucchini (with peel)	2 cups	500 mL
Quartered fresh white mushrooms	2 cups	500 mL
Chopped green pepper	1 3/4 cups	425 mL
Chopped yellow pepper	1 1/2 cups	375 mL
Can of tomato sauce	14 oz.	398 mL
Dried oregano	2 tsp.	10 mL
Salt	1/4 tsp.	1 mL
Pepper	1/8 tsp.	0.5 mL
Can of evaporated milk	13 1/2 oz.	385 mL
Grated Parmesan cheese	1/2 cup	125 mL
Chopped fresh basil	2 tbsp.	30 mL

Heat cooking oil in large deep frying pan or Dutch oven on medium. Add ground beef and onion. Scramble-fry for about 10 minutes until beef is no longer pink. Drain.

Add next 4 ingredients. Cook for about 10 minutes, stirring occasionally, until vegetables are tender-crisp.

Add next 4 ingredients. Stir. Bring to a boil on medium-high. Reduce heat to medium. Boil gently for about 10 minutes, stirring occasionally, until thickened.

Add evaporated milk. Heat and stir for 3 to 4 minutes until hot but not boiling. Remove to large serving bowl.

Sprinkle with Parmesan cheese and basil. Serves 6.

1 serving: 348 Calories; 16.6 g Total Fat (6.2 g Mono, 1.2 g Poly, 7.7 g Sat); 65 mg Cholesterol; 27 g Carbohydrate; 4 g Fibre; 25 g Protein; 795 mg Sodium

Caesar Meat Sauce

Spicy and hot! All the flavour of a well-known cocktail in a very thick, zesty meat sauce. Add your favourite pasta and toss.

Cooking oil	2 tsp.	10 mL
Lean ground beef	1 lb.	454 g
Chopped onion	1 cup	250 mL
Can of tomato sauce	14 oz.	398 mL
Lemon juice	1 tbsp.	15 mL
Granulated sugar	1 tbsp.	15 mL
Worcestershire sauce	1 tbsp.	15 mL
Hot pepper sauce	2 tsp.	10 mL
Celery salt	1/2 tsp.	2 mL
Pepper	1/2 tsp.	2 mL
Vodka (optional)	2 tbsp.	30 mL

Heat cooking oil in large frying pan on medium. Add ground beef and onion. Scramble-fry for about 10 minutes until beef is no longer pink. Drain.

Add next 7 ingredients. Stir. Bring to a boil. Reduce heat to medium-low. Simmer, uncovered, for 5 minutes, stirring occasionally.

Add vodka. Stir. Serves 4.

1 serving: 256 Calories; 12 g Total Fat (5.5 g Mono, 1.1 g Poly, 3.9 g Sat); 59 mg Cholesterol; 15 g Carbohydrate; 2 g Fibre; 23 g Protein; 926 mg Sodium

1. Chuckwagon Chipotle Chili, page 74
2. Cinnamon Chili, page 73
3. Five-Spice Hot Pot, page 141

Props courtesy of: Cherison Enterprises Inc.

Cinnamon Chili

A taste adventure worth trying!

Cooking oil	2 tsp.	10 mL
Lean ground beef	1 lb.	454 g
Chopped onion	1 cup	250 mL
Garlic clove, minced (or 1/4 tsp., 1 mL, powder)	1	1
Chili powder	1 tbsp.	15 mL
Cocoa, sifted if lumpy	2 tsp.	10 mL
Ground cinnamon	1 tsp.	5 mL
Salt	1/2 tsp.	2 mL
Ground allspice	1/4 tsp.	1 mL
Bay leaf	1	1
Can of romano beans, rinsed and drained	19 oz.	540 mL
Can of diced tomatoes (with juice)	14 oz.	398 mL
Can of tomato sauce	7 1/2 oz.	213 mL
Water	1/2 cup	125 mL
Balsamic vinegar	1 tbsp.	15 mL

Heat cooking oil in large frying pan on medium. Add ground beef, onion and garlic. Scramble-fry for about 10 minutes until beef is no longer pink. Drain. Add next 6 ingredients. Heat and stir for about 1 minute until fragrant.

Add remaining 5 ingredients. Stir. Bring to a boil. Reduce heat to medium-low. Simmer, uncovered, for about 20 minutes, stirring occasionally, until slightly thickened. Discard bay leaf. Serves 6.

1 serving: 232 Calories; 8.8 g Total Fat (3.8 g Mono, 0.9 g Poly, 2.8 g Sat); 38 mg Cholesterol; 20 g Carbohydrate; 5 g Fibre; 19 g Protein; 686 mg Sodium

Pictured on page 71.

1. Meatballs In Curry Sauce, page 81
2. Tandoori Chili, page 68
3. Ground Beef Curry, page 140

Props courtesy of: Pier 1 Imports
                The Dazzling Gourmet

Chuckwagon Chipotle Chili

Smoky flavour in warming chili. Potatoes are a hearty addition.
Great for a tailgate party or for a potluck picnic.

Cooking oil	2 tsp.	10 mL
Lean ground beef	1 lb.	454 g
Chopped onion	1 cup	250 mL
Chopped green pepper	1/2 cup	125 mL
Chipotle chili pepper in adobo sauce, chopped (see Tip, below)	1	1
Chili powder	2 tsp.	10 mL
Ground cumin	1/2 tsp.	2 mL
Salt	1/2 tsp.	2 mL
Bay leaf	1	1
Water	3 cups	750 mL
Can of black beans, rinsed and drained	19 oz.	540 mL
Can of diced tomatoes (with juice)	14 oz.	398 mL
Diced peeled potato	1 1/2 cups	375 mL
Frozen kernel corn	1 cup	250 mL
Can of tomato sauce	7 1/2 oz.	213 mL

Heat cooking oil in large deep frying pan or Dutch oven on medium. Add ground beef, onion and green pepper. Scramble-fry for about 10 minutes until beef is no longer pink. Drain.

Add next 5 ingredients. Heat and stir for about 1 minute until fragrant.

Add remaining 6 ingredients. Stir. Bring to a boil on medium-high. Reduce heat to medium. Boil gently, uncovered, for about 30 minutes, stirring occasionally, until potato is tender and sauce is thickened. Discard bay leaf. Serves 6.

1 serving: 290 Calories; 9 g Total Fat (3.9 g Mono, 1.1 g Poly, 2.8 g Sat); 38 mg Cholesterol; 34 g Carbohydrate; 5 g Fibre; 21 g Protein; 687 mg Sodium

Pictured on page 71.

 Chipotle chili peppers are smoked jalapeño peppers. Be sure to wash your hands after handling. To store any leftover chipotle chili peppers, divide into recipe-friendly portions and freeze, with sauce, in airtight containers for up to one year.

Chilies & Sauces

Chili Gumbo

Chili with a creole twist. If you like, add a few drops
of hot pepper sauce for extra heat. Serve with rice.

Bacon slices, diced	4	4
Lean ground beef	1 lb.	454 g
Chopped celery	1 cup	250 mL
Chopped onion	1/2 cup	125 mL
Can of diced tomatoes (with juice)	28 oz.	796 mL
Can of black-eyed peas, rinsed and drained	19 oz.	540 mL
Diced peeled yam (or sweet potato)	2 cups	500 mL
Can of crushed tomatoes	14 oz.	398 mL
Sliced fresh (or frozen, thawed) okra	1 1/2 cups	375 mL
Chopped green pepper	1 cup	250 mL
Prepared beef broth	1 cup	250 mL
Chili powder	1 tbsp.	15 mL
Dried oregano	1 tsp.	5 mL
Dried thyme	1 tsp.	5 mL
Garlic clove, minced (or 1/4 tsp., 1 mL, powder)	1	1
Dried basil	1/2 tsp.	2 mL
Salt	1/2 tsp.	2 mL
Cayenne pepper	1/8 tsp.	0.5 mL
Nutmeg, just a pinch		

Cook bacon in large deep frying pan or Dutch oven on medium until almost crisp.

Add ground beef, celery and onion. Scramble-fry for about 10 minutes until beef is no longer pink. Drain.

Add remaining 15 ingredients. Stir. Bring to a boil on medium-high. Reduce heat to medium-low. Simmer, covered, for about 30 minutes, stirring occasionally, until yam is tender and sauce is slightly thickened. Serves 6.

1 serving: 326 Calories; 9.8 g Total Fat (4 g Mono, 0.9 g Poly, 3.5 g Sat); 41 mg Cholesterol; 39 g Carbohydrate; 7 g Fibre; 22 g Protein; 908 mg Sodium

Pictured on front cover.

Chili And Dumplings

Traditional chunky chili crowned with fluffy dumplings.
A satisfying dish for lunch or dinner!

Cooking oil	2 tsp.	10 mL
Lean ground beef	1 lb.	454 g
Chopped onion	1 cup	250 mL
Garlic clove, minced (or 1/4 tsp., 1 mL, powder)	1	1
Chili powder	1 tbsp.	15 mL
Basil pesto	2 tsp.	10 mL
Ground cumin	1 tsp.	5 mL
Granulated sugar	1 tsp.	5 mL
Dried crushed chilies	1/2 tsp.	2 mL
Salt	1/2 tsp.	2 mL
Can of diced tomatoes (with juice)	14 oz.	398 mL
Can of red kidney beans, rinsed and drained	14 oz.	398 mL
Prepared beef broth	1 1/2 cups	375 mL
Can of tomato sauce	7 1/2 oz.	213 mL
CORNMEAL DUMPLINGS		
All-purpose flour	1/2 cup	125 mL
Yellow cornmeal	1/3 cup	75 mL
Grated Parmesan cheese	3 tbsp.	50 mL
Baking powder	1 tsp.	5 mL
Paprika	1/4 tsp.	1 mL
Large egg	1	1
Milk	2 tbsp.	30 mL
Cooking oil	2 tbsp.	30 mL
Basil pesto	1 tsp.	5 mL

Heat cooking oil in large deep frying pan or Dutch oven on medium. Add ground beef, onion and garlic. Scramble-fry for about 10 minutes until beef is no longer pink. Drain.

Add next 6 ingredients. Heat and stir for about 1 minute until fragrant.

Add next 4 ingredients. Stir. Bring to a boil. Reduce heat to medium-low. Simmer, uncovered, for 10 minutes, stirring occasionally.

(continued on next page)

Chilies & Sauces

Cornmeal Dumplings: Combine first 5 ingredients in medium bowl. Make a well in centre.

Beat remaining 4 ingredients with fork in small bowl until combined. Add to well. Stir until just moistened. Spoon mounds of batter, using about 2 tbsp. (30 mL) for each, in single layer on top of chili. Simmer, covered, for 15 to 20 minutes until wooden pick inserted in centre of dumpling comes out clean. Serves 6.

1 serving: 384 Calories; 16.2 g Total Fat (7.6 g Mono, 2.7 g Poly, 4.1 g Sat); 76 mg Cholesterol; 36 g Carbohydrate; 3 g Fibre; 24 g Protein; 1171 mg Sodium

Bolognese Sauce

This slow-cooker recipe can be adapted to a stovetop method.
Cook in a Dutch oven and simmer, covered, for about
an hour before adding the evaporated milk.

Olive (or cooking) oil	2 tsp.	10 mL
Chopped pancetta (or regular) bacon	4 oz.	113 g
Lean ground beef	2 lbs.	900 g
Finely chopped celery	2 cups	500 mL
Finely chopped carrot	2 cups	500 mL
Finely chopped onion	1 1/2 cups	375 mL
Prepared beef broth	2 cups	500 mL
Dry white (or alcohol-free) wine	1 cup	250 mL
Cans of tomato sauce (14 oz., 398 mL, each)	2	2
Can of evaporated milk	5 1/2 oz.	160 mL

Heat olive oil in large frying pan on medium. Add bacon. Cook for about 4 minutes, stirring occasionally, until almost crisp. Increase heat to medium-high.

Add next 4 ingredients. Scramble-fry for about 10 minutes until ground beef is no longer pink. Drain. Transfer to 4 to 5 quart (4 to 5 L) slow cooker.

Add next 3 ingredients. Stir. Cover. Cook on Low for 6 to 8 hours or on High for 3 to 4 hours. Skim any fat from surface of sauce.

Add evaporated milk. Stir. Cover. Cook on High for another 10 minutes until heated through. Serves 8.

1 serving: 318 Calories; 14.5 g Total Fat (6.5 g Mono, 0.9 g Poly, 5.6 g Sat); 68 mg Cholesterol; 17 g Carbohydrate; 3 g Fibre; 26 g Protein; 998 mg Sodium

Paprika Mushroom Sauce

A mild, stroganoff-style sauce with the added tang of artichokes. Delicious served over rice or egg noodles.

Cooking oil	2 tsp.	10 mL
Lean ground beef	1 lb.	454 g
Cooking oil	1 tsp.	5 mL
Chopped fresh white mushrooms	3 cups	750 mL
Chopped onion	1 cup	250 mL
Paprika	4 tsp.	20 mL
Dry mustard	1 tsp.	5 mL
Pepper	1/4 tsp.	1 mL
All-purpose flour	1 tbsp.	15 mL
Prepared beef broth	2 cups	500 mL
Can of artichoke hearts, drained and quartered	14 oz.	398 mL
Can of diced tomatoes (with juice)	14 oz.	398 mL
Sour cream	1/2 cup	125 mL

Heat first amount of cooking oil in large frying pan or Dutch oven on medium. Add ground beef. Scramble-fry for about 10 minutes until no longer pink. Drain. Transfer to medium bowl. Cover to keep warm.

Heat second amount of cooking oil in same pan. Add next 5 ingredients. Cook for 5 to 10 minutes, stirring often, until onion is softened and liquid is evaporated.

Add flour. Heat and stir for 1 minute. Slowly add broth, stirring constantly. Heat and stir for about 5 minutes until boiling and thickened.

Add beef, artichoke hearts and tomatoes. Stir. Bring to a boil. Heat and stir for about 2 minutes until heated through.

Add sour cream. Heat and stir until hot but not boiling. Serves 4.

1 serving: 364 Calories; 20 g Total Fat (8.6 g Mono, 2.4 g Poly, 7.1 g Sat); 69 mg Cholesterol; 21 g Carbohydrate; 5 g Fibre; 28 g Protein; 829 mg Sodium

Tasty Meatballs

Keep these handy in the freezer to add to your favourite sauce or gravy for a meal that's ready in minutes. We've included them in Mushroom Sauce, page 80, Curry Sauce, page 81, and Pineapple Sauce, page 82.

White (or brown) bread slices, processed into crumbs	2	2
Finely chopped green onion	1/3 cup	75 mL
Milk	2 tbsp.	30 mL
Finely chopped fresh parsley (or 3/4 tsp., 4 mL, flakes)	1 tbsp.	15 mL
Garlic cloves, minced (or 1/2 tsp., 2 mL, powder)	2	2
Seasoned salt	1 tsp.	5 mL
Hot pepper sauce	1/2 tsp.	2 mL
Pepper	1/8 tsp.	0.5 mL
Lean ground beef	1 lb.	454 g

Combine all 8 ingredients in large bowl.

Add ground beef. Mix well. Roll into 1 1/2 inch (3.8 cm) balls. Arrange on greased baking sheet with sides. Bake in 400°F (205°C) oven for about 15 minutes until fully cooked, and internal temperature of beef reaches 160°F (71°C). Makes about 18 meatballs.

1 meatball: 48 Calories; 2.2 g Total Fat (1 g Mono, 0.1 g Poly, 0.9 g Sat); 13 mg Cholesterol; 2 g Carbohydrate; trace Fibre; 5 g Protein; 95 mg Sodium

Paré Pointer

I never repeat gossip, so listen carefully the first time.

Meatballs In Mushroom Sauce

This silky, wine-infused mushroom sauce makes meatballs
a great go-together with mashed potatoes.

Package of dried porcini mushrooms	3/4 oz.	22 g
Boiling water		
Hard margarine (or butter)	1 tbsp.	15 mL
Finely chopped onion	1/4 cup	60 mL
Dry white (or alcohol-free) wine	1/2 cup	125 mL
Parsley flakes	1/2 tsp.	2 mL
Dill weed	1/4 tsp.	1 mL
Pepper	1/4 tsp.	1 mL
All-purpose flour	1 1/2 tbsp.	25 mL
Block of cream cheese, cut up	4 oz.	125 g
Prepared beef broth	1 cup	250 mL
Milk	1 cup	250 mL

Tasty Meatballs (cooked), page 79

Put mushrooms into small bowl. Cover with boiling water. Let stand for about 20 minutes until softened. Drain. Rinse with cold water. Drain well. Finely chop. Set aside.

Melt margarine in large saucepan on medium. Add onion. Cook for 5 to 10 minutes, stirring often, until softened.

Add mushrooms and next 4 ingredients. Stir. Bring to a boil. Reduce heat to low. Simmer, uncovered, for about 3 minutes, stirring often, until liquid is evaporated.

Add flour. Heat and stir for 1 minute.

Add cream cheese. Heat and stir until melted. Slowly add broth, stirring constantly. Add milk. Heat and stir for about 4 minutes until boiling and thickened. Remove from heat.

Put Tasty Meatballs into ungreased 2 quart (2 L) casserole. Pour mushroom mixture over top. Stir until coated. Bake, uncovered, in 350°F (175°C) oven for about 40 minutes until meatballs are heated through. Serves 6.

1 serving: 434 Calories; 24.7 g Total Fat (9.6 g Mono, 1.2 g Poly, 11.8 g Sat); 96 mg Cholesterol; 20 g Carbohydrate; 1 g Fibre; 28 g Protein; 797 mg Sodium

Meatballs In Curry Sauce

This meatball and tomato-based curry combination
is excellent served over rice or noodles.

Cooking oil	3 tbsp.	50 mL
Finely chopped onion	1 1/2 cups	375 mL
Garlic cloves, minced	3	3
Finely grated, peeled gingerroot	2 tsp.	10 mL
Paprika	1 tsp.	5 mL
Turmeric	1 tsp.	5 mL
Ground coriander	1 tsp.	5 mL
Ground cumin	1 tsp.	5 mL
Salt	1/2 tsp.	2 mL
Dried crushed chilies	1/4 tsp.	1 mL
Ground cinnamon	1/8 tsp.	0.5 mL
Ground cloves, just a pinch		
Prepared beef broth	1 1/2 cups	375 mL
Can of tomato sauce	7 1/2 oz.	213 mL
Tasty Meatballs (cooked), page 79		
Plain yogurt	1/2 cup	125 mL

Heat cooking oil in large saucepan on medium. Add onion. Cook for 15 to 20 minutes, stirring often, until caramelized.

Add next 10 ingredients. Heat and stir for about 2 minutes until fragrant.

Add broth and tomato sauce. Stir. Bring to a boil.

Add Tasty Meatballs. Stir. Return to a boil. Reduce heat to medium-low. Simmer, uncovered, for about 45 minutes, stirring occasionally, until sauce is thickened.

Slowly add yogurt, stirring constantly. Heat and stir for about 1 minute until hot but not boiling. Serves 4.

1 serving: 257 Calories; 14.4 g Total Fat (7.2 g Mono, 2.5 g Poly, 3.4 g Sat); 41 mg Cholesterol; 15 g Carbohydrate; 2 g Fibre; 18 g Protein; 932 mg Sodium

Pictured on page 72.

Meatballs In Pineapple Sauce

This pineapple sauce, infused with chili and lime, adds an exotic flair to meatballs. A dominant ginger flavour makes this dish particularly delicious!

Cooking oil	1 tbsp.	15 mL
Finely chopped onion	1/3 cup	75 mL
Finely grated, peeled gingerroot	2 tsp.	10 mL
Can of crushed pineapple, drained and juice reserved	14 oz.	398 mL
Sweet chili sauce	1/2 cup	125 mL
Lime juice	3 tbsp.	50 mL
Minced crystallized ginger	1 tbsp.	15 mL
Soy sauce	2 tsp.	10 mL
Salt	1/4 tsp.	1 mL
Reserved pineapple juice	2/3 cup	150 mL
Cornstarch	2 tsp.	10 mL
Grated lime zest	1/4 tsp.	1 mL

Tasty Meatballs (cooked), page 79

Heat cooking oil in medium saucepan on medium. Add onion. Cook for about 2 minutes, stirring often, until starting to soften. Add ginger. Heat and stir for another 2 to 3 minutes until onion is softened.

Add next 6 ingredients. Stir. Bring to a boil.

Stir reserved pineapple juice and cornstarch in small bowl until smooth. Slowly add to crushed pineapple mixture, stirring constantly. Heat and stir for 2 to 3 minutes until boiling and slightly thickened.

Add lime zest. Stir. Remove from heat.

Put Tasty Meatballs into ungreased 2 quart (2 L) casserole. Pour pineapple mixture over top. Stir until coated. Bake, covered, in 325°F (160°C) oven for about 30 minutes until meatballs are heated through. Serves 6.

1 serving: 368 Calories; 13.7 g Total Fat (6.4 g Mono, 1.5 g Poly, 4.2 g Sat); 59 mg Cholesterol; 39 g Carbohydrate; 4 g Fibre; 24 g Protein; 1237 mg Sodium

Sesame Meatballs

These sesame-coated meatballs are tender on the inside and crunchy on the outside. Pickled ginger adds a tasty touch to the sauce.

Large egg	1	1
Soda cracker crumbs	1/3 cup	75 mL
Sliced green onion	1/4 cup	60 mL
Red curry paste	2 tsp.	10 mL
Salt	1/4 tsp.	1 mL
Pepper	1/4 tsp.	1 mL
Lean ground beef	1 lb.	454 g
Sesame seeds	2/3 cup	150 mL
SWEET AND SOUR SAUCE		
Pineapple juice	1/3 cup	75 mL
Soy sauce	1/4 cup	60 mL
Ketchup	1/4 cup	60 mL
Brown sugar, packed	1/4 cup	60 mL
Balsamic vinegar	2 tbsp.	30 mL
Chopped pickled ginger slices, drained	2 tbsp.	30 mL
Cornstarch	2 tsp.	10 mL

Combine first 6 ingredients in large bowl.

Add ground beef. Mix well. Roll into 1 inch (2.5 cm) balls.

Roll each meatball in sesame seeds in small shallow dish until coated. Arrange on greased baking sheet with sides. Bake in 350°F (175°C) oven for about 20 minutes until fully cooked, and internal temperature of beef reaches 160°F (71°C). Remove to large serving bowl. Cover to keep warm.

Sweet And Sour Sauce: Combine all 7 ingredients in small saucepan. Heat and stir on medium for 6 to 8 minutes until boiling and thickened. Makes about 1 cup (250 mL) sauce. Drizzle over meatballs, or serve on the side. Serves 4.

1 serving: 328 Calories; 16.7 g Total Fat (6.8 g Mono, 4.3 g Poly, 4 g Sat); 75 mg Cholesterol; 27 g Carbohydrate; 4 g Fibre; 20 g Protein; 1068 mg Sodium

Pictured on page 89.

Spicy Lava Meatballs

A spicy cheese surprise oozes like lava from these
meatballs—an explosion of flavour kids of all ages will enjoy.
Serve these as soon as they're cooked for best effect.

Grated Monterey Jack With Jalapeño cheese	1 cup	250 mL
Block of cream cheese, softened	4 oz.	125 g
Crushed buttery crackers	1/4 cup	60 mL
Cajun seasoning	2 tsp.	10 mL
Large egg	1	1
Crushed buttery crackers	1/2 cup	125 mL
Finely chopped green onion	2 tbsp.	30 mL
Worcestershire sauce	1 tbsp.	15 mL
Prepared horseradish	2 tsp.	10 mL
Lean ground beef	1 1/2 lbs.	680 g

Combine first 4 ingredients in small bowl. Roll cheese mixture into 18 inch (45 cm) log. Cut into 1/2 inch (12 mm) slices, for a total of 36 slices. Roll each slice into ball. Arrange on ungreased baking sheet. Freeze for about 1 hour until firm.

Combine next 5 ingredients in large bowl.

Add ground beef. Mix well. Divide into 36 equal portions. Roll into balls. Dent each ball with thumb. Place 1 cheese ball into each dent. Re-roll each ball to completely cover cheese ball with beef mixture. Arrange on greased baking sheet with sides. Broil on top rack in oven for about 15 minutes until fully cooked, and internal temperature of beef reaches 160°F (71°C). Cheese should be oozing from meatballs. Serve immediately. Makes 36 meatballs.

1 meatball: 69 Calories; 4.6 g Total Fat (1.7 g Mono, 0.4 g Poly, 2.2 g Sat); 22 mg Cholesterol; 2 g Carbohydrate; trace Fibre; 5 g Protein; 68 mg Sodium

Vietnamese Noodle Balls

Serve these unique meatballs as an appetizer, or add them to a stir-fry of vegetables and hoisin sauce.

Rice vermicelli	2 oz.	57 g
Hot water		
Large egg, fork-beaten	1	1
Sliced green onion	3 tbsp.	50 mL
Soy sauce	2 tbsp.	30 mL
Fish sauce	2 tbsp.	30 mL
Cornstarch	2 tbsp.	30 mL
Medium sherry	1 tbsp.	15 mL
Garlic clove, minced (or 1/4 tsp., 1 mL, powder)	1	1
Granulated sugar	1 tsp.	5 mL
Sesame oil, for flavour	1 tsp.	5 mL
Pepper	1/2 tsp.	2 mL
Lean ground beef	1 lb.	454 g

Put vermicelli into large bowl. Cover with hot water. Let stand for about 5 minutes until softened. Drain. Coarsely chop. Return to same bowl.

Add next 10 ingredients. Stir.

Add ground beef. Mix well. Roll into 1 inch (2.5 cm) balls. Arrange on greased baking sheet with sides. Bake in 350°F (175°C) oven for 20 to 25 minutes until fully cooked, and internal temperature of beef reaches 160°F (71°C). Makes about 36 meatballs.

1 meatball: 33 Calories; 1.3 g Total Fat (0.6 g Mono, 0.1 g Poly, 0.5 g Sat); 12 mg Cholesterol; 2 g Carbohydrate; 0 g Fibre; 3 g Protein; 123 mg Sodium

Apricot Meatballs

Chewy apricot is hidden inside meatballs
coated with a sweet, smoky sauce. So good!

Dried apricots, halved	18	18
Water		
Large egg	1	1
Finely chopped onion	1/4 cup	60 mL
Cornflake crumbs	1/4 cup	60 mL
Worcestershire sauce	1 tsp.	5 mL
Dried rosemary, crushed	1/2 tsp.	2 mL
Lean ground beef	1 lb.	454 g
APRICOT SAUCE		
Apricot jam	1/2 cup	125 mL
Hickory barbecue sauce	1/4 cup	60 mL
Apple cider vinegar	1 tbsp.	15 mL

Put apricot halves into medium bowl. Cover with water. Let stand for 10 to 15 minutes until softened. Drain. Squeeze out excess water. Blot dry with paper towels. Set aside.

Combine next 5 ingredients in medium bowl.

Add ground beef. Mix well. Divide into 36 equal portions. Roll into balls. Dent each ball with thumb. Place 1 apricot half into each dent. Re-roll each ball to completely cover apricot with beef mixture. Arrange on greased baking sheet with sides. Bake in 400°F (205°C) oven for about 15 minutes until fully cooked, and internal temperature of beef reaches 160°F (71°C). Transfer to greased 2 quart (2 L) casserole.

Apricot Sauce: Combine jam, barbecue sauce and vinegar in small saucepan. Heat and stir on medium for about 3 minutes until heated through. Makes about 1 cup (250 mL) sauce. Pour over meatballs. Stir until coated. Bake, covered, in 350°F (175°C) oven for about 20 minutes until sauce is boiling. Serves 4.

1 serving: 373 Calories; 11.2 g Total Fat (4.8 g Mono, 0.6 g Poly, 4.1 g Sat); 112 mg Cholesterol; 46 g Carbohydrate; 3 g Fibre; 24 g Protein; 290 mg Sodium

Pictured on page 89.

Nacho Meatballs

These Tex-Mex meatballs smothered with spicy cheese sauce are sure to become a favourite. Serve with rice, or tuck the meatballs and sauce inside taco shells or pita breads.

Large egg	1	1
Crushed nacho chips	1/2 cup	125 mL
Medium salsa	1/4 cup	60 mL
Envelope of taco seasoning mix	1 1/4 oz.	35 g
Lean ground beef	1 lb.	454 g
NACHO CHEESE SAUCE		
Hard margarine (or butter)	2 tbsp.	30 mL
All-purpose flour	2 tbsp.	30 mL
Dry mustard	1/2 tsp.	2 mL
Cayenne pepper	1/8 tsp.	0.5 mL
Milk	1 cup	250 mL
Grated sharp Cheddar cheese	1 cup	250 mL

Combine first 4 ingredients in medium bowl.

Add ground beef. Mix well. Roll into 1 inch (2.5 cm) balls. Arrange on greased baking sheet with sides. Bake in 350°F (175°C) oven for about 15 minutes until fully cooked, and internal temperature of beef reaches 160°F (71°C). Remove to large serving bowl. Cover to keep warm.

Nacho Cheese Sauce: Melt margarine in small saucepan on medium. Add flour, mustard and cayenne pepper. Heat and stir for 1 minute.

Slowly add milk, stirring constantly. Heat and stir for about 5 minutes until boiling and thickened. Remove from heat.

Add cheese. Stir until melted. Makes about 1 1/3 cups (325 mL) sauce. Pour over meatballs, or serve on the side. Serves 6.

1 serving: 310 Calories; 19.6 g Total Fat (8.3 g Mono, 1.1 g Poly, 8.2 g Sat); 98 mg Cholesterol; 11 g Carbohydrate; 1 g Fibre; 22 g Protein; 951 mg Sodium

Salsa Porcupines

Forget the chicken dance, these porcupines like to salsa! Old-fashioned meatballs are smothered in a tangy sauce and topped with cheese.

Long grain white rice	1/2 cup	125 mL
Milk	1/2 cup	125 mL
Finely chopped onion	1/4 cup	60 mL
Salt	1 tsp.	5 mL
Pepper	1/4 tsp.	1 mL
Lean ground beef	1 lb.	454 g
Mild salsa	2 cups	500 mL
Water	1/2 cup	125 mL
Grated Monterey Jack cheese	1/2 cup	125 mL

Combine first 5 ingredients in large bowl.

Add ground beef. Mix well. Roll into 1 1/2 inch (3.8 cm) balls. Arrange in greased 9 x 9 inch (22 x 22 cm) pan.

Combine salsa and water in medium bowl. Pour over meatballs. Cover with foil. Bake in 400°F (205°C) oven for about 1 1/4 hours until fully cooked, and internal temperature of beef reaches 160°F (71°C).

Sprinkle with cheese. Serves 4.

1 serving: 438 Calories; 22.5 g Total Fat (8.9 g Mono, 1.1 g Poly, 10 g Sat); 78 mg Cholesterol; 29 g Carbohydrate; 3 g Fibre; 29 g Protein; 1120 mg Sodium

1. Saffron Meatball Casserole, page 39
2. Apricot Meatballs, page 86
3. Sweet and Sour Sauce, page 83
4. Sesame Meatballs, page 83
5. Grilled Meatball Skewers, page 92

Props courtesy of: Anchor Hocking Canada
Cherison Enterprisesu Inc.
Danesco Inc.

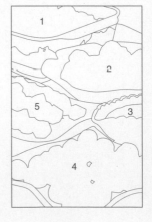

Meatballs

Ginger Meatballs

When you're looking for a taste of the Orient, these meatballs are the ones to try. Add them to stir-fry veggies, or serve them with rice.

Large egg	1	1
Crisp rice cereal	1 cup	250 mL
Ketchup	1/4 cup	60 mL
Jar of pickled ginger slices, drained and finely chopped	1 3/4 oz.	50 g
Finely chopped onion	2 tbsp.	30 mL
Prepared horseradish	1 tbsp.	15 mL
Soy sauce	1 tbsp.	15 mL
Balsamic vinegar	1 tbsp.	15 mL
Lean ground beef	1 lb.	454 g

Combine first 8 ingredients in large bowl.

Add ground beef. Mix well. Roll into 1 1/2 inch (3.8 cm) balls. Arrange on greased baking sheet with sides. Bake in 400°F (205°C) oven for about 20 minutes until fully cooked, and internal temperature of beef reaches 160°F (71°C). Makes about 20 meatballs.

1 meatball: 51 Calories; 2.2 g Total Fat (0.9 g Mono, 0.1 g Poly, 0.8 g Sat); 22 mg Cholesterol; 3 g Carbohydrate; trace Fibre; 5 g Protein; 118 mg Sodium

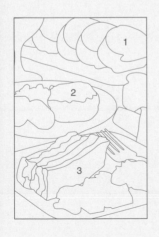

1. Beef And Vegetable Roundup, page 96
2. Gourmet Mini-Meatloaves, page 100
3. Layered Cajun Loaf, page 99

Props courtesy of: Cherison Enterprises Inc.
Danesco Inc.

Grilled Meatball Skewers

For an attractive presentation, arrange these tri-coloured skewers
on a bed of coconut rice. Serve with peanut sauce for dipping.

Large egg	1	1
Graham cracker crumbs	1/3 cup	75 mL
Smooth peanut butter	2 tbsp.	30 mL
Soy sauce	1 tbsp.	15 mL
Garlic clove, minced (or 1/4 tsp., 1 mL, powder)	1	1
Curry powder	1 tsp.	5 mL
Ground ginger	1/2 tsp.	2 mL
Coconut flavouring	1/2 tsp.	2 mL
Lean ground beef	1 lb.	454 g
Can of pineapple chunks, drained	14 oz.	398 mL
Large red pepper, cut into 24 equal pieces	1	1
Bamboo skewers (8 inches, 20 cm, each), soaked in water for 10 minutes	8	8

Combine first 8 ingredients in medium bowl.

Add ground beef. Mix well. Divide into 24 equal portions. Roll into balls.

Thread pineapple, red pepper and meatballs alternately onto skewers, beginning and ending with pineapple on each (see photo, page 89). Preheat gas barbecue to medium. (For other cooking methods, see page 8.) Cook skewers on greased grill for 12 to 15 minutes, turning occasionally, until fully cooked and internal temperature of beef reaches 160°F (71°C). Makes 8 skewers.

1 skewer: 161 Calories; 8.1 g Total Fat (3.6 g Mono, 0.9 g Poly, 2.6 g Sat); 55 mg Cholesterol; 10 g Carbohydrate; 1 g Fibre; 13 g Protein; 210 mg Sodium

Pictured on page 89.

APPETIZER MEATBALL SKEWERS: Soak twenty-four 4 inch (10 cm) bamboo skewers in water for 10 minutes. Thread 1 meatball, 1 pineapple chunk and 1 red pepper piece onto each. Cook as directed.

Meatballs

Meatloaf Classic

A favourite from Casseroles, *this good old-fashioned meatloaf will be a hit with kids and adults alike. Great comfort food!*

Large egg	1	1
Quick-cooking rolled oats	3/4 cup	175 mL
Milk	3/4 cup	175 mL
Minced onion (or 1 tbsp., 15 mL, onion flakes)	1/4 cup	60 mL
Parsley flakes	1 tsp.	5 mL
Worcestershire sauce	1 tsp.	5 mL
Salt	1 1/2 tsp.	7 mL
Pepper	1/4 tsp.	1 mL
Lean ground beef	1 1/2 lbs.	680 g
Grated medium Cheddar cheese	1 cup	250 mL
Ketchup	1/4 cup	60 mL

Combine first 8 ingredients in large bowl.

Add ground beef. Mix well. Press 1/2 of beef mixture into greased 9 x 5 x 3 inch (22 x 12.5 x 7.5 cm) loaf pan.

Sprinkle with cheese. Press remaining beef mixture on top of cheese.

Spread ketchup on top of beef mixture. Bake, uncovered, in 350°F (175°C) oven for 1 1/4 to 1 1/2 hours until fully cooked, and internal temperature of beef reaches 160°F (71°C). Let stand for 10 minutes. Cuts into 12 slices. Serves 6.

1 serving: 416 Calories; 25.8 g Total Fat (10 g Mono, 1.4 g Poly, 11.7 g Sat); 122 mg Cholesterol; 14 g Carbohydrate; 2 g Fibre; 30 g Protein; 955 mg Sodium

Paré Pointer

He offered his girlfriend anything she wanted, so she took everything he had—including his best friend!

Sweet Onion Loaf

*Sweet caramelized onions are baked into this savoury
meatloaf. Topped nicely with a zippy mustard glaze.*

Hard margarine (or butter)	2 tbsp.	30 mL
Olive (or cooking) oil	1 tbsp.	15 mL
Thinly sliced onion	2 cups	500 mL
Balsamic vinegar	1 tbsp.	15 mL
Large egg	1	1
Fine dry bread crumbs	1/2 cup	125 mL
Garlic clove, minced (or 1/4 tsp., 1 mL, powder)	1	1
Dried thyme	1/2 tsp.	2 mL
Seasoned salt	1/2 tsp.	2 mL
Pepper	1/4 tsp.	1 mL
Lean ground beef	2 lbs.	900 g
Dijon mustard	2 tbsp.	30 mL
Liquid honey	2 tbsp.	30 mL
Prepared mustard	1 tbsp.	15 mL

Heat margarine and olive oil in medium frying pan on medium. Add
onion. Cook for 15 to 20 minutes, stirring often, until caramelized.

Add vinegar. Stir. Remove from heat.

Combine next 6 ingredients in large bowl.

Add caramelized onion and ground beef. Mix well. Press into greased
9 x 5 x 3 inch (22 x 12.5 x 7.5 cm) loaf pan. Bake, uncovered, in 350°F
(175°C) oven for 30 minutes. Drain.

Combine last 3 ingredients in small cup. Spread on top of meatloaf. Bake
for another 25 to 30 minutes until fully cooked, and internal temperature
of beef reaches 160°F (71°C). Let stand for 10 minutes. Cuts into 8 slices.

*1 slice: 362 Calories; 23.1 g Total Fat (11.1 g Mono, 1.5 g Poly, 8 g Sat); 91 mg Cholesterol;
14 g Carbohydrate; 1 g Fibre; 24 g Protein; 331 mg Sodium*

Ground Beef Pot Roast

*Easy to make and easy to serve. This homestyle meatloaf
"pot roast," seasoned with horseradish, is a complete meal.*

Large eggs	2	2
Quick-cooking rolled oats	3/4 cup	175 mL
Water	1/3 cup	75 mL
Envelope of dry onion soup mix	1 1/2 oz.	42 g
Prepared horseradish	1 tbsp.	15 mL
Pepper	1/2 tsp.	2 mL
Extra lean ground beef	1 1/2 lbs.	680 g
Baby carrots	3 cups	750 mL
Cubed peeled potato	3 cups	750 mL
Thinly sliced onion	1 1/2 cups	375 mL

Combine first 6 ingredients in large bowl.

Add ground beef. Mix well. Shape into 4 × 6 inch (10 × 15 cm) oval. Put
into greased medium roasting pan.

Arrange remaining 3 ingredients around meatloaf in pan. Bake, covered,
in 350°F (175°C) oven for 1 hour. Remove cover. Bake for another 20 to
30 minutes until fully cooked, and internal temperature of beef reaches
160°F (71°C). Serves 6.

*1 serving: 471 Calories; 19.3 g Total Fat (8.2 g Mono, 1.3 g Poly, 7.1 g Sat); 148 mg Cholesterol;
39 g Carbohydrate; 5 g Fibre; 35 g Protein; 739 mg Sodium*

Paré Pointer
You can tell when the sun gets tired—it sets for awhile.

Beef And Vegetable Roundup

This unique meatloaf is great for a casual dinner. A hint of hickory and a layer of crunchy veggies are rolled up inside.

Large eggs	2	2
Fine dry bread crumbs	2/3 cup	150 mL
Ketchup	1/3 cup	75 mL
Seasoned salt	1 1/2 tsp.	7 mL
Pepper	1/2 tsp.	2 mL
Lean ground beef	2 lbs.	900 g
Thinly sliced onion	1 cup	250 mL
Grated carrot	1 cup	250 mL
Grated zucchini, squeezed dry	1 cup	250 mL
Fine dry bread crumbs	1/3 cup	75 mL
Hickory barbecue sauce	3 tbsp.	50 mL
Ketchup	2 tbsp.	30 mL
Parsley flakes	2 tsp.	10 mL
Hickory barbecue sauce	3 tbsp.	50 mL
Ketchup	2 tbsp.	30 mL

Combine first 5 ingredients in large bowl.

Add ground beef. Mix well. On large sheet of foil, pat out beef mixture to 10 × 15 inch (25 × 38 cm) rectangle.

Combine next 7 ingredients in large bowl. Spread on top of beef rectangle, leaving 1 inch (2.5 cm) edge on 1 long side. Roll up from uncovered long side, jelly-roll style, using foil as guide. Press seam against roll to seal. Place, seam-side down, on greased baking sheet with sides. Bake, uncovered, in 350°F (175°C) oven for 30 minutes.

Combine second amount of barbecue sauce and third amount of ketchup in small cup. Spread on top of meatloaf. Bake for another 25 to 30 minutes until fully cooked, and internal temperature of beef reaches 160°F (71°C). Let stand for 10 minutes. Cuts into 8 slices.

1 slice: 291 Calories; 11.7 g Total Fat (5 g Mono, 0.9 g Poly, 4.3 g Sat); 112 mg Cholesterol; 21 g Carbohydrate; 3 g Fibre; 25 g Protein; 722 mg Sodium

Pictured on page 90.

Ricotta Swiss Wedges

A meatloaf that looks like a cake! You can garnish each
wedge with a potato rosette and top with a cherry tomato—
kids will love a meal that looks like dessert.

Large eggs	2	2
Bacon slices, cooked crisp and crumbled	4	4
Fine dry bread crumbs	3/4 cup	175 mL
Tomato sauce	1/2 cup	125 mL
Medium salsa	1/2 cup	125 mL
Dried basil	1/2 tsp.	2 mL
Dried oregano	1/4 tsp.	1 mL
Dried thyme	1/4 tsp.	1 mL
Salt	1/4 tsp.	1 mL
Pepper	1/4 tsp.	1 mL
Lean ground beef	1 lb.	454 g
Lean ground pork	1/2 lb.	225 g
Ricotta cheese	2 cups	500 mL
Grated Swiss cheese	1 cup	250 mL
Chopped fresh parsley (or 3/4 tsp., 4 mL, flakes)	1 tbsp.	15 mL

Combine first 10 ingredients in large bowl.

Add ground beef and pork. Mix well. Press into greased 9 inch (22 cm) springform pan. Set pan on baking sheet with sides. Bake, uncovered, in 350°F (175°C) oven for about 30 minutes until firm.

Combine remaining 3 ingredients in small bowl. Spread on top of meatloaf. Bake for another 45 to 50 minutes until fully cooked, and internal temperature of meat reaches 160°F (71°C). Let stand for 10 minutes. Cuts into 8 wedges.

1 wedge: 399 Calories; 24.6 g Total Fat (8.7 g Mono, 1.5 g Poly, 12.4 g Sat); 150 mg Cholesterol; 13 g Carbohydrate; 1 g Fibre; 31 g Protein; 503 mg Sodium

Pictured on page 53 and on back cover.

Spinach-Stuffed Meatloaf

Looks as good as it tastes! Stuffed with bacon and spinach and glazed with apricot jam, this meatloaf has a delightfully sweet, smoky flavour.

Bacon slices, diced	4	4
Chopped onion	1/2 cup	125 mL
Garlic clove, minced (or 1/4 tsp., 1 mL, powder)	1	1
Box of frozen chopped spinach, thawed and squeezed dry	10 oz.	300 g
Chopped dried apricot	1/4 cup	60 mL
Pepper	1/2 tsp.	2 mL
Large egg	1	1
Crushed buttery crackers	1/2 cup	125 mL
Balsamic vinegar	2 tbsp.	30 mL
Seasoned salt	1/2 tsp.	2 mL
Lean ground beef	1 lb.	454 g
Apricot jam	1/4 cup	60 mL
Apple cider vinegar	1 1/2 tbsp.	25 mL

Cook bacon in medium frying pan on medium until crisp. Transfer with slotted spoon to paper towels to drain. Set aside.

Heat 1 tbsp. (15 mL) drippings in same pan on medium. Add onion and garlic. Heat and stir for about 3 minutes until onion starts to soften.

Add next 3 ingredients. Stir. Remove from heat. Set aside.

Combine next 4 ingredients in medium bowl. Add ground beef. Mix well. On large sheet of foil, pat out beef mixture to 8 × 11 inch (20 × 28 cm) rectangle. Spoon spinach mixture lengthwise along centre of rectangle. Sprinkle bacon over top. Fold both long sides over stuffing to enclose. Pinch edges to seal. Holding foil, carefully roll meatloaf onto greased wire rack set on greased baking sheet with sides. Seam side should be down. Discard foil. Bake, uncovered, in 350°F (175°C) oven for 30 minutes.

Combine jam and apple cider vinegar in small cup. Spread on top of meatloaf. Bake for another 10 to 15 minutes until fully cooked, and internal temperature of beef reaches 160°F (71°C). Let stand for 10 minutes. Cuts into 8 slices.

1 slice: 225 Calories; 12.3 g Total Fat (5.3 g Mono, 1.1 g Poly, 4.5 g Sat); 62 mg Cholesterol; 15 g Carbohydrate; 1 g Fibre; 14 g Protein; 238 mg Sodium

Pictured on front cover.

Layered Cajun Loaf

Spicy and delicious. Great with rice and steamed veggies.

Large egg	1	1
Grated Monterey Jack cheese	1 cup	250 mL
Soda cracker crumbs	1/2 cup	125 mL
Can of diced green chilies	4 oz.	113 g
Dried thyme	1/4 tsp.	1 mL
Ground coriander	1/4 tsp.	1 mL
Ground marjoram	1/4 tsp.	1 mL
Large egg	1	1
Finely chopped onion	1 cup	250 mL
Soda cracker crumbs	2/3 cup	150 mL
Tomato sauce	1/3 cup	75 mL
Garlic clove, minced (or 1/4 tsp., 1 mL, powder)	1	1
Salt	1/2 tsp.	2 mL
Pepper	1/2 tsp.	2 mL
Lean ground beef	1 1/4 lbs.	560 g
Tomato sauce	1/2 cup	125 mL
Cajun seasoning	1/2 tsp.	2 mL

Combine first 7 ingredients in medium bowl. Divide into 2 equal portions. Set aside.

Combine next 7 ingredients in large bowl.

Add ground beef. Mix well. Divide into 3 equal portions. Starting and ending with beef mixture, press portions of beef and cheese mixtures alternately into greased 9 x 5 x 3 inch (22 x 12.5 x 7.5 cm) loaf pan. Press down lightly. Bake, uncovered, in 350°F (175°C) oven for 30 minutes.

Stir second amount of tomato sauce and seasoning in small bowl. Spread on top of meatloaf. Bake for another 30 to 35 minutes until fully cooked, and internal temperature of beef reaches 160°F (71°C). Let stand for 10 minutes. Cuts into 6 slices.

1 slice: 399 Calories; 23.9 g Total Fat (9.6 g Mono, 1.4 g Poly, 10.3 g Sat); 142 mg Cholesterol; 18 g Carbohydrate; 2 g Fibre; 27 g Protein; 826 mg Sodium

Pictured on page 90.

Gourmet Mini-Meatloaves

Elegant individual meatloaves infused with rich, Italian flavours.
When company's coming, these are sure to impress!

Large egg	1	1
Balsamic vinegar	3 tbsp.	50 mL
Crushed seasoned croutons	1/2 cup	125 mL
Lean ground beef	1 1/2 lbs.	680 g
Block of cream cheese, softened	4 oz.	125 g
Finely chopped prosciutto (or deli) ham	1/2 cup	125 mL
Grated Parmesan cheese	1/3 cup	75 mL
Sun-dried tomato pesto	3 tbsp.	50 mL
Chopped fresh sage (or 3/4 tsp., 4 mL, dried)	1 tbsp.	15 mL
SUN-DRIED TOMATO SAUCE		
Diced Roma (plum) tomato	1 3/4 cups	425 mL
Prepared chicken broth	1 1/4 cups	300 mL
Chopped green onion	1/2 cup	125 mL
Sun-dried tomato pesto	1/4 cup	60 mL
Water	1 tbsp.	15 mL
Cornstarch	1 tbsp.	15 mL

Combine first 3 ingredients in large bowl.

Add ground beef. Mix well. Divide into 8 equal portions. Press into 8 greased 1/2 cup (125 mL) ramekins. Make a well in each, about 1 1/2 inches (3.8 cm) in diameter and 1 inch (2.5 cm) deep.

Combine next 5 ingredients in small bowl. Spoon about 2 tbsp. (30 mL) cheese mixture into each well. Place ramekins on baking sheet. Cover with greased foil. Bake in 350°F (175°C) oven for about 40 minutes until fully cooked, and internal temperature of beef reaches 160°F (71°C). Cool slightly. Lift meatloaves from ramekins to paper towels to drain. Cover to keep warm.

Sun-Dried Tomato Sauce: Combine first 4 ingredients in small saucepan. Bring to a boil on medium. Boil gently for about 5 minutes, stirring occasionally, until tomato is softened.

(continued on next page)

Stir water and cornstarch in small cup until smooth. Slowly add to tomato mixture, stirring constantly. Heat and stir for about 1 minute until boiling and thickened. Makes about 2 1/3 cups (575 mL) sauce. Put meatloaves on dinner plates. Spoon sauce over top. Serves 8.

1 serving: 342 Calories; 23.4 g Total Fat (9.4 g Mono, 1.3 g Poly, 10.4 g Sat); 101 mg Cholesterol; 9 g Carbohydrate; 1 g Fibre; 23 g Protein; 530 mg Sodium

Pictured on page 90.

Lazy Stuffed Meatloaf

A 1950s-style meatloaf, complete with ketchup glaze.
Add some mashed potatoes and you've got comfort food at its best.

Large egg	1	1
Tomato juice	1 cup	250 mL
Fine dry bread crumbs	1/2 cup	125 mL
Finely chopped onion	1/2 cup	125 mL
Prepared horseradish	1 tsp.	5 mL
Celery salt	1/2 tsp.	2 mL
Salt	1/2 tsp.	2 mL
Pepper	1/4 tsp.	1 mL
Box of chicken stove-top stuffing mix, prepared according to package directions	4 1/4 oz.	120 g
Lean ground beef	1 lb.	454 g
Ketchup	3 tbsp.	50 mL
Mustard	1 tbsp.	15 mL

Combine first 8 ingredients in large bowl.

Add prepared stuffing. Stir. Add ground beef. Mix well. Press into greased 2 quart (2 L) casserole.

Combine ketchup and mustard in small cup. Spread on top of beef mixture. Bake, uncovered, in 350°F (175°C) oven for about 1 hour until fully cooked, and internal temperature of beef reaches 160°F (71°C). Serves 6.

1 serving: 362 Calories; 19.1 g Total Fat (8.2 g Mono, 2.7 g Poly, 6.2 g Sat); 79 mg Cholesterol; 28 g Carbohydrate; 3 g Fibre; 19 g Protein; 1103 mg Sodium

Italian Sandwich

Tell your guests to bring their appetite! These attractive,
open-face sandwiches are loaded with Italian flavour.

BRUSCHETTA TOPPING

Diced tomato	3 cups	750 mL
Finely chopped green onion	1/3 cup	75 mL
Chopped fresh basil (or 3/4 tsp., 4 mL, dried)	1 tbsp.	15 mL
Garlic clove, minced (or 1/4 tsp., 1 mL, powder)	1	1
Dried oregano	1/2 tsp.	2 mL
Salt, just a pinch		
Pepper, just a pinch		
Large egg	1	1
Crushed Caesar croutons	1/2 cup	125 mL
Garlic clove, minced (or 1/4 tsp., 1 mL, powder)	1	1
Dried oregano	1/2 tsp.	2 mL
Salt	1/8 tsp.	0.5 mL
Pepper	1/8 tsp.	0.5 mL
Lean ground beef	1 lb.	454 g
Ciabatta rolls (see Note), split	2	2
Balsamic vinegar	2 tbsp.	30 mL
Olive oil	1 tbsp.	15 mL
Provolone (or process mozzarella) cheese slices	8	8

Bruschetta Topping: Combine first 7 ingredients in medium bowl. Makes about 3 1/2 cups (875 mL) topping.

Combine next 6 ingredients in large bowl. Add ground beef. Mix well. Divide into 4 equal portions. Shape into oval patties to fit ciabatta rolls. Place patties on greased baking sheet with sides. Broil on centre rack in oven for 5 to 7 minutes per side until fully cooked, and internal temperature of beef reaches 160°F (71°C).

Place rolls, cut-side up, on separate baking sheet. Brush with vinegar and olive oil. Top each half with 1 patty, Bruschetta Topping and 2 cheese slices. Broil on centre rack for 4 to 5 minutes until cheese is melted and golden. Serves 4.

(continued on next page)

1 serving: 619 Calories; 40.5 g Total Fat (15.9 g Mono, 2.1 g Poly, 18.8 g Sat); 160 mg Cholesterol; 21 g Carbohydrate; 2 g Fibre; 42 g Protein; 903 mg Sodium

Pictured on page 107.

Note: If ciabatta rolls are not available in your grocery store, use other crusty, dense rolls that will support the moist topping without becoming soggy.

Pesto Goat Cheese Wedges

A round loaf of savoury bread holds a large patty. Individual wedges are an attractive, tasty alternative to the traditional hamburger.

Fine dry bread crumbs	1/4 cup	60 mL
Grated Parmesan cheese	3 tbsp.	50 mL
Basil pesto	3 tbsp.	50 mL
Pepper	1/2 tsp.	2 mL
Lean ground beef	1 lb.	454 g
Goat (chèvre) cheese	3/4 cup	175 mL
Mayonnaise	1/4 cup	60 mL
Roasted red peppers, drained, blotted dry, finely chopped	3 tbsp.	50 mL
Herb focaccia bread (10 inch, 25 cm, diameter)	1	1
Shredded lettuce, lightly packed	1 cup	250 mL

Combine first 4 ingredients in medium bowl.

Add ground beef. Mix well. Roll into ball. Place on ungreased 12 inch (30 cm) pizza pan or on baking sheet with sides. Pat out to 10 inch (25 cm) diameter patty. Bake in 350°F (175°C) oven for about 15 minutes until fully cooked, and internal temperature of beef reaches 160°F (71°C). Transfer to large plate. Cover to keep warm.

Combine next 3 ingredients in small bowl.

Cut focaccia bread in half horizontally. Spread goat cheese mixture on both halves. Scatter lettuce over cheese mixture on bottom half. Carefully slide patty onto lettuce. Cover with top half of bread. Cuts into 6 wedges.

1 wedge: 537 Calories; 27.4 g Total Fat (12 g Mono, 4.8 g Poly, 8.7 g Sat); 63 mg Cholesterol; 44 g Carbohydrate; 2 g Fibre; 27 g Protein; 942 mg Sodium

Hummus Pita Pockets

Hummus gives the patties a velvety texture, while the cooling cucumber sauce completes the Mediterranean influence on these scrumptious pitas.

CUCUMBER DILL SAUCE		
Plain yogurt	1/2 cup	125 mL
Finely chopped English cucumber (with peel)	1/2 cup	125 mL
Chopped fresh dill (or 3/4 tsp., 4 mL, dill weed)	1 tbsp.	15 mL
Lemon juice	2 tsp.	10 mL
Garlic clove, minced (or 1/4 tsp., 1 mL, powder)	1	1
Large egg	1	1
Hummus	1/3 cup	75 mL
Fine dry bread crumbs	1/4 cup	60 mL
Milk	2 tbsp.	30 mL
Dried oregano	1/2 tsp.	2 mL
Ground cumin	1/2 tsp.	2 mL
Lean ground beef	1 lb.	454 g
Pita breads (7 inch, 18 cm, diameter)	2	2
Shredded iceberg lettuce, lightly packed	1 cup	250 mL

Cucumber Dill Sauce: Combine first 5 ingredients in medium bowl. Chill. Makes about 7/8 cup (200 mL) sauce.

Combine next 6 ingredients in large bowl.

Add ground beef. Mix well. Divide into 4 equal portions. Shape into 1/2 inch (12 mm) thick oval patties. Preheat gas barbecue to medium. (For other cooking methods, see page 8.) Cook patties on greased grill for 6 to 8 minutes per side until fully cooked, and internal temperature of beef reaches 160°F (71°C). Transfer to large plate. Cover to keep warm.

Cut pita breads in half crosswise. Fill each half with 1/4 cup (60 mL) lettuce and 1 patty. Spoon sauce over patties. Makes 4 pita pockets.

1 pita pocket: 406 Calories; 16.3 g Total Fat (7.3 g Mono, 1.8 g Poly, 5.3 g Sat); 113 mg Cholesterol; 33 g Carbohydrate; 1 g Fibre; 31 g Protein; 389 mg Sodium

Beef Falafel Wraps

A meaty twist on a vegetarian favourite. Dip into Cucumber Dill Sauce,
page 104, to make these even tastier.

Box of falafel mix	10 oz.	283 g
Water	1 1/4 cups	300 mL
Large egg, fork-beaten	1	1
Chopped fresh parsley (or 1 1/2 tsp., 7 mL, flakes)	2 tbsp.	30 mL
Chopped fresh mint leaves (or 3/4 tsp., 4 mL, dried)	1 tbsp.	15 mL
Lean ground beef	1 1/2 lbs.	680 g
Roasted red pepper hummus	1 cup	250 mL
Flour tortillas (9 inch, 22 cm, diameter)	8	8
Shredded lettuce, lightly packed	4 cups	1 L
Diced tomato	1 1/2 cups	375 mL

Put falafel mix into large bowl. Add water. Stir. Let stand for 15 minutes.

Add next 3 ingredients. Stir.

Add ground beef. Mix well. Divide into 24 equal portions. Shape into 3 inch (7.5 cm) diameter patties. Arrange on greased baking sheet with sides. (For other cooking methods, see page 8.) Broil on centre rack in oven for 3 to 4 minutes per side until fully cooked, and internal temperature of beef reaches 160°F (71°C).

Spread 2 tbsp. (30 mL) hummus on 1 tortilla. Layer 1/2 cup (125 mL) lettuce and 3 tbsp. (50 mL) tomato on top of hummus. Arrange 3 patties in horizontal row on top of tomato. Fold sides over filling. Roll up from bottom to enclose. Repeat to make 8 wraps.

1 wrap: 599 Calories; 26.5 g Total Fat (12.8 g Mono, 4.6 g Poly, 6.8 g Sat); 75 mg Cholesterol; 59 g Carbohydrate; 4 g Fibre; 31 g Protein; 902 mg Sodium

Pictured on page 108.

Sloppy Joe Tacos

These sloppy joes have a Mexican flair. Using tomato soup makes them quick and easy. Serve the toppings in separate bowls so guests can help themselves.

Cooking oil	2 tsp.	10 mL
Lean ground beef	1 lb.	454 g
Chopped onion	1 cup	250 mL
Can of condensed tomato soup	10 oz.	284 mL
Chili powder	1 tsp.	5 mL
Salt	3/4 tsp.	4 mL
Pepper	1/4 tsp.	1 mL
Garlic powder	1/4 tsp.	1 mL
Hard taco shells	12	12
Diced tomato	2 cups	500 mL
Shredded lettuce, lightly packed	2 cups	500 mL
Grated medium Cheddar cheese	1 cup	250 mL
Sour cream	1/2 cup	125 mL
Green onions, chopped	6	6

Heat cooking oil in large frying pan on medium. Add ground beef and onion. Scramble-fry for about 10 minutes until beef is no longer pink. Drain.

Add next 5 ingredients. Heat and stir for about 5 minutes until heated through.

Heat taco shells in oven according to package directions. Spoon beef mixture into shells. Layer remaining 5 ingredients on top of beef mixture. Makes 12 tacos.

1 taco: 211 Calories; 12.1 g Total Fat (4.5 g Mono, 1.9 g Poly, 4.8 g Sat); 34 mg Cholesterol; 15 g Carbohydrate; 2 g Fibre; 11 g Protein; 457 mg Sodium

1. Tuscan Barbecue Loaf, page 116
2. Creamy Zucchini Wedges, page 38
3. Italian Sandwich, page 102

Props courtesy of: Cherison Enterprises Inc.
Totally Bamboo

Beef And Bean Burritos

*Simple to make, and on the table in a hurry. This is
an easy recipe to double or triple for a larger group.*

Cooking oil	2 tsp.	10 mL
Lean ground beef	1 lb.	454 g
Chopped onion	1/2 cup	125 mL
Can of refried beans	14 oz.	398 mL
Mild (or medium) salsa	1/2 cup	125 mL
Seasoned salt	1/2 tsp.	2 mL
Flour tortillas (9 inch, 22 cm, diameter)	6	6

Heat cooking oil in large frying pan on medium. Add ground beef and onion. Scramble-fry for about 10 minutes until beef is no longer pink. Drain.

Add next 3 ingredients. Heat and stir for about 3 minutes until heated through.

Spoon about 1/3 cup (75 mL) beef mixture along centre of each tortilla. Fold sides over filling. Roll up from bottom to enclose. Makes 6 burritos.

1 burrito: 391 Calories; 16.9 g Total Fat (7.5 g Mono, 2.2 g Poly, 5.5 g Sat); 48 mg Cholesterol; 37 g Carbohydrate; 6 g Fibre; 22 g Protein; 621 mg Sodium

1. Greek Salad Pizza, page 49
2. Cucumber Dill Sauce, page 104
3. Phyllo Lasagne, page 40
4. Beef Falafel Wraps, page 105

Props courtesy of: Cherison Enterprises Inc.
Totally Bamboo

Thai Beef Wraps

Fragrant mint adds a fresh note to these generously filled wraps. We made four, but you can stretch the filling to make six wraps if you like.

Cooking oil	2 tsp.	10 mL
Lean ground beef	1 lb.	454 g
Garlic clove, minced (or 1/4 tsp., 1 mL, powder)	1	1
Brown sugar, packed	2 tbsp.	30 mL
Lime juice	2 tbsp.	30 mL
Finely grated, peeled gingerroot (or 3/4 tsp., 4 mL, ground ginger)	1 tbsp.	15 mL
Fish sauce (or soy sauce)	1 tbsp.	15 mL
Ground coriander	1 tsp.	5 mL
Sesame oil, for flavour	1 tsp.	5 mL
Chili paste (sambal oelek)	1 tsp.	5 mL
Fresh bean sprouts	2 cups	500 mL
Coarsely grated carrot	1 cup	250 mL
Can of sliced water chestnuts, drained and chopped	8 oz.	227 mL
Sliced green onion	1/2 cup	125 mL
Hoisin sauce	1/4 cup	60 mL
Chopped unsalted peanuts	1/4 cup	60 mL
Chopped fresh mint leaves (or cilantro), optional	2 tbsp.	30 mL
Flour tortillas (9 inch, 22 cm, diameter)	4	4

Heat cooking oil in large frying pan on medium. Add ground beef and garlic. Scramble-fry for about 10 minutes until beef is no longer pink. Drain.

Add next 7 ingredients. Heat and stir for about 2 minutes until brown sugar is dissolved.

Add next 4 ingredients. Heat and stir for about 2 minutes until vegetables are heated through. Remove from heat.

Add next 3 ingredients. Stir.

Spoon about 1 cup (250 mL) beef mixture along centre of each tortilla. Fold sides over filling. Roll up from bottom to enclose. Makes 4 wraps.

1 wrap: 534 Calories; 21.1 g Total Fat (9.7 g Mono, 4.4 g Poly, 5.2 g Sat); 59 mg Cholesterol; 58 g Carbohydrate; 5 g Fibre; 30 g Protein; 910 mg Sodium

Spiced Meatball Pitas

Appetizing and substantial, these pockets are filled with spicy
meatballs that hint of Mediterranean flavours.

CUMIN LIME SAUCE		
Plain yogurt	1 cup	250 mL
Grated English cucumber (with peel)	1/2 cup	125 mL
Lime juice	1 tbsp.	15 mL
Garlic clove, minced (or 1/4 tsp., 1 mL, powder)	1	1
Ground cumin	1/2 tsp.	2 mL
Salt	1/4 tsp.	1 mL
Large egg	1	1
Crushed gingersnaps	1/4 cup	60 mL
Sliced green onion	2 tbsp.	30 mL
Chopped fresh cilantro or parsley (or 1 1/2 tsp., 7 mL, dried)	2 tbsp.	30 mL
Ground cumin	1/2 tsp.	2 mL
Salt	1/2 tsp.	2 mL
Pepper	1/4 tsp.	1 mL
Ground cinnamon	1/4 tsp.	1 mL
Lean ground beef	1 lb.	454 g
Pita breads (7 inch, 18 cm, diameter)	3	3
Chopped or torn lettuce, lightly packed	1 1/2 cups	375 mL
Diced tomato	1/2 cup	125 mL
Diced green pepper	1/2 cup	125 mL

Cumin Lime Sauce: Combine first 6 ingredients in small bowl. Set aside. Makes about 1 1/2 cups (375 mL) sauce.

Combine next 8 ingredients in large bowl.

Add ground beef. Mix well. Roll into 1 inch (2.5 cm) balls. Arrange on greased baking sheet with sides. Bake in 350°F (175°C) oven for about 15 minutes until fully cooked, and internal temperature of beef reaches 160°F (71°C).

Cut pita breads in half crosswise. Fill each half with meatballs and remaining 3 ingredients. Spoon sauce over filling. Serves 6.

1 serving: 270 Calories; 8.8 g Total Fat (3.6 g Mono, 0.7 g Poly, 3.3 g Sat); 78 mg Cholesterol; 26 g Carbohydrate; 1 g Fibre; 21 g Protein; 563 mg Sodium

Teriyaki Lettuce Wraps

Tasty and fun! For a casual presentation, put topping ingredients into individual serving bowls so guests can make their own wraps. Teriyaki Sauce may be used for dipping instead of drizzling inside the wrap.

Large egg	1	1
Fine dry bread crumbs	1/3 cup	75 mL
Soy sauce	1 tbsp.	15 mL
Finely chopped green onion	1 tbsp.	15 mL
Finely grated, peeled gingerroot	1 tsp.	5 mL
(or 1/4 tsp., 1 mL, ground ginger)		
Chinese five-spice powder	1/2 tsp.	2 mL
Garlic clove, minced (or 1/4 tsp., 1 mL,	1	1
powder)		
Lean ground beef	1 lb.	454 g
TERIYAKI SAUCE		
Water	2 tsp.	10 mL
Cornstarch	2 tsp.	10 mL
Soy sauce	1/3 cup	75 mL
Brown sugar, packed	1/3 cup	75 mL
Ketchup	1/3 cup	75 mL
White vinegar	2 1/2 tbsp.	37 mL
Large green leaf lettuce leaves	12	12
Can of sliced water chestnuts, drained	8 oz.	227 mL
and finely chopped		
Grated carrot	1/2 cup	125 mL
Finely chopped green onion	1/2 cup	125 mL
Chopped fresh cilantro or parsley	1/2 cup	125 mL

Combine first 7 ingredients in large bowl.

Add ground beef. Mix well. Divide into 12 equal portions. Shape into 3 inch (7.5 cm) long logs. Place crosswise on greased wire rack set on baking sheet with sides. (For other cooking methods, see page 8.) Broil on centre rack in oven for about 20 minutes, turning once at halftime, until fully cooked, and internal temperature of beef reaches 160°F (71°C). Cool.

(continued on next page)

Teriyaki Sauce: Stir water and cornstarch in small cup until smooth.

Combine next 4 ingredients in small saucepan. Bring to a boil on medium. Slowly add cornstarch mixture, stirring constantly. Heat and stir for about 3 minutes until boiling and thickened. Cool. Makes about 1 cup (250 mL) sauce.

Place 1 beef log crosswise in centre of 1 lettuce leaf. Drizzle with about 1 tbsp. (15 mL) Teriyaki Sauce.

Sprinkle about 2 tsp. (10 mL) of each remaining ingredient over log. Fold sides of leaf over filling. Roll up from bottom to enclose. Repeat to make 12 wraps.

1 wrap: 157 Calories; 6.4 g Total Fat (2.7 g Mono, 0.4 g Poly, 2.5 g Sat); 39 mg Cholesterol; 15 g Carbohydrate; 1 g Fibre; 10 g Protein; 718 mg Sodium

Paré Pointer

Then there are the bankers: they chain up their pens and leave the doors open.

Curried Yam Empanadas

*Pop the frozen dinner roll dough in your refrigerator in the morning,
and you'll have these meal-sized turnovers done for dinner in no time.*

Cooking oil	2 tsp.	10 mL
Extra-lean ground beef	1 lb.	454 g
Finely diced peeled yam	1 cup	250 mL
Finely chopped onion	1/2 cup	125 mL
Curry powder	1/2 tsp.	2 mL
Ground cumin	1/2 tsp.	2 mL
Salt	1/2 tsp.	2 mL
Pepper	1/2 tsp.	2 mL
Ground cinnamon	1/4 tsp.	1 mL
Ground cloves	1/8 tsp.	0.5 mL
Dried cranberries	1/4 cup	60 mL
Chopped slivered almonds, toasted (see Tip, page 129)	1/4 cup	60 mL
Ketchup	3 tbsp.	50 mL
Lime juice	2 tbsp.	30 mL
Chili paste (sambal oelek)	1 tsp.	5 mL
Frozen unbaked dinner rolls, covered, thawed in refrigerator	8	8
Large egg, fork-beaten	1	1

Heat cooking oil in large frying pan on medium. Add next 9 ingredients.
Scramble-fry for about 10 minutes until ground beef is no longer pink and
yam is tender. Drain. Transfer to medium bowl.

Add next 5 ingredients. Stir. Cool.

Roll out 1 dough portion on lightly floured surface to 6 inch (15 cm)
diameter disc. Spoon about 1/3 cup (75 mL) beef mixture onto disc,
leaving 1/2 inch (12 mm) edge. Fold dough over beef mixture. Crimp
edges with fork to seal. Place on greased baking sheet. Repeat with
remaining dough and beef mixture.

Brush tops and sides of empanadas with egg. Bake in 375°F (190°C) oven
for about 20 minutes until golden. Let stand on baking sheet for 5 minutes
before serving. Makes 8 empanadas.

*1 empanada: 295 Calories; 14.8 g Total Fat (7.2 g Mono, 1.6 g Poly, 4.4 g Sat); 59 mg Cholesterol;
26 g Carbohydrate; 3 g Fibre; 15 g Protein; 412 mg Sodium*

Chutney Beef Scones

A tender, golden scone infused with great curry flavour.
Serve this with tomato or mushroom soup for lunch!

Cooking oil	1 tsp.	5 mL
Lean ground beef	1/2 lb.	225 g
Chopped onion	1/4 cup	60 mL
Curry powder	1 tsp.	5 mL
All-purpose flour	2 cups	500 mL
Baking powder	1 tbsp.	15 mL
Baking soda	1/2 tsp.	2 mL
Salt	1/2 tsp.	2 mL
Cold hard margarine (or butter), cut up	1/4 cup	60 mL
Large eggs	2	2
Milk	3/4 cup	175 mL
Grated Swiss cheese	1/2 cup	125 mL
Mango chutney, larger pieces finely chopped	1/4 cup	60 mL

Heat cooking oil in medium frying pan on medium. Add ground beef, onion and curry powder. Scramble-fry for about 10 minutes until beef is no longer pink. Drain. Cool.

Stir next 4 ingredients in large bowl. Cut in margarine until mixture resembles coarse crumbs. Add beef mixture. Stir. Make a well in centre.

Combine remaining 4 ingredients in small bowl. Add to well. Stir until just moistened. Spread evenly in greased 9 inch (22 cm) round pan. Bake in 350°F (175°C) oven for about 30 minutes until golden and wooden pick inserted in centre comes out clean. Let stand in pan for 10 minutes before removing to wire rack to cool. Cuts into 12 wedges. Serves 6.

1 serving: 386 Calories; 17.1 g Total Fat (8.6 g Mono, 1.7 g Poly, 5.4 g Sat); 101 mg Cholesterol; 40 g Carbohydrate; 2 g Fibre; 17 g Protein; 663 mg Sodium

Tuscan Barbecue Loaf

Serve this grilled loaf with salad for a simple
summertime supper. Perfect patio fare.

Large egg	1	1
Chopped fresh white mushrooms	1 cup	250 mL
Chopped onion	1/2 cup	125 mL
Grated zucchini (with peel)	1/2 cup	125 mL
Fine dry bread crumbs	1/2 cup	125 mL
Tomato sauce	1/2 cup	125 mL
Roasted red peppers, drained, blotted dry, finely chopped	1/4 cup	60 mL
Basil pesto	2 tbsp.	30 mL
Garlic clove, minced (or 1/4 tsp., 1 mL, powder)	1	1
Extra-lean ground beef	1 1/2 lbs.	680 g
French bread loaf	1	1
Grated Asiago cheese	1 cup	250 mL
Chopped pine nuts, toasted (see Tip, page 129)	1/2 cup	125 mL
Chopped fresh parsley (or 3/4 tsp., 4 mL, flakes)	1 tbsp.	15 mL

Combine first 9 ingredients in large bowl.

Add ground beef. Mix well.

Cut bread loaf in half horizontally. Spread beef mixture evenly on both halves. Place each half on separate sheet of heavy-duty foil. Bring foil up over sides of bread, leaving tops uncovered. Place on baking sheet. Preheat gas barbecue to medium. Place baking sheet on grill. Close lid. Cook for about 40 minutes until fully cooked.

Sprinkle with remaining 3 ingredients. Cook for another 3 to 5 minutes until cheese is melted. Cut each half into 3 pieces, for a total of 6 pieces.

1 piece: 600 Calories; 27.1 g Total Fat (10.7 g Mono, 4.8 g Poly, 9 g Sat); 110 mg Cholesterol;
53 g Carbohydrate; 6 g Fibre; 38 g Protein; 826 mg Sodium

Pictured on page 107.

Creamy Pepper Quesadillas

Extra-crispy tortilla wedges are stuffed with a creamy Tex-Mex filling.
The chipotle chili pepper gives them a delightfully spicy flavour.

Cooking oil	2 tsp.	10 mL
Lean ground beef	1 lb.	454 g
Finely chopped green pepper	1/4 cup	60 mL
Roasted red peppers, drained, blotted dry, finely chopped	1/4 cup	60 mL
Chipotle chili pepper in adobo sauce, finely chopped (see Tip, page 74)	1	1
Chili powder	1 tsp.	5 mL
Ground cumin	1/2 tsp.	2 mL
Pepper	1/2 tsp.	2 mL
Block of cream cheese, softened	8 oz.	250 g
Flour tortillas (9 inch, 22 cm, diameter)	8	8
Grated Monterey Jack cheese	2 cups	500 mL
Cooking oil	1 tbsp.	15 mL

Heat first amount of cooking oil in large frying pan on medium. Add ground beef. Scramble-fry for about 10 minutes until no longer pink. Drain.

Add next 6 ingredients. Heat and stir for about 2 minutes until fragrant and green pepper is tender-crisp. Remove from heat.

Spread about 2 tbsp. (30 mL) cream cheese on each tortilla. Sprinkle Monterey Jack cheese over 1/2 of cream cheese. Scatter beef mixture over Monterey Jack cheese. Fold tortillas over filling. Press down lightly.

Brush both sides of folded tortillas with second amount of cooking oil. Arrange on 2 greased baking sheets. Bake on separate racks in 400°F (205°C) oven for about 15 minutes, switching position of baking sheets at halftime, until crisp and cheese is melted. Cut each quesadilla into 3 wedges, for a total of 24 wedges. Serves 8.

1 serving: 473 Calories; 30.6 g Total Fat (10.7 g Mono, 2.9 g Poly, 15.1 g Sat); 90 mg Cholesterol; 25 g Carbohydrate; 2 g Fibre; 24 g Protein; 479 mg Sodium

Layered Taco Salad

This salad can be made ahead and refrigerated overnight. Use a glass bowl for best visual impact. Serve with your favourite tortilla chips.

Cooking oil	2 tsp.	10 mL
Lean ground beef	1 lb.	454 g
Finely chopped onion	1/2 cup	125 mL
Taco seasoning mix, stir before measuring	2 tbsp.	30 mL
Mayonnaise	3/4 cup	175 mL
Sour cream	1/2 cup	125 mL
Chopped fresh cilantro or parsley	2 tbsp.	30 mL
Lime juice	2 tbsp.	30 mL
Taco seasoning mix, stir before measuring	1 tbsp.	15 mL
Shredded romaine lettuce, lightly packed	3 1/2 cups	875 mL
Shredded iceberg lettuce, lightly packed	2 1/2 cups	625 mL
Mild salsa	1 cup	250 mL
Chopped yellow or green pepper	1 cup	250 mL
Chopped tomato	1 1/2 cups	375 mL
Grated medium Cheddar cheese	1/2 cup	125 mL
Can of sliced ripe olives, drained	4 1/2 oz.	125 mL
Chopped green onion	1/4 cup	60 mL

Heat cooking oil in large frying pan on medium. Add ground beef and onion. Scramble-fry for about 10 minutes until beef is no longer pink. Drain.

Add first amount of taco seasoning. Heat and stir for 1 minute. Transfer to medium bowl. Cover. Chill until cold.

Combine next 5 ingredients in separate medium bowl. Set aside.

Combine romaine and iceberg lettuce in large serving bowl. Scatter beef mixture over lettuce.

Layer next 3 ingredients, in order given, on top of beef mixture. Spread mayonnaise mixture on top of tomato to side of bowl to seal.

Sprinkle remaining 3 ingredients over top. Serves 8.

1 serving: 357 Calories; 29 g Total Fat (14.3 g Mono, 6.7 g Poly, 6.6 g Sat); 56 mg Cholesterol; 11 g Carbohydrate; 2 g Fibre; 14 g Protein; 931 mg Sodium

Pictured on page 126.

Norway Spinach Salad

Norwegian Gjetost (pronounced YEHT-ohst) cheese has a smooth,
fudge-like texture and a slightly sweet taste that is unequalled.
This salad is sure to impress your guests!

CREAMY CHÈVRE DRESSING		
Mayonnaise	1/4 cup	60 mL
Apple juice	3 tbsp.	50 mL
Goat (chèvre) cheese	1 1/2 oz.	43 g
Apple cider vinegar	1 tbsp.	15 mL
Dry mustard	1/4 tsp.	1 mL
Pepper	1/4 tsp.	1 mL
Cooking oil	2 tsp.	10 mL
Lean ground beef	1 lb.	454 g
Ground allspice	3/4 tsp.	4 mL
Salt	1/2 tsp.	2 mL
Pepper	1/4 tsp.	1 mL
Bag of fresh spinach, stems removed	10 oz.	284 g
Shaved Gjetost (or smoked Gouda) cheese	4 1/2 oz.	125 g
Medium cooking apples (such as McIntosh), with peel and sliced	2	2

Creamy Chèvre Dressing: Process first 6 ingredients in blender or food processor until smooth. Makes about 2/3 cup (150 mL) dressing.

Heat cooking oil in large frying pan on medium. Add next 4 ingredients. Scramble-fry for about 10 minutes until ground beef is no longer pink. Drain. Cool.

Arrange spinach on 4 dinner plates. Top with beef, Gjetost cheese and apple slices. Drizzle with dressing. Serves 4.

1 serving: 513 Calories; 35.8 g Total Fat (15.2 g Mono, 5.4 g Poly, 12.7 g Sat); 111 mg Cholesterol; 16 g Carbohydrate; 3 g Fibre; 33 g Protein; 779 mg Sodium

Caribbean Beef Salad

Doesn't this take you to the tropics? The lime, coconut dressing and mild jerk spices bring this salad to life.

Brown sugar, packed	1/3 cup	75 mL
Dried thyme	1 tsp.	5 mL
Ground ginger	3/4 tsp.	4 mL
Ground cinnamon	1/2 tsp.	2 mL
Ground allspice	1/2 tsp.	2 mL
Ground nutmeg	1/4 tsp.	1 mL
Ground coriander	1/4 tsp.	1 mL
Salt	1/4 tsp.	1 mL
Cayenne pepper	1/4 tsp.	1 mL
Coconut milk (or reconstituted from powder)	1/4 cup	60 mL
Corn syrup (or liquid honey)	2 tbsp.	30 mL
Mayonnaise	2 tbsp.	30 mL
Lime juice	1 tbsp.	15 mL
Large egg	1	1
Medium unsweetened coconut, toasted (see Tip, page 129)	1/2 cup	125 mL
Coconut milk (or reconstituted from powder)	1/3 cup	75 mL
Garlic clove, minced (or 1/4 tsp., 1 mL, powder)	1	1
Pepper	1/4 tsp.	1 mL
Lean ground beef	1 lb.	454 g
Chopped or torn romaine lettuce, lightly packed	4 cups	1 L
Small red onion, halved lengthwise and thinly sliced	1	1
Cubed mango	2 cups	500 mL
Small red pepper, cut into 1 inch (2.5 cm) pieces	1	1
Sultana raisins	1/4 cup	60 mL

(continued on next page)

Soups & Salads

Plain cashews	1/4 cup	60 mL
Medium unsweetened coconut, toasted (see Tip, page 129)	2 tbsp.	30 mL

Lime wedges, for garnish

Combine first 9 ingredients in shallow dish. Transfer 1 tsp. (5 mL) to small bowl.

Add next 4 ingredients to spice mixture in small bowl. Stir. Set aside.

Combine next 5 ingredients in medium bowl.

Add ground beef. Mix well. Divide into 16 equal portions. Shape into 1/2 inch (12 mm) thick patties. Press both sides of each patty into spice mixture in shallow dish. Arrange on greased baking sheet with sides. Broil on top rack in oven for 5 to 7 minutes per side until fully cooked, and internal temperature of beef reaches 160°F (71°C).

Arrange lettuce on 4 dinner plates. Scatter next 4 ingredients over top. Place 4 patties on each salad. Drizzle with coconut milk mixture.

Sprinkle with cashews and second amount of coconut.

Garnish with lime wedges. Serves 4.

1 serving: 687 Calories; 38.5 g Total Fat (11.2 g Mono, 3.5 g Poly, 20.8 g Sat); 115 mg Cholesterol; 65 g Carbohydrate; 5 g Fibre; 27 g Protein; 300 mg Sodium

Pictured on front cover.

Paré Pointer

It's put on the table and someone cuts it, but never eats it.
What is it? A deck of cards!

Soups & Salads   **121**

Continental Rice Salad

Cooking the ground beef with dill weed gives this salad
its deliciously unique flavour. Definitely one to try!

Cooking oil	2 tsp.	10 mL
Lean ground beef	1 lb.	454 g
Chopped onion	1/2 cup	125 mL
Dill weed	1/2 tsp.	2 mL
Cooked converted white rice (about 1 cup, 250 mL, uncooked)	3 cups	750 mL
PARSLEY PEPPERCORN DRESSING		
Olive (or cooking) oil	3 tbsp.	50 mL
Chopped fresh parsley	3 tbsp.	50 mL
White wine vinegar	1 tbsp.	15 mL
Whole green peppercorns, drained and crushed	1 tbsp.	15 mL
Paprika	1/2 tsp.	2 mL
Salt	1/4 tsp.	1 mL
Medium tomatoes, each cut into 8 wedges	3	3
English cucumber (with peel), halved lengthwise and cut into 1/4 inch (6 mm) slices	2 cups	500 mL
Diced green pepper	1 cup	250 mL
Can of artichoke hearts, drained and quartered (optional)	14 oz.	398 mL

Heat cooking oil in large frying pan on medium. Add ground beef, onion and dill weed. Scramble-fry for about 10 minutes until beef is no longer pink. Drain. Remove from heat.

Add rice. Stir. Transfer to extra-large bowl. Cover. Chill for about 2 hours until cold.

Parsley Peppercorn Dressing: Combine first 6 ingredients in jar with tight-fitting lid. Shake well. Makes about 1/3 cup (75 mL) dressing.

Add remaining 4 ingredients to beef mixture. Stir. Drizzle with dressing. Stir. Serves 6.

1 serving: 390 Calories; 20.3 g Total Fat (11 g Mono, 1.7 g Poly, 5.7 g Sat); 42 mg Cholesterol; 34 g Carbohydrate; 2 g Fibre; 18 g Protein; 357 mg Sodium

Pictured on page 126.

Cheesy Meatball Salad

Crunchy meatballs add interesting texture to this salad made
for cheese lovers. The tangy dressing goes great with pasta, too.

PARSLEY PESTO DRESSING

Coarsely chopped fresh parsley	1/2 cup	125 mL
Grated Parmesan cheese	1/3 cup	75 mL
Olive (or cooking) oil	1/3 cup	75 mL
Pine nuts, toasted (see Tip, page 129)	1/4 cup	60 mL
Red wine vinegar	1/4 cup	60 mL
Garlic clove, minced (or 1/4 tsp., 1 mL, powder)	1	1
Salt	1/4 tsp.	1 mL
Pepper	1/8 tsp.	0.5 mL
Grated medium Cheddar cheese	1 1/2 cups	375 mL
Biscuit mix	1/2 cup	125 mL
Seasoned salt	1/2 tsp.	2 mL
Pepper, just a pinch		
Lean ground beef	1/2 lb.	225 g
Bag of mixed salad greens	4 1/2 oz.	128 g
Fresh spinach, stems removed, lightly packed	1 cup	250 mL
Thinly sliced red onion	1/2 cup	125 mL

Parsley Pesto Dressing: Process first 8 ingredients in blender or food processor until smooth. Makes about 2/3 cup (150 mL) dressing.

Combine next 4 ingredients in medium bowl.

Add ground beef. Mix well. Roll into 1 inch (2.5 cm) balls. Arrange on greased baking sheet with sides. Bake in 400°F (205°C) oven for 10 to 15 minutes until fully cooked, and internal temperature of beef reaches 160°F (71°C). Transfer to paper towels to drain. Cover to keep warm.

Arrange salad greens on 6 salad plates. Top with meatballs, spinach and onion. Drizzle with dressing. Serves 6.

1 serving: 413 Calories; 32.8 g Total Fat (15.9 g Mono, 3.7 g Poly, 11.2 g Sat); 55 mg Cholesterol; 12 g Carbohydrate; 2 g Fibre; 20 g Protein; 658 mg Sodium

Hearty Wild Rice Soup

*Earthy mushrooms and a pleasant hint of tarragon complement
the nutty flavour of wild rice. Delicious.*

Cooking oil	2 tsp.	10 mL
Chopped fresh white mushrooms	2 cups	500 mL
Lean ground beef	1 lb.	454 g
Chopped onion	1 cup	250 mL
Dried tarragon leaves	1 tsp.	5 mL
All-purpose flour	3 tbsp.	50 mL
Prepared beef broth	6 cups	1.5 L
Wild rice	2/3 cup	150 mL
Grated carrot	1/2 cup	125 mL

Heat cooking oil in large pot or Dutch oven on medium. Add next
4 ingredients. Scramble-fry for about 10 minutes until ground beef is
no longer pink. Drain.

Add flour. Stir well. Add broth and rice. Stir until boiling. Reduce heat to
medium-low. Simmer, covered, for about 50 minutes, stirring occasionally,
until rice is tender.

Add carrot. Heat and stir for about 2 minutes until carrot is tender-crisp.
Skim any fat from surface of soup. Makes about 8 cups (2 L).

*1 cup (250 mL): 187 Calories; 6.6 g Total Fat (2.9 g Mono, 0.7 g Poly, 2.2 g Sat); 29 mg Cholesterol;
16 g Carbohydrate; 2 g Fibre; 15 g Protein; 646 mg Sodium*

1. Portuguese Soup, page 132
2. Mexican Beef Soup, page 133
3. Hearty Mushroom Soup, page 130

Props courtesy of: Casa Bugatti
Pier 1 Imports
Stokes
The Bay
Totally Bamboo

Potato Fennel Soup

This rich, hearty soup is loaded with vegetables.
Fennel and dill add a refreshing, light flavour.

Cooking oil	2 tsp.	10 mL
Sliced fennel bulb (white part only)	2 cups	500 mL
Lean ground beef	1 lb.	454 g
Diced carrot	1 cup	250 mL
Chopped onion	1/2 cup	125 mL
Prepared beef broth	6 cups	1.5 L
Diced peeled potato	2 cups	500 mL
Chopped fresh dill (or 1/2 tsp., 2 mL, dill weed)	2 tsp.	10 mL
Pepper	1/4 tsp.	1 mL

Heat cooking oil in large pot or Dutch oven on medium. Add next 4 ingredients. Scramble-fry for about 10 minutes until ground beef is no longer pink. Drain.

Add remaining 4 ingredients. Stir. Bring to a boil. Boil gently, covered, for about 15 minutes, stirring occasionally, until potato is tender. Skim any fat from surface of soup. Makes about 9 cups (2.25 L).

1 cup (250 mL): 143 Calories; 5.7 g Total Fat (2.6 g Mono, 0.5 g Poly, 1.9 g Sat); 26 mg Cholesterol; 11 g Carbohydrate; 1 g Fibre; 12 g Protein; 595 mg Sodium

1. Layered Taco Salad, page 118
2. Continental Rice Salad, page 122
3. Chèvre Beef Salad, page 128

Props courtesy of: Cherison Enterprises Inc.
Strahl
The Dazzling Gourmet
Totally Bamboo

Chèvre Beef Salad

*Creamy goat cheese accents savoury beef patties in
a colourful full-meal salad your guests will love.*

BASIL VINAIGRETTE		
Chopped fresh basil	1/2 cup	125 mL
Olive (or cooking) oil	1/3 cup	75 mL
White wine vinegar	1/4 cup	60 mL
Dried oregano	1/2 tsp.	2 mL
Salt, sprinkle		
Pepper, sprinkle		
Large egg	1	1
White bread slice, processed into crumbs	1	1
Balsamic vinegar	2 tbsp.	30 mL
Dried oregano	1 tsp.	5 mL
Garlic clove, minced (or 1/4 tsp., 1 mL, powder)	1	1
Salt	1/8 tsp.	0.5 mL
Pepper, sprinkle		
Lean ground beef	1 lb.	454 g
Cooking oil	2 tsp.	10 mL
Mixed salad greens, lightly packed	8 cups	2 L
Thinly sliced English cucumber (with peel)	3/4 cup	175 mL
Cherry tomatoes, halved	16	16
Thinly sliced yellow pepper	1/2 cup	125 mL
Goat (chèvre) cheese, cut up	4 oz.	113 g

Basil Vinaigrette: Process first 6 ingredients in blender or food processor
until smooth. Makes about 3/4 cup (175 mL) vinaigrette.

Combine next 7 ingredients in large bowl.

Add ground beef. Mix well. Divide into 8 equal portions. Shape into 1/2 inch
(12 mm) thick oval patties.

Heat cooking oil in large frying pan on medium. (For other cooking methods,
see page 8.) Add patties. Cook for about 5 minutes per side until fully
cooked, and internal temperature of beef reaches 160°F (71°C). Transfer to
paper towels to drain. Let stand for 5 minutes. Cut each patty into 4 pieces.

(continued on next page)

Arrange salad greens on 4 dinner plates. Scatter cucumber, tomato and yellow pepper over greens.

Top each salad with 8 patty pieces. Scatter goat cheese over top. Drizzle with vinaigrette. Serves 4.

1 serving: 545 Calories; 41.2 g Total Fat (22 g Mono, 3.7 g Poly, 12.8 g Sat); 135 mg Cholesterol; 14 g Carbohydrate; 3 g Fibre; 32 g Protein; 348 mg Sodium

Pictured on page 126.

 To toast nuts, seeds or coconut, place them in an ungreased shallow frying pan. Heat on medium for 3 to 5 minutes, stirring often, until golden. To bake, spread them evenly in an ungreased shallow pan. Bake in a 350°F (175°C) oven for 5 to 10 minutes, stirring or shaking often, until golden.

Paré Pointer
If you want to light up your yard, plant bulbs.

Hearty Mushroom Soup

Ground beef and pretty pastry "croutons" make this velvety mushroom soup substantial enough to be a meal in itself.

PUFFED TRIANGLES

Package of frozen puff pastry (14 oz., 397 g), thawed according to package directions	1/2	1/2
Large egg, fork-beaten	1	1
Cooking oil	1 tsp.	5 mL
Lean ground beef	1 lb.	454 g
Chopped fresh white mushrooms	5 1/2 cups	1.4 L
Finely chopped onion	2 cups	500 mL
Garlic clove, minced (or 1/4 tsp., 1 mL, powder)	1	1
Prepared beef broth	3 2/3 cups	900 mL
Can of condensed cream of mushroom soup	10 oz.	284 mL
Dry sherry	1/2 cup	125 mL
Chopped fresh tarragon leaves (or 3/4 tsp., 4 mL, dried)	1 tbsp.	15 mL
Salt	1/4 tsp.	1 mL
Pepper	1/8 tsp.	0.5 mL
Sour cream	1 cup	250 mL
Chopped fresh tarragon leaves	2 tbsp.	30 mL

Puffed Triangles: Roll out puff pastry on lightly floured surface to 8 inch (20 cm) square. Brush with egg. Cut pastry lengthwise into thirds, then crosswise into quarters, for a total of 12 rectangles. Cut each rectangle in half diagonally, for a total of 24 triangles. Arrange in single layer on parchment paper-lined baking sheet. Bake in 400°F (205°C) oven for about 15 minutes until puffed and golden. Cool. Makes 24 triangles.

Heat cooking oil in large pot or Dutch oven on medium. Add ground beef. Scramble-fry for about 10 minutes until no longer pink. Drain.

Add next 3 ingredients. Cook for 5 to 10 minutes, stirring often, until onion is softened.

(continued on next page)

Add next 6 ingredients. Stir. Bring to a boil. Boil gently, uncovered, for 20 minutes, stirring occasionally.

Add sour cream. Heat and stir until hot but not boiling. Ladle into 8 soup bowls. Top each with 3 Puffed Triangles. Sprinkle with second amount of tarragon. Serves 8.

1 serving: 372 Calories; 23 g Total Fat (6.7 g Mono, 7.5 g Poly, 7 g Sat); 69 mg Cholesterol; 22 g Carbohydrate; 2 g Fibre; 17 g Protein; 867 mg Sodium

Pictured on page 125.

Italian Meatball Soup

This tasty soup is a creative way to serve pasta with meatballs.

Large egg	1	1
Crushed seasoned croutons	1/4 cup	60 mL
Chopped fresh parsley (or 1 1/2 tsp., 7 mL, flakes)	2 tbsp.	30 mL
Grated Parmesan cheese	2 tbsp.	30 mL
Garlic clove, minced (or 1/4 tsp., 1 mL, powder)	1	1
Lean ground beef	1 lb.	454 g
Prepared beef broth	7 cups	1.75 L
Very small pasta (such as orzo or alpha)	2/3 cup	150 mL
Finely shredded basil	2 tbsp.	30 mL

Combine first 5 ingredients in medium bowl.

Add ground beef. Mix well. Roll into 3/4 inch (2 cm) balls. Arrange on greased baking sheet with sides. Bake in 350°F (175°C) oven for about 15 minutes until fully cooked, and internal temperature of beef reaches 160°F (71°C). Transfer to paper towels to drain. Set aside.

Measure broth into large pot or Dutch oven. Bring to a boil on high. Add pasta. Stir. Reduce heat to medium. Boil gently, uncovered, for 5 to 6 minutes until pasta is tender but firm.

Add meatballs and basil. Heat and stir for about 1 minute until meatballs are heated through. Makes about 8 cups (2 L).

1 cup (250 mL): 209 Calories; 7.1 g Total Fat (2.9 g Mono, 0.5 g Poly, 2.8 g Sat); 58 mg Cholesterol; 18 g Carbohydrate; 1 g Fibre; 17 g Protein; 817 mg Sodium

Portuguese Soup

Adjust this soup to suit your taste. Sprinkle individual servings
with grated Parmesan cheese for added flavour.

Lean ground beef	1/2 lb.	225 g
Chorizo (or hot Italian) sausages, casings removed, chopped	1/2 lb.	225 g
Cooking oil	2 tsp.	10 mL
Chopped onion	3 cups	750 mL
Garlic clove, minced (or 1/4 tsp., 1 mL, powder)	1	1
Low-sodium prepared chicken broth	6 cups	1.5 L
Diced potato (with peel)	3 cups	750 mL
Can of white kidney beans, rinsed and drained	19 oz.	540 mL
Pepper	1/4 tsp.	1 mL
Green kale (see Note), stems removed, chopped, lightly packed	4 cups	1 L

Put ground beef and sausage into medium bowl. Mix well.

Heat cooking oil in large pot or Dutch oven on medium. Add beef mixture, onion and garlic. Scramble-fry for about 10 minutes until meat is no longer pink. Drain.

Add next 4 ingredients. Stir. Bring to a boil on medium-high. Reduce heat to medium-low. Simmer, covered, for about 10 minutes, stirring occasionally, until potato is tender.

Add kale. Cook for about 10 minutes, stirring occasionally, until tender. Makes about 11 1/2 cups (2.9 L).

1 cup (250 mL): 162 Calories; 5.1 g Total Fat (2.3 g Mono, 0.7 g Poly, 1.6 g Sat); 17 mg Cholesterol; 19 g Carbohydrate; 4 g Fibre; 11 g Protein; 493 mg Sodium

Pictured on page 125.

Note: Instead of kale, the same amount of spinach may be used. Spinach cooks much faster than kale. After adding spinach to the soup, cook only for 1 to 2 minutes until spinach is just wilted.

Mexican Beef Soup

Pair this mildly seasoned soup with cornbread muffins or tossed salad.

Cooking oil	2 tsp.	10 mL
Lean ground beef	1 lb.	454 g
Chopped onion	1 cup	250 mL
Chopped green pepper	1 cup	250 mL
Garlic clove, minced (or 1/4 tsp., 1 mL, powder)	1	1
Water	4 cups	1 L
Can of mixed beans, rinsed and drained	19 oz.	540 mL
Can of condensed tomato soup	10 oz.	284 mL
Can of condensed Cheddar cheese soup	10 oz.	284 mL
Taco seasoning mix, stir before measuring	2 tbsp.	30 mL
Can of diced green chilies (optional)	4 oz.	113 g
Sour cream	1 cup	250 mL
Sour cream, for garnish		
Chopped fresh cilantro or parsley, for garnish		

Heat cooking oil in large pot or Dutch oven on medium. Add next 4 ingredients. Scramble-fry for about 10 minutes until ground beef is no longer pink. Drain.

Add next 6 ingredients. Stir. Bring to a boil. Reduce heat to medium-low. Simmer, uncovered, for 15 minutes, stirring occasionally, to blend flavours.

Add first amount of sour cream. Heat and stir until hot but not boiling.

Garnish individual servings with a dollop of sour cream and a sprinkle of cilantro. Makes about 10 cups (2.5 L).

1 cup (250 mL): 221 Calories; 11.4 g Total Fat (4 g Mono, 1 g Poly, 5.4 g Sat); 40 mg Cholesterol; 17 g Carbohydrate; 2 g Fibre; 13 g Protein; 945 mg Sodium

Pictured on page 125.

Sweet Lentil Curry

Accompany this gently sweet curry with a refreshing
cucumber salad to complement its mild spiciness.

Cooking oil	2 tsp.	10 mL
Lean ground beef	1 lb.	454 g
Chopped onion	1/2 cup	125 mL
Diced celery	1/2 cup	125 mL
Curry powder	1 tsp.	5 mL
Dried thyme	1/2 tsp.	2 mL
Ground cumin	1/2 tsp.	2 mL
Pepper	1/2 tsp.	2 mL
Ground cinnamon	1/4 tsp.	1 mL
Can of diced tomatoes (with juice)	14 oz.	398 mL
Cubed peeled sweet potato (or yam)	1 1/2 cups	375 mL
Dried red lentils	1 cup	250 mL
Water	1 cup	250 mL
Frozen concentrated apple juice	1/4 cup	60 mL
Diced peeled apple	1 cup	250 mL
Lemon juice	1 tbsp.	15 mL
Liquid honey	2 tsp.	10 mL

Heat cooking oil in large saucepan or Dutch oven on medium. Add next 8 ingredients. Scramble-fry for about 10 minutes until ground beef is no longer pink. Drain.

Add next 5 ingredients. Stir. Bring to a boil. Reduce heat to medium-low. Simmer, covered, for about 25 minutes, stirring occasionally, until lentils are tender.

Combine apple, lemon juice and honey in small bowl. Add to beef mixture. Stir. Simmer, covered, for another 5 minutes until apple is softened. Serves 4.

1 serving: 515 Calories; 13 g Total Fat (5.6 g Mono, 1.5 g Poly, 4 g Sat); 59 mg Cholesterol; 65 g Carbohydrate; 9 g Fibre; 37 g Protein; 240 mg Sodium

Macaroni Jumble

Kids will love this! Easy to make for supper when there's not a lot of time.

Elbow macaroni	2 cups	500 mL
Cooking oil	2 tsp.	10 mL
Lean ground beef	1 lb.	454 g
Chopped onion	1/3 cup	75 mL
Frozen kernel corn (or 12 oz., 341 mL, can of kernel corn, drained)	1 1/2 cups	375 mL
Can of tomato sauce	7 1/2 oz.	213 mL
Ketchup	1/2 cup	125 mL
Water	1/2 cup	125 mL
Chili powder	2 tsp.	10 mL
Granulated sugar	1/2 tsp.	2 mL
Seasoned salt	1/2 tsp.	2 mL
Grated medium Cheddar cheese	1/2 cup	125 mL

Cook macaroni in boiling salted water in large uncovered saucepan for 8 to 10 minutes, stirring occasionally, until tender but firm. Drain. Set aside.

Heat cooking oil in large frying pan on medium. Add ground beef and onion. Scramble-fry for about 10 minutes until beef is no longer pink. Drain.

Add next 7 ingredients. Heat and stir for about 1 minute until boiling. Reduce heat to medium-low. Simmer, uncovered, for 8 to 10 minutes, stirring occasionally, until slightly thickened. Add macaroni. Heat and stir for about 5 minutes until heated through.

Sprinkle with cheese. Remove from heat. Let stand for about 1 minute until cheese is melted. Serves 4.

1 serving: 576 Calories; 18.5 g Total Fat (7.2 g Mono, 1.9 g Poly, 7.2 g Sat); 74 mg Cholesterol; 70 g Carbohydrate; 5 g Fibre; 35 g Protein; 1013 mg Sodium

Pictured on page 144.

Salisbury Steak

Tender, well-seasoned meat patties are smothered in mushroom sauce.

Fine dry bread crumbs	1/4 cup	60 mL
Finely chopped onion	1/4 cup	60 mL
Water	1/4 cup	60 mL
Celery salt	1/2 tsp.	2 mL
Pepper	1/4 tsp.	1 mL
Garlic powder	1/4 tsp.	1 mL
Dry mustard	1/4 tsp.	1 mL
Lean ground beef	1 lb.	454 g
Cooking oil	2 tsp.	10 mL
MUSHROOM SAUCE		
Prepared beef broth	1/4 cup	60 mL
All-purpose flour	2 tbsp.	30 mL
Prepared beef broth	1 cup	250 mL
Can of sliced mushrooms, drained	10 oz.	284 mL
Worcestershire sauce	1/2 tsp.	2 mL
Dried thyme	1/4 tsp.	1 mL

Combine first 7 ingredients in medium bowl.

Add ground beef. Mix well. Divide into 4 equal portions. Shape into 3/4 inch (2 cm) thick oval patties.

Heat cooking oil in large frying pan on medium. Add patties. Cook for about 5 minutes per side until fully cooked, and internal temperature of beef reaches 160°F (71°C). Remove to large serving platter. Cover to keep warm. Discard drippings, reserving any brown bits in pan.

Mushroom Sauce: Blend first amount of broth with flour in small cup. Set aside.

Slowly pour second amount of broth into same pan on medium, stirring constantly and scraping any brown bits from bottom of pan.

Add remaining 3 ingredients. Stir. Stir flour mixture. Slowly add to mushroom mixture, stirring constantly. Heat and stir for about 5 minutes until boiling and thickened. Makes about 1 1/2 cups (375 mL) sauce. Spoon over patties. Serves 4.

1 serving: 256 Calories; 12.5 g Total Fat (5.8 g Mono, 1.2 g Poly, 4.1 g Sat); 59 mg Cholesterol; 11 g Carbohydrate; 2 g Fibre; 24 g Protein; 670 mg Sodium

Pictured on page 144.

136   Stovetop Dishes

Ginger Beef

Ground beef as ginger beef? You bet! Delicious over chow mein noodles.

Water	2/3 cup	150 mL
Oyster sauce	1/4 cup	60 mL
Granulated sugar	1 tbsp.	15 mL
Cornstarch	2 tsp.	10 mL
Beef bouillon powder	1 tsp.	5 mL
Sesame oil, for flavour	1 tsp.	5 mL
Dried crushed chilies	1/2 tsp.	2 mL
Cornstarch	2 tbsp.	30 mL
Soy sauce	1 tbsp.	15 mL
Finely grated, peeled gingerroot	2 tsp.	10 mL
Garlic clove, minced (or 1/4 tsp., 1 mL, powder)	1	1
Onion powder	1/4 tsp.	1 mL
Extra-lean ground beef	1 lb.	454 g
Cooking oil	1 tbsp.	15 mL
Thinly sliced green pepper	1 cup	250 mL
Green onions, cut into 1/2 inch (12 mm) pieces	6	6

Combine first 7 ingredients in small bowl. Set aside.

Combine next 5 ingredients in medium bowl.

Add ground beef. Mix well.

Heat cooking oil in large frying pan on medium. Add beef mixture. Stir. Cook for about 10 minutes, coarsely breaking up beef, until no longer pink. Drain.

Add green pepper and onion. Heat and stir for 2 minutes. Stir oyster sauce mixture. Add to beef mixture. Heat and stir for about 1 minute until boiling and thickened. Serves 4.

1 serving: 396 Calories; 20.7 g Total Fat (9.5 g Mono, 2.2 g Poly, 6.7 g Sat); 92 mg Cholesterol; 17 g Carbohydrate; 1 g Fibre; 34 g Protein; 1485 mg Sodium

Pictured on page 143.

Sukiyaki Rice Bowl

No need to order in when Asian flavour is what
you're craving. This dish will satisfy!

Water	3 tbsp.	50 mL
Cornstarch	2 tbsp.	30 mL
Cooking oil	2 tsp.	10 mL
Extra-lean ground beef	1 lb.	454 g
Cooking oil	2 tsp.	10 mL
Large onion, halved lengthwise and sliced	1	1
Sliced fresh white mushrooms	1 1/2 cups	375 mL
Shredded suey choy (Chinese cabbage), lightly packed	2 cups	500 mL
Thinly sliced carrot	1 cup	250 mL
Can of bamboo shoots, drained	8 oz.	227 mL
Low-sodium soy sauce	1/2 cup	125 mL
Apple juice	1/2 cup	125 mL
Water	1/2 cup	125 mL
Granulated sugar	2 tbsp.	30 mL
Beef bouillon powder	1 tsp.	5 mL
Green onions, cut into 1 inch (2.5 cm) pieces	4	4
Hot cooked long grain white rice (about 1 1/3 cups, 325 mL, uncooked)	4 cups	1 L
Sliced green onion, for garnish		

Stir first amount of water, and cornstarch in small cup until smooth. Set aside.

Heat first amount of cooking oil in large frying pan on medium. Add ground beef. Scramble-fry for about 10 minutes until no longer pink. Drain. Transfer to medium bowl. Cover to keep warm.

Heat second amount of cooking oil in same pan. Add onion and mushrooms. Cook for 5 to 10 minutes, stirring often, until onion is softened.

Add next 9 ingredients. Stir. Cook, covered, for 2 to 3 minutes until boiling. Add beef. Stir. Stir cornstarch mixture. Add to beef mixture. Heat and stir for 1 to 2 minutes until boiling and thickened.

(continued on next page)

138 Stovetop Dishes

Spoon rice into individual bowls. Spoon beef mixture over rice.

Garnish with second amount of green onion. Serves 6.

1 serving: 486 Calories; 14.3 g Total Fat (6.6 g Mono, 1.6 g Poly, 4.6 g Sat); 61 mg Cholesterol; 59 g Carbohydrate; 3 g Fibre; 28 g Protein; 868 mg Sodium

Pictured on page 143.

Moroccan-Style Beef

A tasty blend of honey and spices complements the slightly sweet fruit flavours in this dish. Serve with couscous for a traditional North African meal.

Cooking oil	1 tsp.	5 mL
Lean ground beef	1 lb.	454 g
Chopped onion	1 1/2 cups	375 mL
Chopped dried apricot	1 cup	250 mL
Chopped dried pitted prunes (or raisins)	1/2 cup	125 mL
All-purpose flour	2 tbsp.	30 mL
Ground cumin	2 tsp.	10 mL
Ground cinnamon	1/2 tsp.	2 mL
Prepared beef broth	4 cups	1 L
Lemon juice	2 tbsp.	30 mL
Liquid honey	1 tbsp.	15 mL
Grated lemon zest	1 tsp.	5 mL
Chopped fresh parsley (or 3/4 tsp., 4 mL, flakes)	1 tbsp.	15 mL

Heat cooking oil in large frying pan on medium. Add ground beef and onion. Scramble-fry for about 10 minutes until beef is no longer pink. Drain.

Add next 5 ingredients. Stir well. Slowly add broth, stirring constantly. Bring to a boil. Reduce heat to medium-low. Simmer, uncovered, for about 20 minutes, stirring occasionally, until sauce is thickened and fruit is softened.

Add next 3 ingredients. Stir. Remove to large serving bowl.

Sprinkle with parsley. Serves 4.

1 serving: 401 Calories; 12.4 g Total Fat (5.3 g Mono, 0.8 g Poly, 4.2 g Sat); 57 mg Cholesterol; 50 g Carbohydrate; 6 g Fibre; 26 g Protein; 894 mg Sodium

Ground Beef Curry

Lots of colour in this flavourful, mild curry. If you've never used sambal oelek before, here's a good place to start. If you're already a fan, add as much as you like.

Cooking oil	1 tsp.	5 mL
Lean ground beef	1 lb.	454 g
Chopped onion	1 cup	250 mL
Garlic clove, minced (or 1/4 tsp., 1 mL, powder)	1	1
All-purpose flour	2 tbsp.	30 mL
Curry powder	2 tbsp.	30 mL
Prepared beef broth	1 1/2 cups	375 mL
Tomato juice	1 1/4 cups	300 mL
Can of chickpeas (garbanzo beans), rinsed and drained	14 oz.	398 mL
Diced tomato	1 1/2 cups	375 mL
Frozen peas, thawed	1 cup	250 mL
Salt	1/4 tsp.	1 mL
Chili paste (sambal oelek), optional	1/2 – 1 tsp.	2 – 5 mL
Plain yogurt	1/2 cup	125 mL
Chopped fresh cilantro or parsley, for garnish		

Heat cooking oil in large frying pan on medium. Add ground beef and onion. Scramble-fry for about 10 minutes until beef is no longer pink. Drain.

Add garlic. Heat and stir for 1 to 2 minutes until fragrant.

Add flour and curry powder. Heat and stir for 1 minute.

Slowly add broth, stirring constantly. Add tomato juice and chickpeas. Stir until boiling. Boil gently, uncovered, for about 15 minutes, stirring occasionally, until thickened.

Add next 4 ingredients. Stir. Cook for about 5 minutes, stirring occasionally, until peas are heated through. Remove from heat.

(continued on next page)

Add yogurt. Stir well. Remove to large serving bowl.

Garnish with cilantro. Serves 6.

1 serving: 262 Calories; 9.2 g Total Fat (3.7 g Mono, 1 g Poly, 3 g Sat); 39 mg Cholesterol; 24 g Carbohydrate; 4 g Fibre; 21 g Protein; 671 mg Sodium

Pictured on page 72.

Five-Spice Hot Pot

Chinese five-spice powder gives this Asian-style dish its distinct flavour. Pair with rice or spring rolls.

Cooking oil	2 tsp.	10 mL
Lean ground beef	1 lb.	454 g
Chopped onion	1/2 cup	125 mL
Garlic clove, minced (or 1/4 tsp., 1 mL, powder)	1	1
Fresh stir-fry vegetable mix	4 cups	1 L
Cans of tomato sauce (14 oz., 398 mL, each)	2	2
Shredded suey choy (Chinese cabbage), lightly packed	2 cups	500 mL
Can of sliced water chestnuts, drained	8 oz.	227 mL
Soy sauce	3 tbsp.	50 mL
Chili powder	1 tsp.	5 mL
Chinese five-spice powder	1/2 tsp.	2 mL
Fresh bean sprouts	1/2 cup	125 mL
Thinly sliced green onion	2 tbsp.	30 mL

Heat cooking oil in large frying pan or wok on medium. Add ground beef, onion and garlic. Scramble-fry for about 10 minutes until beef is no longer pink. Drain.

Add next 7 ingredients. Stir. Bring to a boil. Reduce heat to medium-low. Simmer, uncovered, for about 15 minutes, stirring occasionally, until vegetables are tender-crisp. Remove to large serving bowl.

Sprinkle with bean sprouts and green onion. Serves 6.

1 serving: 230 Calories; 8.6 g Total Fat (3.8 g Mono, 0.9 g Poly, 2.7 g Sat); 38 mg Cholesterol; 22 g Carbohydrate; 4 g Fibre; 19 g Protein; 1434 mg Sodium

Pictured on page 71.

Country Hash Skillet

Thick gravy coats this mildly seasoned beef hash.
A one-dish meal that's on the table in no time.

Cooking oil	2 tsp.	10 mL
Lean ground beef	1 lb.	454 g
Chopped onion	1 cup	250 mL
Chopped celery	1/4 cup	60 mL
All-purpose flour	2 tbsp.	30 mL
Beef bouillon powder	1 tbsp.	15 mL
Celery salt	1/2 tsp.	2 mL
Onion powder	1/2 tsp.	2 mL
Water	1 1/4 cups	300 mL
Frozen hash brown potatoes	2 cups	500 mL
Frozen mixed vegetables	1 1/2 cups	375 mL

Heat cooking oil in large frying pan on medium. Add ground beef, onion and celery. Scramble-fry for about 10 minutes until beef is no longer pink. Drain.

Add next 4 ingredients. Stir. Add water. Heat and stir for about 1 minute until boiling and thickened.

Add potatoes and vegetables. Cook for about 10 minutes, stirring occasionally, until heated through. Serves 4.

1 serving: 365 Calories; 12.9 g Total Fat (5.6 g Mono, 1.5 g Poly, 4.2 g Sat); 59 mg Cholesterol; 37 g Carbohydrate; 5 g Fibre; 26 g Protein; 695 mg Sodium

1. Ginger Beef, page 137
2. Sukiyaki Rice Bowl, page 138
3. Beef With Basil, page 149

Props courtesy of: Casa Bugatti
Cherison Enterprises Inc.
Island Pottery
Out of the Fire Studio

No-Fuss Stroganoff

A delicious stovetop classic that made its debut
in Casseroles. *Spoon over egg noodles or*
mashed potatoes for a hearty meal.

Hard margarine (or butter)	2 tbsp.	30 mL
Lean ground beef	1 lb.	454 g
Finely chopped onion	1 cup	250 mL
All-purpose flour	2 tbsp.	30 mL
Pepper	1/4 tsp.	1 mL
Can of sliced mushrooms, drained	10 oz.	284 mL
Can of condensed cream of chicken soup	10 oz.	284 mL
Sour cream	1/2 cup	125 mL
Grated medium Cheddar cheese	1/4 cup	60 mL

Melt margarine in large frying pan on medium. Add ground beef and onion. Scramble-fry for about 10 minutes until beef is no longer pink. Drain.

Add flour and pepper. Stir well. Add mushrooms. Heat and stir for 2 minutes.

Add soup. Stir. Cook, uncovered, for 10 minutes, stirring occasionally.

Add sour cream and cheese. Heat and stir for 2 to 3 minutes until heated through and cheese is melted. Serves 4.

1 serving: 491 Calories; 35.6 g Total Fat (14.2 g Mono, 4.3 g Poly, 13.8 g Sat); 84 mg Cholesterol; 16 g Carbohydrate; 2 g Fibre; 27 g Protein; 989 mg Sodium

1. Macaroni Jumble, page 135
2. Porcupine Stew, page 64
3. Salisbury Steak, page 136

Props courtesy of: Canhome Global
Casa Bugatti
Emile Henry

Fruity Beef Curry

An attractive, fragrant curry with fantastic flavour! Serve over rice or couscous.

Cooking oil	2 tsp.	10 mL
Lean ground beef	1 lb.	454 g
Salt	1 tsp.	5 mL
Chopped onion	1 1/2 cups	375 mL
Cumin seed	1 tbsp.	15 mL
Coarsely grated, peeled gingerroot	2 tsp.	10 mL
(or 1/2 tsp., 2 mL, ground ginger)		
Turmeric	1 tsp.	5 mL
Ground cardamom	1/2 tsp.	2 mL
Bay leaf	1	1
Ground cloves	1/8 tsp.	0.5 mL
Dried crushed chilies (optional)	1/2 tsp.	2 mL
Medium tomatoes, seeds removed, chopped	3	3
Medium cooking apples (such as McIntosh), peeled and each cut into 6 wedges	2	2
Juice and grated peel of 1 medium lemon, 1/2 of grated peel reserved		
Sultana raisins	1/2 cup	125 mL
Medium bananas, cut into 1 inch (2.5 cm) pieces	2	2
Chopped ripe mango	1 cup	250 mL
Liquid honey	2 tbsp.	30 mL
Raw cashews, toasted (see Tip, page 129)	1/3 cup	75 mL
Reserved grated lemon peel		

Heat cooking oil in large frying pan on medium. Add ground beef and salt. Scramble-fry for about 10 minutes until beef is no longer pink. Drain.

Add next 8 ingredients. Stir. Cook for about 5 minutes, stirring often, until onion is softened.

Add next 4 ingredients. Stir. Cook, covered, for about 5 minutes, stirring twice, until apple just starts to soften.

(continued on next page)

Stovetop Dishes

Add banana, mango and honey. Stir. Cook, covered, for 1 to 2 minutes until heated through and fruit is slightly softened. Discard bay leaf.

Sprinkle individual servings with cashews and reserved lemon peel. Serves 4.

1 serving: 534 Calories; 18.8 g Total Fat (8.9 g Mono, 2.3 g Poly, 5.2 g Sat); 59 mg Cholesterol; 73 g Carbohydrate; 7 g Fibre; 26 g Protein; 656 mg Sodium

Paré Pointer

He jumped off the roof into a pool of cola but wasn't hurt because it was a soft drink.

Saucy Skillet Dinner

Family-friendly, and one of our favourites
from One-Dish Meals. *A thick, rich sauce coats*
spaghetti in this delicious dinner.

Cooking oil	2 tsp.	10 mL
Lean ground beef	1 lb.	454 g
Chopped onion	1 cup	250 mL
Garlic clove, minced (or 1/4 tsp., 1 mL, powder)	1	1
Medium zucchini (with peel), halved lengthwise and sliced	1	1
Chopped fresh white mushrooms	1 cup	250 mL
Tomato pasta sauce	2 cups	500 mL
Water	1 cup	250 mL
Dried basil	1/2 tsp.	2 mL
Granulated sugar	1/2 tsp.	2 mL
Dried whole oregano, just a pinch		
Spaghetti, broken into 1 – 2 inch (2.5 – 5 cm) pieces	6 oz.	170 g
Grated part-skim mozzarella cheese	1/2 cup	125 mL

Heat cooking oil in large frying pan on medium. Add ground beef, onion and garlic. Scramble-fry for about 10 minutes until beef is no longer pink. Drain.

Add zucchini and mushrooms. Cook for 6 to 7 minutes, stirring occasionally, until vegetables are softened.

Add next 5 ingredients. Stir. Bring to a boil.

Add spaghetti. Stir. Reduce heat to medium-low. Simmer, covered, for about 20 minutes until spaghetti is tender but firm and liquid is almost absorbed.

Add cheese. Stir until melted. Serves 4.

1 serving: 537 Calories; 16.6 g Total Fat (6.6 g Mono, 2 g Poly, 5.9 g Sat); 66 mg Cholesterol; 65 g Carbohydrate; 9 g Fibre; 36 g Protein; 226 mg Sodium

Beef With Basil

*A wonderful mingling of aromatic sauces and spices gives
ground beef an exotic flavour. Best served with rice.*

Cooking oil	2 tsp.	10 mL
Lean ground beef	1 lb.	454 g
Cooking oil	1 tbsp.	15 mL
Medium carrots, thinly sliced diagonally	2	2
Cubed green pepper	1 cup	250 mL
Chopped onion	1/2 cup	125 mL
Fresh chili pepper (see Tip, page 47), minced (or 1/2 tsp., 2 mL, dried crushed chilies)	1	1
Garlic clove, minced (or 1/4 tsp., 1 mL, powder)	1	1
Water	1/2 cup	125 mL
Chili sauce	1/3 cup	75 mL
Soy sauce	1 tbsp.	15 mL
Fish sauce (or soy sauce)	1 tbsp.	15 mL
Ground cinnamon	1/2 tsp.	2 mL
Granulated sugar	1/2 tsp.	2 mL
Chopped fresh basil	1/2 cup	125 mL

Heat first amount of cooking oil in large frying pan on medium. Add
ground beef. Scramble-fry for about 10 minutes until no longer pink.
Drain. Transfer to medium bowl. Set aside.

Heat second amount of cooking oil in same pan. Add next 5 ingredients.
Cook for 3 to 4 minutes, stirring often, until vegetables are tender-crisp.

Add beef and next 6 ingredients. Stir. Reduce heat to low. Cook,
uncovered, for 20 to 30 minutes, stirring occasionally, until thickened.

Add basil. Stir. Serves 4.

*1 serving: 299 Calories; 15.5 g Total Fat (7.6 g Mono, 2.2 g Poly, 4.2 g Sat); 59 mg Cholesterol;
17 g Carbohydrate; 4 g Fibre; 23 g Protein; 902 mg Sodium*

Pictured on page 143.

Measurement Tables

Throughout this book measurements are given in Conventional and Metric measure. To compensate for differences between the two measurements due to rounding, a full metric measure is not always used. The cup used is the standard 8 fluid ounce. Temperature is given in degrees Fahrenheit and Celsius. Baking pan measurements are in inches and centimetres as well as quarts and litres. An exact metric conversion is given below as well as the working equivalent (Metric Standard Measure).

Spoons

Conventional Measure	Metric Exact Conversion Millilitre (mL)	Metric Standard Measure Millilitre (mL)
1/8 teaspoon (tsp.)	0.6 mL	0.5 mL
1/4 teaspoon (tsp.)	1.2 mL	1 mL
1/2 teaspoon (tsp.)	2.4 mL	2 mL
1 teaspoon (tsp.)	4.7 mL	5 mL
2 teaspoons (tsp.)	9.4 mL	10 mL
1 tablespoon (tbsp.)	14.2 mL	15 mL

Cups

Conventional Measure	Metric Exact Conversion Millilitre (mL)	Metric Standard Measure Millilitre (mL)
1/4 cup (4 tbsp.)	56.8 mL	60 mL
1/3 cup (5 1/3 tbsp.)	75.6 mL	75 mL
1/2 cup (8 tbsp.)	113.7 mL	125 mL
2/3 cup (10 2/3 tbsp.)	151.2 mL	150 mL
3/4 cup (12 tbsp.)	170.5 mL	175 mL
1 cup (16 tbsp.)	227.3 mL	250 mL
4 1/2 cups	1022.9 mL	1000 mL (1 L)

Oven Temperatures

Fahrenheit (°F)	Celsius (°C)
175°	80°
200°	95°
225°	110°
250°	120°
275°	140°
300°	150°
325°	160°
350°	175°
375°	190°
400°	205°
425°	220°
450°	230°
475°	240°
500°	260°

Dry Measurements

Conventional Measure Ounces (oz.)	Metric Exact Conversion Grams (g)	Metric Standard Measure Grams (g)
1 oz.	28.3 g	28 g
2 oz.	56.7 g	57 g
3 oz.	85.0 g	85 g
4 oz.	113.4 g	125 g
5 oz.	141.7 g	140 g
6 oz.	170.1 g	170 g
7 oz.	198.4 g	200 g
8 oz.	226.8 g	250 g
16 oz.	453.6 g	500 g
32 oz.	907.2 g	1000 g (1 kg)

Pans

Conventional Inches	Metric Centimetres
8x8 inch	20x20 cm
9x9 inch	22x22 cm
9x13 inch	22x33 cm
10x15 inch	25x38 cm
11x17 inch	28x43 cm
8x2 inch round	20x5 cm
9x2 inch round	22x5 cm
10x4 1/2 inch tube	25x11 cm
8x4x3 inch loaf	20x10x7.5 cm
9x5x3 inch loaf	22x12.5x7.5 cm

Casseroles

CANADA & BRITAIN Standard Size Casserole	Exact Metric Measure	UNITED STATES Standard Size Casserole	Exact Metric Measure
1 qt. (5 cups)	1.13 L	1 qt. (4 cups)	900 mL
1 1/2 qts. (7 1/2 cups)	1.69 L	1 1/2 qts. (6 cups)	1.35 L
2 qts. (10 cups)	2.25 L	2 qts. (8 cups)	1.8 L
2 1/2 qts. (12 1/2 cups)	2.81 L	2 1/2 qts. (10 cups)	2.25 L
3 qts. (15 cups)	3.38 L	3 qts. (12 cups)	2.7 L
4 qts. (20 cups)	4.5 L	4 qts. (16 cups)	3.6 L
5 qts. (25 cups)	5.63 L	5 qts. (20 cups)	4.5 L

Recipe Index

A

Appetizer Meatball Skewers 92
Appetizers
   Artichoke Beef Dip 15
   Beefy Potato Cups 14
   Blue Moon Dumplings 19
   Cheeseburger Puffs 11
   Homemade Snack Sausage 16
   Nachos With Avocado Salsa 13
   Pastry Pinwheels 10
   Roquefort Beef Tarts 12
Apricot Meatballs 86
Apricot Sauce 86
Artichoke Beef Dip 15
Avocado Salsa 13

B

Baked Spinach Portobellos 51
Barbecue Loaf, Tuscan 116
Barley Cabbage Rolls, Beef 60
Basil, Beef With 149
Basil Mayonnaise 21
Basil Vinaigrette 128
Beef And Bean Burritos 109
Beef And Cheese Rolls 42
Beef And Vegetable Pie 34
Beef And Vegetable Roundup 96
Beef Barley Cabbage Rolls 60
Beef Corncake 43
Beef Falafel Wraps 105
Beef With Basil 149
Beefy Burrito Bake 55

Beefy Potato Cups 14
Biscuit Crust 58
Biscuit, Giant 24
Blue Moon Dumplings 19
Bolognese Sauce 77
Borscht Burgers 25
Bruschetta Topping 102
Bundles, Surf 'N' Turf 44
Burgers (see also Patties)
   Borscht 25
   Chipotle Jerk 27
   Giant Biscuit 24
   Gouda 20
   Green Chili 23
   Hot Shot 33
   Jalapeño Popper 26
   Mushroom 29
   Pesto Goat Cheese Wedges 103
   Presto Pesto 21
   Teriyaki 22
Burrito Bake, Beefy 55
Burritos, Beef And Bean 109

C

Cabbage Roll Casserole, Lazy 37
Cabbage Rolls, Beef Barley 60
Caesar Meat Sauce 70
Cajun Loaf, Layered 99
Caribbean Beef Salad 120
Casseroles
   Hot Tamale Two-Step 52
   Lazy Cabbage Roll 37
   Saffron Meatball 39
   Tater Tot 45
Cheese Rolls, Beef And 42

151

Cheese Sauce, Nacho. 87

Cheeseburger Pie 58

Cheeseburger Puffs. 11

Cheesy Meatball Salad 123

Chèvre Beef Salad 128

Chèvre Dressing, Creamy. 119

Chili And Dumplings 76

Chili Burgers, Green 23

Chili Gumbo. 75

Chilies

    Chuckwagon Chipotle 74

    Cinnamon 73

    Tandoori 68

Chipotle Chili, Chuckwagon. 74

Chipotle Jerk Burgers 27

Chuckwagon Chipotle Chili 74

Chutney Beef Scones 115

Cinnamon Chili 73

Company's Coming Classics

    Hash Brown Pizza. 59

    Lazy Cabbage Roll Casserole 37

    Meat Sauce 67

    Meatloaf Classic. 93

    No-Fuss Stroganoff 145

    Saucy Skillet Dinner 148

    Shepherd's Pie 48

    Tater Tot Casserole. 45

    Teriyaki Burgers 22

Continental Rice Salad 122

Corncake, Beef. 43

Cornmeal Dumplings. 76

Country Hash Skillet. 142

Creamy Chèvre Dressing 119

Creamy Pepper Quesadillas 117

Creamy Zucchini Wedges. 38

Crust, Biscuit 58

Cucumber Dill Sauce 104

Cumin Lime Sauce 111

Curried Yam Empanadas 114

Curries

    Fruity Beef 146

    Ground Beef 140

    Sweet Lentil. 134

Curry Sauce, Meatballs In. 81

D

Dill Sauce, Cucumber. 104

Dinner, Saucy Skillet. 148

Dip, Artichoke Beef. 15

Dressings

    Creamy Chèvre 119

    Parsley Peppercorn. 122

    Parsley Pesto 123

Dumplings, Blue Moon 19

Dumplings, Cornmeal 76

E

Empanadas, Curried Yam 114

F

Falafel Wraps, Beef. 105

Fennel Soup, Potato. 127

Fiesta Strata 65

Five-Spice Hot Pot 141

Fruity Beef Curry 146

G

Giant Biscuit Burger 24

Ginger Beef 137

152

nger Meatballs 91
nger Salsa, Pineapple 32
at Cheese Wedges, Pesto 103
uda Burgers 20
urmet Mini-Meatloaves 100
eek Salad Pizza 49
een Chili Burgers 23
illed Meatball Skewers 92
illed Tournedos 30
ound Beef Curry 140
ound Beef Pot Roast 95
mbo, Chili 75

H

sh Brown Pizza 59
sh Skillet, Country 142
arty Mushroom Soup 130
arty Wild Rice Soup 124
kory Patties 31
memade Snack Sausage 16
rseradish Mayonnaise 20
t Pot, Five-Spice 141
t Shot Burgers 33
t Tamale Two-Step 52
mmus Pita Pockets 104

I

lian Meatball Soup 131
lian Sandwich 102

J

apeño Popper Burgers 26
k Burgers, Chipotle 27

L

Lasagne, Meaty 62
Lasagne, Phyllo 40
Layered Cajun Loaf 99
Layered Taco Salad 118
Lazy Cabbage Roll Casserole 37
Lazy Stuffed Meatloaf 101
Leek-Crowned Beef Pie 46
Lettuce Wraps, Teriyaki 112
Lentil Curry, Sweet 134
Lime Sauce, Cumin 111
Loaf, Tuscan Barbecue 116

M

Macaroni Jumble 135
Mango Pepper Patties 28
Mango Salsa 28
Mayonnaise, Basil 21
Mayonnaise, Horseradish 20
Mayonnaise, Orange 27
Meat Sauce 67
Meat Sauce, Caesar 70
Meatballs
Appetizer Meatball Skewers 92
Apricot 86
Cheesy Meatball Salad 123
Ginger 91
Grilled Meatball Skewers 92
Italian Meatball Soup 131
Nacho 87
Porcupine Stew 64
Saffron Meatball Casserole 39
Salsa Porcupines 88
Sesame 83

Spiced Meatball Pitas 111

Spicy Lava 84

Tasty 79

Vietnamese Noodle Balls 85

Meatballs In Curry Sauce 81

Meatballs In Mushroom Sauce 80

Meatballs In Pineapple Sauce 82

Meatloaf Classic 93

Meatloaves

   Beef And Vegetable Roundup 96

   Gourmet Mini- 100

   Ground Beef Pot Roast 95

   Layered Cajun Loaf 99

   Lazy Stuffed 101

   Ricotta Swiss Wedges 97

   Spinach-Stuffed 98

   Sweet Onion Loaf 94

Meaty Lasagne 62

Mexican Beef Soup 133

Mini-Meatloaves, Gourmet 100

Moroccan-Style Beef 139

Mushroom Burgers 29

Mushroom Sauce 136

Mushroom Sauce, Meatballs In 80

Mushroom Sauce, Paprika 78

Mushroom Soup, Hearty 130

N

Nacho Cheese Sauce 87

Nacho Meatballs 87

Nachos With Avocado Salsa 13

No-Fuss Stroganoff 145

Noodle Balls, Vietnamese 85

Norway Spinach Salad 119

O

Onion Loaf, Sweet 9

Orange Mayonnaise 2

P

Paprika Mushroom Sauce 7

Parsley Peppercorn Dressing 12

Parsley Pesto Dressing 12

Pastry Pinwheels 1

Patties (see also Burgers)

   Grilled Tournedos 3

   Hickory 3

   Mango Pepper 2

   Pineapple Salsa 3

   Salisbury Steak 13

Pepper Patties, Mango 2

Pepper Quesadillas, Creamy 11

Peppercorn Dressing, Parsley 12

Pesto Burgers, Presto 2

Pesto Dressing, Parsley 12

Pesto Goat Cheese Wedges 10

Phyllo Lasagne 4

Picadillo Pie 5

Pies

   Beef And Vegetable 3

   Cheeseburger 58

   Leek-Crowned Beef 4

   Picadillo 5

   Shepherd's 48

Pineapple Ginger Salsa 3

Pineapple Salsa Patties 3

Pineapple Sauce, Meatballs In 8

Pinwheels, Pastry 1

Pita Pockets, Hummus 104

tas, Spiced Meatball 111

zza, Greek Salad 49

zza, Hash Brown 59

ɔpper Burgers, Jalapeño 26

ɔrcupine Stew 64

ɔrtobellos, Baked Spinach. 51

ɔrtuguese Soup 132

ɔt Roast, Ground Beef 95

ɔtato Cups, Beefy 14

ɔtato Fennel Soup 127

ɾesto Pesto Burgers 21

ʌffed Triangles 130

ʌffs, Cheeseburger 11

Q

ʌuesadillas, Creamy Pepper 117

R

ɪce Bowl, Sukiyaki 138

ɪce Salad, Continental 122

ɪce Soup, Hearty Wild 124

ɪcotta Swiss Wedges 97

ɪolls, Beef And Cheese 42

ɪoquefort Beef Tarts 12

ɪosy Beef Sauce 69

S

affron Meatball Casserole 39

alads

   Caribbean Beef 120

   Cheesy Meatball 123

   Chèvre Beef 128

   Continental Rice 122

Layered Taco 118

Norway Spinach 119

Salisbury Steak 136

Salsa Patties, Pineapple 32

Salsa Porcupines 88

Salsas

   Avocado 13

   Mango 28

   Pineapple Ginger 32

Sandwich, Italian 102

Sauces

   Apricot 86

   Bolognese 77

   Caesar Meat 70

   Cucumber Dill 104

   Cumin Lime 111

   Meat 67

   Mushroom 136

   Nacho Cheese 87

   Paprika Mushroom 78

   Rosy Beef 69

   Sun-Dried Tomato 100

   Sweet And Sour 83

   Teriyaki 112

Saucy Skillet Dinner 148

Sausage, Homemade Snack 16

Scones, Chutney Beef 115

Sesame Meatballs 83

Shepherd's Pie 48

Skewers, Appetizer Meatball 92

Skewers, Grilled Meatball 92

Skillet, Country Hash 142

Skillet Dinner, Saucy 148

Sloppy Ginos 66

Sloppy Joe Tacos 106

Snack Sausage, Homemade 16

155

Soups

    Hearty Mushroom 130

    Hearty Wild Rice. 124

    Italian Meatball 131

    Mexican Beef. 133

    Portuguese. 132

    Potato Fennel. 127

Spiced Meatball Pitas 111

Spicy Lava Meatballs 84

Spinach Portobellos, Baked. 51

Spinach Salad, Norway. 119

Spinach-Stuffed Meatloaf 98

Steak, Salisbury 136

Stew, Porcupine 64

Strata, Fiesta. 65

Stroganoff, No-Fuss 145

Stuffed Meatloaf, Lazy 101

Stuffed Tomatoes, Tuscan. 56

Sukiyaki Rice Bowl 138

Sun-Dried Tomato Sauce 100

Surf 'N' Turf Bundles 44

Sweet And Sour Sauce 83

Sweet Lentil Curry 134

Sweet Onion Loaf. 94

Swiss Wedges, Ricotta 97

T

Taco Salad, Layered 118

Tacos, Sloppy Joe 106

Tamale Two-Step, Hot 52

Tandoori Chili. 68

Tarts, Roquefort Beef 12

Tasty Meatballs. 79

Tater Tot Casserole. 45

Teriyaki Burgers 22

Teriyaki Lettuce Wraps 112

Teriyaki Sauce. 112

Thai Beef Wraps 110

Tomato Sauce, Sun-Dried. 100

Tomatoes, Tuscan Stuffed. 56

Topping, Bruschetta 102

Tournedos, Grilled 30

Tuscan Barbecue Loaf. 116

Tuscan Stuffed Tomatoes 56

V

Vegetable Pie, Beef And 34

Vegetable Roundup, Beef And 96

Vietnamese Noodle Balls 85

Vinaigrette, Basil. 128

W

Wild Rice Soup, Hearty. 124

Wraps

    Beef Falafel. 105

    Teriyaki Lettuce 112

    Thai Beef 110

Y

Yam Empanadas, Curried 114

Z

Zucchini Wedges, Creamy 38

156

Recipe Notes

Recipe Notes

Recipe Notes

Recipe Notes

4-INGREDIENT RECIPES

Company's Coming

National Bestseller

4 Ingredient Recipes

Jean Paré

ORIGINAL SERIES

4-Ingredient
Recipes

Jean Paré

www.companyscoming.com
visit our website

Front Cover

1. Curry Noodle Bowl,
   page 48
2. Tangy Rice Parfaits,
   page 124
3. Spinach Cranberry
   Salad, page 39
4. Tuscan Pull-Aparts,
   page 26

Props courtesy of:
Canhome Global
Casa Bugatti
Totally Bamboo

We gratefully acknowledge the following suppliers for their generous support of our Test and Photography Kitchens:

Broil King Barbecues
Corelle®
Hamilton Beach® Canada
Lagostina®
Proctor Silex® Canada
Tupperware®

Need more recipes?

Six *"sneak preview"* recipes are featured online **with every new book released**.

Visit us at
www.companyscoming.com

Foreword

Let's face it—after a full day of work, the last thing we want to face is a recipe listing 17 ingredients and directions more complicated than a computer manual. No wonder many of us have the phone number of our favourite takeout place memorized!

But what if all you had to do was toss together four ingredients to make a dish that will have your troops gathering eagerly around the table? *4-Ingredient Recipes* is full of easy ideas using convenient foods to prepare great-tasting meals. Our Lemon Tuna Fettuccine, for instance, calls for fettuccine noodles, garlic butter, a lemon and a can of tuna. Add a bowl of salad and you're done! It's so simple that even your kids can get dinner started.

And for tomorrow, try our Ginger Apricot Chicken. Marinate chicken breasts in Italian dressing, ginger and apricot jam in the morning, and you'll be all set for supper.

We've included tasty side dishes such as Salsa Rice, Sweet Onion Squash and Orange Basil Couscous. Get the gang into the kitchen, assign them each a dish and catch up on the day while you put a home-cooked meal on the table.

You'll also find breakfast and lunch ideas, along with mouth-watering desserts. Mudsicle Pie, anyone? How about Ooey Gooey Bars, Blondie Brownies or the divine Chocolate Crunch Cookies (featuring Skor bars as the secret component)? "Just four ingredients," you'll say airily, as you tick them off for your friends.

We've taken advantage of some of the interesting convenience products on your grocery shelves to save you cooking steps. Ingredients run from the everyday, such as peanut butter and cans of condensed soup, to the more exotic, like oyster sauce and chai tea concentrate. As usual, we've come up with delicious, kitchen-tested combinations that will make your four-ingredient dishes a hit with family and friends.

So file away that takeout phone number. With *4-Ingredient Recipes*, you'll be able to whip up simple, nourishing meals faster than your family can argue about pizza toppings. And you won't have to round up toonies for tipping!

Jean Paré

Nutrition Information Guidelines

Each recipe is analyzed using the most current version of the Canadian Nutrient File from Health Canada, which is based on the United States Department of Agriculture (USDA) Nutrient Database.

- If more than one ingredient is listed (such as"hard margarine or butter"), or if a range is given (1 – 2 tsp., 5 – 10 mL), only the first ingredient or first amount is analyzed.
- For meat, poultry and fish, the serving size per person is based on the recommended 4 oz. (113 g) uncooked weight (without bone), which is 2 – 3 oz. (57 – 85 g) cooked weight (without bone)—approximately the size of a deck of playing cards.
- Ingredients indicating "sprinkle," "optional," or "for garnish" are not included in the nutrition information.

Margaret Ng, B.Sc. (Hon.), M.A.
Registered Dietitian

One, Two ... Free Four!

When our test kitchen sat down to plan *4-Ingredient Recipes,* we debated long and hard about what an ingredient was.

"How about water?" asked one. Well, water, though necessary in so many dishes (how do you cook pasta or rice without it?), wasn't really going to count, we decided.

"OK," said another, "but what about the salt we put into the water for pasta?"

"That just brings out the flavour of the pasta," declared a third. "It doesn't create a new flavour, the way basil or oregano would. You can hardly cook pasta without salt!"

After much discussion, we agreed that our "free" ingredients would be water, salt, pepper and the cooking oil needed for frying. All other ingredients had to stand up and be counted.

How We Tested These Recipes

- We use non-stick frying pans in our kitchens.
- A greased frying pan means 1 to 2 tsp. (5 to 10 mL) of cooking oil; well-greased means 1 tbsp. (15 mL) of oil or more.
- When we cook pasta in "boiling salted water," we recommend 1/2 tsp. (2 mL) salt per 4 cups (1 L) water.

- Unless we've indicated otherwise, we've used:
  - 1% milk
  - canola oil as cooking oil
  - the juice of fresh lemons and limes
  - the centre rack in the oven

Guaranteed Great™ Guidelines

For recipe success, follow these cooking tips:

- Read the recipe through.
- Gather and prepare (slice, chop, etc.) your ingredients.
- Use correct wet and dry measures. A liquid measuring cup has a rim to prevent liquids from spilling. A dry measure has no rim, allowing you to level off flour, etc., with a knife.

- To prevent packing the flour, spoon it into a dry measure.
- Don't substitute tub margarine for hard margarine when baking. Tub margarine contains water, which will affect the outcome.
- Use the correct size of saucepan, baking pan or casserole dish indicated in the recipe to avoid under or overcooking.

8

Salmon Cream Quiche

You'll be surprised how easy these elegant appetizers are to make,
and your guests will never know—unless they ask for the recipe!

Tub of smoked salmon spreadable cream cheese	8 oz.	250 g
Milk	1/2 cup	125 mL
Large eggs	2	2
Frozen mini tart shells, thawed	30	30

Process first 3 ingredients and a sprinkle of salt and pepper in blender or food processor until smooth.

Arrange tart shells on baking sheet. Pour cream cheese mixture into shells until almost full. Bake on bottom rack in 350°F (175°C) oven for about 30 minutes until filling is puffed and pastry is golden. Let stand on baking sheet for 10 minutes before removing from foil liners. Makes 30 mini quiche.

1 quiche: 73 Calories; 5.1 g Total Fat (2.1 g Mono, 0.5 g Poly, 2.1 g Sat); 20 mg Cholesterol;
5 g Carbohydrate; 0 g Fibre; 2 g Protein; 125 mg Sodium

Hawaiian Hammies

A good addition to a tropical theme buffet. Provide long cocktail
picks for this sweet and sour nibble so guests can help themselves.

Large green pepper, cut into 1 inch (2.5 cm) pieces	1	1
Ham sausage, cut into 1/4 inch (6 mm) slices	1 1/2 lbs.	680 g
Can of pineapple chunks, drained	14 oz.	398 mL
Sweet and sour sauce	1 1/2 cups	375 mL

Cook green pepper in large well-greased frying pan on medium for about 5 minutes, stirring occasionally, until tender-crisp.

Add remaining 3 ingredients. Stir. Cook for about 5 minutes, stirring occasionally, until heated through. Serves 12.

1 serving: 169 Calories; 7.7 g Total Fat (0.7 g Mono, 0.4 g Poly, 0.1 g Sat); 0 mg Cholesterol;
15 g Carbohydrate; 1 g Fibre; 10 g Protein; 641 mg Sodium

Spinach Cream Triangles

These flaky bundles can be made ahead and frozen. Brushing the pastry sheets with garlic butter instead of margarine will add extra good flavour.

Boxes of frozen chopped spinach (10 oz., 300 g, each), thawed and squeezed dry	2	2
Tub of vegetable light spreadable cream cheese	8 oz.	250 g
Frozen phyllo pastry sheets, thawed according to package directions	12	12
Hard margarine (or butter), melted	1/2 cup	125 mL

Combine spinach, cream cheese and a sprinkle of salt and pepper in medium bowl. Set aside.

Work with pastry sheets 1 at a time. Keep remaining sheets covered with damp tea towel to prevent drying. Place 1 sheet on work surface. Brush with margarine. Place second sheet on top, aligning edges. Brush with margarine. Layer with third pastry sheet. Brush with margarine. Cut lengthwise into 4 equal strips (see diagram 1). Spoon about 2 tbsp. (30 mL) spinach mixture onto end of 1 strip (see diagram 2). Fold pastry over filling to enclose, forming triangle (see diagram 3). Continue folding to end of strip (see diagrams 4, 5 and 6). Place on greased baking sheet. Cover with damp tea towel. Fill and fold remaining 3 strips. Repeat with remaining ingredients to make 16 triangles. Brush tops with remaining margarine. Bake in 350°F (175°C) oven for about 30 minutes until golden. Remove to wire rack to cool. Makes 16 triangles.

1 triangle: 139 Calories; 10 g Total Fat (5.1 g Mono, 1.2 g Poly, 3.1 g Sat); 10 mg Cholesterol; 9 g Carbohydrate; 1 g Fibre; 3 g Protein; 272 mg Sodium

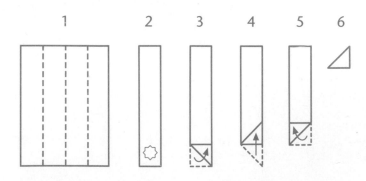

Thai Chicken Salad Wraps

Rice paper rounds are easy to use. You'll have these assembled in no time. Serve with extra peanut sauce for dipping.

Lean ground chicken	1 lb.	454 g
Thai peanut sauce	3/4 cup	175 mL
Rice paper rounds (8 inch, 20 cm, diameter)	12	12
Bag of spring mix lettuce	5 oz.	142 g

Scramble-fry ground chicken in large greased frying pan on medium for about 10 minutes until no longer pink. Drain.

Add peanut sauce. Stir. Cool to room temperature.

Work with rice paper rounds 1 at a time. Soak 1 round in hot water in 9 x 9 inch (22 x 22 cm) pan for about 1 minute until softened. Place on work surface. Put about 1/2 cup (125 mL) lettuce on bottom half of round, leaving 1 inch (2.5 cm) edge. Spoon about 3 tbsp. (50 mL) chicken mixture on top of lettuce. Fold sides over filling. Roll up from bottom to enclose. Press seam against roll to seal. Place, seam-side down, on large serving platter. Cover with damp tea towel to prevent drying. Repeat with remaining ingredients to make 12 wraps. Cut wraps in half crosswise, for a total of 24 pieces.

1 piece: 82 Calories; 5.5 g Total Fat (1.3 g Mono, 0.7 g Poly, 0.8 g Sat); 0 mg Cholesterol; 4 g Carbohydrate; trace Fibre; 5 g Protein; 172 mg Sodium

Paré Pointer

Pigs are great sports fans. They're always rooting.

Taco Beef Snacks

Everyone will love these hand-held pastry pockets filled with
Tex-Mex flavours. Pack any leftovers in the kids' lunch bags the next day!

Lean ground beef	1 lb.	454 g
Grated medium Cheddar cheese	2 cups	500 mL
Envelope of reduced sodium taco seasoning mix	1 1/4 oz.	35 g
Tubes of refrigerator country-style biscuits (10 biscuits per tube), 12 oz. (340 g), each	3	3

Scramble-fry ground beef in large greased frying pan on medium for about 10 minutes until no longer pink. Drain.

Add cheese and taco seasoning. Stir well. Set aside.

Separate biscuits. Pat into 4 inch (10 cm) circles. Spoon beef mixture onto centre of circles. Fold circles in half over filling. Pinch edges to seal. Arrange on 2 greased baking sheets. Bake on separate racks in 350°F (175°C) oven for 15 to 20 minutes, switching position of baking sheets at halftime, until golden. Makes 30 taco snacks.

1 taco snack: 148 Calories; 5.8 g Total Fat (2.3 g Mono, 0.4 g Poly, 2.6 g Sat); 16 mg Cholesterol; 17 g Carbohydrate; trace Fibre; 7 g Protein; 561 mg Sodium

Paré Pointer

Does the transplant recipient of a gambler's
heart now have a cheating heart?

Appetizers

Garlic Lime Pita Chips

Use commercial garlic butter that's flavoured
with wine or herbs for a special touch.

Medium lime	1	1
Garlic butter	1/4 cup	60 mL
Pita breads (3 inch, 7.5 cm, diameter), each split into 2 rounds	18	18
Grated Asiago cheese	1 cup	250 mL

Grate 1 tbsp. (15 mL) lime zest into small bowl. Set aside. Melt butter in small saucepan. Remove from heat. Squeeze and add 1 tbsp. (15 mL) lime juice. Stir.

Brush butter mixture on both sides of pita rounds. Cut each round into 4 wedges. Arrange, split-side up, on 2 ungreased baking sheets with sides.

Add cheese to zest in bowl. Stir. Sprinkle over pita wedges. Bake on separate racks in 350°F (175°C) oven for 12 to 15 minutes, switching position of baking sheets at halftime, until golden. Cool. Serves 12.

1 serving: 156 Calories; 6.9 g Total Fat (1.9 g Mono, 0.4 g Poly, 4.1 g Sat); 20 mg Cholesterol; 18 g Carbohydrate; 1 g Fibre; 5 g Protein; 254 mg Sodium

Pictured on page 17.

Black Olive Spread

This spread is rich and versatile! Serve with crackers, on sandwiches or even toss with pasta. Use a good quality extra-virgin olive oil for best flavour.

Capers, rinsed and drained, divided	3 tbsp.	50 mL
Cans of pitted whole ripe olives (13 oz., 375 mL, each), drained	2	2
Garlic clove, minced (or 1/4 tsp., 1 mL, powder)	1	1
Olive oil	1/4 cup	60 mL

Reserve 1 tsp. (5 mL) capers for garnish. Put remaining capers into blender or food processor.

Add remaining 3 ingredients and a sprinkle of pepper. Process until smooth. Remove to small serving bowl. Garnish with reserved capers. Makes about 1 3/4 cups (425 mL).

2 tbsp. (30 mL): 56 Calories; 5.9 g Total Fat (4.3 g Mono, 0.5 g Poly, 0.8 g Sat); 0 mg Cholesterol; 1 g Carbohydrate; 1 g Fibre; 0 g Protein; 181 mg Sodium

Appetizers

Quesadilla Bites

There's quite a bite to the cheesy filling tucked inside
these warm wedges. Delicious, and easy to prepare!

Tub of vegetable light spreadable cream cheese	8 oz.	250 g
Flour tortillas (9 inch, 22 cm, diameter)	8	8
Grated havarti cheese	2 cups	500 mL
Cans of diced green chilies (4 oz., 113 g, each), drained	2	2

Spread cream cheese on tortillas, leaving 1/2 inch (12 mm) edge. Sprinkle havarti cheese and chilies on half of each tortilla. Fold tortillas in half over filling. Press down lightly. Spray both sides with cooking spray. Arrange on ungreased baking sheets. Bake in 400°F (205°C) oven for about 15 minutes, turning over after 10 minutes, until golden and cheese is melted. Cut each quesadilla into 6 wedges, for a total of 48 wedges.

1 wedge: 62 Calories; 3 g Total Fat (1 g Mono, 0.4 g Poly, 1.5 g Sat); 8 mg Cholesterol; 6 g Carbohydrate; trace Fibre; 3 g Protein; 176 mg Sodium

Spicy Feta Pâté

This creamy cheese pâté has a hint of sweetness and a jalapeño kick.
Good served with crackers or pita chips, or stuffed in celery sticks.

Block of cream cheese, softened	4 oz.	125 g
Crumbled feta cheese	1/2 cup	125 mL
Jellied cranberry sauce	2 tbsp.	30 mL
Jalapeño pepper, finely diced (see Tip, page 15)	1	1

Beat all 4 ingredients in medium bowl until well combined. Makes about 1 cup (250 mL).

2 tbsp. (30 mL): 107 Calories; 9 g Total Fat (2.3 g Mono, 0.3 g Poly, 5.9 g Sat); 32 mg Cholesterol; 3 g Carbohydrate; trace Fibre; 4 g Protein; 240 mg Sodium

Pictured on page 17.

Salmon-Stuffed Brie

A creamy salmon stuffing accented with lemon and dill is sandwiched between layers of Brie. A fancy, easy-to-make appetizer.

Medium lemon	1	1
Tub of smoked salmon spreadable cream cheese	8 oz.	250 g
Chopped fresh dill (or 1/2 tsp., 2 mL, dill weed)	2 tsp.	10 mL
Brie cheese rounds (4 oz., 125 g, each)	2	2

Grate 2 tsp. (10 mL) lemon zest into small bowl. Squeeze and add 2 tsp. (10 mL) lemon juice. Add cream cheese and dill. Beat until smooth.

Cut Brie cheese rounds in half horizontally (see Note). Spread cream cheese mixture on bottom halves. Replace tops. Makes 2 stuffed cheese rounds. Each cheese round cuts into 8 wedges, for a total of 16 wedges.

1 wedge: 88 Calories; 7.4 g Total Fat (2.2 g Mono, 0.2 g Poly, 4.5 g Sat); 25 mg Cholesterol; 1 g Carbohydrate; trace Fibre; 5 g Protein; 207 mg Sodium

Pictured on page 72.

Note: To easily halve a Brie cheese round, encircle the cheese along the centre of its circumference with a length of strong thread or plain dental floss. Crisscross the ends of the thread in front of you. Firmly pull both ends to slide the thread through the cheese.

 Hot peppers contain capsaicin in the seeds and ribs. Removing the seeds and ribs will reduce the heat. Wear rubber gloves when handling hot peppers and avoid touching your eyes. Wash your hands well afterwards.

Cajun Crackers

Kick it up a notch with these invitingly spicy, crisp crackers.
Perfect for dipping, or serve them with soup or salad.

Garlic butter, melted	2 tbsp.	30 mL
Flour tortillas (9 inch, 22 cm, diameter)	4	4
Grated Parmesan cheese	2 tbsp.	30 mL
Cajun seasoning	1 1/2 tsp.	7 mL

Brush butter on both sides of tortillas. Cut each tortilla into 8 wedges. Arrange on 2 ungreased baking sheets with sides.

Sprinkle with Parmesan cheese and seasoning. Bake on separate racks in 350°F (175°C) oven for about 14 minutes, switching position of baking sheets at halftime, until crisp and golden. Cool. Makes 32 crackers.

1 cracker: 33 Calories; 1.4 g Total Fat (0.5 g Mono, 0.2 g Poly, 0.6 g Sat); 2 mg Cholesterol; 4 g Carbohydrate; trace Fibre; 1 g Protein; 70 mg Sodium

1. Spicy Feta Pâté, page 14
2. Five-Spice Nut Crunch, page 129
3. Garlic Lime Pita Chips, page 13

Props courtesy of: Island Pottery Inc.

Appetizers

MMMussels

A treat for seafood lovers. Thai broth subtly infuses plump mussels with a wonderfully fragrant flavour. A gingery mayonnaise provides the perfect accent.

Thai-flavoured prepared chicken broth, divided	1 1/4 cups	300 mL
Fresh mussels, scrubbed and "beards" removed	4 lbs.	1.8 kg
Mayonnaise	1/2 cup	125 mL
Finely chopped pickled ginger slices	2 tbsp.	30 mL

Reserve 2 tbsp. (30 mL) broth in medium bowl. Put mussels into large bowl. Lightly tap any that are opened. Discard any that do not close. Heat remaining broth in large pot or Dutch oven on medium until boiling. Add mussels. Cover. Cook for about 5 minutes, without stirring, until mussels open. Remove mussels with slotted spoon to extra-large bowl. Discard any unopened mussels.

Add mayonnaise and ginger to reserved broth. Stir. Serve with mussels. Serves 10.

1 serving: 232 Calories; 13.1 g Total Fat (6.1 g Mono, 4.1 g Poly, 1.6 g Sat); 52 mg Cholesterol; 7 g Carbohydrate; trace Fibre; 20 g Protein; 621 mg Sodium

1. Orange Cranberry Wedges, page 28
2. Caramel Bubble Buns, page 23
3. Fast Focaccia, page 29

Props courtesy of: Island Pottery Inc.

Nutty Blue Cheese Dip

An all-purpose dip to serve with fresh vegetables. Or shape it into
a log, roll in finely chopped nuts, and chill to serve with crackers.

Block of cream cheese, softened	8 oz.	250 g
Salad dressing (or mayonnaise)	3 tbsp.	50 mL
Crumbled blue cheese	1/4 cup	60 mL
Chopped walnuts, toasted	2 tbsp.	30 mL
(see Tip, page 21)		

Beat cream cheese and salad dressing in medium bowl until smooth.

Add blue cheese and walnuts. Stir well. Makes about 1 1/3 cups (325 mL).

2 tbsp. (30 mL): 121 Calories; 11.7 g Total Fat (3.8 g Mono, 1.5 g Poly, 5.9 g Sat);
29 mg Cholesterol; 1 g Carbohydrate; trace Fibre; 3 g Protein; 146 mg Sodium

Crab Dip

Almonds and water chestnuts add a pleasant crunch
to this creamy dip. Serve with veggies or crackers.

Tub of creamy vegetable dip	10 1/2 oz.	296 mL
Can of sliced water chestnuts, drained and chopped	8 oz.	227 mL
Cans of crabmeat (4 1/4 oz., 120 g, each), drained, cartilage removed, flaked	2	2
Sliced blanched almonds, toasted (see Tip, page 21)	1/2 cup	125 mL

Combine first 3 ingredients in medium bowl. Transfer to serving bowl.

Sprinkle with almonds. Makes about 2 2/3 cups (650 mL).

2 tbsp. (30 mL): 46 Calories; 3.7 g Total Fat (1.5 g Mono, 0.4 g Poly, 1.6 g Sat); 5 mg Cholesterol;
2 g Carbohydrate; trace Fibre; 2 g Protein; 42 mg Sodium

Cheese Nippies

Rich cheese crackers topped with pecans. With a pleasant, spicy flavour, they go nicely with green apple slices or grapes, and a glass of red wine.

Pastry for 2 crust 9 inch (22 cm) pie, your own or a mix		
Container of sharp cold pack Cheddar cheese	9 oz.	250 g
Cayenne pepper	1/2 tsp.	2 mL
Pecan halves, approximately	60	60

Mix first 3 ingredients with pastry blender in large bowl until mixture starts to come together. Turn out onto well-floured surface. Shape into slightly flattened disc. Roll out to 1/8 inch (3 mm) thickness. Cut out circles with 2 inch (5 cm) cookie cutter. Arrange about 2 inches (5 cm) apart on ungreased baking sheet.

Place 1 pecan half on each circle. Bake in 400°F (205°C) oven for 8 to 10 minutes until golden. Makes about 60 crackers.

1 cracker: 51 Calories; 4 g Total Fat (1.9 g Mono, 0.5 g Poly, 1.4 g Sat); 4 mg Cholesterol; 2 g Carbohydrate; trace Fibre; 1 g Protein; 53 mg Sodium

tip *To toast nuts, seeds or coconut, place them in an ungreased shallow frying pan. Heat on medium for 3 to 5 minutes, stirring often, until golden. To bake, spread them evenly in an ungreased shallow pan. Bake in a 350°F (175°C) oven for 5 to 10 minutes, stirring or shaking often, until golden.*

Feta Crescent Swirls

Sweet, buttery pastries filled with zesty cheese.
Serve these with a bowl of soup for a light lunch or supper.

Crumbled feta cheese	1/4 cup	60 mL
Garlic butter	2 tbsp.	30 mL
Sweet chili sauce	2 tbsp.	30 mL
Tubes of refrigerator crescent-style rolls (8 rolls per tube), 8 1/2 oz. (235 g), each	2	2

Combine first 3 ingredients in small bowl. Set aside.

Unroll 1 tube of dough on lightly floured surface. Press perforations together to form 8 × 13 inch (20 × 33 cm) rectangle. Spread cheese mixture on dough, leaving 1/2 inch (12 mm) edge. Unroll second tube of dough on top of cheese mixture, aligning edges with bottom layer. Lightly press perforations together. Lightly press top layer. Pinch dough along edges to seal. Cut crosswise into 12 equal strips (see diagram 1). Twist 1 strip several times. It will lengthen to about 12 inches (30 cm). Loosely coil on baking sheet, tucking end under (see diagram 2). Repeat with remaining strips to make 12 swirls. Bake in 375°F (190°C) oven for 15 to 20 minutes until golden. Makes 12 swirls.

1 swirl: 99 Calories; 6.6 g Total Fat (1.2 g Mono, 0.3 g Poly, 1.7 g Sat); 8 mg Cholesterol; 8 g Carbohydrate; trace Fibre; 2 g Protein; 282 mg Sodium

Pictured on page 89.

1

2

Caramel Bubble Buns

*Sweet caramel glazes a ring of soft, gooey pull-aparts.
You won't believe how simple it is to create this
sweet treat for brunch or coffee break. A real winner!*

Packages of frozen unbaked dinner rolls (1 lb., 454 g, each)	2	2
Hard margarine (or butter)	1/2 cup	125 mL
Brown sugar, packed	1/2 cup	125 mL
Box of butterscotch pudding powder (not instant), 6 serving size	1	1

Thaw covered dough at room temperature for 1 1/2 hours.

Heat and stir margarine and brown sugar in small saucepan on medium for about 6 minutes until boiling. Remove from heat.

Grease 12 cup (3 L) bundt pan. Cut dinner rolls in half. Roll into balls. Arrange 1/2 of balls in pan. Sprinkle with 1/2 of pudding powder. Drizzle with 1/2 of margarine mixture. Arrange remaining balls on top. Sprinkle with remaining pudding powder. Drizzle with remaining margarine mixture. Cover loosely with greased waxed paper and tea towel. Let stand in oven with light on and door closed for about 1 1/2 hours until doubled in size. Bake in 350°F (175°C) oven for about 30 minutes until golden. Let stand in pan on wire rack for 5 minutes before inverting onto large serving plate. Makes about 48 buns.

1 bun: 96 Calories; 3.5 g Total Fat (2 g Mono, 0.4 g Poly, 0.8 g Sat); 0 mg Cholesterol; 15 g Carbohydrate; 1 g Fibre; 2 g Protein; 174 mg Sodium

Pictured on page 18.

Onion Flatbread

This quick bread, with a distinct onion flavour and a poppy seed topping, is great served with soup or stew.

Biscuit mix	2 cups	500 mL
Onion flakes	1 tbsp.	15 mL
Hard margarine (or butter), melted	1 tbsp.	15 mL
Poppy seeds	1/2 tsp.	2 mL

Combine biscuit mix and onion flakes in medium bowl. Make a well in centre. Add 1/2 cup (125 mL) water to well. Stir until soft dough forms. Turn out onto greased baking sheet. Pat out dough to 9 inch (22 cm) circle.

Brush with margarine. Sprinkle with poppy seeds. Bake in 450°F (230°C) oven for about 10 minutes until golden. Cuts into 12 wedges.

1 wedge: 114 Calories; 5.3 g Total Fat (2.3 g Mono, 1.7 g Poly, 1 g Sat); 0 mg Cholesterol; 15 g Carbohydrate; trace Fibre; 2 g Protein; 299 mg Sodium

Variation: Instead of poppy seeds, use ground walnuts or finely chopped fresh rosemary.

Tomato-Topped Biscuits

Cheesy, herb-crusted biscuits topped with fresh tomato. A delight to serve!

Tube of refrigerator country-style biscuits (10 biscuits per tube)	12 oz.	340 g
Basil pesto	1/3 cup	75 mL
Grated mozzarella cheese	1 1/4 cups	300 mL
Large tomatoes, each cut into 5 slices	2	2

Separate biscuits. Pat into 3 1/2 inch (9 cm) circles. Arrange about 2 inches (5 cm) apart on greased baking sheet with sides.

Spread pesto on circles. Sprinkle with cheese. Bake in 375°F (190°C) oven for about 12 minutes until golden and cheese is bubbling.

Top with tomato slices. Sprinkle with pepper. Makes 10 biscuits.

1 biscuit: 163 Calories; 7.8 g Total Fat (3.8 g Mono, 0.8 g Poly, 2.8 g Sat); 12 mg Cholesterol; 18 g Carbohydrate; trace Fibre; 6 g Protein; 485 mg Sodium

Swirled Raisin Braid

This attractive raisin braid is perfect for breakfast
or brunch. Delicious toasted too.

Frozen white bread dough, covered and thawed in refrigerator overnight	1	1
Dark raisins	1/4 cup	60 mL
Cocoa, sifted if lumpy	2 tbsp.	30 mL
Fancy (mild) molasses	1 tbsp.	15 mL

Cut dough into 3 equal portions. Set 1 portion aside.

Combine remaining 3 ingredients and 1 tsp. (5 mL) water in medium bowl. Add 2 dough portions. Knead in bowl for about 3 minutes until dough is marbled with cocoa mixture. Divide in half. Roll into 12 inch (30 cm) long ropes with slightly tapered ends. Roll plain dough portion into 12 inch (30 cm) long rope. Lay ropes side by side, with plain rope in the middle, on work surface. Pinch ropes together at one end. Braid ropes. Pinch together at opposite end. Tuck ends under. Place on greased baking sheet. Cover with greased waxed paper and tea towel. Let stand in oven with light on and door closed for about 1 hour until almost doubled in size. Bake in 350°F (175°C) oven for about 25 minutes until golden and hollow sounding when tapped. Remove to wire rack to cool. Cuts into 20 slices.

1 slice: 70 Calories; 0.9 g Total Fat (0.4 g Mono, 0.2 g Poly, 0.2 g Sat); 0 mg Cholesterol; 14 g Carbohydrate; 1 g Fibre; 2 g Protein; 123 mg Sodium

Pictured on page 53 and on back cover.

Rugelach Roll-Ups

A traditional Hanukkah treat, Rugelach are crescent-shaped cookies filled with fruit and nuts or with jam. Delicious any time, we've filled our version with a tasty combination of raspberry jam and ginger. Yum!

Tube of refrigerator crescent-style rolls (8 rolls per tube)	8 1/2 oz.	235 g
Raspberry jam	1/4 cup	60 mL
Minced crystallized ginger	1 tbsp.	15 mL
Ground almonds	8 tsp.	40 mL

Unroll dough. Separate into triangles.

Combine jam and ginger in small bowl. Spread on triangles, leaving 1/4 inch (6 mm) edge at wide end.

Sprinkle with almonds. Roll up triangles from wide end toward point. Place rolls, point-side down, on greased baking sheet. Bake in 375°F (190°C) oven for 10 to 12 minutes until golden. Makes 8 roll-ups.

1 roll-up: 86 Calories; 3.1 g Total Fat (0.5 g Mono, 0.2 g Poly, 0.1 g Sat); 0 mg Cholesterol; 14 g Carbohydrate; trace Fibre; 1 g Protein; 147 mg Sodium

Pictured on page 54.

Tuscan Pull-Aparts

Soft and savoury, with the rich flavours of ripe olives and Parmesan cheese. Use commercial garlic butter that has added wine or herbs to make these buns extra tasty.

Frozen white bread dough, covered and thawed in refrigerator overnight	1	1
Garlic butter	1/4 cup	60 mL
Grated Parmesan cheese	1/2 cup	125 mL
Can of sliced ripe olives, chopped	4 1/2 oz.	125 mL

(continued on next page)

26   Breads

Cut dough into 12 equal portions. Roll into balls.

Melt butter in small saucepan. Remove from heat. Measure Parmesan cheese into small shallow dish. Dip balls in butter and roll in Parmesan cheese until coated. Arrange 8 balls in greased 9 × 5 × 3 inch (22 × 12.5 × 7.5 cm) loaf pan.

Sprinkle with olives. Place remaining 4 balls along centre of first layer. Drizzle with remaining butter. Sprinkle with remaining Parmesan cheese. Cover with greased waxed paper and tea towel. Let stand in oven with light on and door closed for about 40 minutes until doubled in size. Bake in 350°F (175°C) oven for 25 minutes. Cover loosely with foil. Bake for another 10 minutes. Let stand in pan for 10 minutes before removing to wire rack to cool. Makes 12 pull-aparts.

1 pull-apart: 161 Calories; 7.2 g Total Fat (2.5 g Mono, 0.5 g Poly, 3.7 g Sat); 15 mg Cholesterol; 19 g Carbohydrate; 1 g Fibre; 5 g Protein; 359 mg Sodium

Pictured on front cover.

Garlic Cheese Loaf

This restaurant-style garlic cheese bread speckled with ripe olives has an irresistible flavour! Great served with a main course salad.

Garlic butter, softened	1/3 cup	75 mL
French bread loaf, halved horizontally	1	1
Grated Mexican cheese blend	2 cups	500 mL
Can of sliced ripe olives, chopped	4 1/2 oz.	125 mL

Spread butter on both halves of loaf. Place, buttered-side up, on ungreased baking sheet.

Sprinkle with cheese and olives. Bake in 400°F (205°C) oven for about 15 minutes until cheese is melted and bread is heated through. Cut each half into 16 pieces, for a total of 32 pieces.

1 piece: 88 Calories; 5.1 g Total Fat (1.6 g Mono, 0.3 g Poly, 2.9 g Sat); 13 mg Cholesterol; 8 g Carbohydrate; trace Fibre; 3 g Protein; 165 mg Sodium

Pesto Parmesan Biscuits

Perfect with soup or stew, or serve on the side with an omelet for brunch.

Biscuit mix	2 cups	500 mL
Grated Parmesan cheese	2 tbsp.	30 mL
Milk, divided	2/3 cup	150 mL
Sun-dried tomato pesto	1 tbsp.	15 mL

Combine biscuit mix and Parmesan cheese in medium bowl. Make a well in centre.

Reserve 2 tbsp. (30 mL) milk in small cup. Combine remaining milk and pesto in small bowl. Add to well. Stir until just moistened. Turn out dough onto lightly floured surface. Knead 8 to 10 times. Roll out to 1/2 inch (12 mm) thickness. Cut out circles with lightly floured 2 inch (5 cm) biscuit cutter. Arrange about 1/2 inch (12 mm) apart on greased baking sheet. Brush with reserved milk. Bake in 450°F (230°C) oven for about 10 minutes until firm and golden. Makes about 12 biscuits.

1 biscuit: 115 Calories; 4.8 g Total Fat (1.9 g Mono, 1.6 g Poly, 1.1 g Sat); 1 mg Cholesterol; 15 g Carbohydrate; 0 g Fibre; 3 g Protein; 316 mg Sodium

Pictured on page 36.

Orange Cranberry Wedges

* *Cranberry-studded, scone-like wedges have a delicate orange flavour.*

Large orange	1	1
Biscuit mix	2 cups	500 mL
Orange-flavoured dried cranberries	1 cup	250 mL
Vanilla-flavoured milk	1/3 cup	75 mL

Grate 1 tbsp. (15 mL) orange zest into medium bowl. Add biscuit mix and cranberries. Stir. Make a well in centre.

Squeeze and measure 1/3 cup (75 mL) orange juice into small bowl. Add milk. Stir. Add to well. Stir until just moistened. Spread in greased 8 inch (20 cm) round pan. Bake in 350°F (175°C) oven for about 30 minutes until wooden pick inserted in centre comes out clean. Let stand in pan for 10 minutes before inverting onto wire rack. Cuts into 12 wedges.

1 wedge: 122 Calories; 3.6 g Total Fat (1.3 g Mono, 1.3 g Poly, 0.7 g Sat); 0 mg Cholesterol; 20 g Carbohydrate; 2 g Fibre; 2 g Protein; 292 mg Sodium

Pictured on page 18.

Fast Focaccia

It's a snap to make focaccia bread using biscuit mix.
Garlic-flavoured olive oil infuses the bread with Italian flavours.
Serve with your favourite pasta dish.

Italian seasoning, divided	3 tsp.	15 mL
Biscuit mix	3 cups	750 mL
Milk	1 cup	250 mL
Garlic-flavoured olive oil, divided	3 tbsp.	50 mL

Reserve 1 tsp. (5 mL) seasoning in small cup. Put remaining seasoning into large bowl. Add biscuit mix. Stir. Make a well in centre.

Add milk to well. Stir until just moistened.

Brush 9 x 9 inch (22 x 22 cm) pan with 1 tbsp. (15 mL) olive oil. Press dough into pan. Poke indentations on surface of dough with fingers. Drizzle remaining olive oil over dough. Sprinkle with reserved seasoning. Bake in 400°F (205°C) oven for about 25 minutes until golden, and wooden pick inserted in centre comes out clean. Let stand in pan for 15 minutes. Cut into 4 squares. Cut squares in half diagonally, for a total of 8 triangles.

1 triangle: 281 Calories; 13.3 g Total Fat (6.6 g Mono, 3.4 g Poly, 2.5 g Sat); 1 mg Cholesterol; 35 g Carbohydrate; trace Fibre; 5 g Protein; 857 mg Sodium

Pictured on page 18.

Paré Pointer

What do prisoners use to talk with each other? Cell phones.

Lemon Poppy Seed Biscuits

A quick solution when you're craving something sweet.
These gooey biscuits are sure to satisfy!

Lemon curd (not spread)	2/3 cup	150 mL
Chopped walnuts (or pecans)	2 tbsp.	30 mL
Poppy seeds	1 tbsp.	15 mL
Tube of refrigerator country-style biscuits (10 biscuits per tube)	12 oz.	340 g

Spoon lemon curd into 10 greased muffin cups. Sprinkle with walnuts and poppy seeds.

Separate biscuits. Place in prepared muffin cups. Bake in 425°F (220°C) oven for 12 to 15 minutes until golden. Immediately invert onto wire rack set on baking sheet. Makes 10 biscuits.

1 biscuit: 179 Calories; 6.9 g Total Fat (2.8 g Mono, 1.9 g Poly, 1.6 g Sat); 26 mg Cholesterol; 27 g Carbohydrate; trace Fibre; 4 g Protein; 603 mg Sodium

Parmesan Olive Biscuits

Chopped olives in cheesy biscuits create a nice match for soup or salad.
Kalamata olives in place of ripe olives will produce a bolder, saltier taste.

Biscuit mix	2 cups	500 mL
Grated Parmesan cheese	2/3 cup	150 mL
Can of sliced ripe olives, chopped	4 1/2 oz.	125 mL
Milk	2/3 cup	150 mL

Combine first 3 ingredients in medium bowl. Make a well in centre.

Add milk to well. Stir until just moistened. Drop, using 2 tbsp. (30 mL) for each biscuit, about 2 inches (5 cm) apart onto greased baking sheet. Bake in 450°F (230°C) oven for about 12 minutes until golden. Makes about 15 biscuits.

1 biscuit: 112 Calories; 5.2 g Total Fat (2 g Mono, 1.3 g Poly, 1.6 g Sat); 4 mg Cholesterol; 12 g Carbohydrate; trace Fibre; 4 g Protein; 349 mg Sodium

Pictured on page 108.

Creamy Potato Salad

Smoky bits of bacon and a peppery, creamy dressing coat
chunks of potato and dill pickle in this flavourful salad. Tastes
even better made the day before and chilled overnight.

Red baby potatoes	1 lb.	454 g
Bacon slices, cooked crisp and crumbled	6	6
Peppercorn ranch dressing	1/3 cup	75 mL
Chopped dill pickle (or tangy dill relish)	2 tbsp.	30 mL

Cook potatoes in boiling salted water in medium saucepan until just
tender. Drain. Transfer to medium bowl. Chill, uncovered, for about
2 hours until cold. Cut potatoes into quarters. Return to same bowl.

Add remaining 3 ingredients. Toss gently. Cover. Chill for at least 1 hour
to blend flavours. Makes about 2 1/2 cups (625 mL). Serves 4.

1 serving: 226 Calories; 12.5 g Total Fat (6.5 g Mono, 3.2 g Poly, 2.2 g Sat); 14 mg Cholesterol;
23 g Carbohydrate; 2 g Fibre; 6 g Protein; 351 mg Sodium

Blue Cheese Pear Salad

Toasted pecans complement the bold flavour of blue cheese in this lovely salad.
Juicy pears make this delicious as is, or toss with a sweet vinaigrette.

Mixed salad greens, lightly packed	5 cups	1.25 L
Fresh pears, sliced	2	2
Pecan pieces, toasted (see Tip, page 21)	1/3 cup	75 mL
Crumbled blue cheese	1/3 cup	75 mL

Put all 4 ingredients into large bowl. Toss gently. Makes about 6 1/2 cups
(1.6 L). Serves 4.

1 serving: 172 Calories; 10.9 g Total Fat (5.3 g Mono, 2 g Poly, 2.8 g Sat); 9 mg Cholesterol;
17 g Carbohydrate; 4 g Fibre; 5 g Protein; 182 mg Sodium

Pictured on page 35.

Tomato Bocconcini Salad

Eye-catching! Serve this classic salad with fresh, crusty
baguette slices to dip into the dressing.

Roma (plum) tomatoes, cut into 1/4 inch (6 mm) slices	1 lb.	454 g
Container of bocconcini cheese, cut into 1/4 inch (6 mm) slices	7 oz.	200 g
Chopped fresh basil	1/3 cup	75 mL
Balsamic vinaigrette	1/4 cup	60 mL

Arrange tomato and cheese slices alternately in circular pattern around edge and in centre of large serving platter. Sprinkle generously with salt and freshly ground pepper.

Sprinkle with basil. Drizzle with vinaigrette. Serves 4.

1 serving: 174 Calories; 11.6 g Total Fat (3.5 g Mono, 0.6 g Poly, 6.9 g Sat); 41 mg Cholesterol; 8 g Carbohydrate; 1 g Fibre; 11 g Protein; 205 mg Sodium

Pictured on page 107.

Orange Fennel Salad

A delectable, refreshing salad that's easy to make.

Fennel bulb (white part only), quartered lengthwise and thinly sliced	1	1
Medium oranges, peeled and segmented (see Tip, page 33)	6	6
Maple (or maple-flavoured) syrup	1/4 cup	60 mL
Dijon mustard	1 tbsp.	15 mL

Put fennel and orange segments into large bowl. Toss gently.

Combine syrup and mustard in small cup. Drizzle over salad. Toss gently. Makes about 5 1/2 cups (1.4 L). Serves 6.

1 serving: 113 Calories; 0.4 g Total Fat (0.1 g Mono, 0.1 g Poly, 0.1 g Sat); 0 mg Cholesterol; 28 g Carbohydrate; 2 g Fibre; 2 g Protein; 56 mg Sodium

Curried Broccoli Slaw

Toasting the curry powder gives it a mellow flavour.
A great side for poached fish or roasted chicken.

Curry powder	1 tsp.	5 mL
Ranch dressing	1/2 cup	125 mL
Bag of broccoli slaw	12 oz.	340 g
Pecan pieces, toasted (see Tip, page 21)	1/2 cup	125 mL

Heat and stir curry powder in small frying pan on medium-low for about 5 minutes until fragrant. Transfer to small bowl. Cool.

Add dressing. Stir well.

Put broccoli slaw into large bowl. Add curry mixture. Stir until coated. Chill for at least 1 hour to blend flavours.

Sprinkle with pecan pieces just before serving. Makes about 3 1/2 cups (875 mL). Serves 4.

1 serving: 261 Calories; 22 g Total Fat (13 g Mono, 6.6 g Poly, 1.7 g Sat); 9 mg Cholesterol; 13 g Carbohydrate; 4 g Fibre; 4 g Protein; 254 mg Sodium

 To segment an orange, trim a small slice of peel from both ends so the flesh is exposed. Place the orange, bottom cut-side down, on a cutting board. Remove the peel with a sharp knife, cutting down and around the flesh, leaving as little pith as possible. Over a small bowl, cut on either side of the membranes to release the segments.

Wild Rice Salad

Chilling this salad will bring out the earthy flavours.
Perfect for a picnic or patio lunch.

Package of long grain and wild rice mix (with seasoning packet)	6 1/4 oz.	180 g
Chopped dried cherries	1/2 cup	125 mL
Slivered almonds, toasted (see Tip, page 21)	1/2 cup	125 mL
Blue cheese dressing	1/3 cup	75 mL

Combine rice with seasoning packet and 2 1/2 cups (625 mL) water in medium saucepan. Bring to a boil. Reduce heat to medium-low. Simmer, covered, for about 30 minutes until liquid is absorbed. Remove from heat. Let stand, covered, for 5 minutes. Transfer to large bowl. Cool to room temperature.

Add cherries, almonds and a sprinkle of salt and pepper. Stir. Drizzle with dressing. Stir well. Makes about 4 cups (1 L). Serves 4.

1 serving: 420 Calories; 20.9 g Total Fat (12.1 g Mono, 5.9 g Poly, 1.9 g Sat); 4 mg Cholesterol; 52 g Carbohydrate; 3 g Fibre; 9 g Protein; 722 mg Sodium

1. Lemon Coconut Angel, page 121
2. Polynesian Chicken, page 97
3. Blue Cheese Pear Salad, page 31

Props courtesy of: Casa Bugatti

Antipasto Pasta Salad

Tangy-sweet antipasto flavour coats spiral pasta.
A tasty side salad to serve with baked or grilled herbed chicken.

Rotini (or other spiral) pasta	3 cups	750 mL
Jar of antipasto	9 oz.	250 g
Jar of marinated artichoke hearts, drained and larger pieces cut in half	6 oz.	170 mL
Coarsely crumbled feta cheese	1/2 cup	125 mL

Cook pasta in boiling salted water in large uncovered pot or Dutch oven for 8 to 10 minutes until tender but firm. Drain. Rinse with cold water. Drain well. Put into large bowl.

Add remaining 3 ingredients. Toss gently. Makes about 7 cups (1.75 L). Serves 6.

1 serving: 251 Calories; 3.6 g Total Fat (0.7 g Mono, 0.4 g Poly, 2.2 g Sat); 12 mg Cholesterol; 41 g Carbohydrate; 3 g Fibre; 10 g Protein; 436 mg Sodium

1. Pesto Parmesan Biscuits, page 28
2. Garlic Chicken Pasta, page 92
3. Curry Vegetable Soup, page 45

Props courtesy of: Casa Bugatti

Asian Cucumber Salad

Rice vinegar lends a piquant tang to sweet, dressed cucumbers.
Double the chili paste for added zip.

Rice vinegar	1/4 cup	60 mL
Hoisin sauce	2 tbsp.	30 mL
Chili paste (sambal oelek)	1/2 tsp.	2 mL
Unpeeled English cucumbers, halved lengthwise and cut diagonally into 1/4 inch (6 mm) slices	2	2

Combine first 3 ingredients in large bowl.

Add cucumber. Stir until coated. Chill for 2 to 3 hours, stirring once or twice, to blend flavours. Makes about 4 cups (1 L). Serves 6.

1 serving: 31 Calories; 0.2 g Total Fat (0 g Mono, 0.1 g Poly, 0.1 g Sat); 0 mg Cholesterol; 7 g Carbohydrate; 1 g Fibre; 1 g Protein; 137 mg Sodium

Savoury Apple Slaw

A savoury twist on coleslaw. Serve this with grilled cheese sandwiches,
or try it with a little Cheddar cheese as a wrap filling.

Dijon-flavoured mayonnaise	1/2 cup	125 mL
Tart medium cooking apples (such as Granny Smith), peeled and julienned (see Note)	2	2
Broccoli slaw	2 cups	500 mL
Julienned honey ham	2 cups	500 mL

Put mayonnaise into large bowl. Add apple. Stir gently until coated.

Add broccoli slaw, ham and a sprinkle of salt and pepper. Stir gently. Makes about 5 cups (1.25 L). Serves 6.

1 serving: 240 Calories; 18.3 g Total Fat (9.8 g Mono, 5.5 g Poly, 2.3 g Sat); 35 mg Cholesterol; 9 g Carbohydrate; 2 g Fibre; 11 g Protein; 823 mg Sodium

Note: To julienne, cut into very thin strips that resemble matchsticks.

Spinach Cranberry Salad

This salad can be on the table in no time! Toasted nuts
and dried berries add a delicious boost to greens and juicy oranges.
The brilliant colours say "healthy and fresh."

Bag of fresh spinach	6 oz.	170 g
Pecan halves, toasted (see Tip, page 21)	1/2 cup	125 mL
Orange-flavoured dried cranberries	1/4 cup	60 mL
Medium oranges	3	3

Put first 3 ingredients into large bowl. Toss.

Squeeze juice from 1 orange. Set aside. Peel remaining 2 oranges. Cut oranges crosswise into 1/4 inch (6 mm) slices. Cut slices in half. Add to spinach mixture. Drizzle with juice. Sprinkle with salt and pepper. Toss gently. Makes about 6 1/2 cups (1.6 L). Serves 4.

1 serving: 165 Calories; 10 g Total Fat (6 g Mono, 2.5 g Poly, 0.8 g Sat); 0 mg Cholesterol; 19 g Carbohydrate; 5 g Fibre; 3 g Protein; 34 mg Sodium

Pictured on front cover.

Bruschetta Lentil Salad

Olives, lentils and feta cheese make an appetizing and hearty salad.
Serve with crusty bread to soak up the juices.

Can of lentils, rinsed and drained	19 oz.	540 mL
Bruschetta topping	1 1/2 cups	375 mL
Cubed feta cheese	1 cup	250 mL
Can of sliced ripe olives, drained	4 1/2 oz.	125 mL

Put all 4 ingredients into large bowl. Mix well. Makes about 4 1/2 cups (1.1 L). Serves 6.

1 serving: 150 Calories; 6.9 g Total Fat (1.9 g Mono, 0.4 g Poly, 4.2 g Sat); 24 mg Cholesterol; 15 g Carbohydrate; 4 g Fibre; 9 g Protein; 659 mg Sodium

Feta Beet Salad

*Sweet bites of beet and salty feta cheese create
an interesting salad you're sure to enjoy.*

Bag of mixed salad greens	5 oz.	142 g
Chopped pickled beets (3 tbsp., 50 mL, juice reserved)	1 cup	250 mL
Crumbled feta cheese	1 cup	250 mL
Spicy olive oil with herbs	2 tbsp.	30 mL

Put first 3 ingredients into large bowl. Toss gently.

Combine reserved beet juice and olive oil in small cup. Drizzle over salad.
Toss gently. Makes about 6 cups (1.5 L). Serves 4.

*1 serving: 173 Calories; 11.1 g Total Fat (3.6 g Mono, 0.5 g Poly, 6.5 g Sat); 36 mg Cholesterol;
12 g Carbohydrate; 2 g Fibre; 7 g Protein; 623 mg Sodium*

Couscous Date Salad

*Tangy raspberry vinaigrette offsets sweet dates in this
delicious pilaf-like salad. Good with grilled chicken or kabobs.*

Package of couscous with fruit and nuts	7 oz.	198 g
Chopped unpeeled English cucumber	2 cups	500 mL
Chopped pitted dates	1/2 cup	125 mL
Raspberry vinaigrette	1/4 cup	60 mL

Bring 1 1/2 cups (375 mL) water to a boil in medium saucepan. Add
couscous. Stir. Return to a boil. Remove from heat. Let stand, covered, for
5 minutes. Fluff with a fork. Transfer to large bowl. Chill, uncovered, for
30 minutes.

Add cucumber and dates. Toss. Drizzle with vinaigrette. Toss well. Makes
about 5 cups (1.25 L). Serves 6.

*1 serving: 182 Calories; 2.1 g Total Fat (1.2 g Mono, 0.3 g Poly, 0.3 g Sat); 0 mg Cholesterol;
38 g Carbohydrate; 3 g Fibre; 4 g Protein; 330 mg Sodium*

Pepper Berry Vinaigrette

Match this vinaigrette with a spinach or beet salad,
or drizzle over Blue Cheese Pear Salad, page 31.

Olive (or cooking) oil	1/3 cup	75 mL
Mixed berry jam	1/4 cup	60 mL
Balsamic vinegar	1/4 cup	60 mL
Pepper	1/2 tsp.	2 mL

Process all 4 ingredients in blender or food processor until smooth.
Store in airtight container in refrigerator for up to 1 week. Makes about
3/4 cup (175 mL).

2 tbsp. (30 mL): 142 Calories; 12.1 g Total Fat (8.9 g Mono, 1 g Poly, 1.6 g Sat); 0 mg Cholesterol;
9 g Carbohydrate; trace Fibre; 0 g Protein; 6 mg Sodium

Cranberry Vinaigrette

This is a great way to use up that little bit of leftover cranberry sauce.
Perfect for a romaine lettuce salad with turkey or chicken.

Cooking oil	3 tbsp.	50 mL
Jellied cranberry sauce	2 tbsp.	30 mL
White wine vinegar	1 1/2 tbsp.	25 mL
Dijon mustard	1 tbsp.	15 mL

Combine all 4 ingredients and a sprinkle of salt and pepper in jar with
tight-fitting lid. Shake well. Store in airtight container in refrigerator for up
to 1 week. Makes about 1/2 cup (125 mL).

2 tbsp. (30 mL): 105 Calories; 10.2 g Total Fat (5.9 g Mono, 3.1 g Poly, 0.7 g Sat); 0 mg Cholesterol;
4 g Carbohydrate; trace Fibre; 0 g Protein; 53 mg Sodium

Paré Pointer

Don't try to shoot a mouse that runs out of your stove.
It's out of your range!

Tomato Pesto Dressing

Add this to a pasta or vegetable salad, or use as a marinade.

Sun-dried tomato pesto	1/3 cup	75 mL
Coarsely chopped fresh parsley	1/3 cup	75 mL
Tomato juice	1/3 cup	75 mL
Red wine vinegar	3 tbsp.	50 mL

Process all 4 ingredients in blender or food processor until smooth. Store in airtight container in refrigerator for up to 1 week. Makes about 3/4 cup (175 mL).

2 tbsp. (30 mL): 18 Calories; 0.9 g Total Fat (0.5 g Mono, 0.1 g Poly, 0.1 g Sat); 0 mg Cholesterol; 3 g Carbohydrate; trace Fibre; 1 g Protein; 68 mg Sodium

Orange Sesame Dressing

A great dressing for a spinach salad or oriental-style coleslaw.

Medium orange	1	1
Oyster sauce	3 tbsp.	50 mL
Rice vinegar	3 tbsp.	50 mL
Sesame oil, for flavour	2 tbsp.	30 mL

Grate 1 tsp. (5 mL) orange zest into small bowl. Squeeze and add 1/4 cup (60 mL) orange juice.

Add remaining 3 ingredients. Stir well. Store in airtight container in refrigerator for up to 1 week. Makes about 2/3 cup (150 mL).

2 tbsp. (30 mL): 74 Calories; 5.1 g Total Fat (2 g Mono, 2.1 g Poly, 0.7 g Sat); 0 mg Cholesterol; 7 g Carbohydrate; trace Fibre; 0 g Protein; 211 mg Sodium

Paré Pointer

A long time salesman joined the police force. He wanted to work where the customer is always wrong.

Creamy Bruschetta Dressing

*Puréed bruschetta makes a thick dressing for
any salad, whether green, pasta or vegetable.*

Bruschetta topping	1/2 cup	125 mL
Mayonnaise	1/4 cup	60 mL
Chopped fresh basil (or 3/4 tsp., 4 mL, dried)	1 tbsp.	15 mL
Balsamic vinegar	1 tbsp.	15 mL

Process all 4 ingredients in blender or food processor until smooth.
Store in airtight container in refrigerator for up to 1 week. Makes about
1 cup (250 mL).

*2 tbsp. (30 mL): 55 Calories; 5.7 g Total Fat (3.1 g Mono, 1.9 g Poly, 0.5 g Sat); 4 mg Cholesterol;
1 g Carbohydrate; trace Fibre; 0 g Protein; 79 mg Sodium*

Dijon Chèvre Dressing

*Drizzle this tangy, versatile dressing on potato or shrimp
salad, or serve as a sauce to accompany salmon.*

Goat (chèvre) cheese, cut up	3 oz.	85 g
Dijon-flavoured mayonnaise	1/3 cup	75 mL
Apple cider vinegar	1 1/2 tbsp.	25 mL
Pepper	1/2 tsp.	2 mL

Put all 4 ingredients into blender or food processor. Add 1/4 cup (60 mL)
water. Process until smooth. Store in airtight container in refrigerator for up
to 1 week. Makes about 1 cup (250 mL).

*2 tbsp. (30 mL): 92 Calories; 9.3 g Total Fat (4.6 g Mono, 2.5 g Poly, 2 g Sat); 10 mg Cholesterol;
1 g Carbohydrate; trace Fibre; 1 g Protein; 81 mg Sodium*

Four-Cheese Broccoli Soup

*Thick, rich, creamy—and ready in no time! Have it for
lunch with some Feta Crescent Swirls, page 22.*

Diced onion	1 cup	250 mL
Cans of low-sodium condensed chicken broth (10 oz., 284 mL, each)	2	2
Bag of frozen chopped broccoli, thawed and chopped smaller	16 oz.	455 g
Four-cheese white pasta sauce	1 1/3 cups	325 mL

Heat large greased saucepan on medium. Add onion. Cook for 5 to
10 minutes, stirring often, until softened.

Add remaining 3 ingredients. Stir. Bring to a boil. Reduce heat to medium-
low. Simmer, uncovered, for about 8 minutes, stirring occasionally, until
broccoli is tender. Cool slightly. Process soup in 2 batches in blender or
food processor until smooth. Return to same saucepan. Heat and stir on
medium until heated through. Makes about 5 1/2 cups (1.4 L).

*1 cup (250 mL): 141 Calories; 6.5 g Total Fat (2.4 g Mono, 1.1 g Poly, 2.6 g Sat); 14 mg Cholesterol;
14 g Carbohydrate; 3 g Fibre; 9 g Protein; 951 mg Sodium*

Sausage And Spinach Soup

*A savoury tomato soup laden with sausage, spinach
and herbs. Sure to become a favourite!*

Hot Italian sausages	1/2 lb.	225 g
Can of diced tomatoes with roasted garlic and basil (with juice)	19 oz.	540 mL
Can of condensed chicken broth with garlic and herbs	10 oz.	284 mL
Fresh spinach, stems removed, coarsely chopped, lightly packed	3 cups	750 mL

(continued on next page)

Heat medium greased frying pan on medium. Add sausages. Cook for 5 minutes, turning once. Reduce heat to medium-low. Cook for about 15 minutes, turning once or twice, until no longer pink inside. Transfer to paper towels to drain. Cut sausages lengthwise into quarters, then into 1/2 inch (12 mm) pieces. Set aside.

Combine tomatoes with juice, broth and 2 cups (500 mL) water in large saucepan. Heat and stir on medium until boiling. Reduce heat to medium-low. Add sausage. Stir. Simmer, covered, for 5 minutes.

Add spinach and a sprinkle of salt and pepper. Heat and stir until spinach is wilted. Makes about 7 cups (1.75 L).

1 cup (250 mL): 146 Calories; 10.8 g Total Fat (4.9 g Mono, 1.5 g Poly, 3.8 g Sat); 25 mg Cholesterol; 5 g Carbohydrate; 1 g Fibre; 8 g Protein; 652 mg Sodium

Curry Vegetable Soup

A creamy base and chunky vegetables make a colourful soup for a simple lunch or supper.

Envelope of cream of leek soup mix	2 3/4 oz.	77 g
Curry powder	1 tbsp.	15 mL
Frozen mixed vegetables	1 1/2 cups	375 mL
Milk	1 cup	250 mL

Combine soup mix, curry powder and 3 cups (750 mL) water in large saucepan. Bring to a boil, stirring often. Reduce heat to medium-low. Simmer, covered, for 5 minutes. Increase heat to medium.

Add vegetables, milk and a sprinkle of pepper. Stir. Cook for about 8 minutes, stirring occasionally, until vegetables are tender. Makes about 4 cups (1 L).

1 cup (250 mL): 151 Calories; 3.4 g Total Fat (1.1 g Mono, 0.3 g Poly, 1.5 g Sat); 5 mg Cholesterol; 25 g Carbohydrate; 2 g Fibre; 7 g Protein; 1056 mg Sodium

Pictured on page 36.

Simple Seafood Bisque

Sherry provides a subtle sweetness to this creamy combination.

Can of ready-to-serve New England clam chowder	19 oz.	540 mL
Can of condensed tomato soup	10 oz.	284 mL
Can of crabmeat, drained, cartilage removed, flaked	5 oz.	142 g
Medium sherry	2 tbsp.	30 mL

Process chowder in blender or food processor until smooth. Transfer to medium saucepan.

Add soup. Stir. Add crabmeat and 1 cup (250 mL) water. Stir well. Heat on medium-low, stirring often, until boiling. Remove from heat.

Add sherry. Stir. Makes about 4 2/3 cups (1.15 L).

1 cup (250 mL): 148 Calories; 4.4 g Total Fat (1.3 g Mono, 1 g Poly, 1.6 g Sat); 11 mg Cholesterol; 17 g Carbohydrate; 1 g Fibre; 10 g Protein; 1130 mg Sodium

Ginger Squash Soup

Simmered in broth and ginger, tender squash makes an elegant soup.

Garlic-flavoured olive oil	1 tbsp.	15 mL
Butternut (or acorn) squash, cubed	1 lb.	454 g
Coarsely chopped, peeled gingerroot	1 tbsp.	15 mL
Cans of condensed chicken broth (10 oz., 284 mL, each)	2	2

Heat olive oil in large pot or Dutch oven on medium. Add squash and ginger. Cook for about 15 minutes, stirring occasionally, until squash is softened and lightly browned.

Add broth and 2 1/2 cups (625 mL) water. Stir. Bring to a boil. Reduce heat to medium-low. Simmer, covered, for 20 minutes, stirring occasionally. Remove from heat. Cool slightly. Process soup in 2 batches in blender or food processor until smooth. Return to same pot. Sprinkle with salt and pepper. Heat and stir on medium until heated through. Makes about 6 cups (1.5 L).

1 cup (250 mL): 82 Calories; 3.4 g Total Fat (2.2 g Mono, 0.4 g Poly, 0.6 g Sat); 1 mg Cholesterol; 9 g Carbohydrate; 1 g Fibre; 5 g Protein; 632 mg Sodium

Thai Chicken Soup

Wow! Fragrant Thai flavours blend with smooth coconut milk in this spicy soup.

Boneless, skinless chicken breast halves, cut into 1/4 inch (6 mm) pieces	12 oz.	340 g
Thai peanut sauce	1/2 cup	125 mL
Boxes of Thai-flavoured broth (16 oz., 500 mL, each), or prepared chicken broth	2	2
Can of light coconut milk	14 oz.	398 mL

Heat large greased frying pan on medium. Add chicken and a sprinkle of salt and pepper. Cook for 5 to 10 minutes, stirring often, until no longer pink.

Add peanut sauce. Heat and stir for about 2 minutes until sauce is slightly thickened.

Add broth and coconut milk. Heat and stir until boiling. Makes about 7 cups (1.75 L).

1 cup (250 mL): 213 Calories; 13.9 g Total Fat (3.7 g Mono, 2.2 g Poly, 6.8 g Sat); 28 mg Cholesterol; 5 g Carbohydrate; 1 g Fibre; 18 g Protein; 822 mg Sodium

Pumpkin Soup

This golden orange soup has a velvety texture. Make some Lemon Poppy Seed Biscuits, page 30, and you're set for dinner!

Medium lime	1	1
Can of pumpkin pie filling	19 oz.	540 mL
Ground cumin	1 tsp.	5 mL
Can of evaporated milk	6 oz.	170 mL

Grate 1 tsp. (5 mL) lime zest for garnish. Set aside. Squeeze and measure 3 tbsp. (50 mL) lime juice into medium saucepan.

Add remaining 3 ingredients and 1 1/2 cups (375 mL) water. Sprinkle with salt and pepper. Stir. Heat on medium, stirring occasionally, until heated through. Garnish individual servings with lime zest. Makes about 5 cups (1.25 L).

1 cup (250 mL): 182 Calories; 3.1 g Total Fat (0.9 g Mono, 0.1 g Poly, 1.8 g Sat); 11 mg Cholesterol; 37 g Carbohydrate; trace Fibre; 4 g Protein; 296 mg Sodium

Pictured on page 108.

Shortcut Borscht

Sweet and tangy beet broth is complemented by subtle dill.
Easy to prepare, but tastes like you've been cooking all day.

Prepared beef broth	2 cups	500 mL
Dill weed	1 tsp.	5 mL
Can of diced beets in Harvard sauce	14 oz.	398 mL
Coleslaw mix	1 cup	250 mL

Combine broth, dill and 2 cups (500 mL) water in large saucepan. Heat on medium until boiling.

Add beets with sauce, coleslaw mix and a sprinkle of salt and pepper. Stir. Return to a boil. Boil gently, uncovered, for about 8 minutes, stirring occasionally, until vegetables are softened. Makes about 6 cups (1.5 L).

1 cup (250 mL): 60 Calories; 0.3 g Total Fat (0.1 g Mono, 0 g Poly, 0.1 g Sat); 0 mg Cholesterol; 13 g Carbohydrate; 2 g Fibre; 2 g Protein; 390 mg Sodium

Curry Noodle Bowl

A hearty meal in a bowl! Generous portions of tender
noodles and vegetables in a mild curry broth.

Packages of instant noodles with mushroom or vegetable-flavoured seasoning packet (3 oz., 85 g, each)	2	2
Prepared vegetable broth	4 cups	1 L
Red curry paste	1 tbsp.	15 mL
Fresh stir-fry vegetable mix	4 cups	1 L

Break up noodles into medium bowl. Set aside. Combine seasoning packets, broth and curry paste in large saucepan. Add 2 cups (500 mL) water. Stir. Bring to a boil on high.

Add noodles and vegetables. Stir. Cook for about 3 minutes, stirring occasionally, until noodles are tender but firm and vegetables are tender-crisp. Serves 6.

1 serving: 150 Calories; 2.8 g Total Fat (1 g Mono, 0.7 g Poly, 0.6 g Sat); 27 mg Cholesterol; 25 g Carbohydrate; 2 g Fibre; 8 g Protein; 900 mg Sodium

Pictured on front cover.

Salmon-Sauced Bennies

A twist on eggs Benedict that's on the table in no time!
You'll love the rich taste of the smoked salmon sauce.

Smoked salmon spreadable cream cheese	1/2 cup	125 mL
Dill weed	1/4 tsp.	1 mL
Large eggs	8	8
Whole wheat English muffins, split and toasted	4	4

Combine cream cheese, dill and 2 tbsp. (30 mL) water in small saucepan. Heat and stir on medium-low until smooth. Reduce heat to low. Stir occasionally.

Pour water into large frying pan until 1 1/2 to 2 inches (3.8 to 5 cm) deep. Bring to a boil. Reduce heat to medium-low. Water should continue to simmer (see Note). Break 1 egg into shallow dish. Slip egg into water. Repeat with remaining eggs. Cook for about 4 minutes until whites are set and yolks reach desired doneness.

Remove eggs with slotted spoon, shaking gently to remove excess water. Place on muffin halves. Spoon cream cheese mixture onto eggs. Serves 4.

1 serving: 352 Calories; 17.4 g Total Fat (6 g Mono, 2.1 g Poly, 6.8 g Sat); 450 mg Cholesterol; 29 g Carbohydrate; 4 g Fibre; 21 g Protein; 761 mg Sodium

Pictured on page 53 and on back cover.

Note: To help poached eggs retain their shape, add 1 tsp. (5 mL) white vinegar to the simmering water before adding the eggs.

Maui Oatmeal

A healthy breakfast treat bursting with sweet tropical flavours.

Can of crushed pineapple (with juice)	14 oz.	398 mL
Chopped dried apricot	1/2 cup	125 mL
Medium sweetened coconut	1/2 cup	125 mL
Quick-cooking rolled oats	1 1/2 cups	375 mL

Combine first 3 ingredients in medium saucepan. Add 2 1/2 cups (625 mL) water and a pinch of salt. Heat on medium, stirring occasionally, until boiling.

Add rolled oats. Stir. Reduce heat to medium-low. Heat and stir for about 3 minutes until thickened. Remove from heat. Serve immediately or let stand until desired thickness. Serves 6.

1 serving: 460 Calories; 5.2 g Total Fat (0.9 g Mono, 0.8 g Poly, 2.9 g Sat); 0 mg Cholesterol; 104 g Carbohydrate; 13 g Fibre; 8 g Protein; 34 mg Sodium

Blueberry Cream Pancakes

Plump blueberries pump up pancakes for breakfast.
Cream cheese in the batter makes them even better!

Pancake mix	2 cups	500 mL
Blueberry spreadable cream cheese	1/2 cup	125 mL
Milk	1 1/2 cups	375 mL
Fresh (or frozen) blueberries, approximately	1 cup	250 mL

Measure pancake mix into large bowl. Make a well in centre.

Put cream cheese into small bowl. Slowly add milk, beating constantly with whisk until smooth. Add to well. Stir until just moistened. Batter will be lumpy. Heat large greased frying pan on medium-low. Pour batter into pan, using about 1/4 cup (60 mL) for each pancake.

(continued on next page)

Sprinkle pancakes with a few blueberries. Cook for about 3 minutes until bubbles form on top and edges appear dry. Turn. Cook for about 3 minutes until golden. Remove to large plate. Cover to keep warm. Repeat with remaining ingredients, greasing pan again if necessary to prevent sticking. Makes about 12 pancakes.

1 pancake: 136 Calories; 4.3 g Total Fat (1.6 g Mono, 0.7 g Poly, 1.6 g Sat); 13 mg Cholesterol; 20 g Carbohydrate; 1 g Fibre; 4 g Protein; 366 mg Sodium

Pictured on page 53 and on back cover.

PBJ Ring

Baked with the peanut butter and jam right in it, there's no need to dread the spread of PB and J on the countertops when junior gets hold of this!

Frozen white bread dough, covered and thawed in refrigerator overnight	1	1
Crunchy peanut butter	1/4 cup	60 mL
Berry jam	1/4 cup	60 mL
Hard margarine (or butter), melted	1 tbsp.	15 mL

Roll out dough on lightly floured surface to 6 x 18 inch (15 x 45 cm) rectangle.

Combine peanut butter and jam in small bowl. Spread on dough, leaving 1/2 inch (12 mm) edge. Roll up, jelly-roll style, from 1 long side. Moisten edge with water. Press seam against roll to seal. Shape roll into ring. Pinch ends together to seal. Place, seam-side down, in greased 12 cup (3 L) bundt pan. Cover with greased waxed paper and tea towel. Let stand in oven with light on and door closed for 30 minutes. Bake in 375°F (190°C) oven for about 25 minutes until golden.

Brush with margarine. Let stand in pan for 10 minutes before removing to wire rack to cool. Cuts into 12 pieces.

1 piece: 161 Calories; 5.2 g Total Fat (2.6 g Mono, 1.2 g Poly, 1.1 g Sat); 0 mg Cholesterol; 25 g Carbohydrate; 1 g Fibre; 5 g Protein; 246 mg Sodium

Breakfast Bars

*These healthy bran and blueberry bars can be
individually wrapped and frozen for a carry-along snack.*

Large eggs	2	2
Package of blueberry bran muffin mix	2 lbs.	900 g
Chopped pitted dates	1 cup	250 mL
Chopped pecans, toasted (see Tip, page 21)	1 cup	250 mL

Beat eggs and 2 cups (500 mL) water in large bowl until well combined.
Add muffin mix. Stir until smooth.

Add dates and pecans. Stir well. Spread in greased 9 x 13 inch (22 x 33 cm)
pan. Bake in 350°F (175°C) oven for about 40 minutes until wooden pick
inserted in centre comes out clean. Cuts into 24 bars.

*1 bar: 203 Calories; 8.1 g Total Fat (4.1 g Mono, 2.5 g Poly, 1 g Sat); 18 mg Cholesterol;
30 g Carbohydrate; 1 g Fibre; 3 g Protein; 211 mg Sodium*

Pictured on page 144.

1. Swirled Raisin Braid, page 25
2. Berry Bran Shake, page 56
3. Salmon-Sauced Bennies, page 49
4. Blueberry Cream Pancakes, page 50

Props courtesy of: Danesco Inc.

Baked Berry French Toast

A deliciously different way to prepare French toast.

Tub of berry spreadable cream cheese	8 oz.	250 g
Whole wheat bread slices	12	12
Large eggs	6	6
Milk	1 cup	250 mL

Spread cream cheese on 1 side of 6 bread slices. Cover with remaining slices.

Beat eggs and milk in medium bowl until frothy. Pour just enough egg mixture into well-greased 9 × 13 inch (22 × 33 cm) pan to cover bottom. Arrange sandwiches in pan. Pour remaining egg mixture over top. Bake in 450°F (230°C) oven for about 20 minutes until golden and egg is set. Serves 6.

1 serving: 346 Calories; 18.2 g Total Fat (6.9 g Mono, 2.2 g Poly, 7.2 g Sat); 243 mg Cholesterol; 30 g Carbohydrate; 4 g Fibre; 17 g Protein; 674 mg Sodium

Pictured on page 54.

1. Creamy Ginger Spread, page 57
2. Rugalach Roll-Ups, page 26
3. Huevos Tortillas, page 56
4. Baked Berry French Toast, above

Props courtesy of: Casa Bugatti
Cherison Enterprises Inc.
Danesco Inc.

Breakfast

Huevos Tortillas

A twist on huevos rancheros, *or "rancher's eggs," these saucy wraps are fun to eat and eggs-tremely quick to make!*

Large eggs	8	8
Chunky medium salsa	1/2 cup	125 mL
Grated Mexican cheese blend (or Cheddar cheese)	1 cup	250 mL
Whole wheat flour tortillas (9 inch, 22 cm, diameter)	4	4

Heat large greased frying pan on medium. Beat eggs and a sprinkle of salt and pepper in medium bowl. Pour into pan. Cook for about 4 minutes, stirring occasionally, until set.

Add salsa. Stir. Remove from heat.

Sprinkle cheese along centre of tortillas. Spoon egg mixture on top of cheese. Fold sides over filling. Roll up tortillas from bottom to enclose. Makes 4 wraps.

1 wrap: 492 Calories; 26.6 g Total Fat (9.7 g Mono, 4 g Poly, 10.2 g Sat); 462 mg Cholesterol; 37 g Carbohydrate; 7 g Fibre; 26 g Protein; 687 mg Sodium

Pictured on page 54.

Berry Bran Shake

Breakfast in a glass! The natural sweetness of fruit gets a boost from raisin bran to make a winning breakfast beverage.

Frozen whole strawberries, cut up	2 cups	500 mL
Milk	2 cups	500 mL
Raisin bran cereal	1/2 cup	125 mL
Chopped pitted dates	1/4 cup	60 mL

Process all 4 ingredients in blender or food processor for about 3 minutes until smooth. Makes about 4 cups (1 L).

1 cup (250 mL): 132 Calories; 1.8 g Total Fat (0.4 g Mono, 0.2 g Poly, 0.9 g Sat); 5 mg Cholesterol; 26 g Carbohydrate; 4 g Fibre; 5 g Protein; 109 mg Sodium

Pictured on page 53 and on back cover.

Creamy Ginger Spread

A delicious cream cheese spread for toasted
multi-grain bread, bagels or banana bread.

Block of cream cheese, softened	8 oz.	250 g
Milk	1 tbsp.	15 mL
Liquid honey	1 tbsp.	15 mL
Minced crystallized ginger	3 tbsp.	50 mL

Beat first 3 ingredients in medium bowl until smooth.

Add ginger. Mix well. Makes about 1 1/4 cups (300 mL).

2 tbsp. (30 mL): 98 Calories; 8.4 g Total Fat (2.4 g Mono, 0.3 g Poly, 5.3 g Sat); 26 mg Cholesterol; 74 g Carbohydrate; 0 g Fibre; 2 g Protein; 73 mg Sodium

Pictured on page 54.

Walnut Pear Dip

You'll go nutty for this cheesy, sweetened dip with a hint of cinnamon.
Serve it on toast or crackers, or with apple and pear slices.

Small pear, peeled and grated	1	1
Goat (chèvre) cheese, cut up and softened	4 oz.	125 g
Finely chopped walnuts, toasted (see Tip, page 21)	2 tbsp.	30 mL
Liquid cinnamon honey	1 tbsp.	15 mL

Beat all 4 ingredients with whisk in medium bowl until well combined. Makes about 1 cup (250 mL).

2 tbsp. (30 mL): 79 Calories; 5.6 g Total Fat (1.3 g Mono, 0.8 g Poly, 3.2 g Sat); 12 mg Cholesterol; 4 g Carbohydrate; trace Fibre; 4 g Protein; 78 mg Sodium

Asiago Soufflé

A perfectly domed, golden soufflé is sure to impress!

Milk	1 1/3 cups	325 mL
Minute tapioca	1/4 cup	60 mL
Grated Asiago cheese	1 cup	250 mL
Large eggs, room temperature	4	4

Preheat oven to 350°F (175°C), see Note. Combine milk, tapioca and a generous sprinkle of salt and pepper in small heavy saucepan. Let stand for 5 minutes. Heat and stir on medium for 8 to 10 minutes until boiling. Remove from heat.

Add cheese. Stir until smooth. Set aside.

Separate eggs, putting whites into medium bowl and yolks into large bowl. Beat egg whites until stiff peaks form. Set aside. Beat egg yolks with same beaters for about 1 minute until frothy. Slowly add cheese mixture to egg yolk, beating constantly on low. Fold in 1/4 of egg white until almost combined. Fold in remaining egg white. Carefully pour into greased 6 cup (1.5 L) soufflé dish (round casserole with high, straight side). Smooth top. Set dish in large roasting pan. Slowly pour enough boiling water into pan until water comes halfway up dish. Bake for about 40 minutes, without opening oven door, until soufflé is puffed and top is golden. Serve immediately. Serves 6.

1 serving: 167 Calories; 9.6 g Total Fat (3.3 g Mono, 0.9 g Poly, 4.6 g Sat); 164 mg Cholesterol; 10 g Carbohydrate; trace Fibre; 10 g Protein; 153 mg Sodium

Note: A preheated oven helps to ensure that a soufflé rises successfully. Once the soufflé is prepared, immediately place it in the hot oven to help preserve its "breath."

Sweet Yam Quesadillas

So good! Serve with sour cream or salsa for dipping.

Yams (or sweet potatoes), peeled and diced	3 1/4 lbs.	1.5 kg
Flour tortillas (9 inch, 22 cm, diameter)	8	8
Grated jalapeño Monterey Jack cheese	2 2/3 cups	650 mL
Can of sliced pickled jalapeño peppers, drained and chopped	4 oz.	114 mL

(continued on next page)

Cook yam in boiling salted water in large saucepan until tender. Drain. Add a sprinkle of salt and pepper. Mash.

Spread mashed yam on tortillas. Sprinkle cheese and jalapeño pepper on half of each tortilla. Fold tortillas in half over filling. Press down lightly. Brush both sides with cooking oil. Arrange on ungreased baking sheets. Bake in 400°F (205°C) oven for about 15 minutes, turning over at halftime, until browned and cheese is melted. Cut each quesadilla into 4 wedges, for a total of 32 wedges. Serves 8.

1 serving: 553 Calories; 18.9 g Total Fat (6.6 g Mono, 2.8 g Poly, 8.5 g Sat); 35 mg Cholesterol; 78 g Carbohydrate; 8 g Fibre; 18 g Protein; 611 mg Sodium

---

Cacciatore Sandwiches

Yum! These hearty open-face sandwiches are great for a hot lunch. Cut the bread diagonally for a touch of class.

Boneless, skinless chicken breast halves, cut into 1 inch (2.5 cm) pieces	1 lb.	454 g
Chunky vegetable pasta sauce	2 cups	500 mL
French bread slices (1 inch, 2.5 cm, thick)	4	4
Grated Italian cheese blend (or mozzarella cheese)	1 cup	250 mL

Heat large greased frying pan on medium. Add chicken. Cook for about 10 minutes, stirring occasionally, until no longer pink inside.

Add pasta sauce and a sprinkle of pepper. Stir. Reduce heat to medium-low. Cook, covered, for 10 minutes, stirring occasionally.

Arrange bread slices in ungreased 9 x 13 inch (22 x 33 cm) pan. Broil on centre rack in oven for about 1 minute per side until toasted. Spoon chicken mixture onto toast slices.

Sprinkle with cheese. Broil for another 1 to 2 minutes until cheese is melted and bubbling. Serves 4.

1 serving: 473 Calories; 18.3 g Total Fat (7.5 g Mono, 3.3 g Poly, 5.9 g Sat); 90 mg Cholesterol; 40 g Carbohydrate; 3 g Fibre; 37 g Protein; 982 mg Sodium

Havarti Ham Ring

The enticing combination of cheese, dill, ham and onion spills out of this ring of buttery crescent-roll pastry. Looks lovely on a lunch buffet.

Tubes of refrigerator crescent-style rolls (8 rolls per tube), 8 1/2 oz. (235 g), each	2	2
Grated havarti cheese with dill	1 1/2 cups	375 mL
Finely chopped Black Forest ham	2/3 cup	150 mL
Finely chopped green onion	3 tbsp.	50 mL

Unroll tubes of dough side by side on lightly floured surface, overlapping about 1 inch (2.5 cm). Press perforations and overlapping seam to seal.

Sprinkle cheese over dough, leaving 1/2 inch (12 mm) edge. Scatter ham and onion over cheese. Roll up, jelly-roll style, from 1 long side. Moisten edge with water. Press seam against roll to seal. Place roll, seam-side down, on greased baking sheet. Shape roll into ring. Pinch ends together to seal. Gently stretch ring to 10 inch (25 cm) diameter. Using scissors, make 12 evenly spaced cuts around ring from outside edge to within 1 inch (2.5 cm) of inside edge. Gently turn pieces onto sides in same direction. Pieces will overlap. Bake in 350°F (175°C) oven for about 25 minutes until golden. Let stand for 10 minutes. Cuts into 12 pieces.

1 piece: 133 Calories; 8.3 g Total Fat (1.7 g Mono, 0.4 g Poly, 2.7 g Sat); 19 mg Cholesterol; 8 g Carbohydrate; trace Fibre; 6 g Protein; 421 mg Sodium

Sausage Pandowdy

Pandowdy is usually a deep-dish dessert with sliced apples under a crisp biscuit batter. This is a savoury version with sweet apples and cinnamon that go naturally with pork sausage.

Maple-flavoured pork breakfast sausages	14 oz.	375 g
Chopped onion	1/2 cup	125 mL
Can of apple pie filling	19 oz.	540 mL
Tube of refrigerator crescent-style rolls (8 rolls per tube)	8 1/2 oz.	235 g

(continued on next page)

Cook sausages in large greased frying pan on medium for 8 to 10 minutes, turning occasionally, until no longer pink inside. Transfer with slotted spoon to paper towels to drain. Reserve 1 tsp. (5 mL) drippings in pan. Cut sausage into 1/2 inch (12 mm) pieces.

Heat drippings on medium. Add onion. Cook for about 5 minutes, stirring often, until softened.

Add sausage and pie filling. Stir. Spread in greased 9 x 9 inch (22 x 22 cm) baking dish.

Unroll dough. Separate into triangles. Cut triangles in half. Arrange on top of apple mixture, overlapping if necessary. Bake, uncovered, in 350°F (175°C) oven for about 25 minutes until top is crisp and golden. Let stand for 5 minutes. Serves 4.

1 serving: 377 Calories; 15 g Total Fat (4.5 g Mono, 1.3 g Poly, 3.6 g Sat); 37 mg Cholesterol; 53 g Carbohydrate; 2 g Fibre; 9 g Protein; 692 mg Sodium

Chicken And Cheese Pizza

When you have leftover chicken, make this quick and easy lunch. Enough for one, or serve two by adding soup on the side.

Whole wheat flour tortilla (9 inch, 22 cm, diameter)	1	1
Mild salsa	2 tbsp.	30 mL
Finely chopped cooked chicken	1/2 cup	125 mL
Grated medium Cheddar cheese	1/4 cup	60 mL

Place tortilla on greased baking sheet or 12 inch (30 cm) pizza pan. Spread salsa on tortilla, almost to edge.

Scatter chicken over salsa. Sprinkle with cheese. Bake on bottom rack in 375°F (190°C) oven for about 15 minutes until tortilla is crisp and cheese is melted. Cuts into 6 wedges.

1 wedge: 82 Calories; 3.5 g Total Fat (1.2 g Mono, 0.6 g Poly, 1.5 g Sat); 19 mg Cholesterol; 6 g Carbohydrate; 6 g Fibre; 7 g Protein; 106 mg Sodium

Seafood Quesadillas

When you're expecting a bunch for lunch, serve these seafood quesadillas filled with sweet baby shrimp and creamy cheese. Sure to fill the bill!

Tub of smoked salmon spreadable cream cheese	8 oz.	250 g
Flour tortillas (9 inch, 22 cm, diameter)	8	8
Grated jalapeño Monterey Jack cheese	2 cups	500 mL
Frozen cooked baby shrimp, thawed and blotted dry	2 cups	500 mL

Spread cream cheese on tortillas. Sprinkle Monterey Jack cheese and shrimp over half of each tortilla. Fold tortillas in half over filling. Press down lightly. Brush both sides with cooking oil. Place on ungreased baking sheets. Bake in 400°F (205°C) oven for about 15 minutes until cheese is melted. Cut each quesadilla into 4 wedges, for a total of 32 wedges. Serves 8.

1 serving: 430 Calories; 22 g Total Fat (7.6 g Mono, 3 g Poly, 10.1 g Sat); 112 mg Cholesterol; 35 g Carbohydrate; 2 g Fibre; 22 g Protein; 740 mg Sodium

Hotsy Totsy Casserole

A tasty lunch dish to please the whole family. Potato tots make this casserole simple to put together.

Plain bratwurst sausages, casings removed, chopped	1 lb.	454 g
Can of condensed cream of mushroom soup, divided	10 oz.	284 mL
Frozen peas	1 cup	250 mL
Frozen potato tots (gems or puffs), thawed	4 cups	1 L

(continued on next page)

Scramble-fry sausage in large greased frying pan on medium for about 10 minutes until no longer pink. Transfer to paper towels to drain.

Put 1/2 of soup in medium bowl. Add sausage. Stir. Spread in ungreased 9 x 9 inch (22 x 22 cm) baking dish.

Scatter peas over sausage mixture. Arrange potato tots on top. Combine remaining soup and 1/3 cup (75 mL) water in small bowl. Drizzle over potato tots. Bake, uncovered, in 350°F (175°C) oven for about 1 hour until golden. Serves 4.

1 serving: 482 Calories; 27.3 g Total Fat (10.5 g Mono, 4.7 g Poly, 10.6 g Sat); 33 mg Cholesterol; 44 g Carbohydrate; 5 g Fibre; 14 g Protein; 1730 mg Sodium

---

Feta Shrimp Frittata

A golden-topped, fluffy frittata filled with savoury cheeses and tender shrimp. Lovely served with pasta or a green salad.

Large eggs	8	8
Herb and garlic spreadable cream cheese	1/4 cup	60 mL
Cooked salad shrimp	12 oz.	340 g
Crumbled feta cheese	1 cup	250 mL

Heat large well-greased frying pan on medium. Beat eggs and cream cheese in medium bowl until smooth.

Add shrimp and feta cheese. Stir. Pour into pan. Stir for 5 seconds. Spread evenly in pan. Reduce heat to medium-low. Cook, covered, for about 8 minutes until bottom is golden and top is almost set. Place pan on centre rack in oven (see Note). Broil for about 5 minutes until frittata is browned and set. Cuts into 4 wedges.

1 wedge: 396 Calories; 25 g Total Fat (8.2 g Mono, 2.8 g Poly, 11.4 g Sat); 643 mg Cholesterol; 3 g Carbohydrate; 0 g Fibre; 38 g Protein; 881 mg Sodium

Note: To avoid damaging the frying pan handle in the oven, wrap the handle with foil before placing under the broiler.

Mexican Meatless Lasagne

You'll never miss the meat! This lasagne delivers a spicy kick in tasty layers of soft tortillas, tangy sauce and seasoned, soy-based ground round.

Chunky medium salsa	3 cups	750 mL
Flour tortillas (9 inch, 22 cm, diameter), quartered	4	4
Package of Mexican veggie ground round	12 oz.	340 g
Grated jalapeño Monterey Jack cheese	2 cups	500 mL

Layer all 4 ingredients in greased 8 x 8 inch (20 x 20 cm) pan as follows:

A. 1 cup (250 mL) salsa

B. 8 tortilla quarters, slightly overlapping

C. 1 cup (250 mL) salsa

D. 1/2 of ground round

E. 1 cup (250 mL) cheese

F. 8 tortilla quarters, slightly overlapping

G. 1 cup (250 mL) salsa

H. 1/2 of ground round

I. 1 cup (250 mL) cheese

Bake, covered with greased foil, in 350°F (175°C) oven for about 50 minutes until heated through. Broil, uncovered, on centre rack for about 5 minutes until cheese is golden. Let stand for about 10 minutes until set. Serves 6.

1 serving: 368 Calories; 15.3 g Total Fat (4.7 g Mono, 1.7 g Poly, 8.1 g Sat); 35 mg Cholesterol; 34 g Carbohydrate; 4 g Fibre; 25 g Protein; 1034 mg Sodium

Pictured on page 90.

Polenta Lasagne

Make lunch time fiesta time! Polenta goes well with
Mexican seasonings and tomato. Definitely one to try.

Chunky salsa	2 cups	500 mL
Package of veggie ground round	12 oz.	340 g
Polenta roll, cut into 24 slices	2 1/4 lbs.	1 kg
Grated jalapeño Monterey Jack cheese	2 cups	500 mL

Combine salsa and ground round in large bowl. Spread 1/3 of salsa
mixture in greased 9 × 13 inch (22 × 33 cm) baking dish.

Arrange 12 polenta slices on salsa mixture. Spread another 1/3 of salsa
mixture on top of polenta. Sprinkle with 1/2 of cheese. Layer with
remaining polenta slices, salsa mixture and cheese, in order given. Bake,
uncovered, in 350°F (175°C) oven for about 45 minutes until cheese is
melted and polenta is softened. Serves 6.

1 serving: 368 Calories; 14.3 g Total Fat (4.4 g Mono, 1 g Poly, 7.7 g Sat); 35 mg Cholesterol;
37 g Carbohydrate; 2 g Fibre; 24 g Protein; 725 mg Sodium

Salsa Bean Cakes

Healthy corn and bean cakes are crisp on the outside and soft in the
middle. Serve on hamburger buns with your favourite toppings.

Can of red kidney beans, rinsed and drained	19 oz.	540 mL
Crushed corn tortilla chips	1 cup	250 mL
Medium salsa	1/2 cup	125 mL
Large egg, fork-beaten	1	1

Mash beans with a fork in medium bowl.

Add remaining 3 ingredients. Stir well. Shape into 6 patties to fit buns.
Heat large greased frying pan on medium. Add patties. Cook for about
5 minutes per side until browned and heated through. Serves 6.

1 serving: 142 Calories; 5.7 g Total Fat (3 g Mono, 1.1 g Poly, 1 g Sat); 36 mg Cholesterol;
18 g Carbohydrate; 4 g Fibre; 6 g Protein; 231 mg Sodium

Pictured on page 90.

Meat And Potato Scallop

A satisfying, homestyle casserole that's a snap to put together.

Lean ground beef	1 lb.	454 g
Can of condensed cream of mushroom soup	10 oz.	284 mL
Thinly sliced peeled potato	4 cups	1 L
Thinly sliced onion	1 cup	250 mL

Scramble-fry ground beef in large greased frying pan on medium for about 10 minutes until no longer pink. Drain. Sprinkle with salt and pepper. Stir. Spread in ungreased 2 quart (2 L) casserole.

Combine soup and 3/4 cup (175 mL) water in large bowl. Add potato, onion and a sprinkle of salt and pepper. Stir. Spoon onto beef. Bake, covered, in 350°F (175°C) oven for 1 hour. Bake, uncovered, for another 10 to 15 minutes until top is starting to brown and potato is tender. Serves 4.

1 serving: 391 Calories; 15.3 g Total Fat (5.2 g Mono, 3.1 g Poly, 5.3 g Sat); 59 mg Cholesterol; 38 g Carbohydrate; 3 g Fibre; 25 g Protein; 664 mg Sodium

Quickest Chili

It doesn't get much quicker than this! A simple one-dish meal solution.

Lean ground beef	1 lb.	454 g
Frozen mixed vegetables	2 cups	500 mL
Chili powder	1 tbsp.	15 mL
Cans of baked beans in tomato sauce (14 oz., 398 mL, each)	2	2

Scramble-fry ground beef in large greased frying pan on medium for about 10 minutes until no longer pink. Drain. Sprinkle with salt and pepper. Stir.

(continued on next page)

Add vegetables, chili powder and 1/2 cup (125 mL) water. Heat and stir for 2 minutes.

Add beans. Stir. Reduce heat to medium-low. Cook, uncovered, for 15 minutes, stirring occasionally. Serves 4.

1 serving: 438 Calories; 11.2 g Total Fat (4.2 g Mono, 1 g Poly, 4 g Sat); 59 mg Cholesterol; 58 g Carbohydrate; 20 g Fibre; 34 g Protein; 956 mg Sodium

Barbecued Beef Ribs

Sink your teeth into these! A dark glaze of zesty orange and subtle hickory coats Texas-sized beef ribs, barbecued to perfection. Use twice as much horseradish for a little extra nip.

Beef back ribs, bone-in, cut into 1-bone portions	4 lbs.	1.8 kg
Medium orange	1	1
Hickory barbecue sauce	1 cup	250 mL
Prepared horseradish	1 tbsp.	15 mL

Put ribs into large pot or Dutch oven. Cover with water. Add a sprinkle of salt and pepper. Bring to a boil. Reduce heat to medium-low. Simmer, covered, for about 1 1/2 hours until tender. Drain. Sprinkle ribs with salt and pepper. Set aside.

Grate 1 tsp. (5 mL) orange zest into small bowl. Squeeze and add 1/4 cup (60 mL) orange juice. Add barbecue sauce and horseradish. Stir well. Preheat gas barbecue to medium-high. Place ribs on 1 side of greased grill. Turn off burner under ribs, leaving opposite burner on medium-high. Brush ribs with sauce. Close lid. Cook for about 25 minutes, turning occasionally and brushing with remaining sauce, until ribs are browned and glazed. Serves 6.

1 serving: 308 Calories; 16.5 g Total Fat (7.2 g Mono, 0.8 g Poly, 6.8 g Sat); 74 mg Cholesterol; 7 g Carbohydrate; 3 g Fibre; 31 g Protein; 418 mg Sodium

Stroganoff

Tender, chunky beef and mushrooms in a rich, creamy gravy.
Delicious served with egg noodles or mashed potatoes.

Beef stew meat, cut into 3/4 inch (2 cm) cubes	1 1/2 lbs.	680 g
Sliced fresh white mushrooms	3 cups	750 mL
Envelope of cream of mushroom soup mix	2 1/2 oz.	71 g
Sour cream	1/2 cup	125 mL

Heat large well-greased frying pan or Dutch oven on medium-high. Add beef. Cook for about 10 minutes, stirring occasionally, until browned.

Add mushrooms and a sprinkle of pepper. Cook for about 5 minutes, stirring occasionally, until mushrooms are softened.

Add soup mix. Stir. Slowly add 3 cups (750 mL) water, stirring constantly. Bring to a boil. Reduce heat to medium-low. Simmer, covered, for about 1 1/2 hours, stirring occasionally, until beef is tender.

Add sour cream and another sprinkle of pepper. Heat and stir for 2 to 3 minutes until heated through. Serves 6.

1 serving: 298 Calories; 16.9 g Total Fat (7.1 g Mono, 1.9 g Poly, 6.3 g Sat); 71 mg Cholesterol; 9 g Carbohydrate; trace Fibre; 27 g Protein; 631 mg Sodium

Chutney Steak

Try this tender steak smothered in a sweet, tasty sauce.
Add rice and a salad, and dinner is served!

Boneless beef blade steak, cut into 4 equal pieces	1 lb.	454 g
Prepared beef broth	1 cup	250 mL
Mango chutney, larger pieces chopped	1/2 cup	125 mL
Dijon mustard	3 tbsp.	50 mL

(continued on next page)

Heat medium greased frying pan on medium. Sprinkle both sides of steak pieces with salt and pepper. Add to pan. Cook for about 5 minutes per side until browned.

Combine remaining 3 ingredients in small bowl. Pour over steak. Bring to a boil. Reduce heat to medium-low. Simmer, covered, for about 1 hour until steak is tender. Remove steak to large serving platter. Cover to keep warm. Increase heat to medium. Cook sauce for 2 to 3 minutes, stirring occasionally, until thickened. Skim any fat from surface. Pour sauce over steak. Serves 4.

1 serving: 316 Calories; 21.5 g Total Fat (9.4 g Mono, 1.5 g Poly, 8.1 g Sat); 67 mg Cholesterol; 9 g Carbohydrate; trace Fibre; 21 g Protein; 439 mg Sodium

Easy Pot Roast

The name says it all! Tender beef and vegetables are wonderfully flavoured with a tangy sweet sauce in this one-pot meal. Thicken the sauce for gravy if desired.

Boneless blade (or chuck) roast	3 lbs.	1.4 kg
Potatoes, peeled and quartered	2 lbs.	900 g
Medium carrots, halved	4	4
Steak sauce	1 2/3 cups	400 mL

Place roast in medium roasting pan. Sprinkle with pepper.

Arrange potatoes and carrots around roast in pan. Sprinkle with salt and pepper.

Combine steak sauce and 1 1/2 cups (375 mL) water in small bowl. Pour over roast and vegetables. Cook, covered, in 325°F (160°C) oven for about 2 1/4 hours, turning roast twice, until roast and vegetables are very tender. Remove roast to large serving platter. Cover with foil. Let stand for 10 minutes. Remove vegetables with slotted spoon to large serving bowl. Remove sauce to small serving bowl. Cover both to keep warm. Slice roast. Makes 12 servings (2 to 3 oz., 57 to 85 g, each). Serve with vegetables and sauce. Serves 12.

1 serving: 316 Calories; 17.5 g Total Fat (7.4 g Mono, 0.7 g Poly, 6.8 g Sat); 67 mg Cholesterol; 18 g Carbohydrate; 2 g Fibre; 22 g Protein; 593 mg Sodium

Meaty Potato Bake

A great way to use up leftover beef. Just add a few basic ingredients and supper is underway!

Cubed peeled potato	3 cups	750 mL
Chopped cooked roast beef	2 cups	500 mL
Can of condensed tomato soup	10 oz.	284 mL
Grated sharp Cheddar cheese	1 1/2 cups	375 mL

Combine first 3 ingredients and a sprinkle of pepper in medium bowl. Spread in greased 2 quart (2 L) casserole. Bake, covered, in 350°F (175°C) oven for 1 to 1 1/4 hours until potato is tender.

Sprinkle with cheese. Bake, uncovered, for another 2 to 3 minutes until cheese is melted. Serves 4.

1 serving: 482 Calories; 22.6 g Total Fat (7.1 g Mono, 1.3 g Poly, 12 g Sat); 96 mg Cholesterol; 32 g Carbohydrate; 3 g Fibre; 38 g Protein; 853 mg Sodium

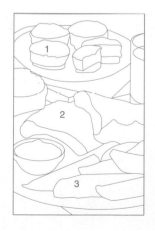

1. Berry Mini-Cheesecakes, page 147
2. Peppered Dry Ribs, page 81
3. Oven Ranch Fries, page 102

Props courtesy of: Cherison Enterprises Inc.

Supper – Beef

"Sweetish" Meatballs

Convenient to toss together in the slow cooker before
running errands for the day. This sweet tomato sauce
with tender meatballs can be served over rice.

Can of condensed tomato soup	10 oz.	284 mL
Brown sugar, packed	3/4 cup	175 mL
White vinegar	1/2 cup	125 mL
Package of frozen cooked meatballs	2 1/4 lbs.	1 kg

Combine first 3 ingredients in medium bowl.

Put meatballs into 4 to 5 quart (4 to 5 L) slow cooker. Sprinkle with salt and pepper. Pour soup mixture over meatballs. Stir until coated. Cook, covered, on Low for 5 to 6 hours or on High for 2 1/2 to 3 hours until heated through. Serves 8.

1 serving: 273 Calories; 5.6 g Total Fat (0.1 g Mono, 0.3 g Poly, 0.1 g Sat); 0 mg Cholesterol; 48 g Carbohydrate; trace Fibre; 9 g Protein; 587 mg Sodium

1. Salmon Lime Patties, page 76
2. Salmon-Stuffed Brie, page 15
3. Shrimp-Stuffed Sole, page 75

Props courtesy of: Danesco Inc.
Totally Bamboo

Pepper Steak

Perfectly peppery, and just plain good! A spicy crust adds a spark to tender, juicy steak. Double the peppercorns for added bite!

Whole mixed (or black) peppercorns, crushed (see Tip, page 75)	1 tbsp.	15 mL
Montreal steak spice	2 tsp.	10 mL
Rib-eye (or strip loin) steaks (4 – 6 oz., 113 – 170 g, each)	2	2
Garlic-flavoured olive oil	2 tbsp.	30 mL

Combine peppercorns and steak spice in small cup. Rub on both sides of steaks. Place on large plate.

Drizzle with olive oil. Let stand for 10 minutes. Preheat gas barbecue to medium-high (see Note). Cook steaks on greased grill for about 4 minutes per side for medium-rare, or until desired doneness. Serves 2.

1 serving: 394 Calories; 32.1 g Total Fat (18.1 g Mono, 1.8 g Poly, 9.4 g Sat); 60 mg Cholesterol; 3 g Carbohydrate; 1 g Fibre; 23 g Protein; 1248 mg Sodium

Note: Steaks may be broiled in the oven. Place steaks on a greased broiler pan. Broil on the top rack for about 4 minutes per side for medium-rare, or until desired doneness.

Onion Beef Ragoût

Beef stew was never so simple, or so good. Serve with mashed potatoes and buttered green beans.

Beef stew meat, cut into 3/4 inch (2 cm) cubes	2 lbs.	900 g
Envelope of green peppercorn sauce mix	1 1/4 oz.	38 g
Medium onions, each cut into 8 wedges	3	3
Dry (or alcohol-free) red wine	1/2 cup	125 mL

Put beef into 4 to 5 quart (4 to 5 L) slow cooker. Sprinkle with sauce mix. Toss until coated. Arrange onion wedges on top of beef.

Combine wine and 1 cup (250 mL) water in small bowl. Pour over onion. Cook, covered, on Low for 8 to 9 hours or on High for 4 to 4 1/2 hours until beef is tender. Serves 8.

1 serving: 235 Calories; 10.3 g Total Fat (4.1 g Mono, 0.4 g Poly, 3.9 g Sat); 62 mg Cholesterol; 6 g Carbohydrate; 1 g Fibre; 26 g Protein; 380 mg Sodium

Shrimp-Stuffed Sole

An elegant dish seasoned with mild garlic and herbs.
Perfect for company.

Frozen uncooked shrimp (peeled and deveined), thawed, blotted dry, finely chopped	1 lb.	454 g
Crushed Caesar-flavoured croutons	1 cup	250 mL
Sole fillets (3 – 4 oz., 85 – 113 g, each), any small bones removed	8	8
Garlic butter, melted	1/4 cup	60 mL

Combine shrimp and crushed croutons in medium bowl.

Place sole fillets on work surface. Spoon shrimp mixture onto centre of fillets. Fold 1 end of each fillet over stuffing and roll up. Place, seam-side down, in greased 9 x 13 inch (22 x 33 cm) baking dish.

Drizzle butter over fillets. Bake, uncovered, in 350°F (175°C) oven for 25 to 30 minutes until shrimp turns pink and fish flakes easily when tested with a fork. Serves 8.

1 serving: 211 Calories; 10 g Total Fat (3.3 g Mono, 1.3 g Poly, 4.5 g Sat); 122 mg Cholesterol; 4 g Carbohydrate; trace Fibre; 25 g Protein; 260 mg Sodium

Pictured on page 72.

 tip To crush peppercorns easily and keep them from spilling, place them in a resealable bag. Do not seal the bag. Use a rolling pin to gently pound and roll the peppercorns until crushed.

Creamy Curry Shrimp

Tender curried shrimp with chunks of
tomato—a perfect topping for rice or pasta.

Frozen uncooked large shrimp (peeled and deveined), thawed and blotted dry	1 lb.	454 g
Curry powder	1 tbsp.	15 mL
Can of diced tomatoes (with juice)	14 oz.	398 mL
Sour cream	1/2 cup	125 mL

Put shrimp into large bowl. Sprinkle with curry powder. Stir well. Heat greased wok or large frying pan on medium-high until very hot. Add shrimp. Stir-fry for about 3 minutes until shrimp just start to turn pink. Transfer to medium bowl.

Heat tomatoes with juice in same wok until boiling. Reduce heat to medium. Boil gently, uncovered, for about 6 minutes, stirring occasionally, until liquid is almost evaporated.

Add shrimp and sour cream. Heat and stir for about 3 minutes until sauce is boiling. Serves 4.

1 serving: 182 Calories; 8.5 g Total Fat (2.8 g Mono, 1.5 g Poly, 3.1 g Sat); 141 mg Cholesterol; 7 g Carbohydrate; 1 g Fibre; 19 g Protein; 304 mg Sodium

Salmon Lime Patties

These are a nice change from conventional beef patties.
Try other salmon varieties for a deeper red colour.

Medium lime	1	1
Cans of skinless, boneless pink salmon (6 oz., 170 g, each), drained	2	2
Large egg, fork-beaten	1	1
Crushed seasoned croutons	1 cup	250 mL

(continued on next page)

Grate 1 tsp. (5 mL) lime zest into medium bowl. Squeeze and add 3 tbsp. (50 mL) lime juice.

Add remaining 3 ingredients and a sprinkle of salt and pepper. Mix well. Shape into six 1/2 inch (12 mm) thick patties. Heat large well-greased frying pan on medium. Add patties. Cook for about 3 minutes per side until browned and heated through. Serves 6.

1 serving: 136 Calories; 8.1 g Total Fat (3.7 g Mono, 2.3 g Poly, 1.6 g Sat); 48 mg Cholesterol; 5 g Carbohydrate; trace Fibre; 10 g Protein; 332 mg Sodium

Pictured on page 72.

Lemon Tuna Fettuccine

Fresh lemon and garlic make tuna fish taste tuna-rrific!

Spinach fettuccine	13 oz.	370 g
Garlic butter, softened	1/4 cup	60 mL
Medium lemon	1	1
Can of white tuna in water, drained and broken up	6 1/2 oz.	184 g

Cook fettuccine in boiling salted water in large uncovered pot or Dutch oven for 8 to 10 minutes, stirring occasionally, until tender but firm. Drain. Return to same pot.

Add butter and a sprinkle of salt and pepper. Stir until butter is melted.

Grate 2 tsp. (10 mL) lemon zest into small bowl. Squeeze and add 2 tbsp. (30 mL) lemon juice. Stir. Add to fettuccine. Toss. Add tuna. Toss well. Serves 4.

1 serving: 509 Calories; 14.9 g Total Fat (4 g Mono, 1.5 g Poly, 8.2 g Sat); 49 mg Cholesterol; 71 g Carbohydrate; 7 g Fibre; 22 g Protein; 304 mg Sodium

Baked Garlic Shrimp

A garlic-lover's delight! Sherry and garlic butter are drizzled over tender shrimp.
Try these with white wine instead of sherry for a different flavour.

White bread slices, processed into crumbs	4	4
Garlic butter	1/3 cup	75 mL
Frozen uncooked large shrimp (peeled and deveined), thawed and blotted dry	1 lb.	454 g
Dry sherry	2 tbsp.	30 mL

Put bread crumbs into small bowl. Melt butter in small saucepan. Add 3 tbsp. (50 mL) butter and a sprinkle of salt and pepper to crumbs. Toss well. Set aside.

Arrange shrimp in ungreased 9 x 9 inch (22 x 22 cm) baking dish. Add sherry to remaining butter. Stir well. Drizzle over shrimp. Sprinkle with crumb mixture. Bake, uncovered, in 325°F (160°C) oven for about 25 minutes until shrimp are pink and curled. Serves 4.

1 serving: 305 Calories; 18.5 g Total Fat (5.3 g Mono, 1.4 g Poly, 10.5 g Sat); 173 mg Cholesterol; 13 g Carbohydrate; 1 g Fibre; 20 g Protein; 425 mg Sodium

Apricot Wasabi Salmon

An elegant entrée for company. A spicy topping of creamy
mayonnaise goes perfectly with this apricot-glazed salmon.

WASABI MAYONNAISE

Mayonnaise	1/2 cup	125 mL
Wasabi paste (Japanese horseradish)	2 tsp.	10 mL
Fresh (or frozen, thawed) salmon fillets, skin removed	1 lb.	454 g
Apricot jam	3 tbsp.	50 mL

(continued on next page)

Wasabi Mayonnaise: Combine mayonnaise and wasabi paste in small bowl. Chill for at least 10 minutes to blend flavours. Makes about 1/2 cup (125 mL) mayonnaise.

Arrange fillets on greased baking sheet with sides. Microwave jam in microwave-safe cup on high (100%) for about 30 seconds until melted. Brush on fillets. Sprinkle with salt and pepper. Broil on top rack in oven for about 8 minutes until fish flakes easily when tested with a fork. Serve with Wasabi Mayonnaise. Serves 4.

1 serving: 412 Calories; 30.6 g Total Fat (15.4 g Mono, 10.7 g Poly, 3.3 g Sat); 80 mg Cholesterol; 10 g Carbohydrate; trace Fibre; 23 g Protein; 209 mg Sodium

---

Zippy Mustard Cod

Reel 'em in for dinner with this one! Mustard and horseradish add zip to this golden, crumb-coated white fish.

Cod fillets, any small bones removed, cut into 4 equal pieces	1 lb.	454 g
Dijon-flavoured mayonnaise	3 tbsp.	50 mL
Prepared horseradish	1 tsp.	5 mL
Crushed seasoned croutons	2/3 cup	150 mL

Arrange fish pieces on greased baking sheet with sides. Sprinkle with salt and pepper.

Combine mayonnaise and horseradish in small cup. Spread on fish. Sprinkle with crushed croutons. Bake in 400°F (205°C) oven for about 15 minutes until fish flakes easily when tested with a fork. Serves 4.

1 serving: 191 Calories; 9.1 g Total Fat (4.6 g Mono, 2.8 g Poly, 1.2 g Sat); 54 mg Cholesterol; 5 g Carbohydrate; trace Fibre; 21 g Protein; 238 mg Sodium

Orange Herb Fish Fillets

Sweet, buttery onion with a mild orange flavour enhances the taste of moist, flaky white fish. A great dish for the supper rush.

White fish (such as cod or sole) fillets, any small bones removed, cut into 4 equal pieces	1 lb.	454 g
Garlic butter	1 tbsp.	15 mL
Finely chopped onion	1/3 cup	75 mL
Orange juice	3 tbsp.	50 mL

Arrange fish pieces in greased 8 × 8 inch (20 × 20 cm) baking dish. Set aside.

Melt butter in small frying pan on medium. Add onion. Cook for about 5 minutes, stirring often, until softened. Remove from heat.

Add orange juice and a sprinkle of salt and pepper. Stir. Spoon onto fish. Bake, uncovered, in 450°F (230°C) oven for about 10 minutes until fish flakes easily when tested with a fork. Serves 4.

1 serving: 240 Calories; 15.5 g Total Fat (4.8 g Mono, 2.8 g Poly, 6.5 g Sat); 92 mg Cholesterol; 2 g Carbohydrate; trace Fibre; 22 g Protein; 148 mg Sodium

 To store fish, wrap loosely and keep in refrigerator. Cook within 24 hours of purchase. Fish wrapped and stored in the freezer will keep for 2 to 3 months.

Glazed Ham Steak

Sweet and tangy mustard sauce livens up smoky ham. Ready in minutes.

Redcurrant jelly	1/3 cup	75 mL
Prepared horseradish	2 tsp.	10 mL
Dijon mustard (with whole seeds)	2 tsp.	10 mL
Ham steak, rind removed, cut into 6 equal pieces	1 1/2 lbs.	680 g

Combine first 3 ingredients in small cup.

Place ham pieces on greased baking sheet. Spread jelly mixture on ham. Broil on top rack in oven for about 8 minutes until heated through and jelly mixture is bubbling. Serves 6.

1 serving: 165 Calories; 5 g Total Fat (2.2 g Mono, 0.6 g Poly, 1.7 g Sat); 51 mg Cholesterol; 7 g Carbohydrate; trace Fibre; 22 g Protein; 1471 mg Sodium

Peppered Dry Ribs

A first-rate feast! These barbecued, lemony-spiced ribs are a savoury solution for a summer supper.

Lemon pepper	1 tbsp.	15 mL
Cajun seasoning	1 1/2 tsp.	7 mL
Brown sugar, packed	1 1/2 tsp.	7 mL
Baby back pork ribs (about 2 racks)	2 1/2 – 3 lbs.	1.1 – 1.4 kg

Combine first 3 ingredients in small bowl. Rub on both sides of ribs. Preheat gas barbecue to medium-high. Turn off burner on 1 side. Place ribs on greased grill over drip pan on unlit side, leaving opposite burner on medium-high. Close lid. Cook for about 45 minutes, turning occasionally, until tender. Cut into 3-bone portions. Serves 4.

1 serving: 519 Calories; 40.7 g Total Fat (18.4 g Mono, 3.2 g Poly, 15.1 g Sat); 162 mg Cholesterol; 3 g Carbohydrate; trace Fibre; 33 g Protein; 769 mg Sodium

Pictured on page 71.

Pork Chops Normandy

A tasty combination for the slow cooker! The peppery, sweet
applesauce is perfect over noodles, rice or mashed potatoes.

Medium cooking apples (such as McIntosh), peeled and quartered	3	3
Boneless pork loin chops (about 1 1/2 lbs., 680 g), trimmed of fat	6	6
Can of condensed cream of mushroom soup	10 oz.	284 mL
Envelope of green peppercorn sauce mix	1 1/4 oz.	38 g

Put apple into 4 to 5 quart (4 to 5 L) slow cooker. Arrange pork chops on top of apple.

Combine soup, sauce mix and 1 1/2 cups (375 mL) water in medium bowl. Pour over chops. Cover. Cook on Low for 8 to 10 hours or on High for 4 to 5 hours until chops are very tender. Remove chops to large serving platter. Process sauce, in slow cooker with hand blender or in blender or food processor, until smooth. Serve with chops. Serves 6.

1 serving: 242 Calories; 9.7 g Total Fat (3 g Mono, 2.4 g Poly, 2.8 g Sat); 52 mg Cholesterol;
16 g Carbohydrate; 1 g Fibre; 22 g Protein; 864 mg Sodium

Celery-Sauced Chops

Seasoned pork chops with lots of sauce for the potatoes.
Add a vegetable or salad, and dinner's complete!

Red baby potatoes, larger ones cut in half	2 lbs.	900 g
Boneless pork loin chops (about 1 1/2 lbs., 680 g), trimmed of fat	6	6
Montreal chicken spice	1/2 – 1 tsp.	2 – 5 mL
Cans of condensed cream of celery soup (10 oz., 284 mL, each)	2	2

(continued on next page)

Put potatoes into 4 to 5 quart (4 to 5 L) slow cooker. Sprinkle with salt and pepper.

Arrange pork chops on top of potatoes. Sprinkle with chicken spice and a pinch of pepper.

Combine soup and 1 can of water in medium bowl. Pour over chops. Cover. Cook on Low for 8 to 10 hours or on High for 4 to 5 hours. Remove chops and potatoes to large serving platter. Process sauce, in slow cooker with hand blender or in blender or food processor, until smooth. Serve with chops and potatoes. Serves 6.

1 serving: 393 Calories; 16.9 g Total Fat (6.5 g Mono, 3.4 g Poly, 5.4 g Sat); 77 mg Cholesterol; 32 g Carbohydrate; 3 g Fibre; 28 g Protein; 869 mg Sodium

Perogy Ham Casserole

Smoky ham and melted cheese smother tender perogies. A comforting casserole that holds its heat well, making this a great potluck choice!

Bag of frozen cheese perogies	2 1/4 lbs.	1 kg
Can of condensed cream of mushroom soup	10 oz.	284 mL
Cubed cooked ham	2 cups	500 mL
Grated medium Cheddar cheese	2 cups	500 mL

Cook perogies in boiling water in large pot or Dutch oven for about 5 minutes until tender. Transfer with slotted spoon to well-greased 9 x 13 inch (22 x 33 cm) baking dish.

Combine soup and 3/4 cup (175 mL) water in small bowl. Pour over perogies. Stir gently until coated. Scatter ham over top. Bake, covered with foil, in 350°F (175°C) oven for about 30 minutes until heated through.

Sprinkle with cheese. Bake, uncovered, for another 12 to 15 minutes until cheese is bubbling. Serves 6.

1 serving: 600 Calories; 27.1 g Total Fat (8.4 g Mono, 3 g Poly, 13 g Sat); 96 mg Cholesterol; 55 g Carbohydrate; 5 g Fibre; 33 g Protein; 1238 mg Sodium

Glazed Pork Roast

Sweet, piquant flavours glaze a juicy pork roast.

Redcurrant jelly	1/2 cup	125 mL
Red jalapeño jelly	1/4 cup	60 mL
Finely chopped pickled ginger slices	1 tbsp.	15 mL
Boneless pork loin roast	2 1/2 – 3 lbs.	1.1 – 1.4 kg

Combine first 3 ingredients in small bowl. Reserve 1/2 in small serving bowl for dipping sauce.

Place roast in small roasting pan. Score diamond pattern in top of roast. Cook, uncovered, in 400°F (205°C) oven for 30 minutes. Brush 1/2 of jelly mixture on roast. Reduce heat to 325°F (160°C). Cook, uncovered, for about 1 hour, brushing twice with remaining jelly mixture, until meat thermometer inserted into thickest part of roast reads 155°F (68°C). Remove from oven. Cover loosely with foil. Let stand for 10 minutes. Internal temperature should rise to at least 160°F (71°C). Slice roast. Makes 12 servings (2 to 3 oz., 57 to 85 g, each). Serve with reserved dipping sauce. Serves 12.

1 serving: 173 Calories; 7.3 g Total Fat (3.4 g Mono, 0.5 g Poly, 2.7 g Sat); 50 mg Cholesterol; 8 g Carbohydrate; trace Fibre; 18 g Protein; 33 mg Sodium

Pictured on page 126.

 tip Invest in a silicone brush for basting. As well as being durable and easy to clean, it won't lose bristles as you're brushing on a glaze or marinade.

Cheesy Red Rice

Tangy tomato and smoky ham accent this simple supper.

Cans of diced tomatoes with Italian spices (14 oz., 398 mL, each), with juice	2	2
Diced deli ham	1 1/2 cups	375 mL
Grated sharp Cheddar cheese, divided	3 cups	750 mL
Instant white rice	1 1/2 cups	375 mL

Put tomatoes with juice into large saucepan. Add a sprinkle of pepper. Stir. Heat on medium, stirring occasionally, until boiling.

Add ham and 1/2 of cheese. Stir. Remove from heat.

Add rice. Stir well. Let stand, covered, for 5 minutes. Sprinkle with remaining cheese. Let stand, covered, until cheese is melted. Serves 4.

1 serving: 762 Calories; 33.2 g Total Fat (9.9 g Mono, 1.4 g Poly, 20 g Sat); 120 mg Cholesterol; 75 g Carbohydrate; 2 g Fibre; 40 g Protein; 1908 mg Sodium

Picante Spareribs

Tender, moist ribs topped with onion and salsa. Simple, and full of flavour.

Pork spareribs	4 lbs.	1.8 kg
Montreal chicken spice	2 tsp.	10 mL
Chopped onion	2 cups	500 mL
Medium salsa	1 1/2 cups	375 mL

Cut ribs into serving-size portions. Arrange, meaty-side up, in large roasting pan. Sprinkle with chicken spice.

Scatter onion over ribs. Spoon salsa over top. Bake, covered, in 325°F (160°C) oven for about 2 hours until ribs are very tender. Serves 6.

1 serving: 584 Calories; 40.8 g Total Fat (17.6 g Mono, 3.8 g Poly, 15.4 g Sat); 156 mg Cholesterol; 9 g Carbohydrate; 2 g Fibre; 44 g Protein; 546 mg Sodium

Aloha Pork Roast

*Tender, succulent pork is glazed with sweet
pineapple and mustard. A tasty tropical delight!*

Honey Dijon mustard	1/4 cup	60 mL
Frozen concentrated pineapple	1/4 cup	60 mL
juice, thawed		
Soy sauce	1 tbsp.	15 mL
Boneless pork loin roast	3 lbs.	1.4 kg

Combine first 3 ingredients in small bowl. Set aside.

Place roast in large roasting pan. Cook, uncovered, in 400°F (205°C) oven
for 30 minutes. Brush 1/2 of mustard mixture on roast. Reduce heat to
325°F (160°C). Cook, uncovered, for about 1 hour, brushing twice with
remaining mustard mixture, until meat thermometer inserted into thickest
part of roast reads 155°F (68°C). Remove from oven. Cover loosely with
foil. Let stand for 10 minutes. Internal temperature should rise to at least
160°F (71°C). Slice roast. Makes 12 servings (2 to 3 oz., 57 to 85 g, each).

*1 serving: 190 Calories; 9.1 g Total Fat (4.1 g Mono, 0.8 g Poly, 3.2 g Sat); 60 mg Cholesterol;
3 g Carbohydrate; 0 g Fibre; 23 g Protein; 192 mg Sodium*

Sweet Onion Bratwurst

*Dark and delicious. Sweet balsamic vinegar and cinnamon
honey take sausages from ordinary to extraordinary!*

Plain bratwurst sausages (about 4 oz., 113 g, each)	4	4
Sliced red onion	2 1/2 cups	625 mL
Balsamic vinegar	2 tbsp.	30 mL
Liquid cinnamon honey	2 tbsp.	30 mL

(continued on next page)

Poke sausages in several places with a fork. Place in large saucepan. Add 1 cup (250 mL) water. Bring to a boil. Boil gently, covered, for 5 minutes. Boil, uncovered, for about 10 minutes until liquid is evaporated. Transfer sausages to large plate. Heat well-greased large frying pan on medium. Add sausages. Cook for 5 to 10 minutes, turning occasionally, until browned. Remove to large serving plate. Cover to keep warm.

Add onion to same pan. Cook for 15 to 20 minutes, stirring often, until caramelized.

Add vinegar and honey. Heat and stir for about 1 minute until vinegar is evaporated. Spoon over sausages. Serves 4.

1 serving: 303 Calories; 17.9 g Total Fat (8.8 g Mono, 2.6 g Poly, 5.4 g Sat); 44 mg Cholesterol; 20 g Carbohydrate; 2 g Fibre; 12 g Protein; 416 mg Sodium

----

Snappy Apple Pork

A taste of home that's a snap to make. Apples and stuffing with pork chops—great any day of the week!

Can of apple pie filling	19 oz.	540 mL
Box of chicken stove-top stuffing mix	4 1/4 oz.	120 g
Hard margarine (or butter), cut up	3 tbsp.	50 mL
Bone-in pork chops, trimmed of fat	1 1/4 lbs.	560 g

Spread pie filling in greased 2 quart (2 L) casserole.

Combine seasoning packet from stuffing mix, margarine and 3/4 cup (175 mL) water in large saucepan. Bring to a boil. Remove from heat. Add stuffing. Stir. Let stand, covered, for about 5 minutes until liquid is absorbed. Fluff with a fork. Spoon onto pie filling in casserole.

Heat well-greased large frying pan on medium-high. Add pork chops. Cook for 1 to 2 minutes per side until browned. Arrange on top of stuffing mixture. Bake, covered, in 350°F (175°C) oven for 20 minutes. Bake, uncovered, for another 8 to 10 minutes until meat thermometer inserted into centre of pork chop reads 160°F (71°C). Serves 4.

1 serving: 501 Calories; 17.9 g Total Fat (10.2 g Mono, 2.6 g Poly, 3.9 g Sat); 58 mg Cholesterol; 62 g Carbohydrate; 1 g Fibre; 24 g Protein; 704 mg Sodium

Minted Lamb Chops

Excellent! Minty marinade gently complements barbecued lamb.

Zesty Italian dressing	1/4 cup	60 mL
Mint jelly	1/4 cup	60 mL
Dried crushed chilies	1/2 tsp.	2 mL
Lamb loin chops	1 1/2 lbs.	680 g

Process first 3 ingredients in blender or food processor until smooth. Transfer to large resealable freezer bag.

Add lamb chops. Seal bag. Turn until coated. Marinate in refrigerator for at least 6 hours or overnight, turning occasionally. Discard marinade. Preheat gas barbecue to medium. Cook chops on greased grill for about 6 minutes per side for medium-rare, or until desired doneness. Serves 4.

1 serving: 347 Calories; 26.1 g Total Fat (11.7 g Mono, 3.2 g Poly, 9.3 g Sat); 96 mg Cholesterol; 4 g Carbohydrate; trace Fibre; 23 g Protein; 191 mg Sodium

Pictured on page 89.

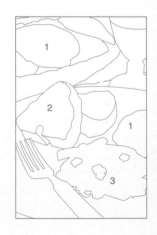

1. Feta Crescent Swirls, page 22
2. Minted Lamb Chops, above
3. Greek Beans, page 102

Props courtesy of: Casa Bugatti

Baked Tomato Chops

Pork chops are topped with cream cheese and
tomato slices, and baked to perfection!

Montreal chicken spice, divided	2 tbsp.	30 mL
Boneless pork loin chops (about 1 lb., 454 g), trimmed of fat	4	4
Chive and onion spreadable cream cheese	1/4 cup	60 mL
Tomato slices (1/4 inch, 6 mm, thick)	8	8

Reserve 1 1/2 tsp. (7 mL) chicken spice in small cup. Rub remaining spice on both sides of pork chops. Arrange in greased 2 quart (2 L) casserole.

Combine cream cheese and 2 tbsp. (30 mL) water in small bowl. Spread on chops.

Top with tomato slices. Sprinkle with reserved spice. Bake, covered, in 350°F (175°C) oven for about 1 hour until chops are very tender. Serves 4.

1 serving: 181 Calories; 8.1 g Total Fat (3.2 g Mono, 0.7 g Poly, 3.5 g Sat); 61 mg Cholesterol; 4 g Carbohydrate; 1 g Fibre; 22 g Protein; 1043 mg Sodium

1. Mexican Meatless Lasagne, page 64
2. Colourful Couscous, page 118
3. Salsa Bean Cakes, page 65

Props courtesy of: Anchor Hocking Canada
Out of the Fire Studio

Garlic Chicken Pasta

Moist pasta with a full garlic presence. A quick, appealing family meal.

Tri-colour fusilli (or other spiral) pasta	3 cups	750 mL
Can of diced tomatoes with roasted garlic and basil (with juice)	19 oz.	540 mL
Diced cooked chicken	2 cups	500 mL
Creamy Caesar dressing	2/3 cup	150 mL

Cook pasta in boiling salted water in large uncovered pot or Dutch oven for 8 to 10 minutes, stirring occasionally, until tender but firm. Drain. Return to same pot. Cover to keep warm.

Combine remaining 3 ingredients in medium saucepan. Heat and stir on medium for 10 to 12 minutes until heated through. Add to pasta. Toss until coated. Serves 4.

1 serving: 719 Calories; 29.1 g Total Fat (2.6 g Mono, 2.2 g Poly, 5.5 g Sat); 94 mg Cholesterol; 74 g Carbohydrate; 4 g Fibre; 40 g Protein; 870 mg Sodium

Pictured on page 36.

Asian Chicken Stir-Fry

Mild oriental flavours coat vegetables and tender chicken.
Stir-fry can't get much easier! Serve with rice.

Boneless, skinless chicken breast halves, cut into 1 inch (2.5 cm) pieces	1 lb.	454 g
Oyster sauce	1/4 cup	60 mL
Hoisin sauce	2 tbsp.	30 mL
Bag of frozen oriental mixed vegetables	17 1/2 oz.	500 g

Heat well-greased wok or large frying pan on medium-high until very hot. Add chicken. Stir-fry for about 8 minutes until no longer pink inside. Reduce heat to medium.

Add both sauces. Stir-fry for 2 minutes. Add vegetables. Stir. Cook, covered, for 6 to 8 minutes, stirring occasionally, until vegetables are tender-crisp. Serves 4.

1 serving: 229 Calories; 5.9 g Total Fat (2.6 g Mono, 1.6 g Poly, 0.9 g Sat); 66 mg Cholesterol; 16 g Carbohydrate; 2 g Fibre; 28 g Protein; 1227 mg Sodium

Savoury Pineapple Chicken

Pretty pineapple-herb topping adds a sweet, mellow flavour to chicken.
Serve over wild rice, jasmine rice or couscous.

Boneless, skinless chicken breast halves (4 – 6 oz., 113 – 170 g, each)	4	4
Can of crushed pineapple (with juice)	14 oz.	398 mL
Cornstarch	2 tsp.	10 mL
Dried savory	1 1/2 tsp.	7 mL

Heat large greased frying pan on medium. Add chicken breast halves. Sprinkle with salt and pepper. Cook for about 5 minutes per side until browned.

Combine remaining 3 ingredients and a sprinkle of salt and pepper in small bowl. Pour over chicken. Stir, scraping any brown bits from bottom of pan. Reduce heat to medium-low. Cook, covered, for about 10 minutes, stirring occasionally, until sauce is thickened and chicken is no longer pink inside. Serves 4.

1 serving: 246 Calories; 4.8 g Total Fat (1.9 g Mono, 1.3 g Poly, 0.8 g Sat); 81 mg Cholesterol; 18 g Carbohydrate; 1 g Fibre; 32 g Protein; 1 mg Sodium

 Make bulk purchases of fresh boneless chicken breasts, less tender steaks and pork ribs. Divide them into meal portions and place them in freezer bags, along with your favourite marinade. Squeeze the air out of the bags, seal, label and freeze. On busy days, remove a bag to the refrigerator in the morning and voila! You're set to go when you get home.

Chicken Corn Spaghetti

This saucy pasta dish can be ready to serve in short order!

Whole wheat spaghetti	6 oz.	170 g
Can of ready-to-serve chicken corn chowder	19 oz.	540 mL
Diced cooked chicken	1 cup	250 mL
Grated Parmesan cheese, divided	1/2 cup	125 mL

Cook spaghetti in boiling salted water in large uncovered pot or Dutch oven for 8 to 10 minutes, stirring occasionally, until tender but firm. Drain. Return to same pot.

Add chowder, chicken and 1/2 cup (125 mL) water. Stir.

Add 1/2 of Parmesan cheese and a sprinkle of salt and pepper. Stir well. Spread in greased 9 × 9 inch (22 × 22 cm) baking dish. Sprinkle with remaining Parmesan cheese. Bake, uncovered, in 425°F (220°C) oven for 15 to 20 minutes until cheese is golden and sauce is bubbling. Serves 4.

1 serving: 402 Calories; 14 g Total Fat (4.8 g Mono, 2 g Poly, 6 g Sat); 65 mg Cholesterol; 42 g Carbohydrate; 4 g Fibre; 29 g Protein; 872 mg Sodium

 Pasta made from regular or whole wheat flour takes the same time to cook, but the whole wheat variety has a delicious nutty flavour and all that extra fibre.

Chicken Alfredo Pie

Quick comfort food that is lip-smacking good!
You'll love the golden crust on this creamy chicken stew.

Boneless, skinless chicken breast halves, cut into 1 inch (2.5 cm) pieces	1 lb.	454 g
Bag of frozen California vegetable mix, thawed and chopped	2 1/4 lbs.	1 kg
Alfredo pasta sauce	1 3/4 cups	425 mL
Package of frozen puff pastry (14 oz., 397 g), thawed according to package directions (see Note)	1/2	1/2

Heat large greased frying pan on medium-high. Add chicken. Heat and stir for 2 to 3 minutes until browned.

Add vegetables. Cook for about 4 minutes, stirring often, until liquid is evaporated and vegetables are tender-crisp.

Add pasta sauce. Stir. Spread in ungreased 9 × 13 inch (22 × 33 cm) baking dish.

Roll out 1 square of pastry on lightly floured surface to 10 × 14 inch (25 × 35 cm) rectangle. Place on top of chicken mixture. Press pastry up side of dish. Cut several small slits in top to allow steam to escape. Bake in 400°F (205°C) oven for about 30 minutes until pastry is golden. Serves 6.

1 serving: 551 Calories; 34.8 g Total Fat (9.6 g Mono, 8.8 g Poly, 14.2 g Sat); 98 mg Cholesterol; 30 g Carbohydrate; 3 g Fibre; 31 g Protein; 519 mg Sodium

Note: Use both squares of puff pastry if you like a thicker crust.

Cranberry Pesto Chicken

This tangy chicken dish is simple to prepare and tastes fantastic.
Serve with Orange Basil Couscous, page 111.

Bone-in chicken thighs, skin removed	3 lbs.	1.4 kg
Whole cranberry sauce	1 cup	250 mL
Barbecue sauce	1/4 cup	60 mL
Basil pesto	1/4 cup	60 mL

Arrange chicken thighs in greased 9 x 13 inch (22 x 33 cm) baking dish. Sprinkle with salt and pepper.

Combine remaining 3 ingredients in medium bowl. Spoon onto chicken. Bake, covered, in 350°F (175°C) oven for 1 hour. Bake, uncovered, for another 25 to 30 minutes until chicken is no longer pink inside. Remove chicken to large serving platter. Skim any fat from surface of sauce. Spoon sauce onto chicken. Serves 6.

1 serving: 280 Calories; 9.9 g Total Fat (4 g Mono, 2.1 g Poly, 2.2 g Sat); 113 mg Cholesterol; 20 g Carbohydrate; 1 g Fibre; 26 g Protein; 105 mg Sodium

Pictured on page 108.

Ginger Apricot Chicken

People will think you've worked all day on this scrumptious grilled chicken dish.

Zesty Italian dressing	2/3 cup	150 mL
Finely grated, peeled gingerroot	1 tbsp.	15 mL
Boneless, skinless chicken breast halves	4	4
(4 – 6 oz., 113 – 170 g, each)		
Apricot jam	1/2 cup	125 mL

Combine dressing and ginger in large resealable freezer bag. Add chicken breast halves. Seal bag. Turn until coated. Marinate in refrigerator for at least 6 hours or overnight, turning occasionally. Drain, reserving 1/3 cup (75 mL) marinade in small saucepan. Discard any remaining marinade.

(continued on next page)

Add jam to reserved marinade. Stir. Heat on medium until boiling. Reduce heat to medium-low. Simmer, uncovered, for at least 5 minutes. Preheat gas barbecue to medium-low (see Note). Cook chicken on greased grill for about 8 minutes per side, turning occasionally and brushing with jam mixture, until no longer pink inside. Serves 4.

1 serving: 453 Calories; 23.9 g Total Fat (12.5 g Mono, 7.7 g Poly, 2.2 g Sat); 102 mg Cholesterol; 29 g Carbohydrate; trace Fibre; 32 g Protein; 506 mg Sodium

Note: Chicken may be broiled in the oven. Place chicken breast halves on a greased broiler pan. Brush with marinade. Broil on the top rack for 8 minutes. Turn. Brush with marinade. Broil for another 8 to 10 minutes until no longer pink inside.

Polynesian Chicken

A few convenient ingredients, and you've got delicious sweet and sour-sauced chicken everyone will love! Use apricot jam instead of marmalade if you prefer.

Bone-in chicken thighs, skin removed	3 lbs.	1.4 kg
Thousand Island dressing	1 cup	250 mL
Orange marmalade	1 cup	250 mL
Envelope of onion soup mix	2 oz.	55 g

Arrange chicken thighs in greased 9 x 13 inch (22 x 33 cm) baking dish.

Combine remaining 3 ingredients in small bowl. Pour over chicken. Bake, covered, in 350°F (175°C) oven for about 1 1/2 hours, turning chicken halfway through cooking time, until no longer pink inside. Remove cover for last 15 minutes to thicken sauce if desired. Serves 6.

1 serving: 519 Calories; 23.4 g Total Fat (11.2 g Mono, 7 g Poly, 3.1 g Sat); 125 mg Cholesterol; 50 g Carbohydrate; 1 g Fibre; 28 g Protein; 1160 mg Sodium

Pictured on page 35.

Cheesy Broccoli Chicken

Cheese, broccoli and tender chicken quickly combine into
a good weeknight casserole. Try it over a baked potato.

Ground chicken	1 lb.	454 g
Frozen chopped broccoli	3 cups	750 mL
Can of condensed broccoli and cheese soup	10 oz.	284 mL
Grated medium Cheddar cheese	1 1/2 cups	375 mL

Scramble-fry ground chicken in large greased frying pan on medium for about 10 minutes until no longer pink.

Add broccoli, soup and a sprinkle of salt and pepper. Stir well. Spread in greased 1 1/2 quart (1.5 L) casserole.

Sprinkle with cheese. Bake, uncovered, in 350°F (175°C) oven for about 40 minutes until sauce is bubbling around edges. Serves 4.

1 serving: 548 Calories; 39.1 g Total Fat (7.4 g Mono, 1.5 g Poly, 13.7 g Sat); 65 mg Cholesterol; 13 g Carbohydrate; 3 g Fibre; 38 g Protein; 954 mg Sodium

Turkey Cannelloni

A great way to use up leftover turkey. Oven-ready pasta tubes and
a simple red pepper sauce make this dish quick and delicious.

Finely chopped red pepper	1 cup	250 mL
Cans of condensed cream of mushroom soup (10 oz., 284 mL, each)	2	2
Chopped cooked turkey	2 1/2 cups	625 mL
Oven-ready cannelloni pasta shells	12	12

Heat medium greased frying pan on medium. Add red pepper. Cook for about 2 minutes, stirring occasionally, until tender-crisp.

(continued on next page)

Add soup. Stir well. Transfer 1/2 cup (125 mL) to medium bowl. Set aside remaining soup mixture in pan.

Add turkey and a sprinkle of pepper to soup mixture in bowl. Stir. Spoon into pasta shells. Arrange in greased 9 x 13 inch (22 x 33 cm) baking dish. Add 2 1/2 cups (625 mL) water and a sprinkle of pepper to soup mixture in pan. Stir well. Pour over shells. Bake, covered, in 350°F (175°C) oven for about 40 minutes until sauce is bubbling. Bake, uncovered, for another 20 to 30 minutes until pasta is tender and sauce is slightly thickened. Serves 4.

1 serving: 446 Calories; 14.9 g Total Fat (2.9 g Mono, 6.5 g Poly, 4.2 g Sat); 112 mg Cholesterol; 36 g Carbohydrate; 2 g Fibre; 40 g Protein; 1299 mg Sodium

Chicken Shake

The Cajun-spiced, crispy coating resembles fried chicken,
without the frying! Increase the Cajun seasoning for extra kick.

Biscuit mix	1/2 cup	125 mL
Cajun seasoning	2 tsp.	10 mL
Poultry seasoning	1 1/2 tsp.	7 mL
Chicken drumsticks (4 – 6 oz., 113 – 170 g, each)	12	12

Combine first 3 ingredients in large resealable freezer bag.

Sprinkle drumsticks with water. Place in bag. Seal. Toss until coated. Arrange drumsticks on greased baking sheet with sides. Spray with cooking spray. Bake in 350°F (175°C) oven for about 1 hour, turning once or twice, until chicken is no longer pink inside and coating is crisp and golden. Serves 6.

1 serving: 349 Calories; 22.7 g Total Fat (8.7 g Mono, 5.3 g Poly, 6.1 g Sat); 119 mg Cholesterol; 8 g Carbohydrate; trace Fibre; 27 g Protein; 250 mg Sodium

Pictured on page 125.

Sweet Orange Chicken

Grilled chicken coated in a dark, sweet sauce.
This barbecue recipe is the perfect choice for dinner
on the deck. Easy to double for a larger group.

Zesty Italian dressing	3/4 cup	175 mL
Brown sugar, packed	1/4 cup	60 mL
Grated orange zest	2 1/2 tsp.	12 mL
Chicken drumsticks (4 – 6 oz.,	12	12
113 – 170 g, each), skin removed		

Combine first 3 ingredients in large resealable freezer bag. Add drumsticks. Seal bag. Turn until coated. Marinate in refrigerator for at least 6 hours or overnight, turning occasionally. Drain marinade into small saucepan. Heat on medium until boiling. Reduce heat to medium-low. Simmer, uncovered, for at least 5 minutes. Preheat gas barbecue to medium-low. Cook chicken on greased grill for about 30 minutes, turning frequently and brushing occasionally with marinade, until no longer pink inside. Serves 6.

1 serving: 391 Calories; 28.1 g Total Fat (14 g Mono, 8.8 g Poly, 3.2 g Sat); 115 mg Cholesterol; 11 g Carbohydrate; trace Fibre; 23 g Protein; 494 mg Sodium

 tip   If a barbecue flare-up occurs, move the food to one side of the grill until flames die down. If you must, a light spritz from a water bottle can control small flames, but serious flare-ups should be doused with baking soda.

Olive Chicken Patties

Olive tapenade adds marvelous Mediterranean flavour
to grilled chicken patties. Tasty with any
relish or a tzatziki cucumber sauce.

Large egg	1	1
Crushed seasoned croutons	3/4 cup	175 mL
Black olive tapenade	1/3 cup	75 mL
Lean ground chicken	1 lb.	454 g

Combine first 3 ingredients in large bowl.

Add ground chicken. Mix well. Shape into four 5 inch (12.5 cm) patties. Preheat gas barbecue to medium (see Note). Cook patties on greased grill for about 7 minutes per side until fully cooked, and internal temperature of chicken reaches 175°F (80°C). Makes 4 patties.

1 patty: 286 Calories; 18.8 g Total Fat (1.8 g Mono, 0.4 g Poly, 0.9 g Sat); 54 mg Cholesterol; 6 g Carbohydrate; 1 g Fibre; 22 g Protein; 252 mg Sodium

Pictured on page 107.

Note: Patties may be broiled in the oven. Place patties on a greased broiler pan. Broil on the top rack for about 7 minutes per side until fully cooked, and internal temperature of chicken reaches 175°F (80°C).

Oven Ranch Fries

Mild ranch seasoning adds tang to tender potatoes. If you want bolder flavour, double the amount of bread crumbs and dressing mix. Serve with sour cream and bacon dip.

Medium unpeeled potatoes, each cut lengthwise into 8 wedges	4	4
Cooking oil	2 tbsp.	30 mL
Fine dry bread crumbs	2 tbsp.	30 mL
Envelope of ranch dressing mix	1 oz.	28 g

Put potato wedges into large bowl. Drizzle with cooking oil. Toss until coated.

Combine bread crumbs and dressing mix in large resealable freezer bag. Add potato wedges in several batches. Seal bag. Toss until coated. Arrange on greased baking sheet. Bake in 375°F (190°C) oven for 45 to 50 minutes until tender and golden. Serves 4.

1 serving: 222 Calories; 9.6 g Total Fat (5.5 g Mono, 2.9 g Poly, 0.8 g Sat); 1 mg Cholesterol; 31 g Carbohydrate; 3 g Fibre; 4 g Protein; 542 mg Sodium

Pictured on page 71.

Greek Beans

Bright green beans are wonderful combined with sweet onion and flavourful feta cheese. Ready in just minutes!

Fresh (or frozen) whole green beans, halved	4 cups	1 L
Garlic butter	2 tbsp.	30 mL
Thinly sliced red onion	1/2 cup	125 mL
Crumbled olive-and-herb-flavoured feta cheese	1/2 cup	125 mL

(continued on next page)

102 Side Dishes

Cook green beans in boiling water in large saucepan for about 3 minutes until bright green. Drain. Set aside.

Melt butter in large frying pan on medium. Add onion. Cook for about 2 minutes, stirring often, until starting to soften. Add beans. Cook for another 3 to 4 minutes, stirring occasionally, until beans are tender-crisp.

Add cheese and a sprinkle of salt and pepper. Stir. Serves 4.

1 serving: 150 Calories; 10.4 g Total Fat (2.6 g Mono, 0.4 g Poly, 6.7 g Sat); 34 mg Cholesterol; 11 g Carbohydrate; 2 g Fibre; 5 g Protein; 296 mg Sodium

Pictured on page 89.

Sweet Potato Sticks

Deliciously seasoned sweet potatoes are good any time!

Fresh medium sweet potatoes (or yams), peeled	2	2
Olive oil	2 tbsp.	30 mL
Montreal chicken spice	2 tsp.	10 mL
Lemon pepper	1 tsp.	5 mL

Cut potatoes lengthwise into 1/2 inch (12 mm) slices. Cut slices lengthwise into 1/2 inch (12 mm) sticks. Put into large bowl. Drizzle with olive oil. Toss until coated.

Combine chicken spice and lemon pepper in large resealable freezer bag. Add potato sticks. Seal bag. Toss until coated. Arrange on greased baking sheet. Bake in 425°F (220°C) oven for 20 to 25 minutes until tender. Serves 4.

1 serving: 209 Calories; 7.3 g Total Fat (5.1 g Mono, 0.8 g Poly, 1 g Sat); 0 mg Cholesterol; 34 g Carbohydrate; 4 g Fibre; 2 g Protein; 463 mg Sodium

Pictured on page 125.

Pineapple Ginger Carrots

Slightly sweetened with a pineapple ginger glaze, these carrots are great paired with rice and baked ham or pork roast.

Hard margarine (or butter)	2 tbsp.	30 mL
Finely grated, peeled gingerroot	1/2 tsp.	2 mL
Bag of baby carrots, larger ones cut in half	1 lb.	454 g
Frozen concentrated pineapple juice	1/3 cup	75 mL

Melt margarine in large frying pan on medium. Add ginger. Heat and stir for about 1 minute until fragrant.

Add carrots and a sprinkle of salt and pepper. Stir until coated. Add concentrated pineapple juice. Stir. Cook, covered, for about 8 minutes until carrots are tender-crisp. Remove cover. Heat and stir for 1 to 2 minutes until liquid is evaporated and carrots are glazed. Serves 4.

1 serving: 146 Calories; 6 g Total Fat (3.8 g Mono, 0.7 g Poly, 1.2 g Sat); 0 mg Cholesterol; 23 g Carbohydrate; 3 g Fibre; 2 g Protein; 108 mg Sodium

Pictured on page 126.

Fruity Stuffing

Serve this baked bread-and-apple stuffing with pork or poultry dishes. Bake it inside a crown roast of pork for an impressive presentation.

Chopped onion	1 1/2 cups	375 mL
Can of apple pie filling	19 oz.	540 mL
Poultry seasoning (or dried sage)	1 tsp.	5 mL
Box of seasoned croutons	6 oz.	170 g

(continued on next page)

Heat large greased frying pan on medium. Add onion. Cook for 5 to 10 minutes, stirring often, until softened. Remove from heat.

Add pie filling. Break up larger pieces of apple with spoon. Add poultry seasoning and a sprinkle of salt and pepper. Stir.

Add croutons and 1/4 cup (60 mL) water. Mix well. Transfer to well-greased 2 quart (2 L) casserole. Bake, covered, in 350°F (175°C) oven for about 45 minutes until heated through and croutons are softened. Serves 6.

1 serving: 262 Calories; 6.9 g Total Fat (3.6 g Mono, 1.2 g Poly, 1.6 g Sat); 1 mg Cholesterol; 48 g Carbohydrate; 3 g Fibre; 4 g Protein; 396 mg Sodium

Wild Rice Medley

Filled with Mediterranean flavours, this double-duty side dish makes an appetizing stuffing for chicken, or a pork or turkey roll.

Package of long grain and wild rice mix (with seasoning packet)	6 1/4 oz.	180 g
Garlic butter	3 tbsp.	50 mL
Chopped onion	1 cup	250 mL
Sun-dried tomatoes in oil, drained and chopped	1/2 cup	125 mL

Combine rice with seasoning packet and 2 1/4 cups (550 mL) water in medium saucepan. Bring to a boil. Reduce heat to medium-low. Simmer, covered, for about 30 minutes until liquid is absorbed. Remove from heat. Let stand, covered, for 5 minutes. Fluff with a fork.

Melt butter in large frying pan on medium. Add onion and sun-dried tomato. Cook for 5 to 10 minutes, stirring often, until onion is softened. Add rice. Heat and stir for about 1 minute until heated through. Serves 4.

1 serving: 285 Calories; 11.5 g Total Fat (4 g Mono, 0.9 g Poly, 5.9 g Sat); 24 mg Cholesterol; 41 g Carbohydrate; 2 g Fibre; 6 g Protein; 596 mg Sodium

Pictured on page 126.

Grilled Dijon Polenta

The mild corn flavour of this roasted side dish will fit at any meal. Use more mustard for a bolder taste.

Prepared chicken broth	4 cups	1 L
Yellow cornmeal	1 1/2 cups	375 mL
Grated Asiago cheese	1/4 cup	60 mL
Dijon mustard	3 tbsp.	50 mL

Combine broth and a sprinkle of salt and pepper in large saucepan. Bring to a boil. Reduce heat to medium. Slowly add cornmeal, stirring constantly. Heat and stir for about 10 minutes until mixture thickens and pulls away from side of saucepan.

Add cheese and mustard. Stir. Line 9 x 9 inch (22 x 22 cm) pan with greased foil. Spread cornmeal mixture in pan. Chill for about 1 hour until firm. Invert onto cutting board. Cut into 4 squares. Cut squares in half diagonally, for a total of 8 triangles. Brush with cooking oil. Preheat gas barbecue to medium. Cook polenta on well-greased grill for about 6 minutes per side until grill marks appear and polenta is heated through. Makes 8 triangles.

1 triangle: 138 Calories; 2.5 g Total Fat (0.8 g Mono, 0.6 g Poly, 0.9 g Sat); 3 mg Cholesterol; 22 g Carbohydrate; 1 g Fibre; 6 g Protein; 505 mg Sodium

Pictured on page 107.

1. Grilled Dijon Polenta, above.
2. Fruit Freeze, page 123
3. Tomato Bocconcini Salad, page 32
4. Olive Chicken Patties, page 101

Props courtesy of: Canhome Global
                    Cherison Enterprises Inc.
                    Pfaltzgraff Canada

Stuffin' Muffins

Serve these hot from the oven with any poultry dish.

Large oranges	2	2
Boxes of chicken stove-top stuffing mix (4 1/4 oz., 120 g, each)	2	2
Chopped pecans, toasted (see Tip, page 21)	1 cup	250 mL
Dried cranberries	1/4 cup	60 mL

Grate 1 tbsp. (15 mL) orange zest into medium saucepan. Squeeze oranges. Transfer juice to 4 cup (1 L) liquid measure. Add enough water to make 2 1/4 cups (550 mL). Add to zest.

Add seasoning packets from stuffing mixes. Stir. Bring to a boil. Add stuffing, pecans and cranberries. Stir. Remove from heat. Let stand for about 10 minutes until liquid is absorbed. Fluff with a fork. Spoon into 12 greased muffin cups. Bake in 350°F (175°C) oven for about 12 minutes until heated through and starting to brown. Makes 12 muffins.

1 muffin: 159 Calories; 7.7 g Total Fat (4.7 g Mono, 1.9 g Poly, 0.7 g Sat); 0 mg Cholesterol; 20 g Carbohydrate; 1 g Fibre; 3 g Protein; 318 mg Sodium

1. Parmesan Olive Biscuits, page 30
2. Pumpkin Soup, page 47
3. Orange Basil Couscous, page 111
4. Cranberry Pesto Chicken, page 96

Props courtesy of: Cherison Enterprises Inc.
Danesco Inc.
Out of the Fire Studio

Saucy Polenta Alfredo

Soft polenta smothered in a rich sauce, accented nicely
with smoky ham. A comforting, cold-weather dish.

Sliced fresh white mushrooms	1 cup	250 mL
Black Forest ham slices, cut into thin strips	6 oz.	170 g
Alfredo pasta sauce	1 3/4 cups	425 mL
Polenta roll, cut into 1/2 inch (12 mm) slices	1 1/8 lbs.	510 g

Heat large greased frying pan on medium-high. Add mushrooms. Heat and stir for 1 minute. Reduce heat to medium-low. Add ham and pasta sauce. Stir. Bring to a boil, stirring occasionally.

Place polenta slices on top of sauce. Boil gently, covered, for about 10 minutes, turning slices over after 5 minutes, until polenta is heated through. Serves 4.

1 serving: 444 Calories; 32.2 g Total Fat (10.3 g Mono, 1.8 g Poly, 18.2 g Sat); 97 mg Cholesterol; 18 g Carbohydrate; 1 g Fibre; 21 g Protein; 1097 mg Sodium

Spinach And Lentil Sauté

A wholesome lentil side dish. Outstanding flavour,
and an attractive addition to any meal.

Garlic butter	1/4 cup	60 mL
Chopped onion	1/2 cup	125 mL
Box of frozen chopped spinach, thawed and squeezed dry	10 oz.	300 g
Can of lentils, rinsed and drained	19 oz.	540 mL

Melt butter in large frying pan on medium-high. Add onion. Cook for about 3 minutes, stirring often, until starting to brown.

Add spinach, lentils and a sprinkle of salt and pepper. Heat and stir for about 2 minutes until heated through. Serves 4.

1 serving: 214 Calories; 12.8 g Total Fat (3.6 g Mono, 0.7 g Poly, 7.7 g Sat); 33 mg Cholesterol; 19 g Carbohydrate; 5 g Fibre; 9 g Protein; 341 mg Sodium

Orange Basil Couscous

Sweet oranges and fragrant basil make delicate couscous an interesting side for pork chops or grilled chicken breasts.

Medium oranges	2	2
Package of couscous with fruit and nuts	7 oz.	198 g
Spicy olive oil with herbs	2 tsp.	10 mL
Chopped fresh basil	1 tbsp.	15 mL

Grate 1/2 tsp. (2 mL) orange zest into medium bowl. Peel and segment oranges (see Tip, page 33). Cut segments into thirds. Add to zest. Stir. Set aside.

Measure 2 cups (500 mL) water into large saucepan. Bring to a boil. Add couscous and olive oil. Stir. Remove from heat. Let stand, covered, for 5 minutes. Fluff with a fork.

Add orange mixture and basil. Stir. Serves 4.

1 serving: 256 Calories; 4.2 g Total Fat (2.1 g Mono, 1.2 g Poly, 0.5 g Sat); 0 mg Cholesterol; 47 g Carbohydrate; 3 g Fibre; 8 g Protein; 470 mg Sodium

Pictured on page 108.

Paré Pointer

The movie had a happy ending. We were all glad it was over.

Salsa Rice

Jazz up long grain rice for a spicy side dish. Cilantro adds a tasty touch!

Long grain white rice	1 cup	250 mL
Can of condensed chicken broth with garlic and herbs	10 oz.	284 mL
Medium salsa	1/2 cup	125 mL
Chopped fresh cilantro or parsley	1 tbsp.	15 mL

Heat medium well-greased saucepan on medium. Add rice. Heat and stir for about 8 minutes until starting to brown.

Add broth, salsa and 1/2 cup (125 mL) water. Stir. Bring to a boil. Reduce heat to medium-low. Simmer, covered, for 15 to 20 minutes, without stirring, until liquid is absorbed and rice is tender.

Sprinkle with cilantro. Fluff with a fork until combined. Serves 4.

1 serving: 122 Calories; 3.3 g Total Fat (1.8 g Mono, 0.9 g Poly, 0.5 g Sat); 1 mg Cholesterol; 18 g Carbohydrate; 1 g Fibre; 5 g Protein; 562 mg Sodium

Creamed Spinach Casserole

This enticing dish can also be served as a spread for crackers. Even the kids will want to eat their spinach!

Boxes of frozen chopped spinach (10 oz., 300 g, each), thawed and squeezed dry	2	2
Tub of vegetable light spreadable cream cheese	8 oz.	250 g
Crushed seasoned croutons	1 cup	250 mL
Hard margarine (or butter), melted	2 tbsp.	30 mL

(continued on next page)

Combine spinach and cream cheese in medium bowl. Spread in greased 1 quart (1 L) casserole.

Combine crushed croutons and margarine in small bowl. Sprinkle over spinach mixture. Bake, uncovered, in 350°F (175°C) oven for about 40 minutes until crumbs are golden. Serves 6.

1 serving: 188 Calories; 14.3 g Total Fat (6.2 g Mono, 1.2 g Poly, 5.9 g Sat); 26 mg Cholesterol; 9 g Carbohydrate; 3 g Fibre; 7 g Protein; 485 mg Sodium

---

Tomato Risotto

This creamy risotto is sublime with just a hint of garlic.
Serve with Italian sausage or grilled herbed chicken breasts.

Vegetable juice	3 cups	750 mL
Garlic butter	1/4 cup	60 mL
Arborio rice	1 1/2 cups	375 mL
Grated Parmesan cheese	3/4 cup	175 mL

Combine juice and 3 cups (750 mL) water in medium saucepan. Bring to a boil. Reduce heat to low. Cover.

Heat butter in large pot or Dutch oven on medium until melted. Add rice. Stir until coated. Add 1 cup (250 mL) juice mixture, stirring constantly until liquid is absorbed. Repeat with remaining juice mixture, 1 cup (250 mL) at a time, until all liquid is absorbed and rice is tender.

Add Parmesan cheese. Stir. Serves 6.

1 serving: 346 Calories; 12.5 g Total Fat (3.6 g Mono, 0.5 g Poly, 7.7 g Sat); 32 mg Cholesterol; 48 g Carbohydrate; 1 g Fibre; 10 g Protein; 797 mg Sodium

---

Paré Pointer
She ran outside and called, "Am I too late for the garbage?"
They replied, "No, just jump in."

Tangy Roasted Mushrooms

Try these mushrooms when you barbecue fish, chicken or pork.

Medium orange	1	1
Balsamic vinegar	1/4 cup	60 mL
Italian seasoning	1/2 tsp.	2 mL
Portobello mushrooms	6	6

Grate 1 tsp. (5 mL) orange zest into small bowl. Squeeze orange. Add juice to zest. Add vinegar and seasoning. Stir.

Discard mushroom stems. Cut mushroom caps into quarters. Arrange, gill-side up, in ungreased 9 × 13 inch (22 × 33 cm) baking dish. Pour orange juice mixture over mushrooms. Bake, uncovered, in 425°F (220°C) oven for 20 minutes. Turn mushrooms over. Bake for another 5 minutes until liquid is absorbed and mushrooms are browned. Sprinkle with salt and pepper. Serves 4.

1 serving: 68 Calories; 1 g Total Fat (0 g Mono, 0.4 g Poly, 0.1 g Sat); 0 mg Cholesterol; 14 g Carbohydrate; 3 g Fibre; 5 g Protein; 58 mg Sodium

Fragrant Rice

A wonderful aroma wafts from this sweetened rice.
Sure to make mouths water.

Large orange	1	1
Converted white rice	1 1/2 cups	375 mL
Chai tea concentrate	1 cup	250 mL
Dark raisins	1/4 cup	60 mL

Grate 2 tsp. (10 mL) orange zest into small bowl. Set aside. Squeeze orange. Transfer juice to 2 cup (500 mL) liquid measure. Add enough water to make 2 cups (500 mL). Pour into medium saucepan.

(continued on next page)

114 Side Dishes

Add rice, tea concentrate and a generous sprinkle of salt. Stir. Bring to a boil. Reduce heat to medium-low. Simmer, covered, for about 18 minutes until liquid is absorbed and rice is tender.

Add orange zest, raisins and a sprinkle of salt and pepper. Stir. Serves 4.

1 serving: 313 Calories; 0.5 g Total Fat (0.1 g Mono, 0.1 g Poly, 0.1 g Sat); 0 mg Cholesterol; 70 g Carbohydrate; 1 g Fibre; 5 g Protein; 6 mg Sodium

Sweet Onion Squash

*Buttery garlic and Parmesan cheese lend
a Mediterranean flair to this delicious side dish.*

Butternut squash, peeled and cubed	1 1/2 lbs.	680 g
Garlic butter	2 tbsp.	30 mL
Chopped onion	1 cup	250 mL
Grated Parmesan cheese	1/4 cup	60 mL

Cook squash in boiling water in large saucepan until tender. Drain. Mash. Cover to keep warm.

Melt butter in medium frying pan on medium. Add onion. Cook for 5 to 10 minutes, stirring often, until onion is softened and starting to brown. Add to squash. Stir well.

Add Parmesan cheese. Stir until cheese is melted. Serves 4.

1 serving: 162 Calories; 8.1 g Total Fat (2.3 g Mono, 0.4 g Poly, 4.9 g Sat); 21 mg Cholesterol; 21 g Carbohydrate; 3 g Fibre; 5 g Protein; 190 mq Sodium

Paré Pointer

*The least expensive plastic surgery is simply cutting up
your credit cards.*

Roasted Onions

Slow roasting gives onions a sweet, mellow flavour. Great with roast beef.

Balsamic vinegar	3 tbsp.	50 mL
Olive oil	2 tbsp.	30 mL
Italian seasoning	1/2 tsp.	2 mL
Sweet medium onions (such as Vidalia), each cut into 12 wedges	3	3

Combine first 3 ingredients and a sprinkle of salt and pepper in large bowl.

Add onion. Toss until coated. Spread on greased baking sheet with sides. Bake in 375°F (190°C) oven for about 30 minutes, stirring occasionally, until softened and browned. Serves 10.

1 serving: 47 Calories; 3.7 g Total Fat (2.6 g Mono, 0.5 g Poly, 0.4 g Sat); 0 mg Cholesterol; 3 g Carbohydrate; 1 g Fibre; 0 g Protein; 21 mg Sodium

Ginger Curry Rice

Vibrant sticky rice with a pleasant, lingering heat.

Finely grated, peeled gingerroot (or 1/2 tsp., 2 mL, ground ginger)	2 tsp.	10 mL
Curry powder	1 tsp.	5 mL
Long grain white rice	1 cup	250 mL
Mango chutney, larger pieces cut smaller	1/4 cup	60 mL

Heat medium well-greaséd saucepan on medium. Add ginger and curry powder. Heat and stir for about 1 minute until fragrant.

Add rice and a sprinkle of salt and pepper. Heat and stir on medium for about 2 minutes until rice is golden. Add 2 cups (500 mL) water. Heat and stir for about 5 minutes until boiling. Reduce heat to medium-low. Simmer, covered, for about 15 minutes until liquid is absorbed and rice is tender.

Add chutney. Stir. Serves 4.

1 serving: 217 Calories; 2.7 g Total Fat (1.5 g Mono, 0.8 g Poly, 0.3 g Sat); 0 mg Cholesterol; 44 g Carbohydrate; 1 g Fibre; 4 g Protein; 3 mg Sodium

Texas-Style Caviar

Everything's bigger in Texas! These zesty black beans look like "giant caviar." Use twice as much cilantro for added fresh flavour. A spicy side for barbecued ribs or chicken.

Can of black beans, rinsed and drained	19 oz.	540 mL
Chipotle chili pepper in adobo sauce, finely chopped (see Note)	1	1
Zesty Italian dressing	1/3 cup	75 mL
Chopped fresh cilantro or parsley	2 tbsp.	30 mL

Combine all 4 ingredients in medium bowl. Cover. Chill for at least 1 hour to blend flavours. Makes about 2 cups (500 mL).

2 tbsp. (30 mL): 53 Calories; 3.5 g Total Fat (1.9 g Mono, 1.2 g Poly, 0.3 g Sat); 3 mg Cholesterol; 4 g Carbohydrate; 1 g Fibre; 1 g Protein; 167 mg Sodium

Note: Store leftover chipotle chili peppers and sauce in a clean jar in the refrigerator for several months.

Glazed Mushrooms

Shiny, teriyaki-glazed mushrooms with a subtle orange accent. There's lots of tasty sauce to drizzle over rice and grilled chicken.

Thick teriyaki basting sauce	1/4 cup	60 mL
Rice vinegar	1 tbsp.	15 mL
Frozen concentrated orange juice, thawed	1 tbsp.	15 mL
Small fresh whole white mushrooms	1 lb.	454 g

Combine first 3 ingredients in small bowl. Set aside.

Heat large greased frying pan on medium. Add mushrooms. Heat and stir for about 10 minutes until starting to brown. Add teriyaki mixture. Heat and stir for about 2 minutes until mushrooms are glazed. Serves 4.

1 serving: 73 Calories; 2.8 g Total Fat (1.4 g Mono, 0.9 g Poly, 0.2 g Sat); 0 mg Cholesterol; 10 g Carbohydrate; 2 g Fibre; 4 g Protein; 740 mg Sodium

Squash-ghetti And Sauce

Once you cook spaghetti squash, you'll discover how it got its name. The flesh separates into thin, slightly firm strands. Smothered in zesty tomato sauce and Parmesan cheese, it's certain to become a favourite!

Spaghetti squash	4 3/4 lbs.	2.2 kg
Medium unpeeled zucchini, quartered lengthwise and cut into 1/2 inch (12 mm) pieces	1	1
Tomato pasta sauce with mushrooms and green pepper	2 3/4 cups	675 mL
Grated Parmesan cheese	1/2 cup	125 mL

Cut squash in half lengthwise. Discard seeds. Place, cut-side down, in microwave-safe 3 quart (3 L) casserole. Cover. Microwave on high (100%) for 20 to 30 minutes until flesh is tender and can be shredded into strands with a fork. Let stand, covered, for about 20 minutes until cool enough to handle. Shred flesh into large serving bowl. Cover to keep warm.

Heat medium greased saucepan on medium. Add zucchini. Cook for about 5 minutes, stirring occasionally, until starting to soften.

Add pasta sauce. Stir. Bring to a boil. Pour over squash. Toss gently until coated.

Sprinkle with Parmesan cheese. Serves 6.

1 serving: 267 Calories; 10.7 g Total Fat (4.3 g Mono, 2.5 g Poly, 2.9 g Sat); 7 mg Cholesterol; 38 g Carbohydrate; 5 g Fibre; 8 g Protein; 807 mg Sodium

Colourful Couscous

This simple-to-make dish is great paired with Tomato Bocconcini Salad, page 32, when you're serving pork chops or grilled chicken.

Vegetable juice	2 cups	500 mL
Packages of couscous with mushrooms (7 oz., 198 g, each)	2	2
Fresh stir-fry vegetable mix	4 cups	1 L
Sun-dried tomato pesto	3 tbsp.	50 mL

(continued on next page)

118 Side Dishes

Combine juice and 2 1/4 cups (550 mL) water in large saucepan. Reserve 1/2 cup (125 mL). Bring juice mixture in pan to a boil.

Add couscous. Stir. Remove from heat. Let stand, covered, for 5 minutes. Fluff with a fork.

Heat greased wok or large frying pan on medium-high. Add vegetables. Stir-fry for 3 minutes.

Add reserved juice mixture and pesto. Stir-fry for another 2 to 3 minutes until vegetables are coated and liquid is evaporated. Add couscous. Stir-fry for about 1 minute until heated through. Serves 6.

1 serving: 306 Calories; 2.8 g Total Fat (1.4 g Mono, 0.8 g Poly, 0.3 g Sat); trace Cholesterol; 60 g Carbohydrate; 4 g Fibre; 11 g Protein; 570 mg Sodium

Pictured on page 90.

Orange Squash Bowls

Sweet, orange couscous sits pretty in squash shells.
A delicious dish that's on the table in about 30 minutes.

Medium acorn squash	2	2
Orange juice	2 1/2 cups	625 mL
Package of couscous with mushrooms	7 oz.	198 g
Chopped dried apricot	1/2 cup	125 mL

Cut both squash in half lengthwise. Discard seeds. Place 2 halves, cut-side down, in microwave-safe 2 quart (2 L) casserole. Pour 1/4 cup (60 mL) water into casserole. Cover. Microwave on high (100%) for about 10 minutes until squash is tender. Repeat with remaining halves. Scoop about 3 tbsp. (50 mL) flesh from each half into small bowl. Set aside. Place shells, cut-side up, on large oven-safe serving platter. Place in 300°F (150°C) oven to keep warm.

Measure orange juice into medium saucepan. Bring to a boil. Add couscous. Stir. Remove from heat. Let stand, covered, for 5 minutes. Fluff with a fork.

Heat large greased frying pan on medium. Add squash flesh, couscous and apricot. Sprinkle with salt and pepper. Heat and stir for about 5 minutes until starting to brown. Spoon into squash shells. Serves 4.

1 serving: 421 Calories; 4.5 g Total Fat (2.2 g Mono, 1.4 g Poly, 0.4 g Sat); 0 mg Cholesterol; 89 g Carbohydrate; 7 g Fibre; 10 g Protein; 177 mg Sodium

Chocolate Hazelnut Angel

*Sweet and crunchy, the chocolate-hazelnut glaze on
this light-textured angel food cake is heavenly!*

Box of angel food cake mix	16 oz.	450 g
Hazelnut liqueur, divided	1/3 cup	75 mL
Flaked hazelnuts (filberts), toasted (see Tip, page 21), divided	2/3 cup	150 mL
Chocolate hazelnut spread	1/2 cup	125 mL

Prepare cake mix according to package directions, adding 2 tbsp. (30 mL)
liqueur to liquid ingredients.

Reserve 2 tbsp. (30 mL) hazelnuts in small cup. Fold remaining hazelnuts
into batter. Spread in ungreased 10 inch (25 cm) angel food tube pan.
Bake in 325°F (160°C) oven for about 55 minutes until wooden pick
inserted in centre of cake comes out clean. Invert cake in pan onto glass
bottle for 2 to 3 hours until cooled completely. Turn upright. Run knife
around inside edge of pan to loosen cake. Remove bottom of pan with
cake. Run knife around tube and bottom of pan to loosen. Invert cake onto
large serving plate.

Combine chocolate spread and remaining liqueur in small saucepan. Heat
and stir on low for about 6 minutes until smooth. Cool slightly. Drizzle over
cake. Sprinkle with reserved hazelnuts. Chill for 30 minutes. Cuts into
12 wedges (see Tip, below).

*1 wedge: 275 Calories; 10.2 g Total Fat (6.1 g Mono, 2.1 g Poly, 1.5 g Sat); 0 mg Cholesterol;
38 g Carbohydrate; 1 g Fibre; 7 g Protein; 330 mg Sodium*

 tip   *The best way to cut an angel food cake is to use a serrated knife and
a gentle sawing motion. Wipe the knife clean after each cut.*

Lemon Coconut Angel

An attractive, three-tiered angel food cake filled
with sweet lemon and coconut. Lovely!

Angel food cake	1	1
Can of lemon pie filling, divided	19 oz.	540 mL
Medium unsweetened coconut, toasted	1 cup	250 mL
(see Tip, page 21)		
Frozen whipped topping, thawed	2 cups	500 mL

Cut cake horizontally into 3 layers. Place largest, bottom layer, cut-side up, on large serving plate.

Reserve 1/2 cup (125 mL) lemon pie filling in small bowl. Put remaining pie filling into separate small bowl. Add 1/2 cup (125 mL) coconut. Stir. Spread 1/2 of coconut mixture on bottom cake layer. Place centre cake layer on top of coconut mixture. Spread with remaining coconut mixture. Cover with smallest, top cake layer, cut-side down.

Add whipped topping to reserved pie filling. Stir. Spread on top and side of cake. Sprinkle with remaining coconut. Chill for about 1 hour until filling is firm. Cuts into 12 wedges (see Tip, page 120).

1 wedge: 272 Calories; 8.7 g Total Fat (0.4 g Mono, 0.2 g Poly, 7.4 g Sat); 0 mg Cholesterol; 47 g Carbohydrate; 1 g Fibre; 4 g Protein; 281 mg Sodium

Pictured on page 35.

Paré Pointer

Bakers make good baseball pitchers because they know their batter.

Chai Ice Cream

Pleasant, mild chai spices add delicate flavour to this light, icy dessert.

Egg yolks (large)	6	6
Granulated sugar	1/2 cup	125 mL
Chai tea concentrate	1/2 cup	125 mL
Half-and-half cream	4 cups	1 L

Beat egg yolks and sugar in large bowl for about 3 minutes until thick and pale. Add tea concentrate. Stir. Set aside.

Heat cream in large heavy saucepan on medium for about 10 minutes until very hot and bubbles appear around edge of saucepan. Slowly add tea mixture, stirring constantly. Heat and stir for about 8 minutes until slightly thickened and mixture coats back of metal spoon. Transfer to large heatproof bowl. Let stand for 30 minutes. Chill, uncovered, for at least 3 hours until very cold. Pour into ice cream maker (see Note). Follow manufacturer's instructions. Makes about 6 cups (1.5 L).

1 cup (250 mL): 329 Calories; 22.2 g Total Fat (6.9 g Mono, 1.3 g Poly, 12.2 g Sat); 269 mg Cholesterol; 25 g Carbohydrate; 0 g Fibre; 8 g Protein; 78 mg Sodium

Note: If you don't have an ice cream maker, spread the mixture in a 9 x 9 inch (22 x 22 cm) pan. Freeze, stirring every hour for 4 hours.

Paré Pointer

The easiest way to see flying saucers is to pinch a waitress.

Fruit Freeze

You'll love the smooth fruit flavour of this refreshing dessert.

Cans of fruit cocktail (14 oz., 398 mL, each), drained and juice reserved	2	2
Box of tropical-flavoured jelly powder (gelatin)	3 oz.	85 g
Vanilla yogurt	1 1/2 cups	375 mL
Egg white (large)	1	1

Measure 1/2 cup (125 mL) reserved juice into small saucepan. Bring to a boil. Remove from heat.

Add jelly powder. Stir until dissolved. Add remaining juice and fruit cocktail. Stir. Add yogurt. Stir well. Process in 2 batches in blender or food processor until smooth. Transfer to medium bowl. Set aside.

Beat egg white in small bowl until stiff peaks form. Gently fold in 1 cup (250 mL) fruit mixture. Fold egg white mixture into remaining fruit mixture in medium bowl. Transfer to 9 × 9 inch (22 × 22 cm) baking dish. Freeze, covered, for about 4 hours until gelled and ice crystals form. Scrape into large bowl. Beat on high until slushy. Pour into large airtight container. Freeze for at least 4 hours until firm. Let stand at room temperature for 15 minutes before serving. Makes about 6 cups (1.5 L).

1 cup (250 mL): 180 Calories; 1.2 g Total Fat (0.3 g Mono, 0 g Poly, 0.8 g Sat); 3 mg Cholesterol; 39 g Carbohydrate; 2 g Fibre; 5 g Protein; 88 mg Sodium

Pictured on page 107.

Paré Pointer

A football coach is desired, hired, wired,
admired, tired, mired—then fired.

Tangy Rice Parfaits

Gorgeous raspberries on top of rice pudding and granola make this a showy dessert. Use vanilla bean yogurt for strongest vanilla flavour.

White basmati rice	3/4 cup	175 mL
Hazelnut and honey granola	1 cup	250 mL
Vanilla yogurt	1 cup	250 mL
Fresh raspberries	2 cups	500 mL

Measure 1 1/2 cups (375 mL) water into medium saucepan. Bring to a boil. Add rice and a sprinkle of salt. Stir. Reduce heat to medium-low. Simmer, covered, for about 15 minutes until water is absorbed. Remove from heat. Let stand, covered, for 5 minutes. Fluff with a fork. Cool.

Put granola into 4 parfait or medium glasses.

Add yogurt to rice. Stir. Spoon on top of granola.

Top with raspberries. Serves 4.

1 serving: 349 Calories; 5.9 g Total Fat (0.5 g Mono, 0.3 g Poly, 0.9 g Sat); 3 mg Cholesterol; 67 g Carbohydrate; 6 g Fibre; 9 g Protein; 86 mg Sodium

Pictured on front cover.

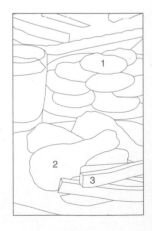

1. Chocolate Crunch Cookies, page 132
2. Chicken Shake, page 99
3. Sweet Potato Sticks, page 103

Props courtesy of: Cherison Enterprises Inc.

Desserts & Snacks

Ooey Gooey Bars

These bars go above and beyond the call of duty to satisfy a sweet tooth!
Macadamia nuts and scrumptious caramel top a chocolate chip cookie base.

Tubes of refrigerator chocolate chip cookie dough (18 oz., 510 g, each)	2	2
Package of caramel apple wraps	6 1/2 oz.	184 g
Coarsely chopped raw macadamia nuts	3/4 cup	175 mL
Skor (or Heath) bars (1 1/2 oz., 39 g, each), chopped	3	3

Let cookie dough stand at room temperature for about 15 minutes until starting to soften. Press into ungreased 9 × 13 inch (22 × 33 cm) pan. Bake in 375ºF (190ºC) oven for about 20 minutes until wooden pick inserted in centre comes out clean.

Arrange caramel wraps on top of cookie in pan to cover. Sprinkle with nuts and Skor pieces. Bake for another 5 minutes until Skor pieces and caramel are melted. Let stand on wire rack for 1 hour. Cuts into 32 bars.

1 bar: 206 Calories; 10.7 g Total Fat (5.2 g Mono, 0.7 g Poly, 3 g Sat); 10 mg Cholesterol; 26 g Carbohydrate; trace Fibre; 2 g Protein; 89 mg Sodium

Pictured on page 126.

1. Ooey Gooey Bars, above
2. Pineapple Ginger Carrots, page 104
3. Wild Rice Medley, page 105
4. Glazed Pork Roast, page 84

Props courtesy of: Casa Bugatti
Danesco Inc.

VIP Cookies

Dark chocolate coats a peanut butter sandwich cookie. Sweet and addictive!
Treat some very important person to a gift of cookies.

Smooth peanut butter	1/2 cup	125 mL
Vanilla wafers	48	48
Semi-sweet chocolate baking squares	8	8
(1 oz., 28 g, each), chopped		
Hard margarine (or butter)	1 tbsp.	15 mL

Spread peanut butter on bottom of 24 wafers. Cover with remaining wafers. Chill for about 1 hour until peanut butter is firm.

Heat chocolate and margarine in small heavy saucepan on lowest heat, stirring often, until chocolate is almost melted. Do not overheat. Remove from heat. Stir until smooth. Transfer to heatproof 1 cup (250 mL) liquid measure set in bowl of hot water. Hot water will prevent chocolate from hardening. Dip cookies into chocolate mixture until coated, allowing excess to drip back into liquid measure. Place on waxed paper-lined cookie sheet. Let stand until set. Drizzle any remaining chocolate in decorative pattern over cookies. Makes 2 dozen (24) cookies.

1 cookie: 118 Calories; 7.4 g Total Fat (3.1 g Mono, 1.2 g Poly, 2.6 g Sat); 5 mg Cholesterol; 13 g Carbohydrate; 1 g Fibre; 2 g Protein; 58 mg Sodium

Pictured on page 143.
Pictured on page 143.

Paré Pointer

Garage sales offer a good service. They distribute
all their junk to lots of other garages.

Five-Spice Nut Crunch

A crunchy snack. These slightly sweet pecans are made for sharing with friends. Easy to double for a party.

Egg white (large)	1	1
Brown sugar, packed	1/3 cup	75 mL
Chinese five-spice powder	2 tsp.	10 mL
Pecan halves	3 cups	750 mL

Beat egg white in large bowl until frothy. Add brown sugar and five-spice powder. Stir well.

Add pecans. Stir until coated. Spread on parchment paper-lined baking sheet with sides. Bake in 350ºF (175ºC) oven for about 15 minutes, stirring occasionally, until golden and dry. Makes about 3 cups (750 mL).

1/4 cup (60 mL): 218 Calories; 19.5 g Total Fat (12.1 g Mono, 4.8 g Poly, 1.6 g Sat); 0 mg Cholesterol; 12 g Carbohydrate; 2 g Fibre; 3 g Protein; 8 mg Sodium

Pictured on page 17.

Blondie Brownies

Crunchy nuts and caramel flavour in a cake-like brownie. A not-too-sweet treat that's ready in a jiffy!

Biscuit mix	2 cups	500 mL
Brown sugar, packed	1 1/2 cups	375 mL
Large eggs	3	3
Chopped pecans	1 cup	250 mL

Beat first 3 ingredients in large bowl for about 3 minutes until smooth.

Add pecans. Stir. Spread in greased 9 x 9 inch (22 x 22 cm) pan. Bake in 350ºF (175ºC) oven for about 30 minutes until wooden pick inserted in centre comes out clean. Let stand on wire rack for 10 minutes. Cuts into 36 squares.

1 square: 98 Calories; 3.9 g Total Fat (2 g Mono, 1.1 g Poly, 0.6 g Sat); 18 mg Cholesterol; 15 g Carbohydrate; trace Fibre; 1 g Protein; 105 mg Sodium

Pictured on page 143.

Grab-And-Go Squares

A sweet, gooey blend of crunchy cereal and chewy dried fruit. Wrap individual squares tightly with plastic wrap, and they're ready to go! Are you?

Raisin bran cereal, coarsely crushed	6 cups	1.5 L
Chopped dried apricot	1/2 cup	125 mL
Hard margarine (or butter)	1/4 cup	60 mL
Package of miniature marshmallows	9 oz.	250 g

Combine cereal and apricot in extra-large bowl.

Melt margarine in large saucepan on medium. Add marshmallows. Heat and stir until smooth. Pour over cereal mixture. Stir until coated. Press in greased 9 x 13 inch (22 x 33 cm) pan. Chill until firm. Cuts into 15 squares.

1 square: 166 Calories; 3.6 g Total Fat (2.1 g Mono, 0.3 g Poly, 0.7 g Sat); 0 mg Cholesterol; 35 g Carbohydrate; 3 g Fibre; 2 g Protein; 186 mg Sodium

Pictured on page 144.

Strawberry Margarita Pie

This creamy strawberry filling tastes just like a strawberry margarita.

Box of strawberry-flavoured jelly powder (gelatin)	3 oz.	85 g
Medium limes	2	2
Frozen whipped topping, thawed	2 cups	500 mL
Chocolate crumb crust (9 inch, 22 cm, diameter)	1	1

Measure 3/4 cup (175 mL) boiling water into large heatproof bowl. Add jelly powder. Stir until dissolved. Grate 1 tsp. (5 mL) lime zest into small bowl. Squeeze lime juice. Add water, if needed, to make 1/2 cup (125 mL). Stir. Add to jelly mixture. Stir. Chill for at least 45 minutes, stirring occasionally, until very thick and starting to set. Beat for about 3 minutes until fluffy.

Fold in whipped topping until just combined. Spread in crumb crust. Chill for at least 2 hours until set. Cuts into 8 wedges.

1 wedge: 249 Calories; 13.7 g Total Fat (4.4 g Mono, 2.3 g Poly, 6.2 g Sat); 0 mg Cholesterol; 31 g Carbohydrate; trace Fibre; 3 g Protein; 220 mg Sodium

Pictured on page 143.

Desserts & Snacks

Hit-The-Trail Bars

Nutty, toasted-oat granola bars are a great snack. Wrap individual bars tightly with plastic wrap so they're ready to hit the trail when you are!

Quick-cooking rolled oats	4 cups	1 L
Coarsely chopped whole (or sliced) natural almonds	2 cups	500 mL
Can of sweetened condensed milk	11 oz.	300 mL
Hard margarine (or butter), melted	1/2 cup	125 mL

Combine rolled oats and almonds in large bowl.

Add condensed milk and margarine. Mix well. Spread in well-greased 10 × 15 inch (25 × 38 cm) jelly roll pan. Bake in 325ºF (160ºC) oven for about 25 minutes until golden. Let stand on wire rack for 5 to 10 minutes until slightly cooled. Cut while still warm into 16 bars.

1 bar: 333 Calories; 18.9 g Total Fat (10.9 g Mono, 3.2 g Poly, 3.7 g Sat); 8 mg Cholesterol; 34 g Carbohydrate; 4 g Fibre; 9 g Protein; 104 mg Sodium

Pictured on page 144.

Frozen Yogurt Tarts

Keep a supply of these creamy berry tarts in your freezer for a quick treat when company drops by.

Frozen mini tart shells, thawed	24	24
Container of blueberry yogurt	6 oz.	175 g
Block of cream cheese, softened	4 oz.	125 g
Blueberry jam	1/2 cup	125 mL

Place tart shells on baking sheet. Bake in 375ºF (190ºC) oven for 10 to 15 minutes until golden. Cool.

Beat remaining 3 ingredients in small bowl until smooth. Spoon into tart shells. Freeze for about 2 hours until firm. Makes 24 tarts.

1 tart: 91 Calories; 5 g Total Fat (2 g Mono, 0.5 g Poly, 2.2 g Sat); 6 mg Cholesterol; 11 g Carbohydrate; trace Fibre; 1 g Protein; 82 mg Sodium

Desserts & Snacks

Snap Brownies

Ready in a snap! These moist treats are just the ticket
when you want something sweet.

Unsweetened chocolate baking squares (1 oz., 28 g, each), chopped	3	3
Can of sweetened condensed milk	11 oz.	300 mL
Finely crushed vanilla wafers (about 48 wafers)	1 2/3 cups	400 mL
Chopped walnuts	1/2 cup	125 mL

Heat chocolate in large heavy saucepan on lowest heat, stirring often, until almost melted. Do not overheat. Remove from heat. Stir until smooth.

Add condensed milk. Stir. Add wafer crumbs and walnuts. Mix well. Spread in greased 8 × 8 inch (20 × 20 cm) pan. Bake in 300ºF (150ºC) oven for about 30 minutes until wooden pick inserted in centre comes out moist but not wet with batter. Do not overbake. Cool. Cuts into 25 squares.

1 square: 117 Calories; 5.9 g Total Fat (1.8 g Mono, 1.4 g Poly, 2.3 g Sat); 10 mg Cholesterol; 15 g Carbohydrate; 1 g Fibre; 3 g Protein; 44 mg Sodium

Pictured on page 143.

Chocolate Crunch Cookies

Easy to make, with outstanding results. Crispy outside, chewy inside—so good!

Large eggs	2	2
Cooking oil	1/4 cup	60 mL
Package of devil's food cake mix (1 layer size)	1	1
Skor (or Heath) bars (1 1/2 oz., 39 g, each), coarsely chopped	3	3

Beat eggs and cooking oil in medium bowl until combined. Add cake mix. Beat until just moistened.

(continued on next page)

Desserts & Snacks

Add Skor pieces. Mix until stiff dough forms. Roll into balls, using 2 tsp. (10 mL) for each cookie. Arrange 2 inches (5 cm) apart on greased cookie sheets. Bake in 350ºF (175ºC) oven for about 10 minutes until tops are domed and cracked. Let stand on cookie sheets for 5 minutes before removing to wire racks to cool. Makes about 4 dozen (48) cookies.

1 cookie: 47 Calories; 3 g Total Fat (1.1 g Mono, 0.6 g Poly, 0.3 g Sat); 10 mg Cholesterol; 5 g Carbohydrate; 0 g Fibre; 1 g Protein; 47 mg Sodium

Pictured on page 125.

Quick Cheesecake Pie

A tangy, light-textured filling in a sweet graham crust.
Delectable cheesecake flavour, without the fuss!

Tub of strawberry light spreadable cream cheese, softened	8 oz.	250 g
Icing (confectioner's) sugar	1 cup	250 mL
Frozen whipped topping, thawed, divided	2 cups	500 mL
Graham cracker crust (9 inch, 22 cm, diameter)	1	1

Beat cream cheese and icing sugar in large bowl until smooth.

Reserve 1/2 cup (125 mL) whipped topping in small bowl. Fold remaining whipped topping into cream cheese mixture. Spread in graham crust. Chill for at least 1 hour until firm. Cut into 6 wedges. Serve with a dollop of reserved whipped topping. Serves 6.

1 serving: 457 Calories; 24.7 g Total Fat (7.5 g Mono, 3.2 g Poly, 12.5 g Sat); 26 mg Cholesterol; 55 g Carbohydrate; 0 g Fibre; 6 g Protein; 525 mg Sodium

Paré Pointer
Lawyers are disbarred, clergy defrocked, electricians delighted, musicians denoted, cowboys deranged, and dry cleaners depressed.

Cranberry Macaroons

You'll be over the moon when you taste these
easy-to-make macaroons! Extra special with tart cranberries.

Egg whites (large), room temperature	2	2
Granulated sugar	3/4 cup	175 mL
Shredded (long thread) coconut	3/4 cup	175 mL
Chopped dried cranberries	3/4 cup	175 mL

Beat egg whites and a pinch of salt in medium bowl until soft peaks form. Add sugar 1 tbsp. (15 mL) at a time, beating constantly until stiff peaks form and sugar is dissolved.

Fold in coconut and cranberries. Drop, using 1 tbsp. (15 mL) for each cookie, about 2 inches (5 cm) apart onto greased cookie sheets. Bake in 325ºF (160ºC) oven for about 15 minutes until golden. Let stand on cookie sheets for 5 minutes before removing to wire racks to cool. Makes about 32 macaroons.

1 macaroon: 40 Calories; 1.5 g Total Fat (0.1 g Mono, 0 g Poly, 1.3 g Sat); 0 mg Cholesterol; 7 g Carbohydrate; 1 g Fibre; 0 g Protein; 4 mg Sodium

Pumpkin Streusel Squares

This delightful cake is moist and cratered in the middle.
Serve with a scoop of ice cream or a dollop of whipped cream.

Box of orange cake mix (2 layer size), divided	1	1
Hard margarine (or butter), melted	3/4 cup	175 mL
Large eggs, divided	3	3
Can of pumpkin pie filling	19 oz.	540 mL

Reserve 3/4 cup (175 mL) cake mix in small bowl. Beat remaining cake mix, margarine, 1 egg and 1/4 cup (60 mL) water in medium bowl for about 1 minute until smooth. Spread in greased 9 x 13 inch (22 x 33 cm) pan.

(continued on next page)

Beat remaining 2 eggs in same bowl until frothy. Add pie filling. Beat well. Pour over batter in pan. Sift reserved cake mix over top. Bake in 350ºF (175ºC) oven for about 45 minutes until set and wooden pick inserted in centre comes out moist but not wet with batter. Do not overbake. Cool. Cuts into 24 squares.

1 square: 182 Calories; 9.2 g Total Fat (5.2 g Mono, 1.6 g Poly, 1.8 g Sat); 27 mg Cholesterol; 24 g Carbohydrate; 0 g Fibre; 2 g Protein; 272 mg Sodium

Express Tropical Trifle

A taste of the tropics—pineapple sweetens the ever-popular banana cream combo and moistens a layer of fluffy vanilla cake.

Package of Twinkies, each halved lengthwise	11 oz.	300 g
Cans of crushed pineapple (14 oz., 398 mL, each), with juice	2	2
Large bananas, sliced	4	4
Frozen whipped topping, thawed	4 cups	1 L

Arrange Twinkie halves, filling-side up, in ungreased 9 x 13 inch (22 x 33 cm) baking dish.

Spoon 1 can of pineapple with juice onto cakes. Scatter banana slices over pineapple. Spoon remaining can of pineapple with juice on top of banana.

Spread whipped topping over pineapple to sides of baking dish. Chill for 2 hours. Serves 12.

1 serving: 252 Calories; 9.8 g Total Fat (1.6 g Mono, 1.1 g Poly, 6.5 g Sat); 4 mg Cholesterol; 42 g Carbohydrate; 1 g Fibre; 2 g Protein; 99 mg Sodium

Paré Pointer

What do you have if you cross a centipede with a parrot?
A walkie–talkie!

Liquid Gold Sauce

This warm sauce will add sparkle to vanilla ice cream or a chocolate dessert. Tastes great over angel food cake and berries too!

Granulated sugar	1 cup	250 mL
Milk	1/2 cup	125 mL
Butter (or hard margarine)	1/4 cup	60 mL
Orange liqueur	2 tbsp.	30 mL

Heat and stir first 3 ingredients in medium saucepan on medium until boiling and sugar is dissolved. Boil gently for 5 minutes. Remove from heat. Add liqueur. Stir. Makes about 1 cup (250 mL).

2 tbsp. (30 mL): 165 Calories; 6.1 g Total Fat (1.8 g Mono, 0.2 g Poly, 3.8 g Sat); 17 mg Cholesterol; 26 g Carbohydrate; 0 g Fibre; 1 g Protein; 68 mg Sodium

Lively Lime Pie

A quick and easy tropical treat! Perfect for a summer luncheon. Keep in the freezer until ready to serve.

Block of cream cheese, softened	8 oz.	250 g
Can of sweetened condensed milk	11 oz.	300 mL
Medium limes	2	2
Graham cracker crust (9 inch, 22 cm, diameter)	1	1

Beat cream cheese in medium bowl for about 3 minutes until smooth. Slowly add condensed milk, beating constantly until combined.

Grate 2 tsp. (10 mL) lime zest into small bowl. Squeeze lime juice. Add water, if needed, to make 1/2 cup (125 mL). Add to cream cheese mixture. Beat well. Spread in graham crust. Freeze for at least 4 hours until firm. Cuts into 8 wedges.

1 wedge: 417 Calories; 22.6 g Total Fat (7.7 g Mono, 2.6 g Poly, 11.1 g Sat); 51 mg Cholesterol; 48 g Carbohydrate; trace Fibre; 8 g Protein; 325 mg Sodium

Brownie Cookies

Dense and delicious two-bite treats. Keep lots on hand—they won't last long!

Unsweetened chocolate baking squares (1 oz., 28 g, each), chopped	2	2
Chocolate hazelnut spread	1/4 cup	60 mL
Graham cracker crumbs	2 cups	500 mL
Can of sweetened condensed milk	11 oz.	300 mL

Melt chocolate in large heavy saucepan on lowest heat, stirring often, until almost melted. Do not overheat. Remove from heat. Add chocolate hazelnut spread. Stir until smooth.

Add graham crumbs and condensed milk. Stir until stiff batter forms. Drop, using 1 tbsp. (15 mL) for each cookie, about 2 inches (5 cm) apart onto greased cookie sheets. Bake in 375ºF (190ºC) oven for 8 to 10 minutes until edges are set. Centres will be soft. Immediately remove to wire racks to cool. Makes about 3 dozen (36) cookies.

1 cookie: 75 Calories; 3.3 g Total Fat (1.3 g Mono, 0.4 g Poly, 1.4 g Sat); 4 mg Cholesterol; 10 g Carbohydrate; trace Fibre; 2 g Protein; 53 mg Sodium

Peanut Butter Fudge

Fluffy fudge quickly made from simple ingredients. Sure to disappear just as fast! Serve chilled.

Granulated sugar	2 cups	500 mL
Milk	1/2 cup	125 mL
Chunky peanut butter	1 1/2 cups	375 mL
Jar of marshmallow creme	7 oz.	198 g

Heat and stir sugar and milk in heavy medium saucepan on medium until boiling and sugar is dissolved. Boil gently for about 3 minutes, stirring constantly, until slightly thickened. Remove from heat.

Add peanut butter and marshmallow creme. Stir until smooth. Spread in greased 8 x 8 inch (20 x 20 cm) pan. Chill for at least 3 hours until set. Cuts into 64 squares.

1 square: 74 Calories; 3.2 g Total Fat (1.5 g Mono, 0.9 g Poly, 0.6 g Sat); 0 mg Cholesterol; 11 g Carbohydrate; trace Fibre; 2 g Protein; 34 mg Sodium

Cranapple Tarts

A fresh, tart filling that's a lovely ruby red. Dress these
up with a whipped cream rosette or a dusting of icing sugar.

Small cooking apples (such as McIntosh), peeled and cut up	2	2
Fresh (or frozen, thawed) cranberries	2 cups	500 mL
White corn syrup	1 cup	250 mL
Unbaked tart shells	24	24

Process first 3 ingredients in blender or food processor until cranberries are finely chopped. Transfer to medium bowl.

Place tart shells on baking sheets. Spoon fruit mixture into shells. Bake in 400°F (205°C) oven for about 20 minutes until pastry is golden and filling is bubbling. Remove to wire racks to cool. Makes 24 tarts.

1 tart: 115 Calories; 4.1 g Total Fat (2 g Mono, 0.5 g Poly, 1.3 g Sat); 0 mg Cholesterol;
20 g Carbohydrate; 1 g Fibre; 1 g Protein; 98 mg Sodium

Butterscotch Pumpkin Pie

This custard-style dessert is a delicious alternative to traditional
pumpkin pie. You can freeze the second pie to enjoy later.

Large eggs	3	3
Butterscotch ripple ice cream, melted	3 cups	750 mL
Can of pumpkin pie filling	19 oz.	540 mL
Graham cracker crusts (9 inch, 22 cm, diameter, each)	2	2

Beat eggs in large bowl until frothy. Add ice cream and pie filling. Stir until smooth.

Pour filling into graham crusts. Bake in 350°F (175°C) oven for about 45 to 50 minutes until filling is set. Let stand on wire racks until cooled completely. Each pie cuts into 8 wedges, for a total of 16 wedges.

1 wedge: 254 Calories; 11.3 g Total Fat (4.6 g Mono, 2.3 g Poly, 3.6 g Sat); 52 mg Cholesterol;
36 g Carbohydrate; 0 g Fibre; 4 g Protein; 284 mg Sodium

Butterscotch Shortbread

Short on time? Here's a speedy answer to what to serve for tea!
The brown sugar creates the butterscotch flavour in this rich shortbread.

Butter, softened	1 cup	250 mL
Brown sugar, packed	2/3 cup	150 mL
All-purpose flour	2 cups	500 mL
Graham cracker crumbs	1/2 cup	125 mL

Cream butter and brown sugar in medium bowl.

Combine flour and graham crumbs in small bowl. Add to butter mixture. Mix until soft, slightly crumbly dough forms. Turn out onto lightly floured surface. Knead for about 2 minutes until smooth. Press into ungreased 8 x 8 inch (20 x 20 cm) pan. Prick top of dough in several places with a fork. Score dough into 12 rectangles with sharp knife. Score rectangles diagonally into 24 triangles. Bake in 300ºF (150ºC) oven for about 30 minutes until edges are golden. Let stand in pan on wire rack until cooled completely. Cut along scoring into 24 triangles.

1 triangle: 144 Calories; 8.4 g Total Fat (2.4 g Mono, 0.4 g Poly, 5.1 g Sat); 22 mg Cholesterol; 16 g Carbohydrate; trace Fibre; 1 g Protein; 97 mg Sodium

Baked Pears

A simple, elegant dessert. Nice as is, or serve with vanilla ice cream.

Fresh pears, peeled, halved lengthwlse, cores removed	4	4
Corn syrup	1/2 cup	125 mL
Lemon juice	2 tbsp.	30 mL
Ground cinnamon	1/2 tsp.	2 mL

Arrange pear halves, cut-side down, in ungreased 3 quart (3 L) casserole. Score decorative pattern on pears.

Combine remaining 3 ingredients in small cup. Pour over pears. Bake, covered, in 350ºF (175ºC) oven for about 30 minutes until tender. Spoon sauce from casserole over individual servings. Serves 4.

1 serving: 170 Calories; 0.1 g Total Fat (0 g Mono, 0 g Poly, 0 g Sat); 0 mg Cholesterol; 46 g Carbohydrate; 3 g Fibre; 0 g Protein; 56 mg Sodium

Desserts & Snacks

Mudsicle Pie

Serve this pie straight from the freezer.

Box of instant chocolate pudding powder (6 serving size)	1	1
Chocolate ice cream, softened	2 cups	500 mL
Chocolate milk	1/2 cup	125 mL
Chocolate crumb crust (9 inch, 22 cm, diameter)	1	1

Beat first 3 ingredients in medium bowl for about 2 minutes until thickened.

Spread filling in crumb crust. Freeze for at least 3 hours until firm. Cuts into 8 wedges.

1 wedge: 304 Calories; 13.2 g Total Fat (5.5 g Mono, 2.4 g Poly, 4.6 g Sat); 13 mg Cholesterol; 45 g Carbohydrate; trace Fibre; 4 g Protein; 527 mg Sodium

Orange Cream Cake

Dust with icing sugar for a pretty finish.

Large oranges	2 – 3	2 – 3
Box of orange cake mix (2 layer size)	1	1
Large eggs	4	4
Envelope of dessert topping (not prepared)	1	1

Grate 2 tbsp. (30 mL) orange zest into large bowl. Squeeze and add 1 cup (250 mL) orange juice.

Add remaining 3 ingredients. Beat on medium for about 2 minutes until smooth. Pour into greased and floured 12 cup (3 L) bundt pan. Bake in 350ºF (175ºC) oven for about 45 minutes until wooden pick inserted in centre of cake comes out clean. Let stand in pan on wire rack for 15 minutes. Tap pan gently on countertop to loosen cake. Invert onto wire rack to cool completely. Cuts into 12 wedges.

1 wedge: 245 Calories; 8.2 g Total Fat (2.8 g Mono, 2.2 g Poly, 2.6 g Sat); 73 mg Cholesterol; 39 g Carbohydrate; trace Fibre; 4 g Protein; 312 mg Sodium

Anise Orange Ice

Heady licorice-scented orange sherbet. Incredibly refreshing!

Granulated sugar	2 1/2 cups	625 mL
Star anise	3	3
Frozen concentrated orange juice	1/2 cup	125 mL
Grated orange zest	1 tsp.	5 mL

Combine sugar, anise and 5 cups (1.25 L) water in medium saucepan. Bring to a boil. Reduce heat to medium. Boil gently for 5 minutes. Remove from heat.

Add concentrated orange juice and zest. Stir. Discard anise. Cool. Chill, covered, for at least 3 hours until very cold. Pour into ice cream maker (see Note). Follow manufacturer's instructions. Makes about 6 cups (1.5 L).

1 cup (250 mL): 381 Calories; 0.1 g Total Fat (0 g Mono, 0 g Poly, 0 g Sat); 0 mg Cholesterol; 98 g Carbohydrate; trace Fibre; 1 g Protein; 2 mg Sodium

Note: If you don't have an ice cream maker, pour the mixture into a 9 x 9 inch (22 x 22 cm) pan. Freeze, stirring every hour for 4 hours. The texture will be flakier, but the flavour will not be affected.

Ginger Cream Fudge

Zippy ginger and a snappy crunch in a smooth white fudge. Makes a great gift!

Can of sweetened condensed milk	11 oz.	300 mL
White chocolate chips	2 1/2 cups	625 mL
Gingersnaps, broken into small pieces	10	10
Minced crystallized ginger	2 tbsp.	30 mL

Heat condensed milk in heavy medium saucepan on medium-low for about 7 minutes, stirring occasionally, until hot but not boiling. Add chocolate chips. Stir until smooth. Remove from heat.

Add gingersnap pieces and ginger. Stir. Spread in greased 8 x 8 inch (20 x 20 cm) pan. Chill for at least 2 hours until firm. Cuts into 64 squares.

1 square: 69 Calories; 2.9 g Total Fat (1 g Mono, 0.1 g Poly, 1.6 g Sat); 4 mg Cholesterol; 10 g Carbohydrate; trace Fibre; 1 g Protein; 32 mg Sodium

Fruity Nut Clusters

A combination of sweet and crunchy in a blond haystack treat.
Keeps well in an airtight container for one week.

White chocolate chips	2 cups	500 mL
Dry chow mein noodles	2/3 cup	150 mL
Salted peanuts	1/2 cup	125 mL
Chopped dried apricot	1/3 cup	75 mL

Heat chocolate chips in heavy medium saucepan on lowest heat, stirring often, until almost melted. Do not overheat. Remove from heat. Stir until smooth.

Add remaining 3 ingredients. Stir until coated. Drop, using 1 tbsp. (15 mL) for each cluster, onto waxed paper-lined baking sheet. Let stand until set. Makes about 22 clusters.

1 cluster: 120 Calories; 7.2 g Total Fat (2.5 g Mono, 0.9 g Poly, 3.2 g Sat); 4 mg Cholesterol; 13 g Carbohydrate; 1 g Fibre; 2 g Protein; 50 mg Sodium

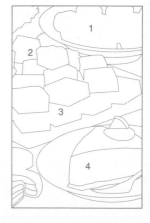

1. VIP Cookies, page 128
2. Blondie Brownies, page 129
3. Snap Brownies, page 132
4. Strawberry Margarita Pie, page 130

Props courtesy of: Casa Bugatti
　　　　　　　　Cherison Enterprises Inc.

Marble Top Snack Cake

A marbled top adds a dramatic flair to these squares. Great with coffee or tea.

Large eggs, divided	5	5
Package of brownie mix	2 lbs.	900 g
Block of cream cheese, softened	8 oz.	250 g
Brown sugar, packed	1/2 cup	125 mL

Beat 3 eggs in large bowl until frothy. Add brownie mix and 1/2 cup (125 mL) water. Beat until smooth. Spread in greased 9 × 13 inch (22 × 33 cm) pan.

Beat cream cheese, brown sugar and remaining 2 eggs in medium bowl until smooth. Pour over brownie mixture. Swirl knife through batter to create marbled effect. Bake in 350°F (175°C) oven for about 50 minutes until wooden pick inserted in centre comes out moist but not wet with batter. Do not overbake. Cool. Cuts into 24 squares.

1 square: 233 Calories; 10.3 g Total Fat (3.3 g Mono, 2.3 g Poly, 3.9 g Sat); 56 mg Cholesterol; 34 g Carbohydrate; 0 g Fibre; 4 g Protein; 159 mg Sodium

1. Hit-The-Trail Bars, page 131
2. Breakfast Bars, page 52
3. Grab-And-Go Squares, page 130

Props courtesy of: Out of the Fire Studio

Crunchy Cherry Cobbler

Cherry and pineapple are tucked under a sweet, crunchy crust that delivers a big vanilla taste. Double the cherries if you want a deeper fruit layer. Serve warm or cold with vanilla ice cream.

Can of cherry pie filling	19 oz.	540 mL
Can of crushed pineapple (with juice)	14 oz.	398 mL
Hard margarine (or butter)	1/2 cup	125 mL
Box of yellow (or white) cake mix (2 layer size)	1	1

Spread cherry pie filling in ungreased 9 x 13 inch (22 x 33 cm) baking dish. Spoon pineapple with juice on top of cherries.

Melt margarine in large saucepan on medium. Remove from heat. Add cake mix. Stir until moistened. Scatter over pineapple in baking dish. Bake in 350°F (175°C) oven for about 50 minutes until golden. Serves 15.

1 serving: 271 Calories; 10.6 g Total Fat (5.9 g Mono, 2.2 g Poly, 2 g Sat); 1 mg Cholesterol; 43 g Carbohydrate; trace Fibre; 2 g Protein; 309 mg Sodium

Fiesta Popcorn

Make this southwestern-style popcorn to share with all your amigos.

Grated Parmesan cheese	1/2 cup	125 mL
Chili powder	1 tbsp.	15 mL
Lemon pepper	1 tsp.	5 mL
Bag of butter-flavoured microwave popcorn	3 1/2 oz.	99 g

Combine first 3 ingredients in small bowl.

Prepare popcorn according to package directions. Put into large bowl. Sprinkle with Parmesan cheese mixture. Toss until coated. Makes about 8 cups (2 L).

1 cup (250 mL): 61 Calories; 3.7 g Total Fat (1 g Mono, 0.8 g Poly, 1.5 g Sat); 5 mg Cholesterol; 4 g Carbohydrate; 1 g Fibre; 3 g Protein; 256 mg Sodium

Desserts & Snacks

Berry Mini-Cheesecakes

Berry jam swirled in creamy cheesecakes. A yummy dessert that freezes well. Keep these on hand for unexpected company.

Cream-filled chocolate cookies	12	12
Tubs of berry spreadable cream cheese (8 oz., 250 g, each)	2	2
Large eggs	2	2
Berry jam	2 tbsp.	30 mL

Line 12 ungreased muffin cups with paper liners. Spray liners with cooking spray. Place cookies in liners.

Beat cream cheese until smooth. Add eggs 1 at a time, beating well after each addition. Spoon onto cookies.

Measure jam into small cup. Stir until smooth. Spoon onto cream cheese mixture. Swirl with wooden pick to create marbled effect. Bake in 325°F (160°C) oven for about 20 minutes until set. Let stand in pan on wire rack for 1 hour. Chill for at least 1 hour until firm. Makes 12 mini-cheesecakes.

1 mini-cheesecake: 161 Calories; 11 g Total Fat (4 g Mono, 0.7 g Poly, 5.3 g Sat); 62 mg Cholesterol; 11 g Carbohydrate; trace Fibre; 5 g Protein; 363 mg Sodium

Pictured on page 71.

Paré Pointer

An accountant solves a problem that you didn't know you had, and explains it in a way that you don't understand.

Berry Shortcake

Strawberry shortcake is even more inviting
with the added goodness of blueberries. Yum!

Vanilla sponge cake, 2 layers (6 inch, 15 cm, diameter)	1	1
Container of frozen strawberries in light syrup, thawed	15 oz.	425 g
Frozen blueberries, thawed	1 1/2 cups	375 mL
Frozen whipped topping, thawed (or whipped cream)	1 cup	250 mL

Place 1 cake layer, flat-side up, on large serving plate. Poke cake in several places with wooden skewer.

Spoon 1/2 of strawberries with syrup onto cake, allowing some syrup to run down side. Sprinkle with 1/2 of blueberries. Cover with second cake layer, flat-side down. Poke second cake layer in several places with wooden skewer. Top with remaining berries and syrup. Chill, covered, for at least 2 hours to allow cake to absorb syrup.

Cut into 6 wedges. Serve with a dollop of whipped topping. Serves 6.

1 serving: 239 Calories; 4.8 g Total Fat (0.6 g Mono, 0.3 g Poly, 3.2 g Sat); 43 mg Cholesterol; 49 g Carbohydrate; 3 g Fibre; 3 g Protein; 106 mg Sodium

Paré Pointer
You know you're in trouble when your
knees buckle but your belt won't.

Measurement Tables

Throughout this book measurements are given in Conventional and Metric measure. To compensate for differences between the two measurements due to rounding, a full metric measure is not always used. The cup used is the standard 8 fluid ounce. Temperature is given in degrees Fahrenheit and Celsius. Baking pan measurements are in inches and centimetres as well as quarts and litres. An exact metric conversion is given below as well as the working equivalent (Metric Standard Measure).

Spoons

Conventional Measure	Metric Exact Conversion Millilitre (mL)	Metric Standard Measure Millilitre (mL)
1/8 teaspoon (tsp.)	0.6 mL	0.5 mL
1/4 teaspoon (tsp.)	1.2 mL	1 mL
1/2 teaspoon (tsp.)	2.4 mL	2 mL
1 teaspoon (tsp.)	4.7 mL	5 mL
2 teaspoons (tsp.)	9.4 mL	10 mL
1 tablespoon (tbsp.)	14.2 mL	15 mL

Cups

Conventional Measure	Metric Exact Conversion Millilitre (mL)	Metric Standard Measure Millilitre (mL)
1/4 cup (4 tbsp.)	56.8 mL	60 mL
1/3 cup (5 1/3 tbsp.)	75.6 mL	75 mL
1/2 cup (8 tbsp.)	113.7 mL	125 mL
2/3 cup (10 2/3 tbsp.)	151.2 mL	150 mL
3/4 cup (12 tbsp.)	170.5 mL	175 mL
1 cup (16 tbsp.)	227.3 mL	250 mL
4 1/2 cups	1022.9 mL	1000 mL (1 L)

Oven Temperatures

Fahrenheit (°F)	Celsius (°C)
175°	80°
200°	95°
225°	110°
250°	120°
275°	140°
300°	150°
325°	160°
350°	175°
375°	190°
400°	205°
425°	220°
450°	230°
475°	240°
500°	260°

Dry Measurements

Conventional Measure Ounces (oz.)	Metric Exact Conversion Grams (g)	Metric Standard Measure Grams (g)
1 oz.	28.3 g	28 g
2 oz.	56.7 g	57 g
3 oz.	85.0 g	85 g
4 oz.	113.4 g	125 g
5 oz.	141.7 g	140 g
6 oz.	170.1 g	170 g
7 oz.	198.4 g	200 g
8 oz.	226.8 g	250 g
16 oz.	453.6 g	500 g
32 oz.	907.2 g	1000 g (1 kg)

Pans

Conventional Inches	Metric Centimetres
8x8 inch	20x20 cm
9x9 inch	22x22 cm
9x13 inch	22x33 cm
10x15 inch	25x38 cm
11x17 inch	28x43 cm
8x2 inch round	20x5 cm
9x2 inch round	22x5 cm
10x4 1/2 inch tube	25x11 cm
8x4x3 inch loaf	20x10x7.5 cm
9x5x3 inch loaf	22x12.5x7.5 cm

Casseroles

CANADA & BRITAIN		UNITED STATES	
Standard Size Casserole	Exact Metric Measure	Standard Size Casserole	Exact Metric Measure
1 qt. (5 cups)	1.13 L	1 qt. (4 cups)	900 mL
1 1/2 qts. (7 1/2 cups)	1.69 L	1 1/2 qts. (6 cups)	1.35 L
2 qts. (10 cups)	2.25 L	2 qts. (8 cups)	1.8 L
2 1/2 qts. (12 1/2 cups)	2.81 L	2 1/2 qts. (10 cups)	2.25 L
3 qts. (15 cups)	3.38 L	3 qts. (12 cups)	2.7 L
4 qts. (20 cups)	4.5 L	4 qts. (16 cups)	3.6 L
5 qts. (25 cups)	5.63 L	5 qts. (20 cups)	4.5 L

Recipe Index

A

Alfredo Pie, Chicken............95
Alfredo, Saucy Polenta.............110
Aloha Pork Roast...............86
Anise Orange Ice................141
Antipasto Pasta Salad.............37
Appetizers
    Black Olive Spread...........13
    Cajun Crackers...........16
    Cheese Nippies.............21
    Crab Dip.............20
    Garlic Lime Pita Chips..........13
    Hawaiian Hammies............9
    Mmmmussels..........19
    Nutty Blue Cheese Dip..........20
    Quesadilla Bites...........14
    Salmon Cream Quiche.........9
    Salmon-Stuffed Brié..........15
    Spicy Feta Pâté...........14
    Spinach Cream Triangles.........10
    Taco Beef Snacks............12
    Thai Chicken Salad Wraps.........11
Apple Pork, Snappy..............87
Apple Slaw, Savoury..............38
Apricot Chicken, Ginger............96
Apricot Wasabi Salmon..........78
Asiago Soufflé...........58
Asian Chicken Stir-Fry..........92
Asian Cucumber Salad............38

B

Bake, Meaty Potato.............70
Baked Berry French Toast...........55
Baked Garlic Shrimp............78
Baked Pears.............139
Baked Tomato Chops............91
Barbecued Beef Ribs.............67
Bars
    Breakfast..........52
    Hit-The-Trail............131
    Ooey Gooey............127
Basil Couscous, Orange...........111
Bean Cakes, Salsa.............65
Beans, Greek.............102
Beef
    Barbecued Beef Ribs...........67
    Chutney Steak...........68
    Easy Pot Roast...........69

Meat And Potato Scallop..............66
Meaty Potato Bake...............70
Onion Beef Ragoût.............74
Pepper Steak..............74
Quickest Chili.............66
Stroganoff.............68
"Sweetish" Meatballs.............73
Taco Beef Snacks.............12
Beet Salad, Feta.............40
Bennies, Salmon-Sauced.............49
Berry Bran Shake.............56
Berry French Toast, Baked.........55
Berry Mini-Cheesecakes............147
Berry Shortcake.............148
Berry Vinaigrette, Pepper.............41
Biscuits
    Lemon Poppy Seed.............30
    Parmesan Olive.............30
    Pesto Parmesan.............28
    Tomato-Topped.............24
Bisque, Simple Seafood............46
Black Olive Spread.............13
Blondie Brownies.............129
Blue Cheese Dip, Nutty............20
Blue Cheese Pear Salad.............31
Blueberry Cream Pancakes............50
Bocconcini Salad, Tomato............32
Borscht, Shortcut.............48
Braid, Swirled Raisin.............25
Bran Shake, Berry.............56
Bratwurst, Sweet Onion............86
Breads
    Caramel Bubble Buns.............23
    Fast Focaccia.............29
    Feta Crescent Swirls.............22
    Garlic Cheese Loaf.............27
    Lemon Poppy Seed Biscuits.............30
    Onion Flatbread.............24
    Orange Cranberry Wedges.............28
    Parmesan Olive Biscuits.............30
    PBJ Ring.............51
    Pesto Parmesan Biscuits.............28
    Rugelach Roll-Ups.............26
    Swirled Raisin Braid.............25
    Tomato-Topped Biscuits.............24
    Tuscan Pull-Aparts.............26
Breakfast
    Baked Berry French Toast.............55
    Berry Bran Shake.............56
    Blueberry Cream Pancakes.............50
    Breakfast Bars.............52

Creamy Ginger Spread 57
Huevos Tortillas 56
Maui Oatmeal 50
PBJ Ring. 51
Salmon-Sauced Bennies. 49
Walnut Pear Dip. 57
eakfast Bars. 52
ie, Salmon-Stuffed 15
occoli
  Cheesy Broccoli Chicken 98
  Curried Broccoli Slaw. 33
  Four-Cheese Broccoli Soup 44
ownie Cookies 137
ownies, Blondie 129
ownies, Snap 132
ruschetta Dressing, Creamy 43
ruschetta Lentil Salad. 39
uns, Caramel Bubble 23
utterscotch Pumpkin Pie 138
utterscotch Shortbread 139

acciatore Sandwiches 59
ajun Crackers. 16
akes
  Berry Mini-Cheesecakes. 147
  Berry Shortcake 148
  Chocolate Hazelnut Angel 120
  Lemon Coconut Angel. 121
  Marble Top Snack 145
  Orange Cream. 140
annelloni, Turkey. 98
aramel Bubble Buns. 23
arrots, Pineapple Ginger 104
asseroles
  Chicken Alfredo Pie 95
  Creamed Spinach 112
  Hotsy Totsy 62
  Meat And Potato Scallop. 66
  Meaty Potato Bake. 70
  Perogy Ham. 83
  Sausage Pandowdy 60
aviar, Texas-Style 117
elery-Sauced Chops. 82
hai Ice Cream 122
heese Broccoli Soup, Four- 44
heese Loaf, Garlic 27
heese Nippies 21
heese Pizza, Chicken And 61
heesecake Pie, Quick. 133
heesecakes, Berry Mini- 147

Cheesy Broccoli Chicken 98
Cheesy Red Rice. 85
Cherry Cobbler, Crunchy 146
Chèvre Dressing, Dijon 43
Chicken Alfredo Pie 95
Chicken And Cheese Pizza 61
Chicken & Poultry
  Asian Chicken Stir-Fry 92
  Cacciatore Sandwiches 59
  Cheesy Broccoli Chicken 98
  Cranberry Pesto Chicken 96
  Garlic Chicken Pasta 92
  Ginger Apricot Chicken 96
  Olive Chicken Patties. 101
  Polynesian Chicken 97
  Savory Pineapple Chicken 93
  Sweet Orange Chicken 100
  Thai Chicken Salad Wraps 11
  Thai Chicken Soup. 47
  Turkey Cannelloni 98
Chicken Corn Spaghetti. 94
Chicken Shake. 99
Chili, Quickest 66
Chips, Garlic Lime Pita. 13
Chocolate Crunch Cookies. 132
Chocolate Hazelnut Angel. 120
Chops
  Baked Tomato 91
  Celery-Sauced 82
  Minted Lamb. 88
  Pork Chops Normandy 82
Chutney Steak 68
Clusters, Fruity Nut 142
Cobbler, Crunchy Cherry. 146
Coconut Angel, Lemon 121
Cod, Zippy Mustard 79
Colourful Couscous 118
Cookies
  Brownie. 137
  Butterscotch Shortbread 139
  Chocolate Crunch 132
  Cranberry Macaroons 134
  Fruity Nut Clusters. 142
  Rugelach Roll-Ups 26
  VIP. 128
Corn Spaghetti, Chicken 94
Couscous, Colourful. 118
Couscous Date Salad 40
Couscous, Orange Basil 111
Crab Dip 20
Crackers, Cajun 16

151

Cranapple Tarts 138
Cranberry Macaroons 134
Cranberry Pesto Chicken 96
Cranberry Salad, Spinach. 39
Cranberry Vinaigrette. 41
Cranberry Wedges, Orange 28
Cream Cake, Orange. 140
Cream Fudge, Ginger 141
Cream Pancakes, Blueberry 50
Cream Quiche, Salmon 9
Cream Triangles, Spinach. 10
Creamed Spinach Casserole. 112
Creamy Bruschetta Dressing 43
Creamy Curry Shrimp 76
Creamy Ginger Spread 57
Creamy Potato Salad 31
Crescent Swirls, Feta 22
Crunchy Cherry Cobbler 146
Cucumber Salad, Asian 38
Curried Broccoli Slaw. 33
Curry Noodle Bowl 48
Curry Rice, Ginger. 116
Curry Shrimp, Creamy. 76
Curry Vegetable Soup 45

D

Date Salad, Couscous 40
Desserts & Snacks (see also Bars, Cakes, Cookies, Pies, Squares)
    Anise Orange Ice 141
    Baked Pears 139
    Chai Ice Cream 122
    Cranapple Tarts 138
    Crunchy Cherry Cobbler 146
    Express Tropical Trifle. 135
    Fiesta Popcorn. 146
    Five-Spice Nut Crunch. 129
    Fruit Freeze 123
    Frozen Yogurt Tarts 131
    Ginger Cream Fudge 141
    Liquid Gold Sauce 136
    Peanut Butter Fudge 137
    Tangy Rice Parfaits. 124
Dijon Chèvre Dressing 43
Dijon Polenta, Grilled. 106
Dips
    Crab 20
    Nutty Blue Cheese. 20
    Walnut Pear. 57
Dry Ribs, Peppered 81

E

Easy Pot Roast 69
Express Tropical Trifle. 135

F

Fast Focaccia 29
Fennel Salad, Orange. 32
Feta Beet Salad 40
Feta Crescent Swirls. 22
Feta Pâté, Spicy 14
Feta Shrimp Frittata 63
Fettuccine, Lemon Tuna. 77
Fiesta Popcorn. 146
Fillets, Orange Herb Fish 80
Fish & Seafood
    Apricot Wasabi Salmon 78
    Baked Garlic Shrimp 78
    Crab Dip 20
    Creamy Curry Shrimp 76
    Feta Shrimp Frittata. 63
    Lemon Tuna Fettuccine 77
    MMMussels 19
    Orange Herb Fish Fillets. 80
    Salmon Cream Quiches. 9
    Salmon Lime Patties. 76
    Salmon-Sauced Bennies. 49
    Salmon-Stuffed Brie. 15
    Seafood Quesadillas. 62
    Shrimp-Stuffed Sole. 75
    Simple Seafood Bisque. 46
    Zippy Mustard Cod 79
Five-Spice Nut Crunch. 129
Flatbread, Onion 24
Focaccia, Fast. 29
Four-Cheese Broccoli Soup 44
Fragrant Rice 114
Freeze, Fruit. 123
French Toast, Baked Berry 55
Fries, Oven Ranch 102
Frittata, Feta Shrimp 63
Frozen Yogurt Tarts 131
Fruit Freeze 123
Fruity Nut Clusters. 142
Fruity Stuffing 104
Fudge, Ginger Cream 141
Fudge, Peanut Butter. 137

G

Garlic Cheese Loaf. 27
Garlic Chicken Pasta 92

152

Garlic Lime Pita Chips 13
Garlic Shrimp, Baked 78
Ginger Apricot Chicken 96
Ginger Carrots, Pineapple 104
Ginger Cream Fudge 141
Ginger Curry Rice 116
Ginger Spread, Creamy 57
Ginger Squash Soup 46
Glazed Ham Steak 81
Glazed Mushrooms 117
Glazed Pork Roast 84
Grab-And-Go Squares 130
Greek Beans 102
Grilled Dijon Polenta 106

H

Ham
    Cheesy Red Rice 85
    Glazed Ham Steak 81
    Havarti Ham Ring 60
    Hawaiian Hammies 9
    Perogy Ham Casserole 83
    Saucy Polenta Alfredo 110
    Savoury Apple Slaw 38
Havarti Ham Ring 60
Hawaiian Hammies 9
Hazelnut Angel, Chocolate 120
Herb Fish Fillets, Orange 80
Hit-The-Trail Bars 131
Hotsy Totsy Casserole 62
Huevos Tortillas 56

I

Ice, Anise Orange 141
Ice Cream, Chai 122

L

Lamb Chops, Minted 88
Lasagne, Mexican Meatless 64
Lasagne, Polenta 65
Lemon Coconut Angel 121
Lemon Poppy Seed Biscuits 30
Lemon Tuna Fettuccine 77
Lentil Salad, Bruschetta 39
Lentil Sauté, Spinach And 110
Lime Patties, Salmon 76
Lime Pie, Lively 136
Lime Pita Chips, Garlic 13
Liquid Gold Sauce 136

Lively Lime Pie 136
Loaf, Garlic Cheese 27
Lunch
    Asiago Soufflé 58
    Cacciatore Sandwiches 59
    Chicken And Cheese Pizza 61
    Feta Shrimp Frittata 63
    Havarti Ham Ring 60
    Hotsy Totsy Casserole 62
    Mexican Meatless Lasagne 64
    Polenta Lasagne 65
    Salsa Bean Cakes 65
    Sausage Pandowdy 60
    Seafood Quesadillas 62
    Sweet Yam Quesadilla 58

M

Macaroons, Cranberry 134
Marble Top Snack Cake 145
Margarita Pie, Strawberry 130
Maui Oatmeal 50
Mayonnaise, Wasabi 78
Meat And Potato Scallop 66
Meatballs, "Sweetish" 73
Meatless Lasagne, Mexican 64
Meaty Potato Bake 70
Mexican Meatless Lasagne 64
Mini-Cheesecakes, Berry 147
Minted Lamb Chops 88
MMMussels 19
Mudsicle Pie 140
Muffins, Stuffin' 109
Mushrooms, Glazed 117
Mushrooms, Tangy Roasted 114
Mustard Cod, Zippy 79

N

Noodle Bowl, Curry 48
Normandy, Pork Chops 82
Nut Clusters, Fruity 142
Nut Crunch, Five-Spice 129
Nutty Blue Cheese Dip 20

O

Oatmeal, Maui 50
Olive Biscuits, Parmesan 30
Olive Chicken Patties 101
Olive Spread, Black 13
Onion Beef Ragoût 74

Onion Bratwurst, Sweet................. 86
Onion Flatbread...................... 24
Onion Squash, Sweet................. 115
Onions, Roasted..................... 116
Ooey Gooey Bars.................... 127
Orange Basil Couscous 111
Orange Chicken, Sweet............... 100
Orange Cranberry Wedges 28
Orange Cream Cake 140
Orange Fennel Salad 32
Orange Herb Fish Fillets............... 80
Orange Ice, Anise 141
Orange Sesame Dressing.............. 42
Orange Squash Bowls 119
Oven Ranch Fries.................... 102

P

Pancakes, Blueberry Cream 50
Pandowdy, Sausage................... 60
Parfaits, Tangy Rice 124
Parmesan Biscuits, Pesto 28
Parmesan Olive Biscuits 30
Pasta
  Antipasto Pasta Salad................ 37
  Chicken Corn Spaghetti.............. 94
  Garlic Chicken..................... 92
  Lemon Tuna Fettuccine 77
  Turkey Cannelloni 98
Pâté, Spicy Feta 14
Patties
  Olive Chicken 101
  Salmon Lime 76
  Salsa Bean Cakes 65
PBJ Ring............................ 51
Peanut Butter Fudge 137
Pear Dip, Walnut 57
Pear Salad, Blue Cheese............... 31
Pears, Baked 139
Pepper Berry Vinaigrette 41
Pepper Steak 74
Peppered Dry Ribs................... 81
Perogy Ham Casserole................ 83
Pesto Chicken, Cranberry............. 96
Pesto Dressing, Tomato 42
Pesto Parmesan Biscuits.............. 28
Picante Spareribs.................... 85
Pies, Savoury
  Chicken Alfredo.................... 95
Pies, Sweet
  Butterscotch Pumpkin 138
  Lively Lime....................... 136

Mudsicle 140
  Quick Cheesecake 133
  Strawberry Margarita.............. 130
Pineapple Chicken, Savory............. 93
Pineapple Ginger Carrots............. 104
Pita Chips, Garlic Lime................ 13
Pizza, Chicken And Cheese 61
Polenta Alfredo, Saucy............... 110
Polenta, Grilled Dijon................ 106
Polenta Lasagne..................... 65
Polynesian Chicken 97
Popcorn, Fiesta 146
Poppy Seed Biscuits, Lemon 30
Pork
  Aloha Pork Roast 86
  Baked Tomato Chops............... 91
  Celery-Sauced Chops............... 82
  Cheesy Red Rice 85
  Glazed Ham Steak 81
  Glazed Pork Roast 84
  Havarti Ham Ring 60
  Hawaiian Hammies 9
  Hotsy Totsy Casserole 62
  Peppered Dry Ribs................. 81
  Perogy Ham Casserole............. 83
  Picante Spareribs 85
  Saucy Polenta Alfredo 110
  Sausage And Spinach Soup 44
  Sausage Pandowdy 60
  Savoury Apple Slaw 38
  Snappy Apple 87
  Sweet Onion Bratwurst 86
Pork Chops Normandy 82
Pot Roast, Easy...................... 69
Potato Bake, Meaty 70
Potato Salad, Creamy 31
Potato Scallop, Meat And 66
Potato Sticks, Sweet................. 103
Pull-Aparts, Tuscan.................. 26
Pumpkin Pie, Butterscotch........... 138
Pumpkin Soup...................... 47
Pumpkin Streusel Squares 134

Q

Quesadilla Bites 14
Quesadillas, Seafood 62
Quesadillas, Sweet Yam 58
Quiche, Salmon Cream 9
Quick Cheesecake Pie 133
Quickest Chili....................... 66

R

goût, Onion Beef 74
isin Braid, Swirled. 25
nch Fries, Oven 102
os
  Barbecued Beef 67
  Peppered Dry 81
  Picante Spareribs. 85
os, Peppered Dry 81
ce
  Cheesy Red 85
  Fragrant. 114
  Ginger Curry 116
  Salsa 112
  Tangy Rice Parfaits. 124
  Tomato Risotto 113
  Wild Rice Medley. 105
  Wild Rice Salad 34
sotto, Tomato 113
ast
  Aloha Pork. 86
  Easy Pot. 69
  Glazed Pork 84
asted Mushrooms, Tangy. 114
asted Onions 116
gelach Roll-Ups 26

S

lad Dressings
  Cranberry Vinaigrette. 41
  Creamy Bruschetta 43
  Dijon Chèvre 43
  Orange Sesame 42
  Pepper Berry Vinaigrette 41
  Tomato Pesto. 42
lads
  Antipasto Pasta 37
  Asian Cucumber 38
  Blue Cheese Pear 31
  Bruschetta Lentil 39
  Couscous Date. 40
  Creamy Potato. 3
  Curried Broccoli Slaw. 33
  Feta Beet 40
  Orange Fennel. 32
  Savoury Apple Slaw 38
  Spinach Cranberry. 39
  Tomato Bocconcini 32
  Wasabi Mayonnaise. 78
  Wild Rice 34
lmon, Apricot Wasabi 78

Salmon Cream Quiche. 9
Salmon Lime Patties. 76
Salmon-Sauced Bennies. 49
Salmon-Stuffed Brie 15
Salsa Bean Cakes 65
Salsa Rice. 112
Sandwiches, Cacciatore 59
Sauce, Liquid Gold. 136
Saucy Polenta Alfredo 110
Sausage And Spinach Soup 44
Sausage Pandowdy 60
Savoury Pineapple Chicken 93
Savory Apple Slaw 38
Scallop, Meat And Potato 66
Seafood Quesadillas. 62
Seafood (see Fish & Seafood)
Sesame Dressing, Orange 42
Shake, Berry Bran. 56
Shortbread, Butterscotch 139
Shortcake, Berry. 148
Shortcut Borscht 48
Shrimp
  Baked Garlic 78
  Creamy Curry 76
  Feta Shrimp Frittata 63
  Seafood Quesadillas. 62
Shrimp-Stuffed Sole. 75
Side Dishes
  Colourful Couscous 118
  Creamed Spinach Casserole. 112
  Fragrant Rice 114
  Fruity Stuffing 104
  Ginger Curry Rice 116
  Glazed Mushrooms 117
  Greek Beans. 102
  Grilled Dijon Polenta 106
  Orange Basil Couscous 111
  Orange Squash Bowls 119
  Oven Ranch Fries. 102
  Pineapple Ginger Carrots. 104
  Roasted Onions 116
  Salsa Rice. 112
  Saucy Polenta Alfredo 110
  Spinach And Lentil Sauté 110
  Squash-ghetti And Sauce. 118
  Stuffin' Muffins 109
  Sweet Onion Squash 115
  Sweet Potato Sticks 103
  Tangy Roasted Mushrooms 114
  Texas-Style "Caviar". 117
  Tomato Risotto 113
  Wild Rice Medley. 105

155

Simple Seafood Bisque................... 46
Slaw, Curried Broccoli 33
Slaw, Savoury Apple.................... 38
Snack Cake, Marble Top 145
Snap Brownies........................ 132
Snappy Apple Pork 87
Sole, Shrimp-Stuffed 75
Soufflé, Asiago....................... 58
Soups
   Curry Noodle Bowl 48
   Curry Vegetable.................... 45
   Four-Cheese Broccoli.............. 44
   Ginger Squash..................... 46
   Pumpkin 47
   Sausage And Spinach............... 44
   Shortcut Borscht 48
   Simple Seafood Bisque.............. 46
   Thai Chicken 47
Spaghetti, Chicken Corn 94
Spareribs, Picante 85
Spicy Feta Pâté 14
Spinach And Lentil Sauté............... 110
Spinach Casserole, Creamed 112
Spinach Cranberry Salad 39
Spinach Cream Triangles 10
Spinach Soup, Sausage And............. 44
Spreads
   Black Olive........................ 13
   Creamy Ginger 57
   Spicy Feta Pâté 14
Squares
   Grab-And-Go...................... 130
   Blondie Brownies.................. 129
   Pumpkin Streusel.................. 134
   Snap Brownies.................... 132
Squash
   Ginger Squash Soup 46
   Orange Squash Bowls 119
   Sweet Onion 115
Squash-ghetti And Sauce............... 118
Steak
   Chutney.......................... 68
   Glazed Ham....................... 81
   Pepper........................... 74
Stir-Fry, Asian Chicken 92
Strawberry Margarita Pie 130
Streusel Squares, Pumpkin.............. 134
Stroganoff 68
Stuffin' Muffins 109
Stuffing, Fruity....................... 104
Sweet Onion Bratwurst 86
Sweet Onion Squash 115
Sweet Orange Chicken 100

Sweet Potato Sticks 103
Sweet Yam Quesadillas 58
"Sweetish" Meatballs.................. 73
Swirled Raisin Braid 25
Swirls, Feta Crescent 22

T

Taco Beef Snacks 12
Tangy Rice Parfaits.................... 124
Tangy Roasted Mushrooms 114
Tarts, Cranapple...................... 138
Tarts, Frozen Yogurt................... 131
Texas-Style Caviar 117
Thai Chicken Salad Wraps 11
Thai Chicken Soup.................... 47
Tomato Bocconcini Salad............... 32
Tomato Chops, Baked 91
Tomato Pesto Dressing 42
Tomato Risotto 113
Tomato-Topped Biscuits................ 24
Tortillas, Huevos..................... 56
Triangles, Spinach Cream.............. 10
Trifle, Express Tropical 135
Tuna Fettuccine, Lemon................ 77
Turkey Cannelloni 98
Tuscan Pull-Aparts 26

V

Vegetable Soup, Curry................. 45
Vegetables (see Side Dishes)
Vinaigrette, Cranberry 41
Vinaigrette, Pepper Berry.............. 41
VIP Cookies 128

W

Walnut Pear Dip....................... 57
Wasabi Mayonnaise.................... 78
Wasabi Salmon, Apricot................ 78
Wild Rice Medley...................... 105
Wild Rice Salad 34
Wraps, Heuvos Tortillas 56
Wraps, Thai Chicken Salad.............. 11

Y

Yam Quesadillas, Sweet 58
Yogurt Tarts, Frozen................... 131

Z

Zippy Mustard Cod 79

156

Recipe Notes

Recipe Notes

Recipe Notes

Recipe Notes

SIMPLE SUPPERS

Company's Coming

National Bestseller

Simple Suppers

Jean Paré

ORIGINAL SERIES

Simple
Suppers

Jean Paré

www.companyscoming.com
visit our website

Front Cover

1. Walnut Green Salad, page 12
2. Pork Marsala, page 134
Props courtesy of: Pfaltzgraff Canada

We gratefully acknowledge the following suppliers for their generous support of our Test and Photography Kitchens:

Broil King Barbecues
Corelle®
Hamilton Beach® Canada
Lagostina®
Proctor Silex® Canada
Tupperware®

Want cooking secrets?

Check out our website for **cooking hints** and **time-saving shortcuts**.

Visit us at

www.companyscoming.com

Table of Contents

Side Salads

Meal Salads

Side Dishes

Beef

Chicken

Fish &
Seafood

Foreword 6

Salads

Side Salads 8

Meal Salads 24

Side Dishes . . . . 38.

Entrees

Beef 64

Chicken 80

Fish & Seafood 98

Lamb 116

Meatless 122

Pork 134

Measurement Tables 149

Recipe Index 150

Recipe Notes 157

Lamb

Meatless

Pork

Foreword

Good things, they say, come in threes—cheers, wishes and wise men, to name, well, three—so it stands to reason that an easy way to organize a delicious dinner is to think in terms of that magical number.

Simple Suppers does just that. It breaks meal-planning down to a trio of necessary elements: vegetables, starches and proteins. Put all three on a plate and you have a full-meal deal that will make a nutritionist smile. What makes this Company's Coming cookbook special, however, is that we've told you how to combine those three elements so you can serve a great-tasting, well-balanced supper every time.

We've divided our table of contents into—you guessed it—three categories: salads, sides and entrees. Some of our meal salads are easy, one-dish meals that are completely balanced on their own. You'll find similarly balanced options in our entree section.

Of course, we also offer a number of tasty one and two-component recipes—all with helpful suggestions on how to incorporate them into a balanced meal. You can follow our suggested combinations or add your own family favourites to create a more personalized dinner medley of vegetables, starch and protein. Our Salmon With Avocado Salsa, for instance, pairs perfectly with our Chipotle Cheese Potatoes from the sides section. And our heavenly Pork Marsala, for example, goes well with your own buttered egg noodles and our Walnut Green Salad for an elegant, guest-friendly dinner.

Each section features all-new recipes prepared in a number of different ways, whether baked, grilled, tossed or cooked on top of the stove. And to keep things really simple, we've made sure that every dish is quick to prepare, so you can get on with your evening.

Now that deserves three cheers!

Jean Paré

Nutrition Information Guidelines

Each recipe is analyzed using the most current version of the Canadian Nutrient File from Health Canada, which is based on the United States Department of Agriculture (USDA) Nutrient Database.

- If more than one ingredient is listed (such as "butter or hard margarine"), or if a range is given (1 – 2 tsp., 5 – 10 mL), only the first ingredient or first amount is analyzed.

- For meat, poultry and fish, the serving size per person is based on the recommended 4 oz. (113 g) uncooked weight (without bone), which is 2 – 3 oz. (57 – 85 g) cooked weight (without bone)—approximately the size of a deck of playing cards.

- Milk used is 1% M.F. (milk fat), unless otherwise stated.

- Cooking oil used is canola oil, unless otherwise stated.

- Ingredients indicating "sprinkle," "optional," or "for garnish" are not included in the nutrition information.

- The fat in recipes and combination foods can vary greatly depending on the sources and types of fats used in each specific ingredient. For these reasons, the amount of saturated, monounsaturated and polyunsaturated fats may not add up to the total fat content.

Vera C. Mazurak, Ph.D.
Nutritionist

Marinated Mushroom Salad

Not "mushroom" on your dinner table? You'll want to make some once you get a glimpse of this eye-catching, Asian-style salad. Marinate the mushrooms while preparing Italian Steak Dinner, page 77. Serve with foccacia bread on the side.

Rice vinegar	3 tbsp.	50 mL
Olive (or cooking) oil	1 tbsp.	15 mL
Soy sauce	1 tbsp.	15 mL
Sesame oil	2 tsp.	10 mL
Olive (or cooking) oil	1 tsp.	5 mL
Halved fresh white mushrooms	8 cups	2 L
Thinly sliced English cucumber (with peel)	1 1/2 cups	375 mL
Finely chopped green onion	2 tbsp.	30 mL
Olive (or cooking) oil	1 1/2 tbsp.	25 mL
Dijon mustard	1 tsp.	5 mL
Mixed salad greens, lightly packed	6 cups	1.5 L
Sesame seeds, toasted (see Tip, page 20)	2 tbsp.	30 mL

Combine first 4 ingredients in small cup. Set aside.

Heat second amount of olive oil in large frying pan on medium. Add mushrooms. Cook for about 10 minutes, stirring occasionally, until softened. Transfer to medium bowl.

Add 2 tbsp. (30 mL) rice vinegar mixture, cucumber and green onion. Toss. Chill for 1 hour.

Add third amount of olive oil and mustard to remaining rice vinegar mixture. Stir.

Put salad greens into large bowl. Drizzle with mustard mixture. Toss. Arrange on 4 large plates. Top with mushroom mixture.

Sprinkle with sesame seeds. Makes 4 salads. Serves 4.

1 serving: 185 Calories; 14.8 g Total Fat (8.8 g Mono, 3.1 g Poly, 2.0 g Sat); 0 mg Cholesterol; 10 g Carbohydrate; 4 g Fibre; 7 g Protein; 376 mg Sodium

Asparagus Cucumber Salad

Smoky grilled asparagus and crisp cucumber make a winning combination in this refreshing sweet and sour salad. Makes a great complement for Satay Chicken Noodles, page 80, or Asian Salmon Burgers, page 104.

Brown sugar, packed	2 tbsp.	30 mL
Mayonnaise	1 tbsp.	15 mL
Soy sauce	1 tbsp.	15 mL
Sesame (or cooking) oil	1 tbsp.	15 mL
Rice vinegar	1 tbsp.	15 mL
Finely grated gingerroot (or 1/4 tsp., 1 mL, ground ginger)	1 tsp.	5 mL
Pepper	1/4 tsp.	1 mL
Fresh asparagus, trimmed of tough ends, cut into 2 inch (5 cm) pieces	1 lb.	454 g
Thinly sliced English cucumber (with peel)	2 cups	500 mL
Sesame seeds, toasted (see Tip, page 20)	1 tsp.	5 mL

Whisk first 7 ingredients in small cup. Set aside.

Cook asparagus in boiling water in covered medium saucepan for 2 to 3 minutes until tender-crisp. Cool under cold running water. Put into medium bowl.

Add cucumber. Toss. Drizzle mayonnaise mixture over salad. Toss.

Sprinkle with sesame seeds. Makes about 3 1/2 cups (875 mL). Serves 4.

1 serving: 122 Calories; 6.8 g Total Fat (3.0 g Mono, 2.6 g Poly, 0.9 g Sat); 2 mg Cholesterol; 15 g Carbohydrate; 2 g Fibre; 3 g Protein; 353 mg Sodium

SMOKY ASPARAGUS SALAD: Preheat gas barbecue to medium. Cook uncut asparagus spears on greased grill for about 5 minutes, turning several times until tender-crisp. Cut into 2 inch (5 cm) pieces.

Pictured on page 107.

Dijon Apple Coleslaw

Apples add a fresh, summery appeal to this crisp, di-jaunty coleslaw. A good match for grilled chicken, beef or pork patties. Add grilled polenta slices for a complete meal.

Mayonnaise	1/4 cup	60 mL
Plain yogurt	1/4 cup	60 mL
Dijon mustard	1 tbsp.	15 mL
Apple cider vinegar	2 tsp.	10 mL
Granulated sugar	2 tsp.	10 mL
Salt	1/4 tsp.	1 mL
Pepper	1/8 tsp.	0.5 mL
Coleslaw mix (about 1 lb., 454 g)	8 cups	2 L
Grated peeled apple	1 cup	250 mL

Combine first 7 ingredients in large bowl.

Add coleslaw and apple. Toss. Makes about 6 cups (1.5 L). Serves 6.

1 serving: 113 Calories; 7.8 g Total Fat (4.2 g Mono, 2.5 g Poly, 0.9 g Sat); 7 mg Cholesterol; 9 g Carbohydrate; 2 g Fibre; 1.5 g Protein; 207 mg Sodium

Grated Carrot Salad

Don't pine away for want of a good side salad! This sweet and tangy carrot slaw is made intriguingly unique with the crunch of toasted pine nuts. A lovely side for Ground Pork Patties, page 145, and mashed potatoes.

Grated carrot	1 1/2 cups	375 mL
Chopped celery	1/4 cup	60 mL
Golden raisins	1/4 cup	60 mL
Pine nuts, toasted (see Tip, page 20)	2 tbsp.	30 mL
Chopped green onion	2 tbsp.	30 mL
HONEY MUSTARD VINAIGRETTE		
Cooking oil	1 tbsp.	15 mL
White vinegar	2 tsp.	10 mL
Liquid honey	2 tsp.	10 mL
Prepared mustard	1 tsp.	5 mL
Salt	1/4 tsp.	1 mL

(continued on next page)

Put first 5 ingredients into medium bowl. Toss.

Honey Mustard Vinaigrette: Combine all 5 ingredients in jar with tight-fitting lid. Shake well. Makes about 2 tbsp. (30 mL) vinaigrette. Drizzle over salad. Toss. Makes about 2 cups (500 mL) salad. Serves 4.

1 serving: 121 Calories; 6.1 g Total Fat (3.0 g Mono, 2.2 g Poly, 0.7 g Sat); 0 mg Cholesterol; 16 g Carbohydrate; 3 g Fibre; 2 g Protein; 197 mg Sodium

Sweet Potato Salad

Spicy, sweet and succulent, this curried potato salad will be an all-star at the family picnic. Makes a marvelous match for Pineapple Pork Kabobs, page 135.

Unpeeled sweet potatoes (or yams), halved crosswise	1 1/2 lbs.	680 g
Chopped green pepper	1/2 cup	125 mL
DRESSING		
Plain yogurt	2 tbsp.	30 mL
Mayonnaise	1 tbsp.	15 mL
Mango chutney, finely chopped	1 tbsp.	15 mL
Frozen concentrated orange juice, thawed	1 1/2 tsp.	7 mL
Curry powder	1/4 tsp.	1 mL
Ground cumin	1/4 tsp.	1 mL
Salt	1/8 tsp.	0.5 mL
Pepper	1/8 tsp.	0.5 mL

Cook sweet potato in boiling salted water in large saucepan until just tender. Drain. Rinse with cold water. Drain well. Remove peel. Cut sweet potato into 1/2 inch (12 mm) pieces. Put into medium bowl.

Add green pepper. Toss.

Dressing: Combine all 8 ingredients in small cup. Add to salad. Toss. Makes about 4 cups (1 L). Serves 4.

1 serving: 223 Calories; 3.6 g Total Fat (1.6 g Mono, 1.2 g Poly, 0.6 g Sat); 3 mg Cholesterol; 45 g Carbohydrate; 6 g Fibre; 3 g Protein; 105 mg Sodium

Walnut Green Salad

Your guests will go nuts for this tangy, crisp and crunchy salad. The citrus vinaigrette makes it a natural fit with Pork Marsala, page 134, and mashed potatoes or rice.

CITRUS BALSAMIC VINAIGRETTE

Balsamic vinaigrette	1/3 cup	75 mL
Orange juice	2 tbsp.	30 mL
Finely chopped green onion	2 tbsp.	30 mL
Grated orange zest	1/4 tsp.	1 mL

SALAD

Mixed salad greens, lightly packed	4 cups	1 L
Fresh spinach leaves, stems removed, lightly packed	4 cups	1 L
Can of mandarin orange segments, drained	10 oz.	284 mL
Thinly sliced radish	1 cup	250 mL
Coarsely chopped walnuts, toasted (see Tip, page 20)	1 cup	250 mL

Citrus Balsamic Vinaigrette: Combine all 4 ingredients in jar with tight-fitting lid. Shake well. Makes about 1/2 cup (125 mL) vinaigrette.

Salad: Put first 4 ingredients into large bowl. Toss. Drizzle with Citrus Balsamic Vinaigrette. Toss.

Sprinkle with walnuts. Makes about 8 cups (2 L). Serves 4.

1 serving: 267 Calories; 20.0 g Total Fat (2.7 g Mono, 14.3 g Poly, 1.9 g Sat); 0 mg Cholesterol; 19 g Carbohydrate; 6 g Fibre; 8 g Protein; 81 mg Sodium

Pictured on front cover.

Paré Pointer

At least when you make mistakes on a computer, you can put them in alphabetical order.

Herbed Potato Salad

A little bit of green makes this avocado and smoky bacon potato salad a unique picnic treat. A great partner for Crispy Chicken Drumettes, page 84, and roasted veggies.

FRESH HERB MAYONNAISE

Mayonnaise	1/3 cup	75 mL
Chopped fresh chives	2 tbsp.	30 mL
Chopped fresh mint	2 tbsp.	30 mL
Chopped fresh parsley	2 tbsp.	30 mL
Dijon mustard	2 tbsp.	30 mL
Salt	1/8 tsp.	0.5 mL
Pepper, sprinkle		

SALAD

Red potatoes, peeled and quartered	3 lbs.	1.4 kg
Bacon slices, cooked crisp and crumbled	4	4
Thinly sliced green onion	1/3 cup	75 mL
Ripe large avocado, chopped	1	1

Fresh Herb Mayonnaise: Combine all 7 ingredients in small bowl. Makes about 1/2 cup (125 mL) mayonnaise.

Salad: Cook potato in boiling salted water in large saucepan until just tender. Drain. Rinse with cold water. Drain well. Cut into 1 inch (2.5 cm) pieces. Put into large bowl.

Add bacon and green onion. Toss. Add Fresh Herb Mayonnaise. Toss.

Scatter avocado over top. Makes about 9 cups (2.25 L). Serves 6.

1 serving: 405 Calories; 21.5 g Total Fat (13.3 g Mono, 5.1 g Poly, 5.7 g Sat); 17 mg Cholesterol; 49 g Carbohydrate; 6 g Fibre; 6 g Protein; 276 mg Sodium

Pictured on page 72.

Vegetable Pearl Salad

Certainly a salad to treasure. Marinated artichokes give pearl barley a unique spin. Simply sensational with Dijon Dill Salmon Patties, page 106.

Water	1 1/2 cups	375 mL
Pearl barley	1/2 cup	125 mL
Salt	1/4 tsp.	1 mL
Diced red pepper	2 cups	500 mL
Quartered fresh white mushrooms	2 cups	500 mL
Jar of marinated artichokes, drained, marinade reserved, chopped	12 oz.	340 mL
Reserved artichoke marinade	1/2 cup	125 mL
Grated Parmesan cheese	2 tbsp.	30 mL
Lemon juice	1 tbsp.	15 mL
Garlic clove, minced (or 1/4 tsp., 1 mL, powder)	1	1
Italian seasoning	1 tsp.	5 mL
Granulated sugar	1 tsp.	5 mL
Salt	1/4 tsp.	1 mL
Pepper, sprinkle		

Chopped fresh basil, for garnish

Combine first 3 ingredients in small saucepan. Bring to a boil. Reduce heat to medium-low. Simmer, partially covered, for about 30 minutes until barley is tender. Drain. Rinse with cold water. Drain well. Transfer to large bowl.

Add next 3 ingredients. Toss.

Process next 8 ingredients in blender or food processor until smooth. Add to barley mixture. Toss.

Garnish with basil. Makes about 6 cups (1.5 L). Serves 6.

1 serving: 123 Calories; 5.1 g Total Fat (0.2 g Mono, 0.2 g Poly, 0.5 g Sat); 2 mg Cholesterol; 20 g Carbohydrate; 5 g Fibre; 3 g Protein; 701 mg Sodium

Rice Noodle Salad

Perfect when you want to experience the lighter side of things—thin noodles, crunchy veggies and mildly-spiced dressing. Pair with Zesty Chicken Kabobs, page 92.

PEANUT DRESSING

Peanut sauce	2/3 cup	150 mL
Soy sauce	2 1/2 tbsp.	37 mL
Chopped fresh cilantro or parsley	1 tbsp.	15 mL
(or 3/4 tsp., 4 mL, dried)		

SALAD

Rice vermicelli	9 oz.	255 g
Shredded bok choy, lightly packed	2 cups	500 mL
Diced red pepper	1 cup	250 mL
Can of sliced water chestnuts,	8 oz.	227 mL
drained and finely chopped		
Grated carrot	1/2 cup	125 mL
Chopped salted peanuts	1/2 cup	125 mL

Peanut Dressing: Combine all 3 ingredients in small bowl. Makes about 2/3 cup (150 mL) dressing.

Salad: Put vermicelli into large bowl. Cover with boiling water. Let stand for about 5 minutes until tender. Drain. Rinse with cold water. Drain well. Return to same bowl.

Add next 4 ingredients. Toss. Drizzle Peanut Dressing over salad. Toss.

Sprinkle with peanuts. Makes about 8 cups (2 L). Serves 4.

1 serving: 380 Calories; 7.3 g Total Fat (trace Mono, 0.1 g Poly, 1.5 g Sat); 0 mg Cholesterol; 65 g Carbohydrate; 4 g Fibre; 11 g Protein; 1574 mg Sodium

Pictured on page 90.

Side Salads

Minted Pea Salad

Fresh mint enhances a simple mix of green peas and chickpeas. Serve with Curry-Spiced Chicken, page 85, and basmati rice—and dinner will be in mint condition!

Frozen peas, thawed	3 cups	750 mL
Can of chickpeas (garbanzo beans), rinsed and drained	19 oz.	540 mL
Chopped fresh mint	3 tbsp.	50 mL
Finely chopped green onion	2 tbsp.	30 mL
SWEET LIME VINAIGRETTE		
Cooking oil	1/3 cup	75 mL
Red wine vinegar	3 tbsp.	50 mL
Granulated sugar	1 tbsp.	15 mL
Garlic clove, minced (or 1/4 tsp., 1 mL, powder)	1	1
Grated lime zest	1 tsp.	5 mL
Lime juice	1 tsp.	5 mL
Salt	1/2 tsp.	2 mL
Pepper	1/4 tsp.	1 mL

Put first 4 ingredients into large bowl. Toss.

Sweet Lime Vinaigrette: Combine all 8 ingredients in jar with tight-fitting lid. Shake well. Makes about 1/2 cup (125 mL) vinaigrette. Drizzle over salad. Toss. Makes about 5 3/4 cups (1.45 L). Serves 4.

1 serving: 472 Calories; 21.2 g Total Fat (11.0 g Mono, 6.9 g Poly, 1.7 g Sat); 0 mg Cholesterol; 56 g Carbohydrate; 11 g Fibre; 18 g Protein; 742 mg Sodium

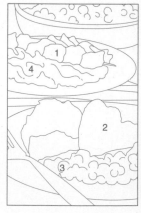

1. Grilled Lamb Kabobs, page 121
2. Curry-Spiced Chicken, page 85
3. Minted Pea Salad, above
4. Cabbage Noodles, page 62

Props courtesy of: Pfaltzgraff Canada

Side Salads

Dill Pasta Salad

Looking for the real dill? This super-easy macaroni salad fits the bill. A versatile side for any barbecue meal—especially Balsamic Skewers, page 99.

Elbow macaroni	1 1/2 cups	375 mL
Chopped tomato	3/4 cup	175 mL
Chopped celery	1/2 cup	125 mL
Grated Parmesan cheese	1/3 cup	75 mL
Chopped red (or green) onion	1/4 cup	60 mL
DRESSING		
Mayonnaise	1/2 cup	125 mL
Tangy dill relish	3 tbsp.	50 mL
Chopped fresh dill (or 3/4 tsp., 4 mL, dried)	1 tbsp.	15 mL
Prepared mustard	1 tsp.	5 mL

Cook macaroni in boiling salted water in large uncovered saucepan for 8 to 10 minutes, stirring occasionally, until tender but firm. Drain. Rinse with cold water. Drain well. Transfer to medium bowl.

Add next 4 ingredients. Toss.

Dressing: Combine all 4 ingredients in small bowl. Add to salad. Toss. Makes about 6 cups (1.5 L). Serves 4.

1 serving: 397 Calories; 25.3 g Total Fat (13.1 g Mono, 7.8 g Poly, 3.7 g Sat); 23 mg Cholesterol; 33 g Carbohydrate; 2 g Fibre; 9 g Protein; 434 mg Sodium

Pictured at left.

1. Cajun Cheese Bread, page 40
2. Dill Pasta Salad, above
3. Balsamic Skewers, page 99

Props courtesy of: Emile Henry

Apple Date Salad

Your first date with this salad will definitely lead to a second...and a third!
Serve this savoury and sweet beauty with roasted pork and stuffing.

BLUE CHEESE DRESSING

Mayonnaise	2 tbsp.	30 mL
Sour cream	2 tbsp.	30 mL
Crumbled blue cheese	1 1/2 tbsp.	25 mL
Apple cider vinegar	1 tbsp.	15 mL
Garlic powder	1/8 tsp.	0.5 mL

SALAD

Medium unpeeled cooking apples (such as McIntosh), diced (see Note)	2	2
Mixed salad greens, lightly packed	6 cups	1.5 L
Chopped pitted dates	1 cup	250 mL
Pecan halves, toasted (see Tip, below)	1/2 cup	125 mL

Blue Cheese Dressing: Combine all 5 ingredients in medium bowl. Makes about 6 tbsp. (100 mL) dressing.

Salad: Put apple into large bowl. Add Blue Cheese Dressing (see Note). Toss until coated.

Add salad greens. Toss.

Sprinkle with dates and pecans. Makes about 10 cups (2.5 L). Serves 8.

1 serving: 171 Calories; 8.9 g Total Fat (4.4 g Mono, 2.5 g Poly, 1.4 g Sat); 6 mg Cholesterol; 23 g Carbohydrate; 4 g Fibre; 2 g Protein; 52 mg Sodium

Note: Wait to dice the apple until just before assembling the salad. Adding dressing to apple as soon as it is cut helps to prevent browning.

 When toasting nuts, seeds or coconut, cooking times will vary for each different ingredient—so never toast them together. For small amounts, place ingredient in an ungreased shallow frying pan. Heat on medium for 3 to 5 minutes, stirring often, until golden. For larger amounts, spread ingredient evenly in an ungreased shallow pan. Bake in a 350°F (175°C) oven for 5 to 10 minutes, stirring or shaking often, until golden.

Potato And Green Bean Salad

There's nothing wrong with a little green. Potatoes and
green beans are accented with subtle flavours of mint
and mustard. A great addition to Cajun Cutlets, page 139.

Red baby potatoes, halved	2 lbs.	900 g
Fresh (or frozen) whole green beans, halved diagonally	1 lb.	454 g
Green onions, sliced diagonally	3	3
Slivered red pepper	1/4 cup	60 mL
MINT MUSTARD DRESSING		
Olive (or cooking) oil	1/4 cup	60 mL
Red wine vinegar	2 tbsp.	30 mL
Liquid honey	1 tbsp.	15 mL
Dijon mustard (with whole seeds)	1 tbsp.	15 mL
Lemon juice	1 tbsp.	15 mL
Finely chopped fresh mint	2 tsp.	10 mL
Salt	1 tsp.	5 mL
Lemon pepper, sprinkle		

Cook potato in boiling salted water in large covered saucepan for 5 minutes.

Add green beans. Reduce heat to medium-low. Simmer, covered, for 5 to 7 minutes until potato is tender and green beans are tender-crisp. Drain. Transfer to large bowl.

Add green onion and red pepper. Toss.

Mint Mustard Dressing: Combine all 8 ingredients in small bowl. Makes about 1/2 cup (125 mL) dressing. Let stand for 10 minutes to blend flavours. Drizzle over salad. Toss. Makes about 5 cups (1.25 L). Serves 4.

1 serving: 364 Calories; 13.7 g Total Fat (10.0 g Mono, 1.2 g Poly, 1.9 g Sat); 0 mg Cholesterol; 54 g Carbohydrate; 7 g Fibre; 8 g Protein; 656 mg Sodium

Jicama Salad

This is one heck of a jicama dish! Jicama (pronounced HEE-kah-mah) is a crunchy, slightly sweet root vegetable that's also fondly known as the Mexican potato. Combined with sweet raisins, almonds and a refreshing citrus vinaigrette, it provides a nice contrast to Polenta-Topped Chili, page 78.

Julienned peeled jicama (see Tip, page 140)	3 cups	750 mL
Medium orange, peeled and chopped	1	1
Chopped fresh parsley	1/2 cup	125 mL
Dark raisins	1/2 cup	125 mL
Sliced almonds, toasted (see Tip, page 20)	1/2 cup	125 mL
SPICY LIME VINAIGRETTE		
Cooking oil	1/4 cup	60 mL
Lime juice	1/4 cup	60 mL
Ground cumin	1/4 tsp.	1 mL
Salt	1/4 tsp.	1 mL
Chili paste (sambal oelek)	1/4 tsp.	1 mL

Put first 5 ingredients into medium bowl. Toss.

Spicy Lime Vinaigrette: Combine all 5 ingredients in jar with tight-fitting lid. Shake well. Makes about 1/2 cup (125 mL) vinaigrette. Drizzle over salad. Toss. Makes about 4 1/2 cups (1.1 L). Serves 6.

1 serving: 207 Calories; 13.3 g Total Fat (7.9 g Mono, 3.7 g Poly, 1.0 g Sat); 0 mg Cholesterol; 22 g Carbohydrate; 5 g Fibre; 3 g Protein; 105 mg Sodium

Pictured on page 53.

Paré Pointer

The prettiest figure in geometry is acute angle.

Pecan Potato Salad

Wow them at the next get together with this highly unusual and superbly stylish potato salad. You're not going to find this one at the deli! Outstanding with Goat Cheese Crostini, page 58, and grilled salmon.

Thinly sliced English cucumber (with peel)	3 cups	750 mL
Cut or torn romaine lettuce, lightly packed	3 cups	750 mL
Can of sweet potatoes, drained and chopped	19 oz.	540 mL
Thinly sliced celery	2 cups	500 mL
Thinly sliced red onion	2/3 cup	150 mL
Coarsely chopped pecans, toasted (see Tip, page 20)	2/3 cup	150 mL
Shaved Asiago (or Parmesan) cheese	1/2 cup	125 mL
TOMATO DRESSING		
Tomato juice	1/2 cup	125 mL
Olive (or cooking) oil	1/4 cup	60 mL
Chopped fresh basil (or 1 1/2 tsp., 7 mL, dried)	2 tbsp.	30 mL
Granulated sugar	2 tsp.	10 mL
Salt	1/2 tsp.	2 mL

Put first 7 ingredients into large bowl. Toss.

Tomato Dressing: Combine all 5 ingredients in jar with tight-fitting lid. Shake well. Makes about 1 cup (250 mL) dressing. Drizzle over salad. Toss. Makes about 12 cups (3 L). Serves 6.

1 serving: 333 Calories; 21.5 g Total Fat (11.8 g Mono, 3.7 g Poly, 3.8 g Sat); 8 mg Cholesterol; 33 g Carbohydrate; 6 g Fibre; 6 g Protein; 429 mg Sodium

Pictured on page 36 and on back cover.

Grilled Beef Tomato Salad

Reach for some Asian-inspired ginger sesame dressing to add a touch of the exotic to this fresh yet hearty steak and tomato meal.

Sesame ginger dressing	3 tbsp.	50 mL
Garlic cloves, minced (or 1/2 tsp., 2 mL, powder)	2	2
Red curry paste	1/2 tsp.	2 mL
Flank steak	1 lb.	454 g
Medium tomatoes, each cut into 8 wedges	3	3
Green onions, sliced	4	4
Sesame ginger dressing	3 tbsp.	50 mL
Chopped fresh cilantro or parsley	2 tbsp.	30 mL
Chopped fresh mint	2 tbsp.	30 mL
Lime juice	2 tbsp.	30 mL
Fresh, thin Chinese-style egg noodles, cut in half	8 oz.	225 g
Sesame ginger dressing	1/3 cup	75 mL
Cut or torn green leaf lettuce, lightly packed	6 cups	1.5 L

Combine first 3 ingredients in small cup.

Brush dressing mixture on both sides of beef. Let stand for 30 minutes. Preheat gas barbecue to medium (see Tip, page 56). Cook beef on greased grill for about 4 minutes per side for medium-rare or until desired doneness. Remove to cutting board. Let stand for 5 minutes. Thinly slice beef diagonally. Put into large bowl.

Add next 6 ingredients. Toss. Set aside.

Cook noodles in boiling salted water in large uncovered saucepan or Dutch oven for about 3 minutes, stirring occasionally, until tender but firm. Drain. Rinse with cold water. Drain well. Transfer to medium bowl.

Drizzle second amount of dressing over noodles. Toss.

Arrange lettuce on 4 large plates. Top with noodles and beef mixture. Serves 4.

1 serving: 611 Calories; 27.6 g Total Fat (3.7 g Mono, 1.2 g Poly, 8.5 g Sat); 103 mg Cholesterol; 59 g Carbohydrate; 6 g Fibre; 37 g Protein; 477 mg Sodium

Pictured on page 90.

Chicken Couscous Salad

Couscous takes an Asian spin in this sweet, tangy, citrusy salad. Best served at room temperature.

Prepared chicken broth	3 cups	750 mL
Box of plain couscous	12 oz.	340 g
Broccoli slaw	4 cups	1 L
(or shredded cabbage with carrot)		
Chopped cooked chicken	2 cups	500 mL
Can of mandarin orange segments, drained	10 oz.	284 mL
Thinly sliced red onion	1/2 cup	125 mL
ORANGE GINGER DRESSING		
Orange juice	6 tbsp.	100 mL
Lemon juice	1/4 cup	60 mL
Olive (or cooking) oil	1/4 cup	60 mL
Finely grated gingerroot (or 3/4 tsp.,	1 tbsp.	15 mL
4 mL, ground ginger)		
Grated orange zest	2 tsp.	10 mL
Garlic cloves, minced (or 1/2 tsp.,	2	2
2 mL, powder)		
Dried crushed chilies	1/4 tsp.	1 mL
Salt	1/4 tsp.	1 mL

Measure broth into medium saucepan. Bring to a boil. Add couscous. Stir. Remove from heat. Let stand, covered, for about 5 minutes until couscous is tender and broth is absorbed. Fluff with a fork. Transfer to large bowl. Cool.

Add next 4 ingredients. Toss.

Orange Ginger Dressing: Combine all 8 ingredients in jar with tight-fitting lid. Shake well. Makes about 1 cup (250 mL) dressing. Drizzle over salad. Toss. Let stand for 15 minutes to blend flavours. Makes about 13 cups (3.25 L). Serves 6.

1 serving: 443 Calories; 13.3 g Total Fat (8.2 g Mono, 1.8 g Poly, 2.4 g Sat); 35 mg Cholesterol; 57 g Carbohydrate; 4 g Fibre; 23 g Protein; 554 mg Sodium

Sunny Rice Salad

This cheerful, yellow salad with mango dressing will brighten everyone's day! Serve on a bed of mixed salad greens for a complete meal.

TANGY MANGO DRESSING

Finely chopped mango chutney	2 tbsp.	30 mL
Water	1 tbsp.	15 mL
Apple cider vinegar	2 tsp.	10 mL
Ketchup	1 tsp.	5 mL
Cooking oil	1 tsp.	5 mL
Salt, sprinkle		
Pepper, sprinkle		

SALAD

Cooked long grain white rice (about 1 cup, 250 mL, uncooked)	3 cups	750 mL
Salad dressing (or mayonnaise)	1/2 cup	125 mL
Turmeric	1/4 tsp.	1 mL
Deli ham, cut into 1/8 inch (3 mm) strips (or 6 1/2 oz., 184 g, can of flaked ham, drained and crumbled)	6 oz.	170 g
Large hard-cooked eggs, quartered lengthwise (or sliced)	6	6
Chopped fresh parsley	2 tbsp.	30 mL

Tangy Mango Dressing: Combine all 7 ingredients in small bowl. Makes about 1/4 cup (60 mL) dressing.

Salad: Combine first 3 ingredients in medium bowl. Spread on large serving plate.

Scatter ham over rice mixture. Arrange egg on top. Drizzle Tangy Mango Dressing over salad.

Sprinkle with parsley. Makes about 5 1/2 cups. Serves 6.

1 serving: 360 Calories; 22.2 g Total Fat (10.8 g Mono, 5.9 g Poly, 3.4 g Sat); 236 mg Cholesterol; 26 g Carbohydrate; trace Fibre; 14 g Protein; 541 mg Sodium

Meal Salads

Grilled Pork And Mango Salad

Hickory, dickory, dock...it's almost six o' clock! Do you know what you're making for dinner? This is it—refreshing, sweet mango and grilled pork tenderloin. Tastes even better with Sun-Dried Tomato Cornbread, page 50.

Pork tenderloin, trimmed of fat	1 lb.	454 g
Chili powder	1 tsp.	5 mL
Hickory barbecue sauce	1/4 cup	60 mL
Cut or torn romaine lettuce, lightly packed	8 cups	2 L
Can of sliced mango in syrup, drained and chopped	14 oz.	398 mL
Thinly sliced red pepper	1 cup	250 mL
SWEET 'N' SPICY DRESSING		
Italian (or ranch) dressing	1/2 cup	125 mL
Lime (or orange) juice	2 tbsp.	30 mL
Liquid honey	2 tbsp.	30 mL
Chili powder	1/2 tsp.	2 mL

Sprinkle all sides of tenderloin with chili powder. Preheat gas barbecue to medium. Place tenderloin on 1 side of greased grill. Turn off burner under tenderloin, leaving opposite burner on medium. Close lid. Cook for 25 minutes, turning occasionally.

Brush tenderloin with barbecue sauce. Cook for another 4 to 5 minutes until meat thermometer inserted into thickest part of tenderloin reads 155°F (68°C). Remove to cutting board. Cover with foil. Let stand for 10 minutes. Cut into 12 slices.

Layer next 3 ingredients on 4 large plates. Top with pork.

Sweet 'N' Spicy Dressing: Combine all 4 ingredients in small bowl. Makes about 3/4 cup (175 mL) dressing. Drizzle over salads. Serves 4.

1 serving: 474 Calories; 23.9 g Total Fat (12.7 g Mono, 7.4 g Poly, 2.6 g Sat); 87 mg Cholesterol; 38 g Carbohydrate; 4 g Fibre; 30 g Protein; 702 mg Sodium

Pictured on page 53.

Tex-Mex Toss

Toss on your sombrero and toss up some fun with this fresh and easy salad!

Cut or torn romaine lettuce, lightly packed	8 cups	2 L
Chopped cooked chicken	3 cups	750 mL
Can of black beans, rinsed and drained	19 oz.	540 mL
Diced medium Cheddar cheese	1 cup	250 mL
Halved cherry tomatoes	1 cup	250 mL
Ranch dressing	2/3 cup	150 mL
Can of sliced black olives	4 1/2 oz.	125 mL
Salsa	1/3 cup	75 mL
Chopped avocado	2 cups	500 mL
Lemon juice	2 tsp.	10 mL
Coarsely crushed nacho chips	2 cups	500 mL

Put first 8 ingredients into extra-large bowl. Toss.

Put avocado into small bowl. Sprinkle with lemon juice. Toss until coated. Scatter over salad.

Sprinkle with chips. Makes about 16 cups (4 L). Serves 6.

1 serving: 660 Calories; 39.5 g Total Fat (13.2 g Mono, 3.4 g Poly, 9.8 g Sat); 80 mg Cholesterol; 45 g Carbohydrate; 13 g Fibre; 35 g Protein; 1016 mg Sodium

Chicken Pita Salad

A super supper salad everyone will enjoy. Light fare for a late evening meal.

Chopped cooked chicken	3 cups	750 mL
Chopped tomato	1 1/2 cups	375 mL
Chopped English cucumber (with peel)	1 1/2 cups	375 mL
Italian dressing	2/3 cup	150 mL
Chopped radish	1/2 cup	125 mL
Chopped fresh parsley	1/3 cup	75 mL
Lemon juice	2 tbsp.	30 mL
Pita bread (7 inch, 18 cm, diameter)	2	2
Italian dressing	1 tbsp.	15 mL

(continued on next page)

Meal Salads

Combine first 7 ingredients in large bowl. Let stand for 10 minutes to blend flavours.

Put pitas on greased baking sheet. Brush with second amount of dressing. Bake in 375°F (190°C) oven for about 6 minutes per side until crisp. Break into irregular 1 to 1 1/2 inch (2.5 to 3.8 cm) pieces. Add to salad. Toss. Makes about 8 cups (2 L). Serves 4.

1 serving: 537 Calories; 35.8 g Total Fat (18.4 g Mono, 11.3 g Poly, 4.0 g Sat); 106 mg Cholesterol; 24 g Carbohydrate; 2 g Fibre; 30 g Protein; 897 mg Sodium

---

Peanut Noodle Salad

*Say nuts to turning on the stove on a hot summer day.
Just the thing when it's too hot to cook.*

Rice vermicelli	9 oz.	255 g
Smooth peanut butter	1/3 cup	75 mL
Brown sugar, packed	1/4 cup	60 mL
Lemon juice	1/4 cup	60 mL
Soy sauce	2 tbsp.	30 mL
Hot water	2 tbsp.	30 mL
Chopped cooked chicken	2 cups	500 mL
Thinly sliced red pepper	2 cups	500 mL
Grated carrot	1 cup	250 mL
Sliced green onion	1/2 cup	125 mL
Heads of butter lettuce, leaves separated	2	2

Put vermicelli into large bowl. Cover with boiling water. Let stand for about 5 minutes until tender. Drain. Rinse with cold water. Drain well. Return to same bowl.

Combine next 5 ingredients in small bowl. Add to vermicelli. Toss until coated.

Add next 4 ingredients. Toss.

Arrange lettuce on 4 large plates. Top with vermicelli mixture. Serves 4.

1 serving: 456 Calories; 5.1 g Total Fat (1.8 g Mono, 1.3 g Poly, 1.4 g Sat); 53 mg Cholesterol; 73 g Carbohydrate; 4 g Fibre; 25 g Protein; 742 mg Sodium

Pork And Pasta Salad

Pork, pasta and peppers, punctuated with a pleasantly creamy buttermilk dressing. Serve at room temperature or chilled with fresh sourdough bread. Cook extra pasta tonight to make light work of this recipe tomorrow.

Olive (or cooking) oil	2 tsp.	10 mL
Pork tenderloin, trimmed of fat and cut into thin strips	3/4 lb.	340 g
Bacon slices, diced	2	2
Pepper, sprinkle		
Sliced fresh white mushrooms	1 1/2 cups	375 mL
Thinly sliced green pepper	1 cup	250 mL
Thinly sliced red pepper	1 cup	250 mL
Cooked medium bow (or other) pasta (about 2 1/4 cups, 550 mL, uncooked)	3 cups	750 mL
BUTTERMILK DRESSING		
Buttermilk	1/3 cup	75 mL
Olive (or cooking) oil	2 tbsp.	30 mL
Red wine vinegar	1 tbsp.	15 mL
Dijon mustard	1 tbsp.	15 mL
Liquid honey	1 tbsp.	15 mL
Chopped fresh oregano (or 3/4 tsp., 4 mL, dried)	1 tbsp.	15 mL

Heat olive oil in large frying pan on medium-high. Add next 3 ingredients. Cook for about 5 minutes, stirring occasionally, until pork is browned.

Add next 3 ingredients. Stir. Cook for about 5 minutes, stirring occasionally, until peppers are tender-crisp. Transfer to large bowl.

Add pasta. Toss.

Buttermilk Dressing: Process all 6 ingredients in blender or food processor until smooth. Makes about 2/3 cup (150 mL) dressing. Drizzle over salad. Toss. Chill. Makes about 8 cups (2 L). Serves 4.

1 serving: 345 Calories; 13.5 g Total Fat (8.3 g Mono, 1.6 g Poly, 2.7 g Sat); 54 mg Cholesterol; 29 g Carbohydrate; 2 g Fibre; 27 g Protein; 189 mg Sodium

Asian Salsa Salad

Are we blending two cultures' cuisines? Absolutely! It's fusion at its finest. Why not have the best of both worlds—in one dish. If you're not a fan of tofu, this salad is sure to make you one.

Chopped tomato	3 cups	750 mL
English cucumber (with peel), seeds removed, diced	1 cup	250 mL
Chopped red onion	1 cup	250 mL
Chopped fresh cilantro or parsley	1/4 cup	60 mL
Rice vinegar	1/4 cup	60 mL
Lime juice	3 tbsp.	50 mL
Sesame (or cooking) oil	1 tbsp.	15 mL
Granulated sugar	1 tbsp.	15 mL
Grated lime zest	1 tsp.	5 mL
Salt	1/2 tsp.	2 mL
Cooked long grain white rice (about 2/3 cup, 150 mL, uncooked)	2 cups	500 mL
Package of firm tofu, cut into 1/2 inch (12 mm) cubes	12 1/2 oz.	350 g
Chopped or torn romaine lettuce, lightly packed	6 cups	1.5 L

Combine first 10 ingredients in large bowl.

Add rice and tofu. Stir gently. Let stand for 30 minutes to blend flavours.

Arrange lettuce on 4 large plates. Top with tofu mixture. Serves 4.

1 serving: 260 Calories; 6.5 g Total Fat (2.0 g Mono, 3.1 g Poly, 1.0 g Sat); 0 mg Cholesterol; 41 g Carbohydrate; 4 g Fibre; 11 g Protein; 343 mg Sodium

Paré Pointer
Huge ships don't sink very often. Only once.

Maple Miso Tofu Salad

Thought miso was only for soup? Think again, this Japanese treat is just as tasty in a salad—especially when it's maple-glazed and served on a colourful bed of vegetables and noodles. Use whichever miso you prefer—the darker it is, the stronger its flavour.

Package of firm tofu	12 1/2 oz.	350 g
Maple (or maple-flavoured) syrup	1/3 cup	75 mL
Miso (see Note)	3 tbsp.	50 mL
Cayenne pepper, sprinkle		
Mixed salad greens, lightly packed	8 cups	2 L
Thinly sliced red pepper	2 cups	500 mL
Dry chow mein noodles	2 cups	500 mL
MAPLE SYRUP VINAIGRETTE		
Cooking oil	2 tbsp.	30 mL
Rice vinegar	1 tbsp.	15 mL
Maple (or maple-flavoured) syrup	1 tbsp.	15 mL
Sesame oil	1 tsp.	5 mL
Soy sauce	1 tsp.	5 mL

Cut tofu crosswise into 8 slices. Let stand on paper towels for about 5 minutes to drain. Arrange tofu on greased foil-lined baking sheet with sides.

Combine next 3 ingredients in small bowl. Brush on tofu. Broil on top rack in oven for about 3 minutes until edges are golden. Turn tofu over. Brush with remaining syrup mixture. Broil for another 3 to 5 minutes until edges are golden.

Put next 3 ingredients into large bowl. Toss.

Maple Syrup Vinaigrette: Combine all 5 ingredients in jar with tight-fitting lid. Shake well. Makes about 1/4 cup (60 mL) vinaigrette. Drizzle over salad. Toss. Arrange on 4 large plates. Top with tofu. Serves 4.

1 serving: 331 Calories; 11.8 g Total Fat (5.1 g Mono, 4.5 g Poly, 1.2 g Sat); 2 mg Cholesterol; 46 g Carbohydrate; 5 g Fibre; 13 g Protein; 700 mg Sodium

Pictured on page 90.

Note: Miso is fermented soy bean paste. It is available in specialty Asian grocery stores.

Spinach Chicken Salad

*It just makes sense that chicken and chickpeas would go together
so well—especially in a feta-studded salad. Serve with garlic toast.
Freeze leftover chickpeas in a small resealable freezer bag
to use another day in a salad, soup or stew.*

Fresh spinach leaves, lightly packed	4 cups	1 L
Canned chickpeas (garbanzo beans), rinsed and drained	1 cup	250 mL
Crumbled feta cheese	1/4 cup	60 mL
Cooking oil	2 tsp.	10 mL
Boneless, skinless chicken breast halves, chopped	3/4 lb.	340 g
Cherry tomatoes	16	16
LEMON OREGANO VINAIGRETTE		
Lemon juice	3 tbsp.	50 mL
Olive (or cooking) oil	4 tsp.	20 mL
Liquid honey	1 tbsp.	15 mL
Dried whole oregano	1 tsp.	5 mL
Ground cumin	1/2 tsp.	2 mL

Put first 3 ingredients into large bowl. Toss. Set aside.

Heat cooking oil in large frying pan on medium-high. Add chicken. Cook for about 5 minutes, stirring often, until no longer pink inside.

Add tomatoes. Heat and stir on medium for about 5 minutes until tomatoes are softened. Add to spinach mixture. Toss.

Lemon Oregano Vinaigrette: Combine all 5 ingredients in jar with tight-fitting lid. Shake well. Makes about 1/3 cup (75 mL) vinaigrette. Drizzle over salad. Toss. Makes about 8 cups (2 L). Serves 4.

1 serving: 292 Calories; 11.7 g Total Fat (5.7 g Mono, 2.1 g Poly, 2.8 g Sat); 58 mg Cholesterol; 21 g Carbohydrate; 4 g Fibre; 27 g Protein; 303 mg Sodium

Pesto Bean Salad

Ciabatta up! Consider all your bases loaded—with bread,
beans and cheese. This is a guaranteed home run!

Cubed ciabatta bread, toasted (see Note)	3 cups	750 mL
Can of red kidney beans, rinsed and drained	19 oz.	540 mL
Chopped tomato	2 cups	500 mL
Diced mozzarella cheese (see Note)	1 cup	250 mL
Thinly sliced red onion	1/2 cup	125 mL
Pine nuts, toasted (see Tip, page 20)	1/4 cup	60 mL
Basil pesto	1/4 cup	60 mL
Italian dressing	1/4 cup	60 mL
Cut or torn romaine lettuce, lightly packed	5 cups	1.25 L

Put first 6 ingredients into large bowl. Toss.

Combine pesto and dressing in small bowl. Add to bread mixture. Toss.

Arrange lettuce on 4 large plates. Top with bean mixture. Serves 4.

1 serving: 624 Calories; 30.1 g Total Fat (9.5 g Mono, 5.9 g Poly, 6.9 g Sat); 37 mg Cholesterol; 64 g Carbohydrate; 17 g Fibre; 26 g Protein; 745 mg Sodium

Pictured at right.

Note: To easily toast bread cubes, spread on an ungreased baking sheet with sides. Bake in a 350°F (175°C) oven for 10 to 12 minutes, tossing once at halftime.

Note: For easier dicing, chill mozzarella cheese in the freezer for 30 minutes.

1. Pesto Bean Salad, above
2. Sicilian Summer Grill, page 82

Props courtesy of: Casa Bugatti

Seafood Spinach Salad

A salad with a healthy helping of two of the sea's best offerings—shrimp and crab. Add Goat Cheese Crostini, page 58, and dinner's complete.

Fresh spinach leaves, lightly packed	7 cups	1.75 L
Cooked salad shrimp	12 oz.	340 g
Grated carrot	1/2 cup	125 mL
Slivered red pepper	1/2 cup	125 mL
Can of crabmeat, drained, cartilage removed, flaked	4 1/4 oz.	120 g
Green onions, sliced	2	2
DILL DRESSING		
Salad dressing (or mayonnaise)	1/2 cup	125 mL
Milk	2 tbsp.	30 mL
Chopped fresh dill (or 1/2 tsp., 2 mL, dried)	2 tsp.	10 mL
Lemon juice	1 tsp.	5 mL
Granulated sugar	3/4 tsp.	4 mL

Put first 6 ingredients into extra-large bowl. Toss.

Dill Dressing: Combine all 5 ingredients in small bowl. Makes about 1/2 cup (125 mL) dressing. Drizzle over salad. Toss. Makes about 8 cups (2 L). Serves 4.

1 serving: 394 Calories; 30.8 g Total Fat (14.4 g Mono, 11.5 g Poly, 3.4 g Sat); 113 mg Cholesterol; 10 g Carbohydrate; 4 g Fibre; 21 g Protein; 630 mg Sodium

Pictured at left and on back cover.

1. Pecan Potato Salad, page 23
2. Seafood Spinach Salad, above
3. Sun-Dried Tomato Crostini, page 59

Props courtesy of: Totally Bamboo

Roasted Garlic Pesto Muffins

Looking for a good side dish? Ever consider muffins? These savoury quick breads were made for mopping up the best part of saucy dishes like chilies or stews. Leave the garlic and onion in their skins for roasting.

Small garlic bulb	1	1
Small onion	1	1
All-purpose flour	2 cups	500 mL
Grated Parmesan cheese	1/4 cup	60 mL
Baking powder	1 tsp.	5 mL
Baking soda	1/2 tsp.	2 mL
Salt	1/2 tsp.	2 mL
Large eggs, fork-beaten	2	2
Buttermilk (or soured milk, see Note)	3/4 cup	175 mL
Butter (or hard margarine), melted	1/4 cup	60 mL
Basil pesto	2 tbsp.	30 mL
Liquid honey	2 tbsp.	30 mL

Trim 1/4 inch (6 mm) from garlic bulb to expose tops of cloves, leaving bulb intact. Trim 1/4 inch (6 mm) from top of onion. Wrap each in greased foil Bake in 375°F (190°C) oven for about 45 minutes until tender. Let stand until cool enough to handle. Squeeze garlic bulb to remove cloves from skin. Discard skin. Put into medium bowl. Mash with a fork. Discard skin from onion. Chop onion. Add to garlic. Stir. Set aside.

Measure next 5 ingredients into large bowl. Stir. Make a well in centre.

Add remaining 5 ingredients to garlic mixture. Stir. Add to well. Stir until just moistened. Fill 12 greased muffin cups 2/3 full. Bake in 375°F (190°C) oven for about 15 minutes until wooden pick inserted in centre of muffin comes out clean. Let stand in pan for 5 minutes. Remove muffins and place on wire racks to cool. Makes 12 muffins.

1 muffin: 170 Calories; 6.9 g Total Fat (1.6 g Mono, 0.4 g Poly, 3.4 g Sat); 44 mg Cholesterol; 22 g Carbohydrate; 1 g Fibre; 5 g Protein; 287 mg Sodium

Pictured on page 144.

Note: To make soured milk, measure 2 tsp. (10 mL) white vinegar or lemon juice into a 1 cup (250 mL) liquid measure. Add enough milk to make 3/4 cup (175 mL). Stir. Let stand for 1 minute.

Oven-Roasted Ratatouille

This versatile dish is inordinately dee-lish. You can't go wrong with tender roasted veggies in a tangy tomato sauce with a hint of orange. Great topping pasta and complementing grilled chicken, pork or beef.

Medium zucchini (with peel), halved lengthwise and cut into 1/2 inch (12 mm) slices	1	1
Medium Asian eggplant (with peel), halved lengthwise and cut into 1/2 inch (12 mm) slices	1	1
Medium red peppers, cut into 1 inch (2.5 cm) pieces	2	2
Medium red onion, coarsely chopped	1	1
Sprigs of fresh rosemary	2	2
Strips of orange peel (2 inches, 5 cm, length, each)	2	2
Garlic cloves, coarsely chopped	3	3
Olive (or cooking) oil	2 tbsp.	30 mL
Tomato sauce	1 cup	250 mL
Salt	1/2 tsp.	2 mL
Pepper	1/4 tsp.	1 mL
Medium tomatoes, chopped	2	2
Chopped fresh basil	1/4 cup	60 mL
Orange juice	2 tbsp.	30 mL

Combine first 7 ingredients in ungreased 9 x 13 inch (22 x 33 cm) baking dish.

Drizzle with olive oil. Toss. Bake, uncovered, in 425°F (220°C) oven for 20 to 25 minutes, stirring occasionally, until vegetables start to soften.

Add next 3 ingredients. Stir. Bake, uncovered, for another 8 to 10 minutes until vegetables are softened. Discard rosemary sprigs and orange peel.

Add remaining 3 ingredients. Stir. Makes about 5 1/2 cups (1.4 L). Serves 6.

1 serving: 97 Calories; 4.9 g Total Fat (3.4 g Mono, 0.6 g Poly, 0.7 g Sat); 0 mg Cholesterol; 13 g Carbohydrate; 3 g Fibre; 2 g Protein; 449 mg Sodium

Cajun Cheese Bread

Topped with spicy jalapeño cheese and Cajun seasoning, this kicky French bread has gone French quarter! Excellent with Balsamic Skewers, page 99.

Butter (or hard margarine), softened	2/3 cup	150 mL
Grated jalapeño Monterey Jack cheese	2/3 cup	150 mL
Cajun seasoning	1 tsp.	5 mL
Parsley flakes	1/2 tsp.	2 mL
French bread loaf, cut into 12 slices	1	1

Combine first 4 ingredients in small bowl.

Spread cheese mixture on 1 side of bread slices. Arrange slices into loaf. Wrap tightly in sheet of heavy-duty (or double layer of regular) foil. Bake in 375°F (190°C) oven for 15 to 20 minutes, until cheese is melted. Makes 12 slices.

1 slice: 203 Calories; 12.5 g Total Fat (3.4 g Mono, 0.7 g Poly, 7.4 g Sat); 31 mg Cholesterol; 18 g Carbohydrate; 1 g Fibre; 5 g Protein; 358 mg Sodium

Pictured on page 18.

GRILLED CAJUN CHEESE BREAD: Preheat gas barbecue to medium. Place foil-wrapped loaf on ungreased grill. Close lid. Cook for about 15 minutes, turning occasionally, until cheese is melted.

Asiago Polenta

This Italian, cornmeal staple is rich and creamy with a hint of nutmeg. A tasty side for Sausage Pepper Skillet, page 142.

Prepared chicken broth	2 cups	500 mL
Water	2 cups	500 mL
Butter (or hard margarine)	2 tbsp.	30 mL
Salt	1/2 tsp.	2 mL
Ground nutmeg	1/4 tsp.	1 mL
Yellow cornmeal	1 cup	250 mL
Grated Asiago cheese	1 cup	250 mL

Combine first 5 ingredients in large saucepan. Bring to a boil.

(continued on next page)

Slowly add cornmeal, stirring constantly. Reduce heat to medium-low. Simmer, covered, for about 5 minutes, stirring often, until thickened.

Add cheese. Stir until melted. Makes about 4 cups (1 L). Serves 4.

1 serving: 307 Calories; 16.0 g Total Fat (1.9 g Mono, 0.6 g Poly, 8.9 g Sat); 40 mg Cholesterol; 28 g Carbohydrate; 2 g Fibre; 11 g Protein; 937 mg Sodium

Pictured on page 143.

Bulgur Vegetables

As an up-and-coming popular grain, bulgur is sure to please the health-conscious when mixed with citrus and fresh herbs. Excellent with Curry-Spiced Chicken, page 85, for a protein-packed meal. Add the leftover chickpeas to a chili or stew.

Boiling water	1 1/4 cups	300 mL
Bulgur, fine grind	3/4 cup	175 mL
Salt	1/2 tsp.	2 mL
Canned chickpeas (garbanzo beans), rinsed and drained	1 cup	250 mL
Frozen peas, thawed	1 cup	250 mL
Diced zucchini (with peel)	1 cup	250 mL
Diced red pepper	1/2 cup	125 mL
Italian dressing	1/3 cup	75 mL
Chopped fresh mint	2 tbsp.	30 mL
Chopped fresh basil	2 tbsp.	30 mL
Chopped fresh parsley	2 tbsp.	30 mL
Grated lemon zest	1 1/2 tsp.	7 mL

Combine first 3 ingredients in medium bowl. Let stand for about 20 minutes until water is absorbed. Fluff with a fork.

Combine next 8 ingredients in large bowl. Add bulgur. Toss.

Sprinkle with lemon zest. Makes about 5 cups (1.25 L). Serves 4.

1 serving: 311 Calories; 14.5 g Total Fat (7.4 g Mono, 5.0 g Poly, 1.1 g Sat); 12.5 mg Cholesterol; 39 g Carbohydrate; 7 g Fibre; 9 g Protein; 735 mg Sodium

Corn-Stuffed Tomatoes

Although there's a lot of corn in it, there's nothing corny about it
—a mild, cheesy filling is just the thing in a ripe, juicy tomato.
A sensational side for Chicken Tortilla Bake, page 95.

Large tomatoes	6	6
Salt, sprinkle		
Chopped onion	1 cup	250 mL
Can of kernel corn, drained	12 oz.	341 mL
Medium salsa	1/4 cup	60 mL
Light vegetable cream cheese	2 tbsp.	30 mL
Grated medium Cheddar cheese	1/4 cup	60 mL
Grated medium Cheddar cheese	1/4 cup	60 mL

Slice 1/4 inch (6 mm) from top of tomatoes. Scoop pulp into small bowl, leaving 1/4 inch (6 mm) thick shells (see Note). Trim bottom of tomatoes to sit flat, being careful not to cut into shells.

Sprinkle inside of tomatoes with salt. Let stand, cut-side down, on paper towels to drain.

Put onion into medium microwave-safe bowl. Microwave on high (100%) for about 2 minutes until softened.

Add next 3 ingredients. Stir until cream cheese is melted.

Add first amount of Cheddar cheese. Stir. Spoon into tomatoes. Arrange in greased 9 x 9 inch (22 x 22 cm) pan.

Sprinkle with second amount of Cheddar cheese. Broil on top rack in oven for about 3 minutes until Cheddar cheese is golden. Serves 6.

1 serving: 141 Calories; 4.8 g Total Fat (1.1 g Mono, 0.6 g Poly, 2.7 g Sat); 13 mg Cholesterol; 21 g Carbohydrate; 4 g Fibre; 6 g Protein; 258 mg Sodium

Note: The tomato pulp is too good to waste—use it in a tomato-based soup or stew.

Fresh Herb Rice

Fresh herbs, a hint of garlic and a lively splash of lemon make ordinary rice fabulously fragrant and flavourful. Excellent with Feta Shrimp Frittata, page 100, and steamed sugar snap peas. If you don't have any cilantro on hand, simply double the parsley.

Butter (or hard margarine)	2 tbsp.	30 mL
Chopped onion	1/2 cup	125 mL
Garlic clove, minced (or 1/4 tsp., 1 mL, powder)	1	1
Long grain white rice	1 1/2 cups	375 mL
Water	2 1/2 cups	625 mL
Dry (or alcohol-free) white wine	1/4 cup	60 mL
Salt	1/2 tsp.	2 mL
Chopped fresh cilantro	2 tbsp.	30 mL
Chopped fresh parsley	2 tbsp.	30 mL
Chopped fresh dill	2 tbsp.	30 mL
Finely chopped green onion	2 tbsp.	30 mL
Grated lemon zest	1 tsp.	5 mL

Melt butter in medium saucepan on medium. Add onion and garlic. Cook for about 5 minutes, stirring often, until onion is softened.

Add rice. Stir until coated.

Add next 3 ingredients. Stir. Bring to a boil. Reduce heat to medium-low. Simmer, covered, for about 20 minutes, without stirring, until rice is tender and liquid is absorbed. Let stand for 5 minutes.

Add remaining 5 ingredients. Stir. Makes about 5 cups (1.25 L). Serves 4.

1 serving: 328 Calories; 6.2 g Total Fat (1.6 g Mono, 0.4 g Poly, 3.7 g Sat); 15 mg Cholesterol; 59 g Carbohydrate; 1 g Fibre; 5 g Protein; 341 mg Sodium

Orange Basil Broccoli

Nobody said broccoli had to be boring! Serve this yummy side
with Bruschetta Steak Loaf, page 67.

Broccoli florets	6 cups	1.5 L
Sliced natural almonds, toasted	3 tbsp.	50 mL
(see Tip, page 20)		
Chopped fresh basil (or 3/4 tsp.,	1 tbsp.	15 mL
4 mL, dried)		
Salt, sprinkle		
Pepper, sprinkle		
Butter (or hard margarine), melted	2 tbsp.	30 mL
Frozen concentrated orange juice, thawed	2 tbsp.	30 mL

Put broccoli into greased 2 quart (2 L) casserole. Sprinkle with next 4 ingredients.

Combine butter and concentrated orange juice in small cup. Drizzle over broccoli. Cook, covered, in 375°F (190°C) oven for 20 to 30 minutes until broccoli is tender-crisp. Serves 4.

1 serving: 121 Calories; 8.3 g Total Fat (2.9 g Mono, 0.9 g Poly, 3.8 g Sat); 15 mg Cholesterol; 10 g Carbohydrate; 4 g Fibre; 4 g Protein; 69 mg Sodium

Pesto Potato Wedges

With a hint of basil pesto, these hearty home-fries are hardly
French—maybe Italian. A great accompaniment for grilled steak
or chicken and your favourite vegetables or salad.

Olive (or cooking) oil	1 tbsp.	15 mL
Seasoned salt	1/2 tsp.	2 mL
Pepper	1/8 tsp.	0.5 mL
Large unpeeled red potatoes,	4	4
each cut into 8 wedges		
Basil pesto	1/4 cup	60 mL

Combine first 3 ingredients in large bowl.

(continued on next page)

Add potato. Toss until coated. Arrange in single layer on greased baking sheet with sides. Bake in 425°F (220°C) oven for about 30 minutes, turning once at halftime, until tender. Remove to same bowl.

Add pesto. Toss until coated. Serves 4.

1 serving: 281 Calories; 11.5 g Total Fat (2.5 g Mono, 0.4 g Poly, 1.8 g Sat); 4 mg Cholesterol; 38 g Carbohydrate; 4 g Fibre; 6 g Protein; 322 mg Sodium

Mediterranean Potatoes

Make merry on the Mediterranean with these well-seasoned, Italian-inspired spuds. Fantastico *with Lamb Meatball Skewers, page 118.*

Medium unpeeled potatoes, quartered	4	4
Grated Parmesan cheese	1/4 cup	60 mL
Sun-dried tomatoes in oil,	3 tbsp.	50 mL
blotted dry and chopped		
Olive (or cooking) oil	2 tbsp.	30 mL
Butter (or hard margarine), softened	2 tbsp.	30 mL
Garlic clove, minced (or 1/4 tsp.,	1	1
1 mL, powder)		
Dried crushed chilies	1/2 tsp.	2 mL
Salt	1/2 tsp.	2 mL
Dried rosemary, crushed	1/4 tsp.	1 mL
Dried whole oregano	1/4 tsp.	1 mL

Cook potato in boiling salted water in medium saucepan for about 10 minutes until partially cooked. Drain.

Combine remaining 9 ingredients in ungreased 2 quart (2 L) casserole. Add potato. Toss until coated. Cook, covered, in 375°F (190°C) oven for about 30 minutes until potato is tender. Serves 4.

1 serving: 218 Calories; 16.8 g Total Fat (8.5 g Mono, 1.2 g Poly, 6.0 g Sat); 20 mg Cholesterol; 12 g Carbohydrate; 5 g Fibre; 7 g Protein; 506 mg Sodium

Roasted Veggie Pockets

These pockets are a perfect fit for hands of all sizes. Partner with Herb-Scented Lamb Kabobs, page 121, for a fantastic Mediterranean-inspired meal.

Ranch dressing	1/4 cup	60 mL
Sliced green onion	2 tbsp.	30 mL
Lime juice	1 tbsp.	15 mL
Finely chopped chipotle pepper in adobo sauce (see Tip, below)	1 tsp.	5 mL
Asian eggplant, cut lengthwise into 1/4 inch (6 mm) slices	1	1
Medium zucchini, cut lengthwise into 1/4 inch (6 mm) slices	1	1
Medium red pepper, quartered	1	1
Olive (or cooking) oil	1 tbsp.	15 mL
Large tomato, cut in half	1	1
Olive (or cooking) oil	2 tsp.	10 mL
Whole wheat pita bread (7 inch, 18 cm, diameter), halved and opened	4	4

Combine first 4 ingredients in small bowl. Set aside.

Brush both sides of eggplant, zucchini and red pepper with first amount of olive oil. Arrange in single layer on greased baking sheet with sides.

Brush cut sides of tomato with second amount of olive oil. Place cut-side up on same baking sheet. Cook vegetables in 400°F (205°C) oven for 5 to 10 minutes until tender-crisp. Chop coarsely. Put into medium bowl. Add dressing mixture. Stir.

Place 1 pita half inside another to make a double-thick pocket. Repeat with remaining pita halves. Fill pockets with vegetable mixture. Serves 4.

1 serving: 336 Calories; 15.5 g Total Fat (4.4 g Mono, 1.3 g Poly, 2.3 g Sat); 4 mg Cholesterol; 46 g Carbohydrate; 8 g Fibre; 8 g Protein; 494 mg Sodium

 Chipotle chili peppers are smoked jalapeno peppers. Be sure to wash your hands after handling. To store any leftover chipotle chili peppers, divide into recipe-friendly portions and freeze, with sauce, in airtight containers for up to one year.

Maple-Glazed Vegetables

Put a truly Canadian spin on veggies by glazing them with
maple syrup. Cut the potatoes about the same size as the carrots
for even cooking. Cook alongside Lemon Herb Chicken, page 88.

Baby carrots	1 lb.	454 g
Baby potatoes, halved or quartered	1 lb.	454 g
Diced onion	1/2 cup	125 mL
Maple (or maple-flavoured) syrup	1/3 cup	75 mL
Finely grated gingerroot (or 1 1/2 tsp., 7 mL, ground ginger)	2 tbsp.	30 mL
Salt	1/2 tsp.	2 mL
Butter (or hard margarine)	2 tbsp.	30 mL
Lemon juice (optional)	2 tbsp.	30 mL
Chopped fresh parsley, for garnish		

Put first 6 ingredients into large bowl. Toss until vegetables are coated. Transfer to greased 2 quart (2 L) casserole.

Spoon dabs of butter, using 1/2 tsp. (2 mL) for each, over vegetable mixture. Bake, covered, in 375°F (190°C) oven for 30 to 40 minutes, stirring once at halftime, until vegetables are tender and glazed. Remove to large serving bowl.

Sprinkle with lemon juice. Toss.

Garnish with parsley. Serves 4.

1 serving: 253 Calories; 5.9 g Total Fat (1.5 g Mono, 0.3 g Poly, 3.6 g Sat); 15 mg Cholesterol;
46 g Carbohydrate; 5 g Fibre; 4 g Protein; 399 mg Sodium

CURRY-GLAZED VEGETABLES: Instead of gingerroot, use 1 to 2 tsp. (5 to 10 mL) curry powder. Sprinkle with orange juice instead of lemon juice.

HONEY-GARLIC GLAZED VEGETABLES: Use liquid honey instead of maple syrup, and dab with garlic butter instead of regular butter.

Braised Celery

The often-unappreciated celery is dressed to impress with the bold flavours of goat cheese and chili. This savoury side is excellent with steamed rice and Artichoke Salmon, page 111.

Cooking oil	1 tbsp.	15 mL
Celery ribs, cut into 1 inch (2.5 cm) pieces	8	8
Dried crushed chilies	1/4 tsp.	1 mL
Salt	1/4 tsp.	1 mL
Prepared chicken broth	3/4 cup	175 mL
Goat (chèvre) cheese	3 tbsp.	50 mL

Heat cooking oil in large frying pan on medium. Add next 3 ingredients. Cook for about 5 minutes, stirring occasionally, until celery starts to soften.

Add broth. Stir. Bring to a boil. Boil gently, uncovered, for about 10 minutes until celery is tender-crisp. Remove with slotted spoon to medium serving bowl. Cover to keep warm. Boil remaining broth for 3 to 5 minutes until reduced to about 1/4 cup (60 mL).

Add cheese. Heat and stir until smooth. Add to celery. Stir. Makes about 4 cups (1 L). Serves 6.

1 serving: 51 Calories; 3.9 g Total Fat (1.8 g Mono, 0.8 g Poly, 1.2 g Sat); 4 mg Cholesterol; 2 g Carbohydrate; 1 g Fibre; 2 g Protein; 265 mg Sodium

Variation: For even bolder flavour, use blue cheese instead of goat cheese.

Balsamic Onions

Tangy and sweet, these onions make an elegant side for any grilled beef, chicken or fish dish—add baked potatoes to make the meal complete.

Large red onions, each cut into 8 wedges	2	2
Balsamic vinegar	1/4 cup	60 mL
Olive (or cooking) oil	2 tbsp.	30 mL
Brown sugar, packed	2 tbsp.	30 mL
Salt	1/2 tsp.	2 mL
Pepper	1/2 tsp.	2 mL

(continued on next page)

Arrange onion in single layer in ungreased 2 quart (2 L) shallow baking dish.

Combine next 3 ingredients in small cup. Drizzle over onion.

Sprinkle with salt and pepper. Bake, covered, in 400°F (205°C) oven for about 45 minutes until onion is softened. Bake, uncovered, for another 10 to 15 minutes until caramelized. Serves 4.

1 serving: 128 Calories; 6.8 g Total Fat (5.0 g Mono, 0.6 g Poly, 0.9 g Sat); 0 mg Cholesterol; 16 g Carbohydrate; 1 g Fibre; 1 g Protein; 303 mg Sodium

Garlicky Mashed Potatoes

Mashed potatoes need not be boring. They're easy to liven up with a little garlic and parsley. No gravy required here! Serve with Sweet Curry Sausages, page 64.

Peeled potatoes, cut up	3 lbs.	1.4 kg
Butter (or hard margarine)	1/3 cup	75 mL
Garlic cloves, minced (or 3/4 tsp., 4 mL, powder)	3	3
Milk	2/3 cup	150 mL
Pepper	1/4 tsp.	1 mL
Chopped fresh parsley (or 3/4 tsp., 4 mL, flakes)	1 tbsp.	15 mL

Cook potato in boiling salted water in large saucepan until tender. Drain.

Cover to keep warm.

Melt butter in small saucepan on medium. Add garlic. Cook for about 2 minutes, stirring constantly, until just golden. Add to potato.

Add milk and pepper. Mash. Remove to large serving bowl.

Sprinkle with parsley. Makes about 6 cups (1.5 L). Serves 4.

1 serving: 423 Calories; 15.2 g Total Fat (3.9 g Mono, 0.7 g Poly, 9.5 g Sat); 40 mg Cholesterol; 67 g Carbohydrate; 6 g Fibre; 7 g Protein; 139 mg Sodium

Sun-Dried Tomato Cornbread

Cornbread is given a modern makeover when it's speckled with sun-dried tomato and cheese. Ideal with Grilled Pork And Mango Salad, page 27.

All-purpose flour	1 1/2 cups	375 mL
Yellow cornmeal	1 cup	250 mL
Granulated sugar	1/4 cup	60 mL
Baking powder	2 tsp.	10 mL
Baking soda	1/2 tsp.	2 mL
Salt	1/2 tsp.	2 mL
Grated havarti cheese	1 cup	250 mL
Large eggs	2	2
Buttermilk (or soured milk, see Note)	1 cup	250 mL
Butter (or hard margarine), melted	1/2 cup	125 mL

Sun-dried tomatoes, softened in
  1/2 cup boiling water for 10 minutes
  before finely chopping
	1/2 cup	125 mL

Measure first 6 ingredients into large bowl. Stir.

Add cheese. Stir. Make a well in centre.

Combine remaining 4 ingredients in medium bowl. Add to well. Stir until just moistened. Spread in greased 8 x 8 inch (20 x 20 cm) pan. Bake in 350°F (175°C) oven for about 35 minutes until wooden pick inserted in centre comes out clean. Cuts into 9 pieces.

1 piece: 332 Calories; 16.5 g Total Fat (3.3 g Mono, 0.8 g Poly, 10.1 g Sat); 80 mg Cholesterol; 37 g Carbohydrate; 2 g Fibre; 8.5 g Protein; 503 mg Sodium

Pictured on page 53.

Note: To make soured milk, measure 1 tbsp. (15 mL) white vinegar or lemon juice into a 1 cup (250 mL) liquid measure. Add enough milk to make 1 cup (250 mL). Stir. Let stand for 1 minute.

Side Dishes

Vegetable Spanish Rice

The refrain in Spain is that this dish is anything but plain! Top this tomato and pepper rice with a little salsa, and serve alongside Nacho-Crusted Haddock, page 109.

Cooking oil	2 tbsp.	30 mL
Finely chopped onion	1 cup	250 mL
Garlic cloves, minced (or 1/2 tsp., 2 mL, powder)	2	2
Long grain white rice	1 1/2 cups	375 mL
Prepared chicken (or vegetable) broth	2 1/2 cups	625 mL
Can of stewed tomatoes	14 oz.	398 mL
Diced green pepper	1 cup	250 mL
Paprika	1/2 tsp.	2 mL
Bay leaf	1	1

Heat cooking oil in large saucepan on medium. Add onion and garlic. Cook for 5 to 10 minutes, stirring often, until onion starts to soften.

Add rice. Stir until coated.

Add remaining 5 ingredients. Stir. Bring to a boil. Reduce heat to medium-low. Simmer, covered, for about 30 minutes, without stirring, until rice is tender and liquid is absorbed. Let stand for 5 minutes. Discard bay leaf. Fluff with a fork. Makes about 7 cups (1.75 L). Serves 6.

1 serving: 240 Calories; 5.2 g Total Fat (2.9 g Mono, 1.5 g Poly, 0.5 g Sat); 0 mg Cholesterol; 43 g Carbohydrate; 1 g Fibre; 6 g Protein; 475 mg Sodium

---

Paré Pointer

After a big heist, the thief hurried home and sawed the legs off his bed. He wanted to lie low for awhile.

Chipotle Cheese Potatoes

With 2 cheeses and smoky chipotle peppers, these potatoes have all the right stuffing! Great with Salmon With Avocado Salsa, page 110.

Large unpeeled baking potatoes	2	2
Chive and onion cream cheese	1/2 cup	125 mL
Grated medium Cheddar cheese	1/2 cup	125 mL
Finely chopped chipotle pepper in adobo sauce (see Tip, page 46)	1/2 tsp.	2 mL
Grated medium Cheddar cheese	1/4 cup	60 mL

Prick potatoes in several places with a fork. Wrap with paper towels. Microwave on high (100%) for about 10 minutes, turning once at halftime, until tender. Cut potatoes in half lengthwise. Scoop pulp into medium bowl, leaving 1/4 inch (6 mm) thick shells. Mash potato pulp.

Add next 3 ingredients. Stir. Spoon into shells. Place in ungreased 9 x 9 inch (22 x 22 cm) baking pan.

Sprinkle with second amount of Cheddar cheese. Bake in 375°F (190°C) oven for 20 to 30 minutes until heated through. Serves 4.

1 serving: 335 Calories; 17.3 g Total Fat (2.0 g Mono, 0.3 g Poly, 11.5 g Sat); 52 mg Cholesterol; 34 g Carbohydrate; 3 g Fibre; 10 g Protein; 282 mg Sodium

GRILLED CHIPOTLE CHEESE POTATOES: Preheat gas barbecue to medium. Place sheet of heavy-duty (or double layer of regular) foil on ungreased grill. Place stuffed potatoes on foil. Close lid. Cook for about 25 minutes until heated through and cheese is golden.

Pictured on page 108.

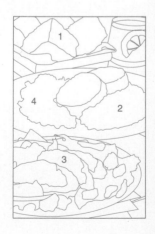

1. Sun-Dried Tomato Cornbread, page 50
2. Polenta-Topped Chili, page 78
3. Grilled Pork And Mango Salad, page 27
4. Jicama Salad, page 22

Spiced Yam Hash

Regular hash browns a bit too blasé? Switch the potatoes for yams and perk the whole thing up with a sweet, spicy heat. Tastes great with Ribbon Zucchini Frittata, page 140.

Cooking oil	2 tbsp.	30 mL
Cubed peeled yam (or sweet potato)	3 cups	750 mL
Chopped green onion	1/2 cup	125 mL
Chopped red pepper	1/2 cup	125 mL
Paprika	1/2 tsp.	2 mL
Chili powder	1/2 tsp.	2 mL
Salt	1/2 tsp.	2 mL
Ground cinnamon	1/8 tsp.	0.5 mL

Heat cooking oil in medium frying pan on medium-high. Add yam. Heat and stir for about 5 minutes until starting to brown. Reduce heat to medium-low.

Add remaining 6 ingredients. Stir. Cook, covered, for about 5 minutes, stirring occasionally, until yam is tender. Makes about 2 1/2 cups (625 mL). Serves 4.

1 serving: 202 Calories; 7.2 g Total Fat (4.0 g Mono, 2.2 g Poly, 0.6 g Sat); 0 mg Cholesterol; 33 g Carbohydrate; 5 g Fibre; 2 g Protein; 308 mg Sodium

Pictured at left.

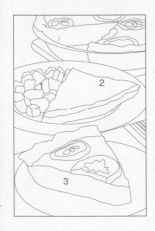

1. Spiced Yam Hash, above
2. Ribbon Zucchini Frittata, page 140
3. Curried Tuna Quiche, page 98

Props courtesy of: The Bay

Potato Vegetable Kabobs

There's always time to enhance the natural flavours of grilled veggies with lime. Make it a citrus-themed night and serve with Margarita Marinated Steak, page 74.

Lime juice	1/4 cup	60 mL
Orange juice	2 tbsp.	30 mL
Sun-dried tomato pesto	2 tbsp.	30 mL
Cooking oil	2 tbsp.	30 mL
White baby potatoes, larger ones cut in half	1 1/2 lbs.	680 g
Large red peppers, cut into 1 1/2 inch (3.8 cm) pieces	2	2
Medium zucchini (with peel), halved lengthwise and cut into 1 inch (2.5 cm) slices	2	2
Bamboo skewers (8 inches, 20 cm, each), soaked in water for 10 minutes	12	12

Combine first 4 ingredients in small cup. Set aside.

Put potatoes on microwave-safe plate. Microwave on high (100%) for about 5 minutes until just tender.

Thread potatoes, red pepper and zucchini alternately onto skewers. Place on large plate. Brush kabobs with half of lime juice mixture. Preheat gas barbecue to medium (see Tip, below). Cook kabobs on greased grill for about 15 minutes, turning once at halftime and brushing with remaining lime juice mixture, until vegetables are tender-crisp. Serves 6.

1 serving: 117 Calories; 5.9 g Total Fat (3.4 g Mono, 1.6 g Poly, 0.5 g Sat); 0 mg Cholesterol; 14 g Carbohydrate; 5 g Fibre; 4 g Protein; 36 mg Sodium

Pictured on page 72.

 Too cold to barbecue? Use the broiler instead! Your food should cook in about the same length of time—and remember to turn or baste as directed. Set your oven rack so that the food is about 3 to 4 inches (7.5 to 10 cm) away from the top element—for most ovens, this is the top rack.

Smashed Celery Spuds

These unique celery, cauliflower and onion potatoes are simply smashing! Serve with Cheese And Pesto Meatloaf, page 70.

Peeled potatoes, cut up	1 1/2 lbs.	680 g
Butter (or hard margarine)	2 tbsp.	30 mL
Chopped cauliflower	2 cups	500 mL
Finely chopped celery	1 cup	250 mL
Finely chopped onion	1/2 cup	125 mL
Prepared chicken broth	1/3 cup	75 mL
Milk	1/4 cup	60 mL
Butter (or hard margarine)	2 tbsp.	30 mL
Pepper	1/4 tsp.	1 mL

Cook potato in boiling salted water in large saucepan until tender. Drain. Return to same saucepan. Heat on medium-low, shaking saucepan, until potato is dry. Remove from heat. Cover to keep warm.

Melt first amount of butter in medium saucepan on medium. Add next 3 ingredients. Cook, covered, for 5 to 10 minutes, stirring occasionally, until vegetables are tender-crisp.

Add broth. Stir. Cook, covered, for 3 to 5 minutes until vegetables are tender. Add to potato.

Add remaining 3 ingredients. Mash. Makes about 4 3/4 cups (1.2 L). Serves 4.

1 serving: 282 Calories; 11.9 g Total Fat (3.1 g Mono, 0.6 g Poly, 7.4 g Sat); 31 mg Cholesterol; 41 g Carbohydrate; 5 g Fibre; 5 g Protein; 490 mg Sodium

Pictured on page 71.

Paré Pointer

When she heard there was going to be some change in the weather, she walked around with an open purse.

Sweet And Spicy Onions

Caramelized onions make a simply sweet (and spicy) side
for Tangy Chicken Potato Bake page 91.

Butter (or hard margarine), softened	3 tbsp.	50 mL
Chili sauce	2 tbsp.	30 mL
Brown sugar, packed	1 tbsp.	15 mL
Worcestershire sauce	1 tsp.	5 mL
Salt	1/8 tsp.	0.5 mL
Pepper	1/8 tsp.	0.5 mL
Medium onions, each cut into 4 wedges	4	4
Grated Parmesan cheese	2 tsp.	10 mL

Melt butter in large frying pan on medium. Add next 5 ingredients. Heat and stir until bubbling.

Add onion. Stir to coat. Cook, covered, for about 30 minutes, stirring occasionally, until onion is very soft and caramelized.

Sprinkle with cheese. Makes about 3 cups (750 mL). Serves 4.

1 serving: 142 Calories; 9.0 g Total Fat (2.3 g Mono, 0.4 g Poly, 5.6 g Sat); 23 mg Cholesterol; 15 g Carbohydrate; 2 g Fibre; 2 g Protein; 161 mg Sodium

Goat Cheese Crostini

Looking for something light for dinner? Serve with Seafood Spinach Salad, page 37, and you're all set. Need an appealing appetizer? Slice the baguette on the diagonal for a stylish presentation and double the recipe to use the entire loaf.

Baguette bread slices (about 1/2 inch, 12 mm, thick)	12	12
Olive (or cooking) oil	2 tbsp.	30 mL
Balsamic vinegar	1 tsp.	5 mL
Goat (chèvre) cheese, room temperature	1/2 cup	125 mL
Coarsely ground pepper	1/4 tsp.	1 mL

Arrange bread slices on ungreased baking sheet with sides.

(continued on next page)

Side Dishes

Combine olive oil and vinegar in small cup. Brush on bread. Bake in 350°F (175°C) oven for about 10 minutes until toasted.

Spread cheese on toast. Broil on top rack in oven for about 2 minutes until cheese is melted.

Sprinkle with pepper. Serves 4 to 6.

1 serving: 336 Calories; 10.7 g Total Fat (5.9 g Mono, 0.7 g Poly, 3.6 g Sat); 9 mg Cholesterol; 47 g Carbohydrate; 1 g Fibre; 11 g Protein; 624 mg Sodium

SUN-DRIED TOMATO CROSTINI: Combine goat cheese with 1 tbsp. (15 mL) sun-dried tomato pesto before spreading on toast.

Pictured on page 36 and on back cover.

Lemon Pepper Greens

This crisp and colourful side will leave other dishes green with envy.
Simply sinful with Scallop "Orzotto," page 103.

Butter (or hard margarine)	1 tbsp.	15 mL
Cooking oil	1 tsp.	5 mL
Sugar snap peas, trimmed	2 cups	500 mL
Chopped fresh (or frozen) green beans	2 cups	500 mL
Fresh asparagus, trimmed of tough ends	1 lb.	454 g
and cut into 1 inch (2.5 cm) pieces		
Lemon juice	1 tbsp.	15 mL
Lemon pepper	1 tsp.	5 mL
Pine nuts, toasted	2 tbsp.	30 mL
(see Tip, page 20), optional		

Heat wok or large frying pan on medium-high until very hot. Add butter and cooking oil. Add next 3 ingredients. Stir-fry for 3 to 4 minutes until vegetables are tender-crisp.

Add remaining 3 ingredients. Stir. Makes about 5 cups (1.25 L). Serves 4.

1 serving: 112 Calories; 4.3 g Total Fat (1.4 g Mono, 0.6 g Poly, 1.9 g Sat); 8 mg Cholesterol; 15 g Carbohydrate; 5 g Fibre; 5 g Protein; 64 mg Sodium

Lemon-Kissed Couscous

They'll be lining up to kiss the cook when you serve them this colourful couscous.
Delightful when served warm or cold with Satay Pork Skewers, page 141.

Cooking oil	1 tsp.	5 mL
Chopped fennel bulb (white part only)	1 1/4 cups	300 mL
Garlic clove, minced (or 1/4 tsp., 1 mL, powder)	1	1
Prepared chicken broth	1 1/2 cups	375 mL
Frozen peas	1 cup	250 mL
Plain couscous	1 cup	250 mL
Diced tomato	3/4 cup	175 mL
Dark raisins	1/2 cup	125 mL
Lemon juice	2 tbsp.	30 mL
Grated lemon zest	1/2 tsp.	2 mL

Heat cooking oil in large frying pan on medium. Add fennel and garlic. Cook for about 5 minutes, stirring often, until fennel is tender-crisp.

Add broth and peas. Stir. Bring to a boil.

Add remaining 5 ingredients. Stir. Remove from heat. Let stand, covered, for about 5 minutes until couscous is tender and broth is absorbed. Fluff with a fork. Makes about 5 cups (1.25 L). Serves 4.

1 serving: 332 Calories; 2.5 g Total Fat (1.0 g Mono, 0.7 g Poly, 0.4 g Sat); 0 mg Cholesterol; 68 g Carbohydrate; 8 g Fibre; 12 g Protein; 401 mg Sodium

Paré Pointer

Cross a termite and a praying mantis and you get
a bug that says grace before eating your house.

Baked Fragrant Rice

With a name like this, you know your kitchen is going to smell wonderful once you get cooking. Pair with Pork In Plum Sauce, page 137.

Cooking oil	2 tbsp.	30 mL
Chopped onion	1 cup	250 mL
Long grain white rice	1 1/2 cups	375 mL
Garlic clove, minced (or 1/4 tsp., 1 mL, powder)	1	1
Finely grated gingerroot (or 1/8 tsp., 0.5 mL, ground ginger)	1/2 tsp.	2 mL
Garam masala (see Tip, below)	1/2 tsp.	2 mL
Chopped butternut squash	2 1/2 cups	625 mL
Prepared chicken broth	2 1/2 cups	625 mL
Chopped pistachios	1/4 cup	60 mL

Heat cooking oil in large frying pan on medium. Add onion. Cook for 5 to 10 minutes, stirring often, until softened.

Add next 4 ingredients. Heat and stir for about 3 minutes until fragrant. Transfer to ungreased 2 quart (2 L) casserole.

Add remaining 3 ingredients. Stir. Bake, covered, in 375°F (190°C) oven for about 1 hour until squash and rice are tender and broth is absorbed. Fluff with a fork. Makes about 8 cups (2 L). Serves 6.

1 serving: 295 Calories; 7.6 g Total Fat (4.1 g Mono, 2.2 g Poly, 0.8 g Sat); 0 mg Cholesterol; 52 g Carbohydrate; 3 g Fibre; 7 g Protein; 328 mg Sodium

 If you don't keep garam masala on hand, add just a pinch each of ground cumin, coriander, pepper, cardamom, cinnamon and cloves.

Cabbage Noodles

An unexpected combination of coleslaw and noodles makes a super simple side for supper. Excellent with Herb-Scented Lamb Kabobs, page 121.

Broad egg noodles	3 cups	750 mL
Olive (or cooking) oil	1 tbsp.	15 mL
Butter (or hard margarine)	1 tbsp.	15 mL
Coleslaw mix (about 1 lb., 454 g)	8 cups	2 L
Thinly sliced onion	1 cup	250 mL
Granulated sugar	1 tbsp.	15 mL
Garlic clove, minced (or 1/4 tsp., 1 mL, powder)	1	1
Salt	1/2 tsp.	2 mL
Pepper	1/4 tsp.	1 mL

Cook noodles in boiling salted water in large uncovered saucepan for 6 to 8 minutes, stirring occasionally, until tender but firm. Drain. Return to same pot. Cover to keep warm.

Heat olive oil and butter in Dutch oven on medium. Add remaining 6 ingredients. Cook, covered, for about 10 minutes, stirring occasionally, until coleslaw is softened. Add noodles. Stir. Makes about 6 cups (1.5 L). Serves 4.

1 serving: 223 Calories; 7.5 g Total Fat (3.6 g Mono, 0.8 g Poly, 2.6 g Sat); 31 mg Cholesterol; 33 g Carbohydrate; 4 g Fibre; 6 g Protein; 353 mg Sodium

Pictured on page 17.

Sweet Sugar Peas

Indulge your sweet tooth with this quick and easy side of tender-crisp pea pods coated in a sweet, gingery glaze. Delicious with Peanut Chicken Rice Bake, page 87.

Frozen concentrated orange juice, thawed	2 tbsp.	30 mL
Water	1 tbsp.	15 mL
Soy sauce	2 tsp.	10 mL
Cornstarch	1 tsp.	5 mL
Ground ginger	1/4 tsp.	1 mL
Cooking oil	2 tsp.	10 mL
Sugar snap peas, trimmed	5 cups	1.25 L

(continued on next page)

Combine first 5 ingredients in small cup.

Heat cooking oil in large frying pan on medium. Add peas. Heat and stir for about 5 minutes until tender-crisp. Stir cornstarch mixture. Add to peas. Heat and stir for about 1 minute until sauce is thickened. Makes about 4 cups (1 L). Serves 6.

1 serving: 80 Calories; 1.5 g Total Fat (0.9 g Mono, 0.5 g Poly, 0.1 g Sat); 0 mg Cholesterol; 12 g Carbohydrate; 3 g Fibre; 3 g Protein; 160 mg Sodium

Creamed Spinach

Put a whole new spin on spinach with the addition of prosciutto and nutmeg. Serve with Moroccan Pot Roast, page 66, and steamed carrots.

Cooking oil	2 tbsp.	30 mL
Chopped prosciutto (or deli) ham	1/2 cup	125 mL
Butter (or hard margarine)	1/4 cup	60 mL
Finely chopped onion	1 1/3 cups	325 mL
Garlic cloves, minced (or 1 tsp., 5 mL, powder)	4	4
Coarsely chopped fresh spinach, lightly packed	12 cups	3 L
Sour cream	1 cup	250 mL
Ground nutmeg	1/2 tsp.	2 mL

Heat cooking oil in Dutch oven on medium. Add ham. Heat and stir for 3 to 5 minutes until crisp. Transfer to small bowl. Set aside. Reduce heat to medium-low.

Melt butter in same pan. Add onion and garlic. Cook for about 5 minutes, stirring often, until onion is softened.

Add spinach. Heat and stir for 1 to 2 minutes until spinach is almost wilted.

Add ham, sour cream and nutmeg. Heat and stir for 1 minute. Makes about 4 cups (1 L). Serves 8.

1 serving: 195 Calories; 15.9 g Total Fat (3.5 g Mono, 1.3 g Poly, 7.9 g Sat); 46 mg Cholesterol; 6 g Carbohydrate; 1 g Fibre; 7 g Protein; 467 mg Sodium

Sweet Curry Sausages

Just call them Bangalore Bangers! Ordinary sausages go
down India way with apple, raisins and a coconut curry flavour.
Great with Garlicky Mashed Potatoes, page 49.

Prepared chicken broth	1/4 cup	60 mL
Cornstarch	1 tsp.	5 mL
Cooking oil	2 tsp.	10 mL
Beef sausages, casings removed, cut into 1 inch (2.5 cm) pieces	1 lb.	454 g
Chopped peeled tart apple (such as Granny Smith)	2 cups	500 mL
Sliced onion	1 cup	250 mL
Garlic cloves, minced (or 1/2 tsp., 2 mL, powder)	2	2
Finely grated gingerroot (or 1/4 tsp., 1 mL, ground ginger)	1 tsp.	5 mL
Curry powder	1 1/2 tbsp.	25 mL
Can of light coconut milk	14 oz.	398 mL
Dark raisins	1/3 cup	75 mL

Stir broth into cornstarch in small cup. Set aside.

Heat cooking oil in large frying pan on medium-high. Add sausage. Cook for about 5 minutes, stirring occasionally, until browned. Drain. Reduce heat to medium.

Add next 4 ingredients. Cook for about 5 minutes, stirring occasionally, until apple starts to soften.

Add curry powder. Heat and stir for about 1 minute until fragrant.

Add coconut milk and raisins. Stir. Bring to a boil. Reduce heat to medium. Boil gently, uncovered, for about 5 minutes, stirring occasionally, until apple is tender. Stir cornstarch mixture. Add to sausage mixture. Heat and stir for about 1 minute until boiling and thickened. Makes about 4 cups (1 L). Serves 4.

1 serving: 553 Calories; 40.9 g Total Fat (15.8 g Mono, 1.7 g Poly, 18.1 g Sat); 93 mg Cholesterol; 25 g Carbohydrate; 2 g Fibre; 22 g Protein; 792 mg Sodium

Family Fajitas

Every aspiring señor and señorita loves a steak-filled fajita.
Serve with all the fixings that make do-it-yourself fajitas
so fun—lettuce, grated cheese, sour cream and salsa.

Paprika	1 tsp.	5 mL
Seasoned salt	1/2 tsp.	2 mL
Garlic powder	1/2 tsp.	2 mL
Ground cumin	1/2 tsp.	2 mL
Dry mustard	1/4 tsp.	1 mL
Cayenne pepper, just a pinch		
Flour tortillas (7 1/2 inch, 19 cm, diameter)	8	8
Cooking oil	1 tbsp.	15 mL
Beef top sirloin steak, cut into short strips	1 lb.	454 g
Cooking oil	1 tsp.	5 mL
Sliced fresh white mushrooms	2 cups	500 mL
Thinly sliced onion	1 cup	250 mL
Thinly sliced red pepper	1 cup	250 mL
Thinly sliced yellow pepper	1 cup	250 mL

Combine first 6 ingredients in small cup. Set aside.

Wrap tortillas in foil. Heat in 425°F (220°C) oven for 10 to 15 minutes until warm.

Heat first amount of cooking oil in large frying pan on medium. Add beef. Sprinkle with 2 tsp. (10 mL) spice mixture. Stir. Cook for about 5 minutes, stirring occasionally, until beef is browned. Transfer to large bowl. Set aside.

Heat second amount of cooking oil in same frying pan. Add mushrooms and onion. Cook for 5 to 10 minutes, stirring often, until onion is softened.

Add red and yellow peppers. Stir. Sprinkle with remaining spice mixture. Cook for about 5 minutes, stirring occasionally, until peppers are tender-crisp. Add beef. Heat and stir until heated through. Arrange beef mixture down centre of tortillas. Fold bottom ends of tortillas over filling. Fold in sides, slightly overlapping, leaving top ends open. Serves 4.

1 serving: 618 Calories; 23.6 g Total Fat (11.0 g Mono, 3.5 g Poly, 6.5 g Sat); 83 mg Cholesterol; 57 g Carbohydrate; 5 g Fibre; 43 g Protein; 871 mg Sodium

Moroccan Pot Roast

Spice up your Sunday night roast with exotic flavours—your taste buds will be rockin' to the Moroccan experience. Steam some carrots and serve with Creamed Spinach, page 63.

Olive (or cooking) oil	2 tbsp.	30 mL
Ground cumin	1 tsp.	5 mL
Ground coriander	1 tsp.	5 mL
Ground ginger	1 tsp.	5 mL
Granulated sugar	1 tsp.	5 mL
Salt	1 tsp.	5 mL
Garlic powder	1/2 tsp.	2 mL
Ground cinnamon	1/2 tsp.	2 mL
Boneless beef cross-rib roast	3 lbs.	1.4 kg
Red baby potatoes, larger ones cut in half	2 lbs.	900 g
Prepared beef broth	1 cup	250 mL
Water	1/3 cup	75 mL
All-purpose flour	2 tbsp.	30 mL

Combine first 8 ingredients in small bowl.

Rub spice mixture on roast. Place on greased wire rack set in large roasting pan. Bake, uncovered, in 450°F (230°C) oven for about 30 minutes, turning once at halftime, until browned. Reduce heat to 350°F (175°C).

Arrange potatoes around roast in pan. Bake, covered, for another 1 to 1 1/2 hours until potatoes are tender and meat thermometer inserted into thickest part of roast reads 160°F (71°C) for medium or until desired doneness. Remove roast to cutting board. Cover with foil. Let stand for 10 minutes. Stir potatoes gently in pan until coated with drippings. Remove with slotted spoon to large serving bowl. Cover to keep warm.

Transfer remaining drippings to medium saucepan. Add broth. Stir. Bring to a boil.

Stir water into flour in small cup until smooth. Slowly add to broth mixture, stirring constantly until boiling and thickened. Strain through sieve into small serving bowl. Cut roast into thin slices. Makes 12 servings (2 to 3 oz., 57 to 85 g each, cooked weight). Serve with potatoes and gravy. Serves 12.

1 serving: 383 Calories; 27.0 g Total Fat (12.1 g Mono, 1.2 g Poly, 10.3 g Sat); 70 mg Cholesterol; 14 g Carbohydrate; 1 g Fibre; 20 g Protein; 320 mg Sodium

Bruschetta Steak Loaf

Plain old steak sandwiches are given a makeover with fresh tomatoes and peppers. Sure to please when served with Orange Basil Broccoli, page 44. Use the remaining bread another day to make garlic toast.

French bread loaf	1/2	1/2
Sun-dried tomato pesto	1/4 cup	60 mL
Chopped tomato	1 1/2 cups	375 mL
Finely diced green pepper	1/2 cup	125 mL
Finely chopped green onion	2 tbsp.	30 mL
Italian dressing	1 tbsp.	15 mL
Italian dressing	1/4 cup	60 mL
Beef strip loin steak, cut crosswise into short strips	1 lb.	454 g
Pepper	1/2 tsp.	2 mL
Chopped fresh basil	2 tbsp.	30 mL

Cut bread in half lengthwise. Cut crosswise to make 4 pieces. Place cut-side up on ungreased baking sheet. Broil on centre rack in oven for about 1 minute until golden. Spread pesto on cut sides of bread.

Combine next 4 ingredients in medium bowl. Spoon tomato mixture over pesto.

Heat 2 tbsp. (30 mL) dressing in large frying pan on medium-high. Add beef. Sprinkle with pepper. Stir-fry for 3 to 4 minutes until desired doneness. Remove from heat. Stir in remaining dressing. Spoon beef over tomato mixture.

Sprinkle with basil. Serves 4.

1 serving: 743 Calories; 36.5 g Total Fat (17.7 g Mono, 6.2 g Poly, 9.0 g Sat); 75 mg Cholesterol; 68 g Carbohydrate; 6 g Fibre; 35 g Protein; 1097 mg Sodium

Tortellini Chili Bake

A can of chili, a package of fresh tortellini and some chopped-up veggies are all you need for a hearty meal on busy evenings. Sprinkle with sliced green onion or grated Cheddar cheese for a colourful, tasty garnish.

Chopped tomato	2 cups	500 mL
Tomato juice	2 cups	500 mL
Can of chili (see Note)	15 oz.	425 g
Chopped green pepper	1 1/3 cups	325 mL
Finely chopped onion	1/4 cup	60 mL
Cream cheese, cut up	1/4 cup	60 mL
Package of fresh beef-filled tortellini	12 1/2 oz.	350 g

Combine first 6 ingredients in greased 2 quart (2 L) casserole.

Add tortellini. Stir gently. Bake, covered, in 425°F (220°C) oven for about 45 minutes, stirring once at halftime, until tortellini is tender but firm. Makes about 8 cups (2 L). Serves 4.

1 serving: 392 Calories; 15.3 g Total Fat (4.0 g Mono, 0.7 g Poly, 8.2 g Sat); 61 mg Cholesterol; 51 g Carbohydrate; 8 g Fibre; 17 g Protein; 1380 mg Sodium

Pictured on page 89.

Note: Instead of canned chili, use 2 cups (500 mL) leftover chili.

Paré Pointer

If oxygen was only discovered in the seventeen hundreds, what did people breathe before then?

Beef And Bowtie Pasta

Bowtie pasta is all dressed up with tangy balsamic vinaigrette and sharp Dijon. Serve this meaty pasta with a side of veggies or over fresh spinach leaves for a complete meal. Can be chilled or served at room temperature.

Medium bow pasta	2 1/2 cups	625 mL
Diced red pepper	1/4 cup	60 mL
Chopped fresh parsley	1/4 cup	60 mL
Cooking oil	1 tbsp.	15 mL
Beef top sirloin steak, cut diagonally into 1/4 inch (6 mm) slices	1 lb.	454 g
Balsamic vinaigrette	1/2 cup	125 mL
Dijon mustard (with whole seeds)	2 tbsp.	30 mL
Capers (optional)	2 tbsp.	30 mL

Cook pasta in boiling salted water in large uncovered saucepan or Dutch oven for 8 to 10 minutes, stirring occasionally, until tender but firm. Drain. Rinse with cold water. Drain well. Transfer to large bowl.

Add red pepper and parsley. Toss. Set aside.

Heat cooking oil in large frying pan on medium-high. Add beef. Cook for 3 minutes, stirring constantly.

Add remaining 3 ingredients. Cook for 1 to 2 minutes, scraping any brown bits from bottom of pan, until desired doneness. Add to pasta mixture. Toss. Makes about 6 cups (1.5 L). Serves 4.

1 serving: 506 Calories; 26.5 g Total Fat (8.2 g Mono, 1.6 g Poly, 7.2 g Sat); 53 mg Cholesterol; 36 g Carbohydrate; 1 g Fibre; 29 g Protein; 461 mg Sodium

Cheese And Pesto Meatloaf

Is your family pesto-ing you for dinner? Pesto them back with this hearty meatloaf. Perfect served with Smashed Celery Spuds, page 57. And you'll have just enough meatloaf left over for sandwiches the next day!

Large eggs, fork-beaten	2	2
Finely chopped onion	3/4 cup	175 mL
Fine dry bread crumbs	2/3 cup	150 mL
Finely chopped green pepper	1/2 cup	125 mL
Grated carrot	1/2 cup	125 mL
Sun-dried tomato pesto	3 tbsp.	50 mL
Salt	1 tsp.	5 mL
Pepper	1/2 tsp.	2 mL
Lean ground beef	1 1/2 lbs.	680 g
Sun-dried tomato pesto	2 tbsp.	30 mL
Grated medium Cheddar cheese	1/2 cup	125 mL

Combine first 8 ingredients in large bowl.

Add beef. Mix well. Press into ungreased 9 x 5 x 3 inch (22 x 12.5 x 7.5 cm) loaf pan. Bake in 350°F (175°C) oven for about 1 hour until fully cooked, and internal temperature of beef reaches 160°F (71°C).

Spread second amount of pesto on meatloaf. Sprinkle with cheese. Bake for another 5 to 10 minutes until cheese is melted. Let stand for 10 minutes. Serves 6.

1 serving: 398 Calories; 23.7 g Total Fat (10.5 g Mono, 1.3 g Poly, 9.2 g Sat); 140 mg Cholesterol; 17 g Carbohydrate; 2 g Fibre; 29 g Protein; 698 mg Sodium

Pictured at right.

1. Cheese and Pesto Meatloaf, above
2. Smashed Celery Spuds, page 57
3. Pork Pot Roast, page 138

Props courtesy of: Cherison Enterprises Inc.
Danesco Inc.
Pfaltzgraff Canada

Meatball Shepherd's Pie

Shepherd's pie is extra-fun for the family when meatballs are involved. Customize this dish by using your favourite pasta sauce and cheese, or try meatballs made with ground chicken or turkey.

Frozen cooked meatballs	32	32
Roasted garlic pasta sauce	2 cups	500 mL
Chopped zucchini (with peel)	2 cups	500 mL
Chopped green pepper	1 cup	250 mL
Frozen hash brown potatoes	3 cups	750 mL
Crumbled feta cheese	1 cup	250 mL
Sour cream	1/2 cup	125 mL
Grated Parmesan cheese	1/4 cup	60 mL
Dried oregano	1/2 tsp.	2 mL

Combine first 4 ingredients in ungreased 2 quart (2 L) casserole.

Combine remaining 5 ingredients in large bowl. Spoon onto meatball mixture. Bake, covered, in 375°F (190°C) oven for 1 hour. Bake, uncovered, for another 20 to 30 minutes until heated through. Serves 4.

1 serving: 630 Calories; 31.8 g Total Fat (8.7 g Mono, 1.5 g Poly, 16.0 g Sat); 154 mg Cholesterol; 52 g Carbohydrate; 6 g Fibre; 34 g Protein; 1021 mg Sodium

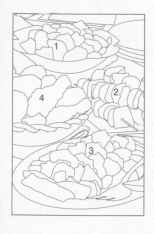

1. Herbed Potato Salad, page 13
2. Potato Vegetable Kabobs, page 56
3. Margarita Marinated Steak, page 74
4. Crispy Chicken Drumettes, page 84

Props courtesy of: Stokes

Margarita Marinated Steak

Give a less-tender cut of meat the spa treatment with a long soak
in a refreshing lime-scented marinade, and watch it become tender
and juicy. Complete this makeover with a pitcher of margaritas
and Potato Vegetable Kabobs, page 56, on the side.

Frozen concentrated limeade, thawed	1/3 cup	75 mL
Water	1/3 cup	75 mL
Cooking oil	1/4 cup	60 mL
Chopped fresh cilantro	1/4 cup	60 mL
Cajun seasoning	3 tbsp.	50 mL
Garlic cloves, minced (or 3/4 tsp., 4 mL, powder)	3	3
Ground cumin	1 tsp.	5 mL
Boneless beef round steak, trimmed of fat	1 1/2 lbs.	680 g
Chopped avocado	1 cup	250 mL
Chopped orange	3/4 cup	175 mL
Finely chopped red onion	1/4 cup	60 mL

Combine first 7 ingredients in small bowl. Reserve 2 tbsp. (30 mL) in small cup.

Put beef into large resealable freezer bag. Add remaining limeade mixture. Seal bag. Turn until coated. Let stand in refrigerator for at least 6 hours or overnight, turning occasionally. Drain. Preheat gas barbecue to medium (see Tip, page 56). Cook beef on greased grill for about 3 minutes per side for medium-rare or until desired doneness. Remove to cutting board. Cover to keep warm.

Combine remaining 3 ingredients in small bowl. Add reserved limeade mixture. Toss until coated. Cut beef diagonally into 1/4 inch (6 mm) slices. Arrange on large serving plate. Top with avocado mixture. Serves 6.

1 serving: 268 Calories; 13.7 g Total Fat (7.1 g Mono, 1.4 g Poly, 3.8 g Sat); 55 mg Cholesterol; 8 g Carbohydrate; 2 g Fibre; 28 g Protein; 269 mg Sodium

Pictured on page 72.

Beef And Mushroom Arugula

Arugula, popular for its peppery mustard flavour,
is a must try for the stir-fry fan. Pair with pasta.

Cooking oil	1 tsp.	5 mL
Beef rib-eye steak, cut into 1 inch (2.5 cm) pieces	1 lb.	454 g
Butter (or hard margarine)	2 tbsp.	30 mL
Chopped onion	1/3 cup	75 mL
Garlic clove, minced (or 1/4 tsp., 1 mL, powder)	1	1
Sliced brown (or white) mushrooms	2 cups	500 mL
Fresh arugula, stems removed, coarsely chopped, lightly packed	4 cups	1 L
Sour cream	1/4 cup	60 mL
Salt	1/4 tsp.	1 mL
Pepper	1/8 tsp.	0.5 mL

Heat cooking oil in large frying pan on medium-high. Add beef. Cook for about 3 minutes, stirring occasionally, until desired doneness. Transfer to large bowl. Set aside.

Melt butter in same frying pan on medium. Add onion and garlic. Cook for about 5 minutes, stirring often, until onion is softened.

Add mushrooms. Stir. Cook for 5 to 10 minutes, stirring occasionally, until mushrooms are softened.

Add beef and remaining 4 ingredients. Heat and stir for about 1 minute until heated through and arugula is wilted. Makes about 4 cups (1 L). Serves 4.

1 serving: 373 Calories; 28.0 g Total Fat (10.1 g Mono, 1.3 g Poly, 13.0 g Sat); 85 mg Cholesterol; 4 g Carbohydrate; 1 g Fibre; 25 g Protein; 259 mg Sodium

Hamburger Pizza

This hamburger-pizza combo upgrades all notions of the takeout favourite.
Sure to thrill kids of all ages. Easily doubled, if you're so inclined.

Cooking oil	1 tsp.	5 mL
Sliced fresh white mushrooms	1 cup	250 mL
Chopped onion	1/2 cup	125 mL
Lean ground beef	1/4 lb.	113 g
Dried basil	1/4 tsp.	1 mL
Prebaked pizza crust (12 inch, 30 cm, diameter)	1	1
Pizza (or pasta) sauce	1/4 cup	60 mL
Grated Parmesan cheese	1/4 cup	60 mL
Medium tomato, seeds removed, chopped	1	1
Grated mozzarella cheese	1 cup	250 mL

Heat cooking oil in medium frying pan on medium. Add next 4 ingredients. Scramble-fry for about 10 minutes until beef is no longer pink. Remove from heat. Drain.

Place pizza crust on 12 inch (30 cm) pizza pan. Spread pizza sauce on crust almost to edge.

Sprinkle with Parmesan cheese.

Scatter beef mixture, tomato and mozzarella cheese over top. Bake in 450°F (230°C) oven for 10 to 15 minutes until crust is crisp and cheese is melted. Serves 4.

1 serving: 436 Calories; 15.4 g Total Fat (4.0 g Mono, 0.8 g Poly, 6.5 g Sat); 43 mg Cholesterol; 50 g Carbohydrate; 3 g Fibre; 24 g Protein; 791 mg Sodium

Italian Steak Dinner

They'll think they've been to Tuscany after they've dined on this
delectable dinner! Fabulous with Marinated Mushroom Salad, page 8.

Jar of marinated artichoke hearts, drained, liquid reserved, finely chopped	6 oz.	170 mL
Sun-dried tomatoes, softened in boiling water for 10 minutes before finely chopping	1/4 cup	60 mL
Reserved artichoke liquid	1/3 cup	75 mL
Pepper	1 tsp.	5 mL
Fennel seed	1/2 tsp.	2 mL
Dried oregano	1/2 tsp.	2 mL
Beef strip loin steak, cut into 4 equal pieces	1 lb.	454 g
Polenta roll, cut into 8 slices	1.1 lbs.	500 g
Olive (or cooking) oil	1 tbsp.	15 mL

Put artichoke hearts and sun-dried tomato into small bowl. Add half of artichoke marinade. Stir. Set aside.

Add next 3 ingredients to remaining artichoke marinade. Stir.

Brush both sides of beef with fennel mixture.

Brush both sides of polenta with olive oil. Place steak and polenta on greased broiler pan. Broil on top rack in oven for 3 to 5 minutes per side for medium-rare or until desired doneness. Transfer to large serving plate. Top polenta with artichoke mixture. Serves 4.

1 serving: 420 Calories; 23.9 g Total Fat (9.8 g Mono, 1.0 g Poly, 7.4 g Sat); 62 mg Cholesterol; 26 g Carbohydrate; 2 g Fibre; 26 g Protein; 252 mg Sodium

Polenta-Topped Chili

Smoky, hickory-flavoured chili gets even better with the addition of unconventional polenta patties. Garnish with lime wedges, and add Jicama Salad, page 22, for a marvelous Mexican-inspired meal!

Cooking oil	2 tsp.	10 mL
Lean ground beef	1 lb.	454 g
Chopped onion	1 cup	250 mL
Garlic cloves, minced (or 1/2 tsp., 2 mL, powder)	2	2
Cans of black beans (19 oz., 540 mL, each), rinsed and drained	2	2
Can of crushed tomatoes	28 oz.	796 mL
Hickory barbecue sauce	1/4 cup	60 mL
Chili powder	2 tbsp.	30 mL
Seasoned salt	1/2 tsp.	2 mL
Polenta roll, cut into 12 slices	2.2 lbs.	1 kg
Grated jalapeño Monterey Jack cheese	1 cup	250 mL

Heat cooking oil in large frying pan on medium. Add next 3 ingredients. Scramble-fry for about 10 minutes until beef is no longer pink.

Add next 5 ingredients. Stir. Bring to a boil. Transfer to ungreased 9 x 13 inch (22 x 33 cm) baking dish.

Arrange polenta on chili. Bake, uncovered, in 350°F (175°C) oven for about 20 minutes until polenta is heated through.

Sprinkle with cheese. Bake, uncovered, for another 10 to 12 minutes until cheese is bubbling. Makes about 8 cups (2 L). Serves 6.

1 serving: 672 Calories; 19.7 g Total Fat (7.4 g Mono, 1.7 g Poly, 8.2 g Sat); 62 mg Cholesterol; 86 g Carbohydrate; 16 g Fibre; 41 g Protein; 1000 mg Sodium

Pictured on page 53.

Variation: For a different presentation, cut polenta into small cubes. Scatter over top of chili.

Meatball And Potato Kabobs

About the easiest kabobs you can make, this meat(ball)
and potatoes meal-on-a-stick will be ready in no time.

Baby potatoes, halved	12	12
Cooking oil	1 tbsp.	15 mL
Italian seasoning	2 tsp.	10 mL
Frozen cooked meatballs, thawed	36	36
Pepper	1/4 tsp.	1 mL
Red pepper pieces (1 inch, 2.5 cm, size)	48	48
Bamboo skewers (8 inches, 20 cm, each), soaked in water for 10 minutes	12	12
Barbecue sauce	1/4 cup	60 mL

Put potato into medium microwave-safe bowl. Microwave on high (100%) for about 5 minutes until just tender.

Drizzle with cooking oil. Sprinkle with seasoning. Toss until coated. Set aside.

Put meatballs into large bowl. Sprinkle with pepper. Toss until coated.

Thread potato, meatballs and red pepper alternately onto skewers. Place kabobs on greased broiler pan.

Brush kabobs with barbecue sauce. Broil on centre rack in oven for 20 to 25 minutes, turning occasionally, until meatballs are heated through and potato is tender. Serves 4.

1 serving: 351 Calories; 18.8 g Total Fat (8.5 g Mono, 2.0 g Poly, 5.5 g Sat); 94 mg Cholesterol; 22 g Carbohydrate; 6 g Fibre; 23 g Protein; 310 mg Sodium

GRILLED MEATBALL AND POTATO KABOBS: Preheat gas barbecue to medium. Cook kabobs on greased grill for about 15 minutes, turning occasionally, until meatballs are heated through and potato is tender.

Satay Chicken Noodles

Sweet and spicy chicken takes a rest on a delicate bed of angel hair pasta.
Simply Thai-rrific with Asparagus Cucumber Salad, page 9.

Angel hair pasta, broken up	8 oz.	225 g
Sesame (or cooking) oil	1 tbsp.	15 mL
Water	1/4 cup	60 mL
Sweet chili sauce	2 tbsp.	30 mL
Chunky peanut butter	2 tbsp.	30 mL
Soy sauce	2 tbsp.	30 mL
Rice vinegar	1 tbsp.	15 mL
Cooking oil	1 tbsp.	15 mL
Boneless, skinless chicken breast halves, cut crosswise into 1/4 inch (6 mm) slices	1 lb.	454 g
Finely grated gingerroot (or 1/2 tsp., 2 mL, ground ginger)	2 tsp.	10 mL
Garlic clove, minced (or 1/4 tsp., 1 mL, powder)	1	1

Cook pasta in boiling salted water in large uncovered saucepan or Dutch oven for 6 to 8 minutes, stirring occasionally, until tender but firm. Drain. Transfer to large bowl.

Drizzle with sesame oil. Toss. Set aside.

Combine next 5 ingredients in small bowl.

Heat cooking oil in large frying pan on medium-high. Add remaining 3 ingredients. Cook for 3 to 5 minutes, stirring constantly, until chicken is no longer pink inside. Add peanut butter mixture. Heat and stir for 1 to 2 minutes until coated. Add pasta. Toss until heated through. Makes about 6 cups (1.5 L). Serves 4.

1 serving: 452 Calories; 13.6 g Total Fat (5.7 g Mono, 4.0 g Poly, 1.9 g Sat); 66 mg Cholesterol; 44 g Carbohydrate; 2 g Fibre; 36 g Protein; 762 mg Sodium

Hawaiian Burgers

Take a vacation from boring beef burgers with this
sweet and savoury chicken variation. Aloha!

Salad dressing (or mayonnaise)	2 tbsp.	30 mL
Thick teriyaki basting sauce	2 tbsp.	30 mL
Chicken breast cutlets	4	4
(4 – 6 oz., 113 – 170 g, each)		
Thick teriyaki basting sauce	1/4 cup	60 mL
Cooking oil	2 tsp.	10 mL
Deli ham slices (about 4 oz., 113 g)	4	4
Deli part-skim mozzarella cheese slices	4	4
(about 3 oz., 85 g)		
Canned pineapple slices, drained	4	4
Kaiser rolls, split	4	4
Lettuce leaves	8	8
Tomato slices	4	4

Combine salad dressing and first amount of teriyaki sauce in small cup.
Set aside.

Brush both sides of chicken with second amount of teriyaki sauce. Heat oil
in large frying pan on medium. Add chicken. Cook for about 4 minutes per
side until no longer pink inside.

Place ham and cheese slices over chicken. Cook, covered, for 1 to 2 minutes
until cheese is melted. Remove to large plate. Cover to keep warm.

Cook pineapple in same frying pan for about 1 minute per side until
heated through and starting to brown.

Spread salad dressing mixture on rolls. Serve chicken, topped with
pineapple, lettuce and tomato, in rolls. Serves 4.

1 serving: 527 Calories; 16.8 g Total Fat (6.7 g Mono, 4.1 g Poly, 4.2 g Sat); 94 mg Cholesterol;
49 g Carbohydrate; 2 g Fibre; 43 g Protein; 1517 mg Sodium

Sicilian Summer Grill

This tasty Italian treat may just be the grill of your dreams!
For a sensational supper in no time, start cooking the chicken
while you prepare the polenta and tomato. If your barbecue is
big enough, cook the polenta and tomato at the same time.

Boneless, skinless chicken thighs	8	8
(about 3 oz., 85 g, each)		
Seasoned salt	1 tsp.	5 mL
Pepper	1/2 tsp.	2 mL
Polenta roll, cut into 8 slices	1.1 lbs.	500 g
Basil pesto	1/4 cup	60 mL
Crumbled feta cheese (optional)	6 tbsp.	100 mL
Roma (plum) tomatoes, halved lengthwise	4	4
Olive (or cooking) oil	1 tbsp.	15 mL
Salt	1/4 tsp.	1 mL
Pepper	1/8 tsp.	0.5 mL

Sprinkle chicken with seasoned salt and first amount of pepper. Preheat gas barbecue to medium (see Tip, page 56). Cook chicken on greased grill for about 20 minutes, turning occasionally, until no longer pink inside. Remove to large serving plate. Cover to keep warm.

Brush both sides of polenta with pesto. Cook on greased grill for about 5 minutes until bottom is golden and grill marks appear. Turn polenta over.

Sprinkle with cheese. Cook for another 4 to 5 minutes until bottom is golden. Remove to same plate. Cover to keep warm.

Put tomato into medium bowl. Add olive oil. Sprinkle with salt and pepper. Toss gently until coated. Cook tomato, cut-side down, on greased grill for about 5 minutes until bottom starts to brown. Turn tomato over. Cook for another 4 to 5 minutes until slightly softened. Remove to same plate. Serves 4.

1 serving: 291 Calories; 12.3 g Total Fat (5.8 g Mono, 2.3 g Poly, 2.9 g Sat); 74 mg Cholesterol; 22 g Carbohydrate; 1 g Fibre; 23 g Protein; 568 mg Sodium

Pictured on page 35.

Island Chicken Casserole

*Forget the road—this chicken has gone clear across the Pacific
and returned loaded with tropical flavours. A meal in
itself, but even better with steamed rice.*

Red jalapeño jelly	1/2 cup	125 mL
Frozen concentrated orange juice	1/4 cup	60 mL
Thick teriyaki basting sauce	1/4 cup	60 mL
Garlic cloves, minced (or 1/2 tsp., 2 mL, powder)	2	2
Curry powder	1 tsp.	5 mL
Cubed peeled yam (or sweet potato)	3 cups	750 mL
Coarsely chopped onion	2 cups	500 mL
Can of pineapple chunks, drained	14 oz.	398 mL
Coarsely chopped green pepper	1 1/2 cups	375 mL
Bone-in chicken thighs (5 – 6 oz., 140 – 170 g, each)	8	8

Heat jelly in small saucepan on medium until melted. Remove from heat.

Add next 4 ingredients. Stir.

Put next 4 ingredients into greased 9 x 13 inch (22 x 33 cm) baking dish.
Add 1/4 cup (60 mL) jelly mixture. Stir until coated.

Arrange chicken on vegetables. Spoon remaining jelly mixture onto
chicken. Bake, uncovered, in 375°F (190°C) oven for about 1 hour until
vegetables are tender and chicken is no longer pink inside. Serves 4.

*1 serving: 674 Calories; 17.0 g Total Fat (6.3 g Mono, 4.0 g Poly, 4.7 g Sat); 143 mg Cholesterol;
87 g Carbohydrate; 8 g Fibre; 44 g Protein; 554 mg Sodium*

Pictured on page 126.

Olive Chicken Bake

*Olive lovers rejoice, a Greek feast awaits! Serve with
steamed rice or potatoes for a complete meal.*

Boneless, skinless chicken breast halves (4 – 6 oz., 113 – 170 g, each)	4	4
Diced eggplant (with peel)	2 cups	500 mL
Sun-dried tomato pesto	1/2 cup	125 mL
Chopped kalamata olives	1/2 cup	125 mL
Dried oregano	1 1/2 tsp.	7 mL
Garlic clove, minced (or 1/4 tsp., 1 mL, powder)	1	1
Pepper	1/2 tsp.	2 mL
Crumbled feta cheese	1/3 cup	75 mL

Put chicken into greased 2 quart (2 L) shallow baking dish.

Combine next 6 ingredients in medium bowl. Spoon onto chicken. Bake,
uncovered, in 400°F (205°C) oven for about 30 minutes until chicken is
no longer pink inside.

Sprinkle with cheese. Serves 4.

*1 serving: 291 Calories; 12.9 g Total Fat (6.4 g Mono, 1.7 g Poly, 3.5 g Sat); 77 mg Cholesterol;
16 g Carbohydrate; 5 g Fibre; 31 g Protein; 471 mg Sodium*

Crispy Chicken Drumettes

*Backyard picnic anyone? Serve these crispy kid-pleasers with Herbed
Potato Salad, page 13, and corn on the cob. Let the fun begin!*

Salad dressing (or mayonnaise)	3/4 cup	175 mL
Chicken drumettes (or split chicken wings, tips discarded)	3 lbs.	1.4 kg
Crushed Ritz crackers (about 30)	1 cup	250 mL
Fine dry bread crumbs	3/4 cup	175 mL
Parsley flakes	2 tsp.	10 mL
Seasoned salt	2 tsp.	10 mL

(continued on next page)

84   Entrees – Chicken

Measure salad dressing into large bowl. Add chicken. Toss until coated.

Combine remaining 4 ingredients in small bowl. Put half of crumb mixture into large resealable freezer bag. Add half of chicken. Seal bag. Toss until coated. Arrange chicken on greased baking sheet with sides. Repeat with remaining crumb mixture and chicken. Discard any remaining crumb mixture. Bake in 375°F (190°C) oven for about 45 minutes until crumb coating is crisp and chicken is no longer pink inside. Makes about 24 drumettes (or 36 wing pieces). Serves 6.

1 serving: 619 Calories; 38.2 g Total Fat (17.6 g Mono, 11.1 g Poly, 6.6 g Sat); 193 mg Cholesterol; 19 g Carbohydrate; 1 g Fibre; 47 g Protein; 1075 mg Sodium

Pictured on page 72.

Curry-Spiced Chicken

Curry the favour of your household with this spicy and sweet marinated chicken. Terrific with fresh rolls and Minted Pea Salad, page 16, or Bulgur Vegetables, page 41.

Plain yogurt	1/2 cup	125 mL
Mango chutney, chopped	2 tbsp.	30 mL
Cooking oil	2 tbsp.	30 mL
Garam masala (see Tip, page 61)	1 tsp.	5 mL
Chili paste (sambal oelek)	1/2 tsp.	2 mL
Ground cumin	1/4 tsp.	1 mL
Turmeric	1/4 tsp.	1 mL
Salt	1/4 tsp.	1 mL
Boneless, skinless chicken breast halves (4 – 6 oz., 113 – 170 g, each)	4	4

Combine first 8 ingredients in small bowl.

Score top of chicken with sharp knife. Put into large resealable freezer bag. Add yogurt mixture. Seal bag. Turn until coated. Let stand in refrigerator for at least 6 hours or overnight, turning occasionally. Drain. Preheat gas barbecue to medium (see Tip, page 56). Place chicken on greased grill. Close lid. Cook for 6 to 8 minutes per side until chicken is no longer pink inside. Serves 4.

1 serving: 151 Calories; 3.8 g Total Fat (1.5 g Mono, 0.9 g Poly, 0.8 g Sat); 67 mg Cholesterol; 1 g Carbohydrate; trace Fibre; 26 g Protein; 104 mg Sodium

Pictured on page 17.

Chicken And Couscous

*Opposites really do attract. Cooling mint and warming
chili make a delightful pair in this easy recipe.*

Cooking oil	1 tbsp.	15 mL
Boneless, skinless chicken breast halves, cut crosswise into thin slices (see Tip, page 87)	1 lb.	454 g
Chopped red onion	1 cup	250 mL
Chopped zucchini (with peel)	1 cup	250 mL
Grated carrot	1 cup	250 mL
Ground cumin	1 tsp.	5 mL
Dried crushed chilies	1/2 tsp.	2 mL
Montreal chicken spice	1/4 tsp.	1 mL
Pepper, sprinkle		
Prepared chicken broth	1 1/2 cups	375 mL
Orange juice	1/2 cup	125 mL
Frozen peas	1/2 cup	125 mL
Chopped fresh mint (or 3/4 tsp., 4 mL, dried)	1 tbsp.	15 mL
Grated orange zest	1 tsp.	5 mL
Plain couscous	1 cup	250 mL

Heat cooking oil in large frying pan on medium-high. Add chicken.
Cook for about 5 minutes, stirring occasionally, until browned. Reduce
heat to medium.

Add next 7 ingredients. Stir. Cook for about 5 minutes, stirring often,
until onion starts to soften.

Add next 5 ingredients. Stir. Bring to a boil.

Add couscous. Stir. Remove from heat. Let stand, covered, for about
5 minutes until couscous is tender and broth is absorbed. Fluff with
a fork. Makes about 6 cups (1.5 L). Serves 4.

*1 serving: 410 Calories; 6.5 g Total Fat (2.8 g Mono, 1.8 g Poly, 1.0 g Sat); 66 mg Cholesterol;
50 g Carbohydrate; 5 g Fibre; 36 g Protein; 427 mg Sodium*

Peanut Chicken Rice Bake

Working for peanuts isn't bad if you get to use them in dishes like this. This easy and warming casserole will provide comfort to all. Serve with Sweet Sugar Peas, page 62, for a crunchy contrast.

Prepared chicken broth	2 1/2 cups	625 mL
Long grain white rice	1 1/2 cups	375 mL
Cooking oil	1 tbsp.	15 mL
Garlic clove, minced (or 1/4 tsp., 1 mL, powder)	1	1
Boneless, skinless chicken thighs (about 3 oz., 85 g, each)	12	12
Diced onion	3/4 cup	175 mL
Diced red pepper	3/4 cup	175 mL
Peanut sauce	1 cup	250 mL

Combine first 4 ingredients in greased 9 x 13 inch (22 x 33 cm) baking dish.

Arrange chicken on rice mixture. Sprinkle with onion and red pepper.

Spoon peanut sauce over top. Bake, covered, in 375°F (190°C) oven for about 1 hour until rice is tender, broth is absorbed and chicken is no longer pink inside. Serves 6.

1 serving: 506 Calories; 22.0 g Total Fat (9.8 g Mono, 5.6 g Poly, 4.8 g Sat); 76 mg Cholesterol; 45 g Carbohydrate; 2 g Fibre; 32 g Protein; 486 mg Sodium

 To slice meat easily, before cutting place in freezer for about 30 minutes until just starting to freeze. If using from frozen state, partially thaw before cutting.

Lemon Herb Chicken

This subtly seasoned chicken is wonderful with Maple-Glazed Vegetables, page 47. Marinate the chicken overnight if you like.

Olive (or cooking) oil	1/4 cup	60 mL
Liquid honey	1/4 cup	60 mL
Lemon juice	3 tbsp.	50 mL
Chopped fresh oregano (or 1 1/2 tsp., 7 mL, dried)	2 tbsp.	30 mL
Grated lemon zest	1 tbsp.	15 mL
Ground cumin	1 tbsp.	15 mL
Garlic cloves, minced (or 1/2 tsp., 2 mL, powder)	2	2
Salt	1/2 tsp.	2 mL
Chicken drumsticks (3 – 5 oz., 85 – 140 g, each)	12	12

Combine first 8 ingredients in small bowl. Reserve 3 tbsp. (50 mL) of olive oil mixture in small cup for basting sauce.

Put chicken into large resealable freezer bag. Add remaining olive oil mixture. Seal bag. Turn until coated. Let stand in refrigerator for 2 hours, turning occasionally. Drain. Place chicken on greased wire rack set in foil-lined baking sheet with sides. Bake in 375°F (190°C) oven for about 40 minutes, turning occasionally and brushing with basting sauce, until no longer pink inside. Serves 4.

1 serving: 499 Calories; 21.9 g Total Fat (8.7 g Mono, 4.7 g Poly, 5.1 g Sat); 262 mg Cholesterol; 6 g Carbohydrate; trace Fibre; 65 g Protein; 397 mg Sodium

1. Tortellini Chili Bake, page 68
2. Creamy Chicken Shrimp Penne, page 97

Props courtesy of: Casa Bugatti
Cherison Enterprises Inc.

Tangy Chicken Potato Bake

This mustard-flavoured chicken and potato dish is a must-have for a great dinner. Serve with Sweet And Spicy Onions, page 58.

Italian dressing	1/2 cup	125 mL
Honey Dijon mustard	1/4 cup	60 mL
Chopped fresh basil (or 1 1/2 tsp., 7 mL, dried)	2 tbsp.	30 mL
Boneless, skinless chicken breast halves (4 – 6 oz., 113 – 170 g, each)	4	4
Medium unpeeled potatoes, cut into 3/4 inch (2 cm) cubes	4	4
Salt, sprinkle		
Pepper, sprinkle		

Combine first 3 ingredients in small bowl. Reserve half of dressing mixture in small cup.

Put chicken into large resealable freezer bag. Add remaining dressing mixture. Seal bag. Turn until coated. Let stand in refrigerator for 2 hours. Drain.

Put potato into medium bowl. Add reserved dressing mixture, salt and pepper. Toss until coated. Arrange chicken breasts in centre of greased 9 x 13 inch (22 cm x 33 cm) baking dish. Arrange potato around chicken. Cover with foil. Cook in 375°F (190°C) oven for about 45 minutes until chicken is no longer pink inside and potato is tender. Serves 4.

1 serving: 297 Calories; 14.5 g Total Fat (7.5 g Mono, 4.6 g Poly, 1.4 g Sat); 78 mg Cholesterol; 12 g Carbohydrate; 8 g Fibre; 29 g Protein; 494 mg Sodium

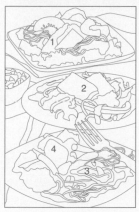

1. Grilled Beef Tomato Salad, page 24
2. Maple Miso Tofu Salad, page 32
3. Rice Noodle Salad, page 15
4. Grilled Chicken Kabobs, page 92

Props courtesy of: Stokes
Totally Bamboo

Zesty Chicken Kabobs

Savour the Asian flavour! Excellent with Rice Noodle Salad, page 15.

Soy sauce	1/4 cup	60 mL
Water	1/4 cup	60 mL
Brown sugar, packed	2 tbsp.	30 mL
Grated orange zest	2 tsp.	10 mL
Garlic cloves, minced (or 1/2 tsp., 2 mL, powder)	2	2
Finely grated gingerroot (or 1/4 tsp., 1 mL, ground ginger)	1 tsp.	5 mL
Pepper	1/2 tsp.	2 mL
Boneless, skinless chicken thighs, cut into 1 inch (2.5 cm) pieces	1 lb.	454 g
Green onions, cut into 1 inch (2.5 cm) pieces	6	6
Bamboo skewers (8 inches, 20 cm, each), soaked in water for 10 minutes	8	8

Combine first 7 ingredients in small bowl. Reserve half of soy sauce mixture in small cup for basting sauce.

Put chicken into medium resealable freezer bag. Add remaining soy sauce mixture. Seal bag. Turn until coated. Let stand in refrigerator for 30 minutes, turning occasionally. Drain.

Thread green onion and chicken alternately onto skewers, beginning and ending with green onion. Place kabobs on greased broiler pan. Brush with basting sauce. Broil on top rack in oven for 10 to 12 minutes, turning occasionally and brushing with any remaining basting sauce, until chicken is no longer pink inside. Serves 4.

1 serving: 231 Calories; 12.2 g Total Fat (4.8 g Mono, 2.7 g Poly, 3.4 g Sat); 73 mg Cholesterol; 9 g Carbohydrate; 1 g Fibre; 21 g Protein; 1058 mg Sodium

GRILLED CHICKEN KABOBS: Preheat gas barbecue to medium. Cook kabobs on greased grill for 10 to 12 minutes, turning occasionally and brushing with any remaining basting sauce, until chicken is no longer pink inside.

Pictured on page 90.

Baked Lemon Chicken

Tangy lemon enhances herbed chicken and vegetables.
An aromatic oven-baked meal that's sure to be a hit.

Olive (or cooking) oil	1 tbsp.	15 mL
Boneless, skinless chicken thighs	12	12
(about 3 oz., 85 g, each)		
Red baby potatoes, larger ones cut in half	1 1/2 lbs.	680 g
Small fresh whole white mushrooms	2 cups	500 mL
Small onion, cut into 8 wedges	1	1
Lemon juice	3 tbsp.	50 mL
Olive (or cooking) oil	3 tbsp.	50 mL
Water	3 tbsp.	50 mL
Grated lemon zest	1 tbsp.	15 mL
Dried oregano	2 1/2 tsp.	12 mL
Dried rosemary, crushed	1 tsp.	5 mL
Salt	1/2 tsp.	2 mL
Pepper	1/4 tsp.	1 mL
Baby carrots	2 cups	500 mL

Heat first amount of olive oil in large frying pan on medium-high. Add chicken. Cook for about 3 minutes per side until browned. Transfer to greased 3 quart (3 L) casserole.

Add next 3 ingredients.

Combine next 8 ingredients in small cup. Drizzle over chicken and vegetables. Toss until coated. Bake, uncovered, in 400°F (205°C) oven for 20 minutes.

Add carrots. Bake, covered, for another 25 to 30 minutes until chicken is no longer pink inside and carrots are tender-crisp. Serves 6.

1 serving: 360 Calories; 17.8 g Total Fat (9.9 g Mono, 2.8 g Poly, 3.7 g Sat); 74 mg Cholesterol; 26 g Carbohydrate; 4 g Fibre; 24 g Protein; 294 mg Sodium

Confetti Rice And Chicken

Time to celebrate the little dining pleasures in life—we've even included the confetti! Tender chicken atop rice with festive flecks of cranberry and vegetables is certain to get the party started.

Boneless, skinless chicken thighs (about 3 oz., 85 g, each)	8	8
Seasoned salt	1/2 tsp.	2 mL
Pepper	1/4 tsp.	1 mL
Cooking oil	1 tbsp.	15 mL
Prepared chicken broth	2 cups	500 mL
Grated peeled yam (or sweet potato)	1 1/2 cups	375 mL
Converted white rice	1 cup	250 mL
Grated carrot	1 cup	250 mL
Dried cranberries	3/4 cup	175 mL
Finely chopped onion	1/2 cup	125 mL
Butter (or hard margarine), melted	1 tbsp.	15 mL
Dried thyme	1 tsp.	5 mL

Sprinkle chicken with seasoned salt and pepper.

Heat cooking oil in large frying pan on medium-high. Add chicken. Cook for about 5 minutes per side until browned. Remove from heat.

Combine remaining 8 ingredients in ungreased 2 quart (2 L) casserole. Arrange chicken on rice mixture. Bake, covered, in 350°F (175°C) oven for about 1 hour until rice is tender and broth is absorbed. Serves 4.

1 serving: 569 Calories; 16.5 g Total Fat (6.5 g Mono, 3.6 g Poly, 4.8 g Sat); 82 mg Cholesterol; 77 g Carbohydrate; 6 g Fibre; 28 g Protein; 679 mg Sodium

Chicken Tortilla Bake

A saucy casserole with southwestern flair. Make it a fiesta with Corn-Stuffed Tomatoes, page 42.

Diced cooked chicken	1 1/2 cups	375 mL
Can of condensed cream of mushroom soup	10 oz.	284 mL
Chopped onion	1 cup	250 mL
Milk	2/3 cup	150 mL
Can of diced green chilies	4 oz.	113 g
Corn tortillas (6 inch, 15 cm, diameter), each cut into 4 wedges	6	6
Grated medium Cheddar cheese	1 1/2 cups	375 mL

Combine first 5 ingredients in medium bowl.

Arrange half of tortilla wedges in greased 2 quart (2 L) casserole. Layer with half of chicken mixture.

Sprinkle with half of cheese. Repeat with remaining ingredients. Bake, uncovered, in 350°F (175°C) oven for about 50 minutes until heated through and cheese is bubbling. Serves 6.

1 serving: 301 Calories; 15.9 g Total Fat (3.8 g Mono, 1.2 g Poly, 7.9 g Sat); 61 mg Cholesterol; 20 g Carbohydrate; 3 g Fibre; 20 g Protein; 651 mg Sodium

---

Paré Pointer

No wonder their coffee tastes like mud. It was ground ten minutes ago.

Jiffy Jambalaya

Spice up dinner tonight with this traditional Cajun meal and laissez les bons temps rouler (let the good times roll). Smoky sausage and tender chicken flavour this mildly-spiced jambalaya blend.

Cooking oil	1 tbsp.	15 mL
Chopped celery	1 cup	250 mL
Chopped onion	1 cup	250 mL
Chopped green pepper	1 cup	250 mL
Smoked ham sausage, cut into 1/2 inch (12 mm) slices	5 oz.	140 g
Can of diced tomatoes (with juice)	14 oz.	398 mL
Prepared chicken broth	1 1/2 cups	375 mL
Long grain white rice	1 1/4 cups	300 mL
Cajun seasoning	1 tbsp.	15 mL
Cayenne pepper	1/2 tsp.	2 mL
Precooked whole roasted chicken (see Note)	2 1/2 – 3 lbs.	1.1 – 1.4 kg

Chopped fresh parsley, for garnish

Heat cooking oil in large saucepan or Dutch oven on medium-high. Add next 4 ingredients. Cook for 5 to 10 minutes, stirring occasionally, until vegetables start to soften and sausage is heated through.

Add next 5 ingredients. Stir. Bring to a boil. Reduce heat to medium-low. Simmer, covered, for about 20 minutes, without stirring, until rice is tender and liquid is absorbed. Let stand for 5 minutes. Fluff with a fork.

Remove chicken from bones. Chop coarsely. Add to rice mixture. Stir. Remove to large serving dish.

Garnish with parsley. Makes about 9 cups (2.4 L). Serves 6.

1 serving: 608 Calories; 23.0 g Total Fat (9.8 g Mono, 4.6 g Poly, 6.5 g Sat); 158 mg Cholesterol; 39 g Carbohydrate; 2 g Fibre; 58 g Protein; 1160 mg Sodium

Pictured on page 125.

Note: If you have leftover cooked chicken, use 4 cups (1 L) chopped cooked chicken in place of the precooked whole roasted chicken.

Creamy Chicken Shrimp Penne

*A penne for your thoughts? Pile chicken, shrimp, spinach and tomatoes
on top of penne and we know what you'll be thinking—simply delicious!*

Penne pasta	4 cups	1 L
Olive (or cooking) oil	2 tsp.	10 mL
Boneless, skinless chicken breast halves, cut crosswise into slices	1 lb.	454 g
Garlic cloves, minced (or 1/2 tsp., 2 mL, powder)	2	2
Dry (or alcohol-free) white wine	1/4 cup	60 mL
Can of evaporated milk	13 1/2 oz.	385 mL
Salt	1/2 tsp.	2 mL
Cayenne pepper	1/4 tsp.	1 mL
Frozen, uncooked medium shrimp (peeled and deveined), thawed	1/2 lb.	225 g
Chopped fresh spinach, lightly packed	1 cup	250 mL
Grated Parmesan cheese	1/2 cup	125 mL
Roma (plum) tomatoes, chopped	3	3

Cook pasta in boiling salted water in large uncovered saucepan or Dutch
oven for 8 to 10 minutes, stirring occasionally, until tender but firm. Drain.
Return to same saucepan. Cover to keep warm.

Heat olive oil in large frying pan on medium. Add chicken and garlic. Cook
for 5 to 10 minutes, stirring occasionally, until chicken is no longer pink
inside and starts to brown. Add to pasta. Toss. Cover to keep warm.

Add wine to same frying pan. Heat and stir, scraping any brown bits from
bottom of pan. Bring to a boil. Reduce heat to medium. Boil gently for
about 1 minute until reduced by half.

Add next 3 ingredients. Stir. Boil gently for 5 minutes, stirring often.

Add shrimp. Stir. Cook, uncovered, for about 3 minutes until shrimp turn pink.

Add remaining 3 ingredients. Heat and stir for about 1 minute until spinach is
wilted. Add to pasta mixture. Toss. Makes about 10 1/2 cups (2.6 L). Serves 4.

*1 serving: 625 Calories; 17.4 g Total Fat (5.7 g Mono, 1.4 g Poly, 7.9 g Sat); 190 mg Cholesterol;
54 g Carbohydrate; 2 g Fibre; 57 g Protein; 782 mg Sodium*

Pictured on page 89.

Curried Tuna Quiche

It's not a silly notion at all! Fusilli pasta adds an attractive and unusual touch to traditional quiche. Serve with a green salad. To lighten your work, use a pre-grated mozzarella and Cheddar cheese blend.

Pastry for 9 inch (22 cm) pie shell

Cooked fusilli pasta (about 2/3 cup, 150 mL, uncooked)	1 cup	250 mL
Grated zucchini (with peel), squeezed dry	1 cup	250 mL
Can of flaked white tuna in water, drained	6 oz.	170 g
Grated mozzarella cheese	1/2 cup	125 mL
Grated medium Cheddar cheese	1/2 cup	125 mL
Large eggs	3	3
All-purpose flour	1 tbsp.	15 mL
Curry powder	1 tsp.	5 mL
Salt	1/2 tsp.	2 mL
Pepper	1/4 tsp.	1 mL
Skim evaporated milk	1 1/4 cups	300 mL
Roma (plum) tomatoes, sliced	2	2

Roll out pastry on lightly floured surface to 1/8 inch (3 mm) thickness. Line 9 inch (22 cm) pie plate. Trim and crimp decorative edge.

Scatter next 5 ingredients in pie shell. Set aside.

Beat next 5 ingredients in medium bowl until smooth.

Add evaporated milk. Stir. Pour into pie shell.

Top with tomato. Bake on bottom rack in 350°F (175°C) oven for 60 to 65 minutes until knife inserted in centre comes out clean. Let stand for 10 minutes. Serves 6.

1 serving: 388 Calories; 19.6 g Total Fat (2.9 g Mono, 0.9 g Poly, 7.1 g Sat); 124 mg Cholesterol; 30 g Carbohydrate; 1 g Fibre; 21 g Protein; 566 mg Sodium

Pictured on page 54.

Balsamic Skewers

A delicious basting sauce is only a bottle of balsamic vinaigrette away—
perfect for succulent shrimp. Use thick-stalked asparagus in this recipe
for best results on the grill. Cajun Cheese Bread, page 40, or
Dill Pasta Salad, page 19, will finish this meal nicely.

Frozen, uncooked large shrimp (peeled and deveined), thawed	1 lb.	454 g
Bamboo skewers (8 inches, 20 cm, each), soaked in water for 10 minutes	8	8
Can of whole baby corn, drained and cut into 1 inch (2.5 cm) pieces	14 oz.	398 mL
Fresh asparagus, trimmed of tough ends and cut into 1 inch (2.5 cm) pieces	3/4 lb.	340 g
Green onions (white parts only), cut into 1 inch (2.5 cm) pieces	6	6
Large red pepper, cut into 1 inch (2.5 cm) pieces	1	1
Bamboo skewers (8 inches, 20 cm, each), soaked in water for 10 minutes	8	8
Balsamic vinaigrette	1/2 cup	125 mL

Thread shrimp onto first 8 skewers (see Note). Place skewers on ungreased baking sheet with sides.

Thread next 4 ingredients alternately onto next 8 skewers. Place on same baking sheet.

Brush skewers with vinaigrette. Preheat gas barbecue to medium (see Tip, page 56). Cook vegetable skewers on greased grill for about 8 minutes, turning once at halftime, until vegetables are tender-crisp. Cook shrimp skewers on greased grill for about 2 minutes per side until shrimp turn pink. Serves 4.

1 serving: 355 Calories; 11.6 g Total Fat (0.7 g Mono, 1.5 g Poly, 1.6 g Sat); 172 mg Cholesterol; 38 g Carbohydrate; 5 g Fibre; 29 g Protein; 491 mg Sodium

Note: Thread shrimp body and tail through the skewers to ensure even cooking.

Pictured on page 18.

Salmon French Loaf

Say bonjour to this warm take on the classic salmon salad sandwich. It's just as good baked in the oven or served cold. Serve with your favourite pickles and Walnut Green Salad, page 12.

Cans of red (or pink) salmon (7 1/2 oz., 213 g, each), drained, skin and round bones removed	2	2
Block of cream cheese, softened	8 oz.	250 g
Roasted red peppers, blotted dry and diced	1/2 cup	125 mL
Green onions, sliced	2	2
Grated lemon zest	1 tsp.	5 mL
Pepper	1 tsp.	5 mL
French bread loaf, halved lengthwise	1	1

Combine first 6 ingredients in large bowl.

Spread salmon mixture on bottom half of loaf. Cover with top half. Secure with 6 wooden picks evenly spaced apart. Wrap tightly in sheet of heavy-duty (or double layer of regular) foil. Bake in 375°F (190°C) oven for 20 to 30 minutes until heated through. Cut crosswise between wooden picks into 6 pieces. Serves 6.

1 serving: 476 Calories; 23.2 g Total Fat (4.6 g Mono, 1.0 g Poly, 10.5 g Sat); 87 mg Cholesterol; 42 g Carbohydrate; 2 g Fibre; 25 g Protein; 1037 mg Sodium

Feta Shrimp Frittata

This delightful frittata makes a nice, light meal when served with Fresh Herb Rice, page 43, and your favourite salad.

Cooking oil	1 tbsp.	15 mL
Chopped green pepper	1 cup	250 mL
Chopped onion	1/4 cup	60 mL
Large eggs	8	8
Herb and garlic cream cheese	1/4 cup	60 mL
Cooked salad shrimp	3/4 lb.	340 g
Crumbled feta cheese	1 cup	250 mL
Pepper	1/2 tsp.	2 mL

(continued on next page)

Heat cooking oil in large frying pan on medium. Add green pepper and onion. Cook for 5 to 10 minutes, stirring often, until vegetables are softened.

Beat eggs and cream cheese in medium bowl until smooth. Add remaining 3 ingredients. Stir. Pour over vegetables in frying pan. Stir for 5 seconds. Spread egg mixture evenly in pan. Reduce heat to medium-low. Cook, covered, for about 10 minutes until bottom is golden and top is almost set. Broil on centre rack in oven (see Tip, page 115) for 2 to 3 minutes until frittata is golden and set. Serves 4.

1 serving: 456 Calories; 33.0 g Total Fat (10.2 g Mono, 6.7 g Poly, 12.6 g Sat); 518 mg Cholesterol; 8 g Carbohydrate; 1 g Fibre; 31 g Protein; 806 mg Sodium

Orzo Shrimp Packets

Pasta on the barbecue? You bet! You'll love this flavourful shrimp and orzo combination.

Chopped tomato	2 cups	500 mL
Sliced leek (white part only)	1 cup	250 mL
Dry (or alcohol-free) white wine	1/4 cup	60 mL
Olive (or cooking) oil	1 tbsp.	15 mL
Parsley flakes	1 tbsp.	15 mL
Garlic cloves, minced (or 3/4 tsp., 4 mL, powder)	3	3
Salt	1/2 tsp.	2 mL
Granulated sugar	1/4 tsp.	1 mL
Cooked orzo (about 1 1/2 cups, 375 mL, uncooked)	3 cups	750 mL
Frozen, uncooked medium shrimp (peeled and deveined), thawed	1 lb.	454 g

Combine first 8 ingredients in large bowl.

Add orzo and shrimp. Stir. Transfer to four greased sheets of heavy-duty (or double layer of regular) foil. Fold edges of foil together over shrimp mixture to enclose. Fold ends to seal completely. Preheat gas barbecue to medium. Place packets on ungreased grill. Close lid. Cook for about 15 minutes, turning once at halftime, until shrimp turn pink. Serves 4.

1 serving: 451 Calories; 6.6 g Total Fat (2.8 g Mono, 1.2 g Poly, 1.2 g Sat); 172 mg Cholesterol; 61 g Carbohydrate; 4 g Fibre; 34 g Protein; 475 mg Sodium

Tarragon Shrimp Linguine

Dahling! Dinner is simply divine when tarragon and
white wine accent a buttery shrimp-and-pasta toss.

Linguine	12 oz.	340 g
Cooking oil	1 tbsp.	15 mL
Frozen, uncooked large shrimp (peeled and deveined), thawed	1 lb.	454 g
Julienned carrot (see Tip, page 140)	2 cups	500 mL
Prepared chicken broth	1 cup	250 mL
Dry (or alcohol-free) white wine	1/3 cup	75 mL
Lemon juice	1 tbsp.	15 mL
Chopped fresh tarragon (or 1/4 tsp., 1 mL, dried)	1 tsp.	5 mL
Water	2 tbsp.	30 mL
Cornstarch	2 tsp.	10 mL
Chopped fresh chives	1/4 cup	60 mL
Butter (or hard margarine)	1 tbsp.	15 mL

Cook pasta in boiling salted water in large uncovered saucepan or Dutch oven for 8 to 10 minutes, stirring occasionally, until tender but firm. Drain. Return to same saucepan. Cover to keep warm.

Heat cooking oil in large frying pan on medium-high. Add shrimp. Heat and stir for 2 to 3 minutes until shrimp turn pink. Transfer to small bowl. Set aside.

Combine next 5 ingredients in same frying pan. Bring to a boil. Reduce heat to medium. Cook, covered, for about 3 minutes until carrot is tender-crisp.

Stir water into cornstarch in small cup. Stir into carrot mixture. Add shrimp. Heat and stir for about 1 minute until sauce is boiling and thickened and shrimp are heated through. Remove from heat.

Add chives and butter. Heat and stir until butter is melted. Add to pasta. Toss. Makes about 7 cups (1.75 L). Serves 4.

1 serving: 542 Calories; 9.9 g Total Fat (3.2 g Mono, 2.0 g Poly, 2.9 g Sat); 180 mg Cholesterol; 73 g Carbohydrate; 4 g Fibre; 37 g Protein; 429 mg Sodium

Scallop "Orzotto"

Our pasta version of risotto. Made with orzo, tiny rice-shaped pasta,
this dish is rich, creamy and loaded with scallops and mushrooms. Lemon
Pepper Greens, page 59, will add a delightful splash of colour to this meal.

Orzo	2 cups	500 mL
Garlic butter	1 tbsp.	15 mL
Sliced fresh white mushrooms	1 1/2 cups	375 mL
Prepared chicken broth	1 1/2 cups	375 mL
Grated lemon zest	1/2 tsp.	2 mL
Dried oregano	1/4 tsp.	1 mL
Fresh (or frozen, thawed) small bay scallops	2 cups	500 mL
Grated Parmesan cheese	1/2 cup	125 mL
Garlic butter	1 tbsp.	15 mL
Lemon juice	1 tbsp.	15 mL
Pepper	1/4 tsp.	1 mL

Cook orzo in boiling salted water in large uncovered saucepan or Dutch oven for about 5 minutes, stirring occasionally, until almost tender. Drain. Rinse with cold water. Drain well. Set aside.

Melt first amount of garlic butter in same saucepan on medium. Add mushrooms. Cook for about 5 minutes, stirring occasionally, until softened.

Add orzo and next 3 ingredients. Stir. Bring to a boil. Reduce heat to medium-low. Simmer, uncovered, for 5 minutes, stirring constantly.

Add scallops. Heat and stir for about 5 minutes until scallops are opaque and broth is absorbed.

Add remaining 4 ingredients. Heat and stir until butter is melted. Makes about 6 1/2 cups (1.6 L). Serves 4.

1 serving: 538 Calories; 11.9 g Total Fat (1.4 g Mono, 0.5 g Poly, 5.5 g Sat); 57 mg Cholesterol;
68 g Carbohydrate; 3 g Fibre; 38 g Protein; 767 mg Sodium

Asian Salmon Burgers

This Asian-inspired dish will go over swimmingly! Top with lettuce,
tomato and add Asparagus Cucumber Salad, page 9, on the side.

Mayonnaise	2 tbsp.	30 mL
Chopped pickled ginger	1 tbsp.	15 mL
Wasabi paste (Japanese horseradish)	1/2 tsp.	2 mL
Large egg, fork-beaten	1	1
Finely chopped green onion	1/4 cup	60 mL
Soy sauce	1 tbsp.	15 mL
Finely grated gingerroot (or 1/4 tsp., 1 mL, ground ginger)	1 1/2 tsp.	7 mL
Honey Dijon mustard	1 tsp.	5 mL
Fresh (or frozen, thawed) salmon fillet, skin and any small bones removed, coarsely chopped	1 lb.	454 g
Fine dry bread crumbs	1/2 cup	125 mL
Onion buns, split	4	4

Combine first 3 ingredients in small cup. Chill.

Combine next 5 ingredients in medium bowl. Set aside.

Put fish into food processor. Process with on/off motion until finely chopped.

Add bread crumbs. Process with on/off motion until combined. Add to egg
mixture. Mix well. Divide into 4 equal portions. Shape into 4 inch (10 cm)
diameter patties. Place on greased broiler pan. Broil on top rack in oven for
about 5 minutes per side until golden and set. Remove to large plate.
Cover to keep warm.

Place buns cut-side up on same broiler pan. Broil on top rack in oven for
1 to 2 minutes until golden. Serve patties, topped with mayonnaise mixture,
in buns. Serves 4.

1 serving: 512 Calories; 17.7 g Total Fat (6.3 g Mono, 5.1 g Poly, 3.2 g Sat); 123 mg Cholesterol;
51 g Carbohydrate; 3 g Fibre; 34 g Protein; 1155 mg Sodium

GRILLED SALMON BURGERS: Preheat gas barbecue to medium. Cook patties
on greased grill for about 5 minutes per side until golden and set. Toast buns
cut-side down on greased grill. Serve grilled patties, topped with mayonnaise
mixture, in buns.

Pictured on page 107.

Salmon Polenta Skewers

Polenta, ham-wrapped salmon and tender-crisp vegetables make quite an eye-catching meal. But don't fret, this is easy. You'll have dinner on the table faster than you can say "kabob's your uncle!" Serve with grilled vegetables or salad.

Italian dressing	1/4 cup	60 mL
Sun-dried tomato pesto	1 tbsp.	15 mL
Deli ham slices, each cut into 4 strips (about 1 inch, 2.5 cm, wide)	4	4
Fresh (or frozen, thawed) salmon fillet, skin removed, cut into 1 1/2 inch (3.8 cm) cubes	1 lb.	454 g
Zucchini slices (with peel), cut 1 inch, 2.5 cm, thick, halved crosswise	8	8
Polenta cubes (1 inch, 2.5 cm, size)	16	16
Red pepper pieces (1 inch, 2.5 cm, size)	16	16
Bamboo skewers (8 inches, 20 cm, each), soaked in water for 10 minutes	8	8

Combine dressing and pesto in small cup. Set aside.

Wrap ham strips around fish pieces.

Thread fish and next 3 ingredients alternately onto skewers. Place on large plate. Brush skewers with pesto mixture. Preheat gas barbecue to medium (see Tip, page 56). Cook skewers on greased grill for 10 to 12 minutes, turning occasionally, until vegetables are tender-crisp and fish flakes easily when tested with a fork. Serves 4.

1 serving: 421 Calories; 19.5 g Total Fat (8.5 g Mono, 6.4 g Poly, 2.0 g Sat); 112 mg Cholesterol; 21 g Carbohydrate; 1 g Fibre; 41 g Protein; 1520 mg Sodium

Pictured on page 107.

Paré Pointer
He tried to book a trip to the moon but it was already full.

Dijon Dill Salmon Patties

Salmon patties are made simply sensational when paired with Dijon mustard and dill. A perfect match for Vegetable Pearl Salad, page 14.

Large eggs, fork-beaten	2	2
Crushed Ritz crackers (about 24)	3/4 cup	175 mL
Finely chopped green onion	1/2 cup	125 mL
Honey Dijon mustard	2 tbsp.	30 mL
Chopped fresh dill	2 tbsp.	30 mL
(or 1 1/2 tsp., 7 mL, dried)		
Grated lemon zest	2 tsp.	10 mL
Cans of pink salmon (6 1/2 oz., 184 g, each), drained, skin and round bones removed	4	4
Cooking oil	2 tbsp.	30 mL

Lemon wedges, for garnish

Combine first 6 ingredients in medium bowl.

Add salmon. Mix well. Divide into 6 equal portions. Shape into 4 inch (10 cm) diameter patties.

Heat 1 tbsp. (15 mL) cooking oil in large frying pan on medium. Add 3 patties. Cook for about 3 minutes per side until golden. Remove to large serving plate. Cover to keep warm. Repeat with remaining cooking oil and patties.

Garnish with lemon wedges. Serves 6.

1 serving: 281 Calories; 13.6 g Total Fat (4.5 g Mono, 2.2 g Poly, 2.0 g Sat); 151 mg Cholesterol; 8 g Carbohydrate; 1 g Fibre; 34 g Protein; 688 mg Sodium

1. Smoky Asparagus Salad, page 9
2. Grilled Salmon Burgers, page 104
3. Salmon Polenta Skewers, page 105

Props courtesy of: Cherison Enterprises Inc.
Emile Henry

Nacho-Crusted Haddock

Definitely nacho ordinary fish sticks! Serve alongside Vegetable Spanish Rice, page 51, for a meal the whole family will love.

Haddock fillets, any small bones removed, cut into 6 equal pieces	1 1/2 lbs.	680 g
Mayonnaise	2 tbsp.	30 mL
Finely chopped cilantro or parsley (or 3/4 tsp., 4 mL, dried)	1 tbsp.	15 mL
Crushed cheese-flavoured tortilla chips	1 cup	250 mL
Grated medium Cheddar cheese	1/3 cup	75 mL
Lime juice	1 tbsp.	15 mL
Grated lime zest	1/2 tsp.	2 mL

Arrange fish on greased foil-lined baking sheet with sides.

Combine mayonnaise and cilantro in small cup. Spread on fish.

Combine remaining 4 ingredients in small bowl. Spoon onto fish. Press down lightly with back of spoon. Bake in 375°F (190°C) oven for 8 to 10 minutes until fish flakes easily when tested with a fork. Serves 6.

1 serving: 281 Calories; 12.9 g Total Fat (6.5 g Mono, 2.4 g Poly, 3.0 g Sat); 74 mg Cholesterol; 16 g Carbohydrate; 1 g Fibre; 25 g Protein; 314 mg Sodium

Pictured at left.

1. Grilled Salmon With Avocado Salsa, page 110
2. Grilled Chipotle Cheese Potatoes, page 52
3. Nacho-Crusted Haddock, above
4. Vegetable Spanish Rice, page 51

Props courtesy of: Pfaltzgraff Canada
Stokes

Salmon With Avocado Salsa

Forget the guacamole, avocado salsa is where it's at. Chunks of avocado and cucumber atop lemon pepper salmon will have you feeling cool on those hot summer nights. Nicely complemented by Chipotle Cheese Potatoes, page 52.

Fresh (or frozen, thawed) salmon fillets (about 4 oz., 113 g, each), skin removed	4	4
Lemon pepper	1 tsp.	5 mL
CUCUMBER AVOCADO SALSA		
English cucumber (with peel), seeds removed, diced	1 1/2 cups	375 mL
Ripe medium avocado, chopped	1	1
Lime juice	1/3 cup	75 mL
Chopped red onion	1/4 cup	60 mL
Chopped fresh cilantro or parsley	1/4 cup	60 mL
Liquid honey	1 tbsp.	15 mL
Finely chopped fresh jalapeño pepper (see Tip, below)	1 tsp.	5 mL

Sprinkle fish with lemon pepper. Place on greased broiler pan. Broil on top rack in oven for 2 to 4 minutes per side, depending on thickness, until fish flakes easily when tested with a fork.

Cucumber Avocado Salsa: Combine all 7 ingredients in medium bowl. Makes about 2 1/2 cups (625 mL) salsa. Serve with fish. Serves 4.

1 serving: 257 Calories; 14.8 g Total Fat (2.4 g Mono, 2.9 g Poly, 1.8 g Sat); 62 mg Cholesterol; 11 g Carbohydrate; 2 g Fibre; 24 g Protein; 84 mg Sodium

GRILLED SALMON WITH AVOCADO SALSA: Preheat gas barbecue to medium-high. Cook fish on greased grill for 2 to 4 minutes per side, depending on thickness, until fish flakes easily when tested with a fork.

Pictured on page 108.

 Hot peppers contain capsaicin in the seeds and ribs. Removing the seeds and ribs will reduce the heat. Wear rubber gloves when handling hot peppers and avoid touching your eyes. Wash your hands well afterwards.

Artichoke Salmon

Artichoke is always an artful choice when it comes to impressing guests. They'll be full of accolades when they taste the smoky bacon and artichoke stuffing atop sensational salmon. Serve with wild rice and Braised Celery, page 48.

Bacon slices, diced	2	2
Sliced fresh white mushrooms	2 cups	500 mL
Chopped onion	1/2 cup	125 mL
Large egg, fork-beaten	1	1
Seasoned croutons	1 1/2 cups	375 mL
Jar of marinated artichoke hearts, drained and chopped	6 oz.	170 mL
Prepared chicken broth	1/4 cup	60 mL
Grated Parmesan cheese	1/4 cup	60 mL
Fresh (or frozen, thawed) salmon fillet, with skin, any small bones removed	2 lbs.	900 g

Cook bacon in large frying pan on medium until crisp.

Add mushrooms and onion. Cook for 5 to 10 minutes, stirring often, until onion is softened. Transfer to large bowl.

Add next 5 ingredients. Stir until croutons are moistened.

Place fish, skin-side down, on greased baking sheet. Spoon crouton mixture on top. Press down lightly with back of spoon. Bake in 375°F (190°C) oven for about 20 minutes until fish flakes easily when tested with a fork. Serves 6.

1 serving: 341 Calories; 16.0 g Total Fat (5.3 g Mono, 4.4 g Poly, 3.4 g Sat); 120 mg Cholesterol; 12 g Carbohydrate; 2 g Fibre; 37 g Protein; 467 mg Sodium

Paré Pointer

How come a lawyer writes a 90 page document and calls it a brief?

Shrimp Fried Rice

*Got rice? If you have leftover rice in the fridge, you can have dinner
on the table in minutes (results are better if the rice is cold).
Serve with steamed sugar snap peas on the side.*

Cooking oil	1 tbsp.	15 mL
Sliced celery	1/2 cup	125 mL
Garlic clove, minced (or 1/4 tsp.,	1	1
1 mL, powder)		
Finely grated gingerroot (or 1/8 tsp.,	1/2 tsp.	2 mL
0.5 mL, ground ginger)		
Cooking oil	1 tbsp.	15 mL
Large eggs	4	4
Pepper, sprinkle		
Cooked long grain white rice	4 cups	1 L
(about 1 1/3 cups, 325 mL, uncooked)		
Sliced green onion	1 cup	250 mL
Soy sauce	2 tbsp.	30 mL
Cooked baby shrimp	1 lb.	454 g
Frozen peas, thawed	1 cup	250 mL

Heat wok or large frying pan on medium-high until very hot. Add first
amount of cooking oil. Add next 3 ingredients. Stir-fry for about 1 minute
until celery is softened. Transfer to small bowl. Set aside.

Add second amount of cooking oil to hot wok. Break eggs into wok.
Sprinkle with pepper. Break yolks. Cook for 1 to 2 minutes until eggs start
to set. Turn eggs over. Stir-fry for 1 to 2 minutes until egg starts to brown.

Add next 3 ingredients. Stir-fry for about 5 minutes until rice starts to brown.

Add celery mixture, shrimp and peas. Stir-fry for about 3 minutes until
heated through. Makes about 8 cups (2 L). Serves 4.

*1 serving: 503 Calories; 14.4 g Total Fat (6.6 g Mono, 3.7 g Poly, 2.6 g Sat); 359 mg Cholesterol;
54 g Carbohydrate; 3 g Fibre; 37 g Protein; 944 mg Sodium*

Sole Packets

The pirate in you will take great delight in this buried treasure
of tender sole hidden under fragrant coconut and curry couscous.

Sole fillets, any small bones removed, divided into 4 equal portions	1 lb.	454 g
Salt	1/4 tsp.	1 mL
Pepper	1/8 tsp.	0.5 mL
Prepared chicken broth	1 cup	250 mL
Coconut milk (or reconstituted from powder)	1/2 cup	125 mL
Granulated sugar	2 tbsp.	30 mL
Curry powder	1 tbsp.	15 mL
Finely grated gingerroot (or 1/2 tsp., 2 mL, ground ginger)	2 tsp.	10 mL
Parsley flakes	2 tsp.	10 mL
Salt	1/4 tsp.	1 mL
Frozen peas	2 cups	500 mL
Plain couscous	1 1/2 cups	375 mL

Sprinkle fish with first amount of salt and pepper. Place on 4 greased sheets of heavy-duty (or double layer of regular) foil. Set aside.

Combine next 7 ingredients in large bowl.

Add peas and couscous. Stir. Spoon onto fish. Fold edges of foil together over couscous mixture to enclose. Fold ends to seal completely. Preheat gas barbecue to medium. Place packets on ungreased grill. Close lid. Cook for 15 to 20 minutes, turning once at halftime, until fish flakes easily when tested with a fork. Serves 4.

1 serving: 516 Calories; 9.0 g Total Fat (0.9 g Mono, 0.9 g Poly, 6.3 g Sat); 54 mg Cholesterol; 72 g Carbohydrate; 6 g Fibre; 36 g Protein; 671 mg Sodium

Oven Salmon Scallop

To the table they'll gallop for a taste of this scallop! Salmon,
potatoes and vegetables are smothered in a creamy
sauce—especially nice on a cold, blustery day!

Thinly sliced peeled potato (about 1 1/2 lbs., 680 g)	4 cups	1 L
Thinly sliced carrot	1 cup	250 mL
Thinly sliced onion	1 cup	250 mL
Thinly sliced celery	3/4 cup	175 mL
Fresh (or frozen, thawed) salmon fillets, skin removed, cut into 1 inch (2.5 cm) pieces	1 lb.	454 g
Milk	2 cups	500 mL
Envelope of leek soup mix	2 3/4 oz.	77 g

Layer half of first 4 ingredients, in order given, in greased 9 x 13 inch
(22 x 33 cm) baking dish.

Arrange fish on celery. Layer remaining vegetables on top. Set aside.

Heat milk in small saucepan on medium until hot but not boiling. Slowly
add soup mix, stirring constantly until thickened. Pour over vegetables,
poking with knife in several places to bottom of baking dish to allow soup
mixture to flow through. Bake, covered, in 350°F (175°C) oven for about
1 hour until vegetables are tender and fish flakes easily when tested with
a fork. Serves 4.

1 serving: 459 Calories; 10.9 g Total Fat (3.6 g Mono, 3.2 g Poly, 3.0 g Sat); 70 mg Cholesterol;
58 g Carbohydrate; 5 g Fibre; 32 g Protein; 1149 mg Sodium

Paré Pointer

If a traffic light could talk it would say, "Don't look now, I'm changing."

Sole Skillet

This meal's got sole! Lemony, zesty fish
looks mighty fine atop a bed of tasty rice.

Vegetable cocktail (or tomato) juice	2 cups	500 mL
Long grain white rice	1 1/2 cups	375 mL
Diced red pepper	1 1/2 cups	375 mL
Water	1 cup	250 mL
Dried basil	2 tsp.	10 mL
Salt	1/4 tsp.	1 mL
Mayonnaise	1/4 cup	60 mL
Grated lemon zest	2 tsp.	10 mL
Garlic powder	1/8 tsp.	0.5 mL
Pepper	1/8 tsp.	0.5 mL
Sole fillets, any small bones removed, blotted dry	1 lb.	454 g

Combine first 6 ingredients in large frying pan. Bring to a boil. Reduce heat to medium-low. Simmer, covered, for 20 to 30 minutes, without stirring, until rice is tender and liquid is absorbed. Let stand for 5 minutes. Fluff with a fork.

Stir next 4 ingredients in small bowl.

Spread mayonnaise mixture on both sides of fish. Arrange on rice in pan. Broil on centre rack in oven (see Tip, below) for about 5 minutes until fish flakes easily when tested with a fork. Serves 4.

1 serving: 492 Calories; 13.1 g Total Fat (6.6 g Mono, 4.3 g Poly, 1.5 g Sat); 63 mg Cholesterol; 64 g Carbohydrate; 3 g Fibre; 28 g Protein; 641 mg Sodium

 tip When baking or broiling food in a frying pan with a handle that isn't ovenproof, wrap the handle in foil and keep it to the front of the oven, away from the element.

Saucepan Lamb Stew

*Mary had a little lamb, it's true. But what they never told you
was that everywhere that Mary went her saucepan was sure to go, too.
After all, Mary was classically trained at Le Cordon Bleu. And you thought
she was just a sweet little shepherdess! The trick to this treat is using
thyme, rather than spending too much time prepping ingredients.*

Stewing lamb	1 lb.	454 g
All-purpose flour	2 tbsp.	30 mL
Salt	1/2 tsp.	2 mL
Pepper	1/2 tsp.	2 mL
Cooking oil	1 tbsp.	15 mL
Cooking oil	1 tsp.	5 mL
Chopped onion	1 cup	250 mL
Dry (or alcohol-free) red wine	1/4 cup	60 mL
Prepared beef broth	2 1/2 cups	625 mL
Tomato paste (see Tip, page 117)	1 tbsp.	15 mL
Dried thyme	1 tsp.	5 mL
Baby carrots	2 cups	500 mL
Red baby potatoes, halved	1 lb.	454 g
Water	2 tbsp.	30 mL
All-purpose flour	2 tbsp.	30 mL

Put first 4 ingredients into large resealable freezer bag. Seal bag. Toss until
coated. Remove lamb. Discard any remaining flour mixture.

Heat first amount of cooking oil in large saucepan on medium. Cook lamb
in 2 batches for about 5 minutes per batch, stirring occasionally, until
browned. Transfer to large plate. Set aside.

Heat second amount of cooking oil in same saucepan. Add onion. Cook for
5 to 10 minutes, stirring often, until softened.

Add wine. Heat and stir for 1 minute, scraping any brown bits from
bottom of saucepan.

Add lamb and next 3 ingredients. Stir. Bring to a boil. Reduce heat to
medium-low. Simmer, covered, for 30 minutes.

(continued on next page)

Add carrots and potato. Stir. Bring to a boil. Reduce heat to medium-low. Simmer, covered, for 20 to 30 minutes until lamb and potato are tender.

Stir water into flour in small cup until smooth. Slowly add to lamb mixture, stirring constantly until boiling and thickened. Makes about 6 1/2 cups (1.6 L). Serves 4.

1 serving: 375 Calories; 11.2 g Total Fat (5.3 g Mono, 2.0 g Poly, 2.7 g Sat); 74 mg Cholesterol; 36 g Carbohydrate; 4 g Fibre; 29 g Protein; 899 mg Sodium

Pictured on page 144.

SAUCEPAN BEEF STEW: Use same amount of stewing beef instead of lamb.

 If a recipe calls for less than an entire can of tomato paste, freeze the unopened can for 30 minutes. Open both ends and push the contents through one end. Slice off only what you need. Freeze the remaining paste in a resealable freezer bag or plastic wrap for future use.

Lamb Meatball Skewers

If you haven't tried ground lamb, here's your chance. This easy-to-make entree is a fun initiation for the whole family. Pair with Mediterranean Potatoes, page 45.

Large egg, fork-beaten	1	1
Fine dry bread crumbs	1/4 cup	60 mL
Dried oregano	1/2 tsp.	2 mL
Lemon pepper	1/2 tsp.	2 mL
Seasoned salt	1/2 tsp.	2 mL
Ground nutmeg	1/4 tsp.	1 mL
Ground cinnamon	1/4 tsp.	1 mL
Lean ground lamb	1 lb.	454 g
Medium onion, cut into 24 equal pieces	1	1
Large green pepper, cut into 24 equal pieces	1	1
Large red pepper, cut into 24 equal pieces	1	1
Bamboo skewers (8 inches, 20 cm, each), soaked in water for 10 minutes	8	8
Italian dressing	1/2 cup	125 mL

Combine first 7 ingredients in medium bowl.

Add lamb. Mix well. Divide into 24 equal portions. Roll into balls.

Thread meatballs and next 3 ingredients alternately onto skewers. Place on greased wire rack set in foil-lined baking sheet with sides.

Brush skewers with dressing. Bake in 375°F (190°C) oven for about 30 minutes, turning occasionally and brushing with any remaining dressing, until meatballs are fully cooked, and internal temperature of lamb reaches 160°F (71°C). Serves 4.

1 serving: 580 Calories; 48.7 g Total Fat (22.9 g Mono, 9.2 g Poly, 13.6 g Sat); 149 mg Cholesterol; 14 g Carbohydrate; 2 g Fibre; 22 g Protein; 796 mg Sodium

GRILLED MEATBALL SKEWERS: Preheat gas barbecue to medium. Cook skewers on greased grill for about 15 minutes, turning occasionally and brushing with any remaining dressing, until meatballs are fully cooked, and internal temperature of lamb reaches 160°F (71°C).

Okra And Lamb Casserole

*A favourite of all true belles and beaus, okra makes a tasty
and unexpected contribution to this tomato casserole. Steam
some rice, put it on the table and faster than you can say
"I'll never be hungry again," dinner will be gone with the wind!*

Cooking oil	1 tsp.	5 mL
Lean ground lamb	1 lb.	454 g
Cooking oil	1 tbsp.	15 mL
Fresh (or frozen) okra, cut into 1/2 inch (12 mm) pieces	1 lb.	454 g
Chopped green pepper	1 cup	250 mL
Chopped onion	1/2 cup	125 mL
Can of diced tomatoes (with juice)	14 oz.	398 mL
Granulated sugar	1 tsp.	5 mL
Garlic and herb no-salt seasoning	1 tsp.	5 mL
Dried basil	1/2 tsp.	2 mL
Pepper	1/4 tsp.	1 mL

Heat first amount of cooking oil in large frying pan on medium. Add lamb.
Scramble-fry for 5 to 10 minutes until no longer pink. Drain. Transfer to
paper towel-lined plate.

Heat second amount of cooking oil in same frying pan. Add okra. Cook for
about 5 minutes, stirring occasionally, until starting to brown.

Add green pepper and onion. Cook for about 5 minutes, stirring often, until
onion is softened.

Add lamb and remaining 5 ingredients. Stir. Transfer to ungreased 2 quart
(2 L) casserole. Bake, covered, in 350°F (175°C) oven for about 45 minutes
until boiling. Let stand for about 10 minutes until sauce is slightly thickened.
Stir. Makes about 7 cups (1.75 L). Serves 4.

*1 serving: 434 Calories; 31.3 g Total Fat (13.6 g Mono, 3.5 g Poly, 11.9 g Sat); 83 mg Cholesterol;
18 g Carbohydrate; 5 g Fibre; 22 g Protein; 348 mg Sodium*

Lamb Orzo Stew

Don't know what to make for dinner? Well don't go on the lam just yet.
Go to the lamb, instead, and make this easy, saucy, risotto-like stew.
Serve with buns or garlic bread to sop up the delicious sauce.

Cooking oil	2 tsp.	10 mL
Lamb shanks (see Note)	2 1/2 lbs.	1.1 kg
Chopped onion	2 cups	500 mL
Chopped carrot	1 cup	250 mL
Can of tomato paste	5 1/2 oz.	156 mL
Dry (or alcohol-free) red wine	1 cup	250 mL
Prepared chicken broth	2 cups	500 mL
Water	2 cups	500 mL
Lemon juice	1/4 cup	60 mL
Liquid honey	1 tbsp.	15 mL
Dried rosemary, crushed	1 tsp.	5 mL
Salt	1/4 tsp.	1 mL
Orzo	1 1/2 cups	375 mL
Chopped red pepper	1 cup	250 mL

Heat cooking oil in Dutch oven on medium-high. Add lamb. Cook for 3 to 4 minutes per side until browned.

Add onion and carrot. Cook for about 5 minutes, stirring often, until onion starts to soften.

Add tomato paste. Stir, scraping any brown bits from bottom of pan. Add wine. Heat and stir for 1 minute.

Add next 6 ingredients. Stir. Bring to a boil. Reduce heat to medium-low. Simmer, covered, for about 2 hours until lamb is tender. Transfer lamb to cutting board.

Add orzo and red pepper to broth mixture. Stir. Cook, covered, for 10 to 12 minutes, stirring occasionally, until orzo is tender. Remove shanks to cutting board using slotted spoon. Remove lamb from bones. Discard bones. Chop. Add to orzo mixture. Heat and stir until heated through. Makes about 7 cups (1.75 L). Serves 6.

1 serving: 680 Calories; 28.3 g Total Fat (11.5 g Mono, 2.7 g Poly, 11.5 g Sat); 136 mg Cholesterol; 53 g Carbohydrate; 4 g Fibre; 46 g Protein; 536 mg Sodium

Note: Lamb shanks are commonly found in frozen bulk packages.

Herb-Scented Lamb Kabobs

Making dinner can be quite a job, so get some help from this easy kabob! The tender lamb infused with fragrant herbs is made to be set atop Cabbage Noodles, page 62, or served alongside Roasted Veggie Pockets, page 46.

Olive (or cooking) oil	1/3 cup	75 mL
Red wine vinegar	1/4 cup	60 mL
Dried oregano	1 1/2 tsp.	7 mL
Garlic clove, minced (or 1/4 tsp.,	1	1
1 mL, powder)		
Lemon pepper	1 tsp.	5 mL
Ground coriander	1/2 tsp.	2 mL
Stewing lamb, trimmed of fat	1 lb.	454 g
Bamboo skewers (8 inches, 20 cm, each),	4	4
soaked in water for 10 minutes		

Combine first 6 ingredients in small bowl. Reserve half of olive oil mixture in small cup for basting sauce.

Put lamb into large resealable freezer bag. Add remaining olive oil mixture. Seal bag. Turn until coated. Let stand in refrigerator for at least 6 hours or overnight, turning occasionally. Drain.

Thread lamb onto skewers. Place on greased broiler pan. Brush kabobs with basting sauce. Broil kabobs on top rack in oven for about 10 minutes, turning once at halftime and brushing with any remaining basting sauce, until desired doneness. Serves 4.

1 serving: 268 Calories; 18.8 g Total Fat (11.9 g Mono, 1.6 g Poly, 3.9 g Sat); 74 mg Cholesterol; trace Carbohydrate; trace Fibre; 23 g Protein; 97 mg Sodium

GRILLED LAMB KABOBS: Preheat gas barbecue to medium. Cook kabobs on greased grill for about 10 minutes, turning once at halftime and brushing with any remaining basting sauce, until desired doneness.

Pictured on page 17.

Couscous And Beans

Couscous goes Greek when it's loaded with olives, cucumber and feta—it's a tasty twist!

Prepared vegetable (or chicken) broth	1 1/2 cups	375 mL
Plain couscous	1 1/2 cups	375 mL
Can of mixed beans, rinsed and drained	19 oz.	540 mL
Chopped tomato	2 cups	500 mL
Chopped red pepper	1 cup	250 mL
Chopped English cucumber (with peel)	1 cup	250 mL
Chopped kalamata olives	1/4 cup	60 mL
Olive (or cooking) oil	6 tbsp.	100 mL
Balsamic vinegar	3 tbsp.	50 mL
Chopped fresh basil	2 tbsp.	30 mL
Garlic clove, minced (or 1/4 tsp., 1 mL, powder)	1	1
Pepper	1/4 tsp.	1 mL
Crumbled feta cheese	1 cup	250 mL

Measure broth into medium saucepan. Bring to a boil. Add couscous. Stir. Remove from heat. Let stand, covered, for about 5 minutes until couscous is tender and broth is absorbed. Fluff with a fork. Transfer to large bowl. Cool.

Add next 5 ingredients. Toss.

Whisk next 5 ingredients in small bowl until combined. Add to couscous mixture. Toss.

Sprinkle with cheese. Makes 10 cups (2.25 L). Serves 4.

1 serving: 746 Calories; 31.9 g Total Fat (17.9 g Mono, 3.0 g Poly, 9.1 g Sat); 35 mg Cholesterol; 89 g Carbohydrate; 10 g Fibre; 26 g Protein; 1170 mg Sodium

Cottage Broccoli Bake

Tender-crisp broccoli is blanketed with two cheeses and a buttery crumb topping.
Perfect when the mercury's dropping and you're looking for a little warmth.
For our deluxe version of mac 'n' cheese, spoon over hot, buttered macaroni.

Broccoli florets	6 cups	1.5 L
Large eggs	2	2
2% cottage cheese	1 cup	250 mL
Grated sharp (or medium) Cheddar cheese	1 cup	250 mL
Finely chopped green onion	1 tbsp.	15 mL
Lemon pepper	1/2 tsp.	2 mL
Butter (or hard margarine)	2 tbsp.	30 mL
Fine dry bread crumbs	1/3 cup	75 mL
Cornflake crumbs	3 tbsp.	50 mL

Cook broccoli in boiling water in large saucepan until just tender. Drain. Transfer to ungreased 2 quart (2 L) baking dish.

Combine next 5 ingredients in medium bowl. Spoon onto broccoli.

Melt butter in small saucepan. Add bread crumbs and cornflake crumbs. Stir until well mixed. Sprinkle over cottage cheese mixture. Bake, uncovered, in 375°F (190°C) oven for about 30 minutes until golden and set. Serves 6.

1 serving: 218 Calories; 12.7 g Total Fat (2.1 g Mono, 0.6 g Poly, 7.5 g Sat); 92 mg Cholesterol; 12 g Carbohydrate; 2 g Fibre; 14 g Protein; 419 mg Sodium

---

Paré Pointer
A hit and run is only legal in baseball.

Curried Baked Chickpeas

This creative curry combo will keep the compliments coming. This sweet apple,
tender chickpea and dark raisin dish is excellent served over steamed rice.

Cans of chickpeas (garbanzo beans), 19 oz. (540 mL), each, rinsed and drained	2	2
Chopped peeled tart apple (such as Granny Smith)	1 cup	250 mL
Chopped onion	3/4 cup	175 mL
Dark raisins	1/2 cup	125 mL
Liquid honey	1/2 cup	125 mL
Sweet pickle relish	1/3 cup	75 mL
Prepared chicken broth	1/4 cup	60 mL
Dijon mustard	1 tbsp.	15 mL
Curry powder	1 tsp.	5 mL

Chopped fresh parsley, for garnish

Combine first 9 ingredients in ungreased 2 quart (2 L) casserole. Bake,
covered, in 325°F (160°C) oven for about 45 minutes until apple is tender.

Garnish with parsley. Makes about 5 1/2 cups (1.4 L). Serves 4.

1 serving: 790 Calories; 6.1 g Total Fat (1.6 g Mono, 2.5 g Poly, 0.7 g Sat); 0 mg Cholesterol;
177 g Carbohydrate; 12 g Fibre; 19 g Protein; 2147 mg Sodium

1. Pork Noodle Stri-Fry, page 147
2. Jiffy Jambalaya, page 96

Props courtesy of: Cherison Enterprises Inc.
Stokes

Teriyaki Tofu Pizza

A light, crisp alternative to heavy pizzas. It's a must-try for teriyaki lovers.
Using a ready-made pizza crust makes prep a breeze.

Prebaked pizza crust	1	1
(12 inch, 30 cm, diameter)		
Thick teriyaki basting sauce	1/3 cup	75 mL
Coarsely grated firm tofu	1 1/3 cups	325 mL
Canned pineapple tidbits, drained	2/3 cup	150 mL
Medium green or red pepper, sliced	1	1
Grated mozzarella cheese	3/4 cup	175 mL
Fresh bean sprouts	1 cup	250 mL
Thinly sliced green onion	2 tbsp.	30 mL

Place pizza crust on greased 12 inch (30 cm) pizza pan. Spread teriyaki sauce on crust, leaving 1/2 inch (12 mm) edge.

Scatter next 3 ingredients over sauce.

Sprinkle with cheese. Bake on centre rack in 475°F (240°C) oven for about 10 minutes until cheese is melted and golden.

Top with bean sprouts and onion. Serves 4.

1 serving: 410 Calories; 10.8 g Total Fat (1.7 g Mono, 1.0 g Poly, 4.0 g Sat); 17 mg Cholesterol; 60 g Carbohydrate; 3 g Fibre; 19 g Protein; 1105 mg Sodium

Pictured at left.

TERIYAKI CHICKEN PIZZA: Use chopped cooked chicken instead of tofu.

1. Island Chicken Casserole, page 83
2. Ginger Maple Pork, page 148
3. Teriyaki Tofu Pizza, above

Props courtesy of: Cherison Enterprises Inc.
Totally Bamboo

Spicy Vegetable Omelettes

This hot little treat is far too spicy for breakfast fare—this fiery fave deserves a place at the dinner table! Enough for two but easy to double for four. Make a complete meal with whole grain toast on the side.

Cooking oil	1 tsp.	5 mL
Sliced fresh white mushrooms	1 cup	250 mL
Chopped green onion	3 tbsp.	50 mL
Chopped tomato	1 cup	250 mL
Chili paste (sambal oelek)	1 tsp.	5 mL
Fresh spinach leaves, lightly packed	1 cup	250 mL
Chopped fresh parsley (or 2 1/4 tsp., 11 mL, flakes)	3 tbsp.	50 mL
Balsamic vinegar	1 tsp.	5 mL
Pepper, sprinkle		
Large eggs	4	4
Milk	2 tbsp.	30 mL
Grated Parmesan cheese	2 tbsp.	30 mL

Heat cooking oil in medium frying pan on medium. Add mushrooms and green onion. Cook for 5 to 10 minutes, stirring occasionally, until mushrooms are softened.

Add tomato and chili paste. Heat and stir for about 2 minutes until tomato is heated through.

Add next 4 ingredients. Heat and stir for about 1 minute until spinach is just wilted. Remove from heat. Cover to keep warm.

Beat 2 eggs and 1 tbsp. (15 mL) milk in small bowl. Spray small (8 inch, 20 cm) non-stick frying pan with cooking spray. Heat on medium until hot. Pour egg mixture into pan. Reduce heat to medium-low. When starting to set at outside edge, tilt pan and gently lift cooked egg mixture with spatula, easing around pan from outside edge in. Allow uncooked egg mixture to flow onto bottom of pan until egg is softly set. Slide onto large serving plate.

Drain spinach mixture. Spread half of spinach mixture on half of omelette. Sprinkle with 1 tbsp. (15 mL) cheese. Fold omelette in half over filling. Cover to keep warm. Repeat with remaining ingredients. Serves 2.

1 serving: 238 Calories; 14.7 g Total Fat (6.3 g Mono, 2.4 g Poly, 4.6 g Sat); 378 mg Cholesterol; 9 g Carbohydrate; 3 g Fibre; 18 g Protein; 282 mg Sodium

Entrees – Meatless

Mushroom Pasta Wedges

This angel hair pasta pizza is a decidedly different
dinner delight. Serve with Sweet Sugar Peas, page 62.

Angel hair pasta	8 oz.	225 g
Large eggs	4	4
2% cottage cheese	1/2 cup	125 mL
Grated Parmesan cheese	1/4 cup	60 mL
Basil pesto	1/4 cup	60 mL
Pepper	1/2 tsp.	2 mL
Olive (or cooking) oil	2 tsp.	10 mL
Sliced fresh white mushrooms	3 cups	750 mL
Green onions, sliced	2	2
Grated Parmesan cheese	1/4 cup	60 mL

Cook pasta in boiling salted water in large uncovered saucepan or Dutch oven for 6 to 8 minutes, stirring occasionally, until tender but firm. Drain. Return to same saucepan.

Process next 5 ingredients in blender or food processor until smooth. Add to pasta. Toss.

Heat olive oil in medium frying pan on medium-high. Add mushrooms. Cook for about 10 minutes, stirring occasionally, until softened and liquid is evaporated. Add to pasta mixture.

Add green onion. Toss. Spread pasta mixture in greased foil-lined 12 inch (30 cm) pizza pan. Press pasta mixture firmly with back of spoon.

Sprinkle with second amount of Parmesan cheese. Bake in 375°F (190°C) oven for 35 to 40 minutes until edge is golden. Let stand for 10 minutes. Serves 6.

1 serving: 319 Calories; 13.6 g Total Fat (3.4 g Mono, 0.8 g Poly, 3.9 g Sat); 135 mg Cholesterol; 30 g Carbohydrate; 1 g Fibre; 17 g Protein; 363 mg Sodium

Barley-Stuffed Peppers

Your vegetarian friends will weep for joy when they see these
wholesome stuffed peppers filled with barley, mushrooms and
havarti cheese. This is how you do vegetarian right!

Cooking (or olive) oil	1 tbsp.	15 mL
Chopped fresh white mushrooms	2 cups	500 mL
Pearl barley	1 cup	250 mL
Garlic cloves, minced (or 1/2 tsp., 2 mL, powder)	2	2
Prepared vegetable (or chicken) broth	2 1/2 cups	625 mL
Package of veggie ground round (see Note)	12 oz.	340 g
Vegetable cocktail juice	1 cup	250 mL
Italian seasoning	1 tsp.	5 mL
Sliced green onion	1/4 cup	60 mL
Large red peppers, halved lengthwise	4	4
Grated havarti cheese	1 1/2 cups	375 mL

Heat cooking oil in large frying pan on medium-high. Add next 3 ingredients. Cook for about 5 minutes, stirring occasionally, until barley is toasted and mushrooms are softened.

Add next 4 ingredients. Stir. Bring to a boil. Reduce heat to medium. Boil gently, uncovered, for about 30 minutes, stirring occasionally, until barley is almost tender. Remove from heat.

Add green onion. Stir.

Arrange red pepper halves in greased 9 x 13 inch (22 x 33 cm) baking dish. Fill with barley mixture.

Sprinkle with cheese. Bake in 400°F (205°C) oven for 15 to 20 minutes until red pepper is tender-crisp and cheese is melted. Serves 4.

1 serving: 573 Calories; 20.8 g Total Fat (2.5 g Mono, 1.8 g Poly, 11.3 g Sat); 38 mg Cholesterol; 61 g Carbohydrate; 17 g Fibre; 34 g Protein; 1319 mg Sodium

Note: Veggie ground round is available in the produce section of your grocery store.

Potato Egg Muffins

A muffin for a dinner entree? You bet! Full of potatoes and cheese, this savoury delight is made to please. Outstanding with a green salad for a nice, light meal.

Chive and onion cream cheese	3 tbsp.	50 mL
Milk	3 tbsp.	50 mL
Large eggs	4	4
Frozen shredded hash brown potatoes	4 cups	1 L
Grated mozzarella cheese	3/4 cup	175 mL
Sliced green onion	1/4 cup	60 mL
Salt	1/2 tsp.	2 mL
Pepper	1/4 tsp.	1 mL

Mash cream cheese and milk with fork in small bowl.

Beat eggs in medium bowl until frothy. Add cream cheese mixture. Stir.

Add remaining 5 ingredients. Stir. Spoon into 8 greased muffin cups. Bake in 350°F (175°C) oven for 30 to 35 minutes until golden and set. Let stand in pan on wire rack for 5 minutes. Run knife around edges of muffin cups to loosen. Serves 4.

1 serving: 356 Calories; 14.9 g Total Fat (3.7 g Mono, 1.5 g Poly, 7.5 g Sat); 215 mg Cholesterol; 40 g Carbohydrate; 4 g Fibre; 16 g Protein; 541 mg Sodium

SMOKED SALMON EGG MUFFINS: Use smoked salmon cream cheese instead of chive and onion.

VEGETABLE ASIAGO EGG MUFFINS: Use vegetable cream cheese instead of chive and onion, and grated Asiago cheese instead of mozzarella.

ROASTED PEPPER EGG MUFFINS: Use roasted red pepper cream cheese instead of chive and onion, and grated Swiss cheese instead of mozzarella.

Greek Couscous Pizza

The toppings are all Greek to us, but the crust is a crunchy combination of walnuts and couscous—you may never go back to plain old pizza dough again.

CRUST		
Prepared vegetable broth	3/4 cup	175 mL
Plain couscous	3/4 cup	175 mL
Finely chopped walnuts	1 cup	250 mL
Grated mozzarella cheese	1/2 cup	125 mL
Large egg, fork-beaten	1	1
TOPPING		
Cooking oil	1 tsp.	5 mL
Sliced fresh white mushrooms	1 1/2 cups	375 mL
Can of diced tomatoes, drained	14 oz.	398 mL
Thinly sliced zucchini (with peel)	1 1/2 cups	375 mL
Italian seasoning	1/2 tsp.	2 mL
Grated mozzarella cheese	1 cup	250 mL
Crumbled feta cheese	1/2 cup	125 mL

Crust: Measure broth into small saucepan. Bring to a boil. Add couscous. Stir. Remove from heat. Let stand, covered, for about 5 minutes until couscous is tender and broth is absorbed. Fluff with a fork.

Add next 3 ingredients. Stir. Press into bottom and up side of greased 12 inch (30 cm) pizza pan. Bake in 400°F (205°C) oven for about 10 minutes until set and golden.

Topping: Heat cooking oil in large frying pan on medium-high. Add mushrooms. Cook for about 5 minutes, stirring occasionally, until softened and liquid is evaporated. Reduce heat to medium.

Add next 3 ingredients. Cook for about 5 minutes, stirring occasionally, until zucchini is tender. Spread on couscous crust.

Sprinkle with mozzarella and feta cheese. Bake in 400°F (205°C) oven for about 15 minutes until cheese is melted and golden. Serves 6.

1 serving: 377 Calories; 24.1 g Total Fat (5.1 g Mono, 10.2 g Poly, 7.4 g Sat); 66 mg Cholesterol; 27 g Carbohydrate; 3 g Fibre; 16 g Protein; 513 mg Sodium

Potato Tofu Frittata

Whether it's brunch, lunch or dinner, a frittata fits the bill.
Flavoured with basil, tomato and leek, this meatless dish doesn't
skimp on taste. Serve with the green salad of your choice.

Red baby potatoes, quartered	6 oz.	170 g
Cooking oil	1 tbsp.	15 mL
Sliced leek (white part only)	1 1/2 cups	375 mL
Coarsely grated firm tofu	1 1/3 cups	325 mL
Green onions, sliced	2	2
Large eggs	6	6
Chopped fresh basil	1/4 cup	60 mL
Salt, sprinkle		
Pepper, sprinkle		
Roma (plum) tomatoes, sliced	2	2
Chopped fresh basil, for garnish		

Cook potato in boiling salted water in small saucepan until tender. Drain.

Heat cooking oil in large frying pan on medium. Add leek. Cook for about 5 minutes, stirring often, until tender.

Add potato, tofu and onion. Cook for about 3 minutes, stirring occasionally, until onion is softened.

Beat eggs in medium bowl until frothy. Add next 3 ingredients. Stir. Pour over potato mixture. Do not stir. Reduce heat to medium-low. Cook, covered, for about 5 minutes until bottom is golden and top is almost set. Remove from heat.

Arrange tomato on top. Broil on centre rack in oven for 3 to 4 minutes until frittata is set (see Tip, page 115).

Garnish with basil. Serves 4.

1 serving: 229 Calories; 12.3 g Total Fat (5.5 g Mono, 2.9 g Poly, 2.8 g Sat); 279 mg Cholesterol; 16 g Carbohydrate; 2 g Fibre; 14 g Protein; 120 mg Sodium

Pork Marsala ·

An elegant wine-simmered dish that's remarkably easy to prepare.
Serve over buttered egg noodles or creamy mashed potatoes
with Walnut Green Salad, page 12, on the side.

All-purpose flour	1/4 cup	60 mL
Salt	1/4 tsp.	1 mL
Pepper	1/8 tsp.	0.5 mL
Pork tenderloin, trimmed of fat and cut diagonally into 1/4 inch (6 mm) slices	1 lb.	454 g
Olive (or cooking) oil	1 tbsp.	15 mL
Butter (or hard margarine)	1 tbsp.	15 mL
Sliced fresh white mushrooms	2 cups	500 mL
Prepared chicken broth	1 cup	250 mL
Marsala wine	1/4 cup	60 mL
Chopped fresh parsley, for garnish		

Combine first 3 ingredients in small shallow dish.

Press both sides of pork in flour mixture. Transfer pork to large plate. Set remaining flour mixture aside.

Heat olive oil and butter in large frying pan on medium-high. Add pork. Cook for about 1 minute per side until browned. Transfer to separate large plate. Reduce heat to medium.

Cook mushrooms in same frying pan for about 5 minutes, stirring occasionally, until softened and liquid is evaporated. Sprinkle with remaining flour mixture. Heat and stir for 1 minute.

Slowly add broth and wine, stirring constantly and scraping any brown bits from bottom of pan. Heat and stir for about 5 minutes until boiling and thickened. Add pork. Reduce heat to medium-low. Simmer, covered, for about 10 minutes, stirring occasionally, until desired doneness. Remove to large serving bowl.

Garnish with parsley. Makes about 6 cups (1.5 L). Serves 4.

1 serving: 266 Calories; 9.6 g Total Fat (4.7 g Mono, 0.9 g Poly, 3.4 g Sat); 74 mg Cholesterol; 9 g Carbohydrate; 1 g Fibre; 30 g Protein; 420 mg Sodium

Pictured on front cover.

Pineapple Pork Kabobs

The islands await. Coconut, pineapple and pork—sounds like a luau to us! Serve with Sweet Potato Salad, page 11.

Can of coconut milk	14 oz.	398 mL
Sweet chili sauce	2 tbsp.	30 mL
Brown sugar, packed	1 tbsp.	15 mL
Grated lime zest	1 tsp.	5 mL
Fish (or soy) sauce	1 tsp.	5 mL
Finely grated gingerroot (or 1/4 tsp., 1 mL, ground ginger)	1 tsp.	5 mL
Pork tenderloin, trimmed of fat and cubed	1 lb.	454 g
Cubed fresh pineapple (or 14 oz., 398 mL, can of pineapple chunks, drained)	3 cups	750 mL
Bamboo skewers (8 inches, 20 cm, each), soaked in water for 10 minutes	8	8

Combine first 6 ingredients in large bowl.

Add pork. Stir. Let stand, covered, in refrigerator for 3 to 5 hours. Drain coconut milk mixture into small saucepan. Bring to a boil on medium. Boil gently, uncovered, for at least 5 minutes, stirring occasionally, until slightly thickened.

Thread pork and pineapple alternately onto skewers. Place on greased broiler pan. Broil on centre rack in oven for 20 to 25 minutes, turning occasionally and brushing with coconut milk mixture, until desired doneness. Serves 4.

1 serving: 409 Calories; 24.2 g Total Fat (2.2 g Mono, 0.6 g Poly, 19.8 g Sat); 67 mg Cholesterol; 21 g Carbohydrate; 2 g Fibre; 30 g Protein; 188 mg Sodium

GRILLED PINEAPPLE PORK KABOBS: Preheat gas barbecue to medium. Cook kabobs on greased grill for about 15 minutes, turning occasionally and brushing with coconut milk mixture, until desired doneness.

Island Pork Fajitas

Mango, lime and jalapeño pepper give these fajitas
a tasty Caribbean flair, while jicama adds a great crunchy texture.
The pork may be marinated overnight in the refrigerator.

Diced red onion	1/2 cup	125 mL
Fresh jalapeño peppers, finely diced (see Tip, page 46)	2	2
Garlic cloves, minced (or 3/4 tsp., 4 mL, powder)	3	3
Chili powder	2 tsp.	10 mL
Chopped fresh (or frozen) mango	1 1/4 cups	300 mL
Diced peeled jicama	1 cup	250 mL
Chopped fresh cilantro or parsley	2 tbsp.	30 mL
Lime juice	2 tbsp.	30 mL
Lime juice	3 tbsp.	50 mL
Boneless centre-cut pork chops	1 lb.	454 g
Flour tortillas (9 inch, 22 cm, diameter), see Note	8	8
Fresh spinach leaves, lightly packed	2 cups	500 mL

Combine first 4 ingredients in medium bowl. Transfer half of onion mixture to large resealable freezer bag.

Add next 4 ingredients to remaining onion mixture in bowl. Stir. Chill.

Add second amount of lime juice to onion mixture in freezer bag. Shake gently until combined.

Add pork. Seal bag. Turn until coated. Let stand in refrigerator for at least 2 hours. Arrange pork on greased broiler pan. Broil on top rack in oven for about 5 minutes per side until desired doneness. Remove to cutting board. Let stand for 5 minutes. Cut into thin slices.

Arrange pork down centre of tortillas.

Top with mango mixture and spinach. Fold bottom ends of tortillas over filling. Fold in sides, slightly overlapping, leaving top ends open. Serves 4.

1 serving: 680 Calories; 24.4 g Total Fat (11.2 g Mono, 3.7 g Poly, 7.4 g Sat); 76 mg Cholesterol; 80 g Carbohydrate; 8 g Fibre; 35 g Protein; 878 mg Sodium

(continued on next page)

Note: Tortillas may be wrapped in foil and heated in the oven if desired.

GRILLED PORK FAJITAS: Preheat gas barbecue to medium. Cook pork on greased grill for 3 to 5 minutes per side until desired doneness. Remove to cutting board. Let stand for 5 minutes. Cut into thin slices.

Pork In Plum Sauce

Plum delicious! This easy-to-make dish is
delectable with Baked Fragrant Rice, page 61.

Water	1/3 cup	75 mL
Soy sauce	2 tbsp.	30 mL
Hoisin sauce	2 tbsp.	30 mL
Cornstarch	1 tbsp.	15 mL
Dry sherry	1 tbsp.	15 mL
Sesame oil	2 tsp.	10 mL
Pork tenderloin, trimmed of fat, halved, lengthwise, cut into 1/4 inch (6 mm) slices	1 1/2 lbs.	680 g
Plum sauce	1 cup	250 mL
Chili paste (sambal oelek)	1 tsp.	5 mL
Pepper	1/4 tsp.	1 mL
Cooking oil	1 tbsp.	15 mL
Green onion, thinly sliced	1	1

Combine first 6 ingredients in large bowl.

Add pork. Stir until coated. Let stand, covered, in refrigerator for 1 hour. Drain, reserving soy sauce mixture in medium saucepan.

Add next 3 ingredients to soy sauce mixture. Stir. Bring to a boil. Reduce heat to medium. Boil gently for at least 5 minutes until slightly thickened.

Heat wok or large frying pan on medium-high until very hot. Add cooking oil. Add pork. Stir-fry for 3 minutes. Add plum sauce mixture. Cook for 1 to 2 minutes until desired doneness. Remove to large serving bowl.

Sprinkle with green onion. Makes about 4 cups (1 L). Serves 6.

1 serving: 290 Calories; 7.3 g Total Fat (3.4 g Mono, 2.0 g Poly, 1.5 g Sat); 67 mg Cholesterol; 26 g Carbohydrate; 1 g Fibre; 28 g Protein; 850 mg Sodium

Pork Pot Roast

*Call it the roast with the most. The flavours of Dijon and pickling spice add
a tangy twist to the traditional pot roast. Serve with pickled beets on the side.*

Cooking oil	1 tsp.	5 mL
Boneless pork shoulder butt roast	3 lbs.	1.4 kg
Medium onions, quartered	3	3
Apple juice	1 cup	250 mL
Dijon mustard	1 tbsp.	15 mL
Mixed pickling spice	1 tbsp.	15 mL
Cubed yellow turnip	3 cups	750 mL
Salt	1/2 tsp.	2 mL
Frozen Brussels sprouts, thawed	3 cups	750 mL
Large peeled yams (or sweet potatoes), quartered lengthwise and cut into 2 inch (5 cm) pieces	3	3
Water	1/4 cup	60 mL
All-purpose flour	1 1/2 tbsp.	25 mL

Heat cooking oil in large frying pan on medium-high. Add roast. Cook for
about 5 minutes, turning occasionally, until browned on all sides. Transfer
to large roasting pan. Set aside. Reduce heat to medium.

Cook onion in same frying pan for about 5 minutes, stirring often,
until browned.

Add next 3 ingredients. Heat and stir for 1 minute, scraping any brown bits
from bottom of pan. Poke holes in roast with a meat fork. Pour apple juice
mixture over top.

Arrange turnip around roast in pan. Sprinkle with salt. Cook, covered, in
350°F (175°C) oven for 1 hour.

Add Brussels sprouts and yam. Cook, covered, for another 40 to 50 minutes
until vegetables are tender and meat thermometer inserted into thickest
part of roast reads at least 155°F (68°C) or desired doneness. Remove roast
to cutting board. Cover with foil. Let stand for 10 minutes. Remove
vegetables to large serving bowl. Cover to keep warm. Strain drippings
through sieve into small saucepan. Skim any fat from surface. Bring to
a boil on medium.

(continued on next page)

Entrees – Pork

Stir water into flour in small cup until smooth. Slowly add to drippings, stirring constantly until boiling and thickened. Slice roast. Makes 12 servings (2 to 3 oz., 57 to 85 g each, cooked weight). Serve with vegetables and gravy. Serves 12.

1 serving: 305 Calories; 15.1 g Total Fat (6.5 g Mono, 1.6 g Poly, 5.4 g Sat); 51 mg Cholesterol; 24 g Carbohydrate; 3 g Fibre; 19 g Protein; 200 mg Sodium

Pictured on page 71.

Cajun Cutlets

The kindest cut(let) of all! Top with a squeeze of lemon and serve with Potato And Green Bean Salad, page 21. Or sandwich in ciabatta buns, top with your favourite condiments and serve coleslaw on the side.

All-purpose flour	1/3 cup	75 mL
Cajun seasoning	1 tsp.	5 mL
Salt	1/2 tsp.	2 mL
Pepper	1/4 tsp.	1 mL
Large egg	1	1
Milk	3 tbsp.	50 mL
Fine dry bread crumbs	3/4 cup	175 mL
Grated Parmesan cheese	2 tbsp.	30 mL
Pork cutlets (about 4 oz., 113 g, each)	4	4
Cooking oil	2 tbsp.	30 mL
Lemon wedges, for garnish		

Combine first 4 ingredients in small shallow dish.

Beat egg and milk in small bowl.

Stir bread crumbs and cheese in separate small shallow dish.

Press both sides of pork in flour mixture. Dip into egg mixture. Press in crumb mixture until coated. Heat cooking oil in large frying pan on medium. Add pork. Cook for about 3 minutes per side until desired doneness and crumb coating is golden. Remove to large serving plate.

Garnish with lemon wedges. Serves 4.

1 serving: 488 Calories; 31.0 g Total Fat (14.6 g Mono, 4.7 g Poly, 9.0 g Sat); 117 mg Cholesterol; 23 g Carbohydrate; 1 g Fibre; 27 g Protein; 750 mg Sodium

Pictured on page 143.

Ribbon Zucchini Frittata

A smoky ham and cheese frittata that's all dressed up in ribbons
of green. Superbly satisfying with Spiced Yam Hash, page 55.

Olive (or cooking) oil	1 1/2 tbsp.	25 mL
Large zucchini (with peel), cut lengthwise into 1/4 inch (6 mm) slices	1	1
Large eggs	8	8
Julienned deli ham (see Tip, below)	1 cup	250 mL
Grated sharp Cheddar cheese	1/2 cup	125 mL
Chopped fresh parsley	3 tbsp.	50 mL
Milk	1 tbsp.	15 mL
Salt	1/8 tsp.	0.5 mL
Pepper	1/4 tsp.	1 mL
Olive (or cooking) oil	1 1/2 tsp.	7 mL
Grated sharp Cheddar cheese	1/2 cup	125 mL
Ground nutmeg	1/4 tsp.	1 mL

Heat first amount of olive oil in large frying pan on medium-high. Add and cook zucchini in several batches for 2 to 3 minutes per side until browned. Transfer to large plate. Set aside.

Beat eggs in large bowl until frothy.

Add next 6 ingredients. Stir.

Heat second amount of olive oil in same frying pan on medium. Add egg mixture. Reduce heat to medium-low. Cook, covered, for about 10 minutes until bottom is golden and top is almost set. Remove from heat.

Arrange zucchini on top. Sprinkle with second amount of cheese and nutmeg. Broil on centre rack in oven for 2 to 3 minutes until cheese is melted and golden (see Tip, page 115). Serves 4.

1 serving: 363 Calories; 26.3 g Total Fat (9.3 g Mono, 2.1 g Poly, 10.1 g Sat); 413 mg Cholesterol; 6 g Carbohydrate; 1 g Fibre; 26 g Protein; 853 mg Sodium

Pictured on page 54.

 tip   To julienne, cut into very thin strips that resemble matchsticks.

Satay Pork Skewers

Serve these coconut, lime and chili-marinated skewers to your dinner guests and they just might satay all night! A veritable feast with Lemon-Kissed Couscous, page 60.

Prepared chicken broth	1/2 cup	125 mL
Smooth peanut butter	1/4 cup	60 mL
Sweet chili sauce	2 tbsp.	30 mL
Coconut milk powder	2 tbsp.	30 mL
Lime juice	4 tsp.	20 mL
Mirin (see Note), or rice vinegar	1 tbsp.	15 mL
Hoisin sauce	1 tbsp.	15 mL
Finely grated gingerroot (or 1/4 tsp., 1 mL, ground ginger)	1 1/2 tsp.	7 mL
Pepper	1/4 tsp.	1 mL
Pork tenderloin, trimmed of fat, halved lengthwise, cut diagonally into 1/4 inch (6 mm) slices	1 lb.	454 g
Bamboo skewers (8 inches, 20 cm, each), soaked in water for 10 minutes	16	16

Process first 9 ingredients in blender or food processor until smooth. Reserve half of broth mixture in small bowl for dipping sauce. Chill.

Put pork into large resealable freezer bag. Add remaining broth mixture. Seal bag. Turn until coated. Let stand in refrigerator for at least 3 hours, turning occasionally. Drain.

Thread pork, accordion-style, onto skewers. Place skewers on greased broiler pan. Broil on top rack in oven for about 2 minutes per side until desired doneness. Serve with warmed dipping sauce. Serves 4.

1 serving: 252 Calories; 10.8 g Total Fat (4.3 g Mono, 2.1 g Poly, 3.8 g Sat); 67 mg Cholesterol; 6 g Carbohydrate; 1 g Fibre; 31 g Protein; 186 mg Sodium

Note: Mirin is a Japanese sweet cooking rice wine. It is available in specialty Asian grocery stores.

GRILLED PORK SKEWERS: Preheat gas barbecue to medium-high. Cook skewers on greased grill for about 2 minutes per side until desired doneness and grill marks appear. Serve with warmed dipping sauce.

Sausage Pepper Skillet

Peppers abound in this colourful skillet. First-rate with Asiago Polenta, page 40.

Olive (or cooking) oil	2 tsp.	10 mL
Hot Italian sausages, cut into 1 inch (2.5 cm) pieces	1 lb.	454 g
Sliced green pepper	1 1/2 cups	375 mL
Sliced red pepper	1 1/2 cups	375 mL
Sliced orange pepper	1 1/2 cups	375 mL
Sliced red onion	3/4 cup	175 mL
Prepared chicken broth	1/2 cup	125 mL
Balsamic vinegar	3 tbsp.	50 mL
Sun-dried tomatoes, softened in boiling water for 10 minutes before chopping	2 tbsp.	30 mL

Heat olive oil in large frying pan on medium. Add sausage. Cook for 6 to 8 minutes, stirring often, until browned. Transfer with slotted spoon to paper towels to drain.

Heat 2 tsp. (10 mL) drippings in same frying pan. Add next 4 ingredients. Stir. Cook, covered, for 5 to 10 minutes, stirring occasionally, until onion is softened and peppers are tender-crisp.

Add sausage and remaining 3 ingredients. Heat and stir for about 5 minutes, scraping any brown bits from bottom of pan, until heated through. Makes about 6 cups (1.5 L). Serves 4.

1 serving: 460 Calories; 32.7 g Total Fat (15.6 g Mono, 4.3 g Poly, 11.0 g Sat); 90 mg Cholesterol; 16 g Carbohydrate; 3 g Fibre; 26 g Protein; 1190 mg Sodium

Pictured at right.

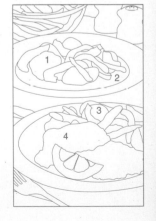

1. Sausage Pepper Skillet, above
2. Asiago Polenta, page 40
3. Potato And Green Bean Salad, page 21
4. Cajun Cutlets, page 139

Ground Pork Patties

*Delicious, thick, juicy patties with a boisterous barbecue flavour—
the secret's in the oyster sauce. Grated Carrot Salad, page 10, and
French fries or mashed potatoes will make dinner complete.*

Large egg, fork-beaten	1	1
Fine dry bread crumbs	1/3 cup	75 mL
Finely chopped onion	1/4 cup	60 mL
Barbecue sauce	3 tbsp.	50 mL
Ketchup	3 tbsp.	50 mL
Oyster sauce	1 tbsp.	15 mL
Garlic cloves, minced (or 1/2 tsp., 2 mL, powder)	2	2
Salt	1/2 tsp.	2 mL
Pepper	1/4 tsp.	1 mL
Lean ground pork	1 lb.	454 g

Combine first 9 ingredients in large bowl.

Add pork. Mix well. Divide into 12 equal portions. Shape into 3 inch (7.5 cm)
diameter patties. Arrange on greased broiler pan. Broil on centre rack in
oven for 6 to 8 minutes per side until no longer pink inside. Serves 4.

*1 serving: 220 Calories; 8.0 g Total Fat (0.8 g Mono, 0.4 g Poly, 3.0 g Sat); 112 mg Cholesterol;
13 g Carbohydrate; 1 g Fibre; 25 g Protein; 733 mg Sodium*

1. Saucepan Lamb Stew, page 116
2. Roasted Garlic Pesto Muffins, page 38
3. Chorizo Sausage Gnocchi, page 146

Props courtesy of: Danesco Inc.
Out of the Fire Studio

Chorizo Sausage Gnocchi

Gnocchi, gnocchi. Who's there? Company called—and now that they're here—
with this hearty pasta dish on the table, there'll be lots of good cheer!

Cooking oil	1/2 tsp.	2 mL
Chorizo sausages, cut into 1/4 inch (6 mm) slices	2	2
Cooking oil	1 tbsp.	15 mL
Chopped eggplant (with peel)	2 cups	500 mL
Sliced fresh white mushrooms	1 cup	250 mL
Chopped onion	1 cup	250 mL
Garlic cloves, minced (or 1/2 tsp., 2 mL, powder)	2	2
Tomato pasta sauce	2 cups	500 mL
Chopped fresh parsley (or 1 tbsp., 15 mL, flakes)	1/4 cup	60 mL
Salt	1/4 tsp.	1 mL
Pepper	1/4 tsp.	1 mL
Package of fresh gnocchi	16 1/2 oz.	500 g

Grated Cheddar cheese, for garnish

Heat first amount of cooking oil in large frying pan on medium-high. Add sausage. Cook for about 5 minutes, stirring occasionally, until browned. Transfer with slotted spoon to paper towels to drain. Discard drippings.

Heat second amount of cooking oil in same pan on medium. Add next 4 ingredients. Cook for 5 to 10 minutes, stirring often, until onion is softened.

Add sausage and next 4 ingredients. Heat and stir for about 2 minutes until heated through.

Cook gnocchi in boiling salted water in large uncovered saucepan for about 1 minute until just tender. Transfer with slotted spoon to sausage mixture. Stir gently.

Garnish individual servings with cheese. Makes about 6 1/2 cups (1.6 L). Serves 4.

1 serving: 405 Calories; 23.7 g Total Fat (7.6 g Mono, 1.9 g Poly, 9.6 g Sat); 38 mg Cholesterol; 40 g Carbohydrate; 6 g Fibre; 10 g Protein; 1038 mg Sodium

Pictured on page 144.

Pork Noodle Stir-Fry

Use your noodles and spend as little time making dinner as possible! Try it with your favourite vegetables or save time with a precut veggie blend from your grocery store.

Fresh, thin Chinese-style egg noodles, cut in half	8 oz.	225 g
Sesame (or cooking) oil	1 tbsp.	15 mL
Boneless pork loin chops, trimmed of fat and cut crosswise into thin strips	1 lb.	454 g
Sesame (or cooking) oil	2 tsp.	10 mL
Fresh mixed stir-fry vegetables	5 cups	1.25 L
Prepared chicken broth	1/2 cup	125 mL
Garlic cloves, minced (or 1/2 tsp., 2 mL, powder)	2	2
Finely grated gingerroot (or 1/2 tsp., 2 mL, ground ginger)	2 tsp.	10 mL
Sweet chili sauce	1/4 cup	60 mL
Hoisin sauce	1/4 cup	60 mL

Cook noodles in boiling salted water in large uncovered saucepan or Dutch oven for about 3 minutes, stirring occasionally, until tender but firm. Drain, reserving 1 cup (250 mL) cooking water.

Heat wok or large frying pan on medium-high until very hot. Add first amount of sesame oil. Add pork. Stir-fry for about 5 minutes until browned. Transfer to large plate. Set aside.

Add second amount of sesame oil to hot wok. Add next 4 ingredients. Stir-fry for about 3 minutes until vegetables start to soften.

Add reserved cooking water, chili sauce and hoisin sauce. Stir. Add noodles and pork. Toss. Cook, covered, for about 2 minutes until vegetables are tender-crisp and noodles are heated through. Makes about 8 cups (2 L). Serves 4.

1 serving: 416 Calories; 11.9 g Total Fat (4.5 g Mono, 3.1 g Poly, 2.7 g Sat); 81 mg Cholesterol; 43 g Carbohydrate; 3 g Fibre; 33 g Protein; 564 mg Sodium

Pictured on page 125.

Ginger Maple Pork

Pork tenderloin is paired with a packet of flavourful rice. Garnish the
rice with sliced green onion, and complete with a salad on the side.

Maple (or maple-flavoured) syrup	1/3 cup	75 mL
Finely grated gingerroot (or 3/4 tsp., 4 mL, ground ginger)	1 tbsp.	15 mL
Garlic clove, minced (or 1/4 tsp., 1 mL, powder)	1	1
Pork tenderloin, trimmed of fat	1 lb.	454 g
Salt	1/4 tsp.	1 mL
Pepper	1/8 tsp.	0.5 mL
Cooked long grain white rice (about 2/3 cup, 150 mL, uncooked)	2 cups	500 mL
Chopped fresh spinach, lightly packed	1/2 cup	125 mL
Thinly sliced green onion	2 tbsp.	30 mL
Sliced natural almonds, toasted (see Tip, page 20)	2 tbsp.	30 mL
Rice vinegar	2 tsp.	10 mL
Finely grated gingerroot (or 1/8 tsp., 0.5 mL, ground ginger)	1/2 tsp.	2 mL
Salt	1/4 tsp.	1 mL
Sesame oil (optional)	1/2 tsp.	2 mL

Combine first 3 ingredients in small bowl. Set aside.

Sprinkle tenderloin with first amount of salt and pepper. Preheat gas
barbecue to medium. Cook tenderloin on greased grill for 15 minutes,
turning occasionally. Brush with syrup mixture. Cook for another 15 to
20 minutes until meat thermometer inserted into thickest part of tenderloin
reads at least 155°F (68°C) or desired doneness. Remove to cutting board.
Cover with foil. Let stand for 10 minutes.

Combine remaining 8 ingredients in medium bowl. Transfer to greased
sheet of heavy-duty (or double layer of regular) foil. Fold edges of foil
together over rice mixture to enclose. Fold ends to seal completely. Place
packet, seam-side up, on ungreased grill. Cook for about 15 minutes until
heated through. Cut tenderloin into 12 slices. Serve with rice. Serves 4.

1 serving: 337 Calories; 5.2 g Total Fat (2.5 g Mono, 1.0 g Poly, 1.3 g Sat); 67 mg Cholesterol;
41 g Carbohydrate; 1 g Fibre; 30 g Protein; 356 mg Sodium

Pictured on page 126.

Measurement Tables

Throughout this book measurements are given in Conventional and Metric measure. To compensate for differences between the two measurements due to rounding, a full metric measure is not always used. The cup used is the standard 8 fluid ounce. Temperature is given in degrees Fahrenheit and Celsius. Baking pan measurements are in inches and centimetres as well as quarts and litres. An exact metric conversion is given below as well as the working equivalent (Metric Standard Measure).

Spoons

Conventional Measure	Metric Exact Conversion Millilitre (mL)	Metric Standard Measure Millilitre (mL)
1/8 teaspoon (tsp.)	0.6 mL	0.5 mL
1/4 teaspoon (tsp.)	1.2 mL	1 mL
1/2 teaspoon (tsp.)	2.4 mL	2 mL
1 teaspoon (tsp.)	4.7 mL	5 mL
2 teaspoons (tsp.)	9.4 mL	10 mL
1 tablespoon (tbsp.)	14.2 mL	15 mL

Cups

Conventional Measure	Metric Exact Conversion Millilitre (mL)	Metric Standard Measure Millilitre (mL)
1/4 cup (4 tbsp.)	56.8 mL	60 mL
1/3 cup (5 1/3 tbsp.)	75.6 mL	75 mL
1/2 cup (8 tbsp.)	113.7 mL	125 mL
2/3 cup (10 2/3 tbsp.)	151.2 mL	150 mL
3/4 cup (12 tbsp.)	170.5 mL	175 mL
1 cup (16 tbsp.)	227.3 mL	250 mL
4 1/2 cups	1022.9 mL	1000 mL (1 L)

Oven Temperatures

Fahrenheit (°F)	Celsius (°C)
175°	80°
200°	95°
225°	110°
250°	120°
275°	140°
300°	150°
325°	160°
350°	175°
375°	190°
400°	205°
425°	220°
450°	230°
475°	240°
500°	260°

Dry Measurements

Conventional Measure Ounces (oz.)	Metric Exact Conversion Grams (g)	Metric Standard Measure Grams (g)
1 oz.	28.3 g	28 g
2 oz.	56.7 g	57 g
3 oz.	85.0 g	85 g
4 oz.	113.4 g	125 g
5 oz.	141.7 g	140 g
6 oz.	170.1 g	170 g
7 oz.	198.4 g	200 g
8 oz.	226.8 g	250 g
16 oz.	453.6 g	500 g
32 oz.	907.2 g	1000 g (1 kg)

Pans

Conventional Inches	Metric Centimetres
x8 inch	20x20 cm
x9 inch	22x22 cm
x13 inch	22x33 cm
0x15 inch	25x38 cm
1x17 inch	28x43 cm
x2 inch round	20x5 cm
x2 inch round	22x5 cm
0x4 1/2 inch tube	25x11 cm
x4x3 inch loaf	20x10x7.5 cm
x5x3 inch loaf	22x12.5x7.5 cm

Casseroles

CANADA & BRITAIN		UNITED STATES	
Standard Size Casserole	Exact Metric Measure	Standard Size Casserole	Exact Metric Measure
1 qt. (5 cups)	1.13 L	1 qt. (4 cups)	900 mL
1 1/2 qts. (7 1/2 cups)	1.69 L	1 1/2 qts. (6 cups)	1.35 L
2 qts. (10 cups)	2.25 L	2 qts. (8 cups)	1.8 L
2 1/2 qts. (12 1/2 cups)	2.81 L	2 1/2 qts. (10 cups)	2.25 L
3 qts. (15 cups)	3.38 L	3 qts. (12 cups)	2.7 L
4 qts. (20 cups)	4.5 L	4 qts. (16 cups)	3.6 L
5 qts. (25 cups)	5.63 L	5 qts. (20 cups)	4.5 L

Recipe Index

A

Apple Coleslaw, Dijon 10
Apple Date Salad 20
Artichoke Salmon 111
Arugula, Beef And Mushroom 75
Asiago Egg Muffins, Vegetable 131
Asiago Polenta 40
Asian Salmon Burgers 104
Asian Salsa Salad 31
Asparagus Cucumber Salad 9
Asparagus Salad, Smoky 9
Avocado Salsa, Cucumber 110
Avocado Salsa, Grilled Salmon With 110
Avocado Salsa, Salmon With 110

B

Baked Fragrant Rice 61
Baked Lemon Chicken 93
Balsamic Onions 48
Balsamic Skewers 99
Balsamic Vinaigrette, Citrus 12
Barley-Stuffed Peppers 130
Basil Broccoli, Orange 44
Bean Salad, Pesto 34
Bean Salad, Potato And Green 21
Beans, Couscous And 122
Beef
 Beef And Bowtie Pasta 69
 Beef And Mushroom Arugula 75
 Bruschetta Steak Loaf 67
 Cheese And Pesto Meatloaf 70
 Family Fajitas 65
 Grilled Beef Tomato Salad 24
 Grilled Meatball And Potato Kabobs 79
 Hamburger Pizza 76
 Italian Steak Dinner 77
 Margarita Marinated Steak 74
 Meatball And Potato Kabobs 79
 Meatball Shepherd's Pie 73
 Moroccan Pot Roast 66
 Polenta-Topped Chili 78
 Saucepan Beef Stew 117
 Sweet Curry Sausages 64
 Tortellini Chili Bake 68

Beef And Bowtie Pasta 69
Beef And Mushroom Arugula 75
Blue Cheese Dressing 20
Bowtie Pasta, Beef And 69
Braised Celery 48
Bread, Cajun Cheese 40
Bread, Grilled Cajun Cheese 40
Broccoli Bake, Cottage 123
Broccoli, Orange Basil 44
Bruschetta Steak Loaf 67
Bulgur Vegetables 41
Burgers & Patties
 Asian Salmon Burgers 104
 Dijon Dill Salmon Patties 106
 Grilled Salmon Burgers 104
 Ground Pork Patties 145
 Hawaiian Burgers 81
Buttermilk Dressing 30

C

Cabbage Noodles 62
Cajun Cheese Bread 40
Cajun Cheese Bread, Grilled 40
Cajun Cutlets 139
Carrot Salad, Grated 10
Casserole, Island Chicken 83
Casserole, Okra And Lamb 119
Celery, Braised 48
Celery Spuds, Smashed 57
Cheese And Pesto Meatloaf 70
Cheese Bread, Cajun 40
Cheese Bread, Grilled Cajun 40
Cheese Crostini, Goat 58
Cheese Dressing, Blue 20
Cheese Potatoes, Chipotle 52
Cheese Potatoes, Grilled Chipotle 52
Chicken
 Baked Lemon Chicken 93
 Chicken And Couscous 86
 Chicken Couscous Salad 25
 Chicken Pita Salad 28
 Chicken Tortilla Bake 95
 Confetti Rice And Chicken 94
 Creamy Chicken Shrimp Penne 97
 Crispy Chicken Drumettes 84
 Curry-Spiced Chicken 85
 Grilled Chicken Kabobs 92

Hawaiian Burgers 81
Island Chicken Casserole. 83
Jiffy Jambalaya. 96
Lemon Herb Chicken 88
Olive Chicken Bake. 84
Peanut Chicken Rice Bake 87
Peanut Noodle Salad 29
Satay Chicken Noodles. 80
Sicilian Summer Grill. 82
Spinach Chicken Salad 33
Tangy Chicken Potato Bake 91
Teriyaki Chicken Pizza. 127
Tex-Mex Toss. 28
Zesty Chicken Kabobs. 92
ᴨicken And Couscous 86
ᴨicken Couscous Salad 25
ᴨicken Pita Salad 28
ᴨicken Tortilla Bake 95
ᴨickpeas, Curried Baked 124
ᴨili Bake, Tortellini 68
ᴨili, Polenta-Topped 78
ᴨipotle Cheese Potatoes 52
ᴨipotle Cheese Potatoes, Grilled. 52
ᴨorizo Sausage Gnocchi 146
ᴨrus Balsamic Vinaigrette 12
ᴨleslaw, Dijon Apple 10
ᴨnfetti Rice And Chicken. 94
ᴨrnbread, Sun-Dried Tomato 50
ᴨrn-Stuffed Tomatoes 42
ᴨttage Broccoli Bake 123
ᴨuscous
    Chicken And Couscous. 86
    Chicken Couscous Salad. 25
    Couscous And Beans 122
    Greek Couscous Pizza. 132
    Lemon-Kissed Couscous 60
    Sole Packets. 113
ᴨuscous And Beans 122
ᴨeamed Spinach 63
ᴨeamy Chicken Shrimp Penne 97
ᴨspy Chicken Drumettes. 84
ᴨstini, Goat Cheese 58
ᴨstini, Sun-Dried Tomato. 59
ᴨcumber Avocado Salsa 110
ᴨcumber Salad, Asparagus 9
ᴨrried Baked Chickpeas. 124
ᴨrried Tuna Quiche 98
ᴨrry-Glazed Vegetables 47

Curry Sausages, Sweet. 64
Curry-Spiced Chicken 85
Cutlets, Cajun 139

D

Date Salad, Apple 20
Dijon Apple Coleslaw. 10
Dijon Dill Salmon Patties. 106
Dill Dressing. 37
Dill Pasta Salad. 19
Dill Salmon Patties, Dijon 106
Dressing, see also Vinaigrette
    Blue Cheese. 20
    Buttermilk 30
    Dill. 37
    Fresh Herb Mayonnaise 13
    Mint Mustard 21
    Orange Ginger 25
    Peanut. 15
    Sweet 'N' Spicy. 27
    Tangy Mango 26
    Tomato 23
Drumettes, Crispy Chicken 84

E

Egg Muffins, Potato. 131
Egg Muffins, Roasted Pepper 131
Egg Muffins, Smoked Salmon. 131
Egg Muffins, Vegetable Asiago 131

F

Fajitas
    Family 65
    Grilled Pork 137
    Island Pork. 136
Family Fajitas 65
Feta Shrimp Frittata 100
Fish & Seafood
    Artichoke Salmon 111
    Asian Salmon Burgers. 104
    Balsamic Skewers 99
    Creamy Chicken Shrimp Penne 97
    Curried Tuna Quiche. 98
    Dijon Dill Salmon Patties. 106
    Feta Shrimp Frittata 100
    Grilled Salmon Burgers. 104

151

Grilled Salmon With Avocado Salsa 110
Nacho-Crusted Haddock 109
Orzo Shrimp Packets. 101
Oven Salmon Scallop 114
Salmon French Loaf 100
Salmon Polenta Skewers. 105
Salmon With Avocado Salsa 110
Scallop "Orzotto" 103
Seafood Spinach Salad 37
Shrimp Fried Rice 112
Smoked Salmon Egg Muffins 131
Sole Packets. 113
Sole Skillet. 115
Tarragon Shrimp Linguine 102
Fragrant Rice, Baked 61
French Loaf, Salmon 100
Fresh Herb Mayonnaise. 13
Fresh Herb Rice 43
Fried Rice, Shrimp 112
Frittata
    Feta Shrimp. 100
    Potato Tofu 133
    Ribbon Zucchini 140

G

Garlic Pesto Muffins, Roasted 38
Garlicky Mashed Potatoes 49
Ginger Dressing, Orange. 25
Ginger Maple Pork 148
Gnocchi, Chorizo Sausage. 146
Goat Cheese Crostini. 58
Grated Carrot Salad. 10
Greek Couscous Pizza 132
Green Bean Salad, Potato And 21
Green Salad, Walnut 12
Greens, Lemon Pepper 59
Grill, Sicilian Summer. 82
Grilled Beef Tomato Salad 24
Grilled Cajun Cheese Bread. 40
Grilled Chicken Kabobs 92
Grilled Chipotle Cheese Potatoes 52
Grilled Lamb Kabobs. 121
Grilled Meatball And Potato Kabobs. 79
Grilled Meatball Skewers 118
Grilled Pineapple Pork Kabobs. 135
Grilled Pork And Mango Salad 27
Grilled Pork Fajitas 137
Grilled Pork Skewers 141

Grilled Salmon Burgers 104
Grilled Salmon With Avocado Salsa. 110
Ground Pork Patties. 145

H

Haddock, Nacho-Crusted 109
Hamburger Pizza 76
Hash, Spiced Yam 55
Hawaiian Burgers 81
Herb Chicken, Lemon 88
Herb Mayonnaise, Fresh 13
Herb Rice, Fresh 43
Herb-Scented Lamb Kabobs 121
Herbed Potato Salad 13
Honey-Garlic Glazed Vegetables 47
Honey Mustard Vinaigrette 10

I

Island Chicken Casserole 83
Island Pork Fajitas. 136
Italian Steak Dinner 77

J

Jambalaya, Jiffy. 96
Jicama Salad. 22
Jiffy Jambalaya 96

K

Kabobs & Skewers
    Balsamic Skewers 99
    Grilled Chicken Kabobs. 92
    Grilled Lamb Kabobs 121
    Grilled Meatball And Potato Kabobs 79
    Grilled Meatball Skewers. 118
    Grilled Pineapple Pork Kabobs 135
    Grilled Pork Skewers 141
    Herb-Scented Lamb Kabobs. 121
    Lamb Meatball Skewers 118
    Meatball And Potato Kabobs 79
    Pineapple Pork Kabobs. 135
    Potato Vegetable Kabobs 50
    Salmon Polenta Skewers. 105
    Satay Pork Skewers 14
    Zesty Chicken Kabobs. 91

152

L

mb
Grilled Lamb Kabobs 121
Grilled Meatball Skewers. 118
Herb-Scented Lamb Kabobs 121
Lamb Meatball Skewers 118
Lamb Orzo Stew. 120
Okra And Lamb Casserole 119
Saucepan Lamb Stew. 116
mb Meatball Skewers. 118
mb Orzo Stew 120
mon Chicken, Baked 93
mon Herb Chicken. 88
mon-Kissed Couscous 60
mon Oregano Vinaigrette 33
mon Pepper Greens. 59
ne Vinaigrette, Spicy 22
ne Vinaigrette, Sweet. 16
nguine, Tarragon Shrimp 102
af, Bruschetta Steak 67
af, Salmon French 100

M

ango Dressing, Tangy. 26
ango Salad, Grilled Pork And . . . . : 27
aple-Glazed Vegetables 47
aple Miso Tofu Salad 32
aple Pork, Ginger 148
aple Syrup Vinaigrette 32
argarita Marinated Steak 74
arinated Mushroom Salad 8
arinated Steak, Margarita. 74
arsala, Pork. 134
ashed Potatoes, Garlicky 49
ayonnaise, Fresh Herb 13
eatball And Potato Kabobs. 79
eatball And Potato Kabobs, Grilled 79
eatball Shepherd's Pie 73
eatball Skewers, Grilled 118
eatball Skewers, Lamb 118
eatless Entrees
Asian Salsa Salad. 31
Barley-Stuffed Peppers 130
Cottage Broccoli Bake. 123
Couscous And Beans . . . . : 122
Curried Baked Chickpeas 124
Greek Couscous Pizza. 132
Maple Miso Tofu Salad 32
Mushroom Pasta Wedges. 129
Pesto Bean Salad. 34
Potato Egg Muffins. 131
Potato Tofu Frittata 133
Roasted Pepper Egg Muffins. 131
Spicy Vegetable Omelettes. 128
Teriyaki Tofu Pizza . . . . \ 127
Vegetable Asiago Egg Muffins 131
Meatloaf, Cheese And Pesto 70
Mediterranean Potatoes. 45
Mint Mustard Dressing 21
Minted Pea Salad. 16
Miso Tofu Salad, Maple. 32
Moroccan Pot Roast 66
Muffins
Potato Egg 131
Roasted Garlic Pesto 38
Roasted Pepper Egg 131
Smoked Salmon Egg 131
Vegetable Asiago Egg 131
Mushroom Arugula, Beef And. 75
Mushroom Pasta Wedges 129
Mushroom Salad, Marinated. 8
Mustard Dressing, Mint. 21
Mustard Vinaigrette, Honey. 10

N

Nacho-Crusted Haddock. 109
Noodle Salad, Peanut 29
Noodle Salad, Rice. 15
Noodle Stir-Fry, Pork 147
Noodles, Cabbage. 62
Noodles, Satay Chicken. 80

O

Okra And Lamb Casserole. 119
Olive Chicken Bake 84
Omelettes, Spicy Vegetable. 128
Onions, Balsamic. 48
Onions, Sweet And Spicy. 58
Orange Basil Broccoli. 44
Orange Ginger Dressing 25
Oregano Vinaigrette, Lemon. 33
Orzo Shrimp Packets 101

Orzo Stew, Lamb............................120
"Orzotto," Scallop.........................103
Oven-Roasted Ratatouille....................39
Oven Salmon Scallop 114

P

Packets, Orzo Shrimp 101
Packets, Sole 113
Pasta Salad, Dill 19
Pasta Salad, Pork And 30
Pasta Wedges, Mushroom....................129
Pasta, Beef And Bowtie 69
Patties, see Burgers & Patties
Pea Salad, Minted 16
Peanut Chicken Rice Bake 87
Peanut Dressing............................15
Peanut Noodle Salad.........................29
Pearl Salad, Vegetable 14
Peas, Sweet Sugar 62
Pecan Potato Salad 23
Penne, Creamy Chicken Shrimp................97
Pepper Egg Muffins, Roasted 131
Pepper Greens, Lemon 59
Pepper Skillet, Sausage 142
Peppers, Barley-Stuffed 130
Pesto Bean Salad 34
Pesto Meatloaf, Cheese And 70
Pesto Muffins, Roasted Garlic 38
Pesto Potato Wedges........................44
Pie, Meatball Shepherd's 73
Pineapple Pork Kabobs 135
Pineapple Pork Kabobs, Grilled 135
Pita Salad, Chicken 28
Pizza
    Greek Couscous 132
    Hamburger..............................76
    Teriyaki Chicken 127
    Teriyaki Tofu 127
Plum Sauce, Pork In........................137
Pockets, Roasted Veggie 46
Polenta, Asiago 40
Polenta Skewers, Salmon....................105
Polenta-Topped Chili 78
Pork
    Cajun Cutlets 139
    Chorizo Sausage Gnocchi..................146
    Ginger Maple Pork 148
    Grilled Pineapple Pork Kabobs 135

Grilled Pork And Mango Salad 27
Grilled Pork Fajitas.........................137
Grilled Pork Skewers 141
Ground Pork Patties 145
Hawaiian Burgers 81
Island Pork Fajitas 136
Jiffy Jambalaya.............................96
Pineapple Pork Kabobs 135
Pork And Pasta Salad 30
Pork In Plum Sauce.........................137
Pork Marsala 134
Pork Noodle Stir-Fry 147
Pork Pot Roast.............................138
Ribbon Zucchini Frittata 140
Salmon Polenta Skewers....................105
Satay Pork Skewers.........................141
Sausage Pepper Skillet 142
Sunny Rice Salad...........................26
Pork And Pasta Salad.........................30
Pork In Plum Sauce.........................137
Pork Marsala 134
Pork Noodle Stir-Fry 147
Pork Pot Roast.............................138
Pot Roast, Moroccan 66
Pot Roast, Pork............................138
Potato And Green Bean Salad.................21
Potato Bake, Tangy Chicken 91
Potato Egg Muffins 131
Potato Kabobs, Grilled Meatball And 79
Potato Kabobs, Meatball And 79
Potato Salad, Herbed........................13
Potato Salad, Pecan.........................23
Potato Tofu Frittata 133
Potato Vegetable Kabobs.....................56
Potato Wedges, Pesto 44
Potatoes, Chipotle Cheese....................52
Potatoes, Garlicky Mashed 49
Potatoes, Grilled Chipotle Cheese..............52
Potatoes, Mediterranean 49

Q

Quiche, Curried Tuna 98

R

Ratatouille, Oven-Roasted 39
Ribbon Zucchini Frittata 140
Rice And Chicken, Confetti 94

154

e And Pork, Coconut 149
e Bake, Peanut Chicken....................... 87
e Noodle Salad 15
e Salad, Sunny............................... 26
e, Baked Fragrant 61
e, Fresh Herb................................ 43
e, Shrimp Fried 112
e, Vegetable Spanish......................... 51
ast, Moroccan Pot 66
ast, Pork Pot................................138
asted Garlic Pesto Muffins.................... 38
asted Pepper Egg Muffins 131
asted Veggie Pockets......................... 46

ads (Meal)
Asian Salsa.................................. 31
Chicken Couscous............................ 25
Chicken Pita 28
Grilled Beef Tomato 24
Grilled Pork And Mango...................... 27
Maple Miso Tofu............................ 32
Peanut Noodle 29
Pesto Bean.................................. 34
Pork And Pasta 30
Seafood Spinach............................. 37
Spinach Chicken 33
Sunny Rice.................................. 26
Tex-Mex Toss................................ 28
ads (Side)
Apple Date 20
Asparagus Cucumber 9
Dijon Apple Coleslaw 10
Dill Pasta 19
Grated Carrot 10
Herbed Potato............................... 13
Jicama 22
Marinated Mushroom......................... 8
Minted Pea 16
Pecan Potato................................ 23
Potato And Green Bean 21
Rice Noodle................................. 15
Smoky Asparagus 9
Sweet Potato................................ 11
Vegetable Pearl 14
Walnut Green 12
mon, see Fish & Seafood
mon French Loaf.............................100

Salmon Polenta Skewers 105
Salmon With Avocado Salsa 110
Salsa, Cucumber Avocado.....................110
Salsa, Grilled Salmon With Avocado 110
Salsa Salad, Asian........................... 31
Salsa, Salmon With Avocado..................110
Satay Chicken Noodles 80
Satay Pork Skewers 141
Sauce, Pork In Plum.........................137
Saucepan Beef Stew 117
Saucepan Lamb Stew 116
Sausage Gnocchi, Chorizo....................146
Sausage Pepper Skillet.......................142
Sausages, Sweet Curry....................... 64
Scallop "Orzotto" 103
Scallop, Oven Salmon 114
Seafood Spinach Salad 37
Shepherd's Pie, Meatball 73
Shrimp, see Fish & Seafood
Shrimp Fried Rice...........................112
Sicilian Summer Grill 82
Sides
    Asiago Polenta........................... 40
    Baked Fragrant Rice 61
    Balsamic Onions 48
    Braised Celery 48
    Bulgur Vegetables 41
    Cabbage Noodles 62
    Cajun Cheese Bread 40
    Chipotle Cheese Potatoes................. 52
    Corn-Stuffed Tomatoes.................... 42
    Creamed Spinach 63
    Curry-Glazed Vegetables.................. 47
    Fresh Herb Rice.......................... 43
    Garlicky Mashed Potatoes................. 49
    Goat Cheese Crostini 58
    Grilled Cajun Cheese Bread 40
    Grilled Chipotle Cheese Potatoes.......... 52
    Honey-Garlic Glazed Vegetables........... 47
    Lemon Pepper Greens 59
    Lemon-Kissed Couscous 60
    Maple-Glazed Vegetables 47
    Mediterranean Potatoes 45
    Orange Basil Broccoli 44
    Oven-Roasted Ratatouille 39
    Pesto Potato Wedges 44
    Potato Vegetable Kabobs 56
    Roasted Garlic Pesto Muffins 38

Roasted Veggie Pockets 46
Smashed Celery Spuds 57
Spiced Yam Hash 55
Sun-Dried Tomato Cornbread 50
Sun-Dried Tomato Crostini 59
Sweet And Spicy Onions 58
Sweet Sugar Peas 62
Vegetable Spanish Rice 51
Skewers, see Kabobs & Skewers
Skillet, Sausage Pepper 142
Skillet, Sole 115
Smashed Celery Spuds 57
Smoked Salmon Egg Muffins 131
Smoky Asparagus Salad 9
Sole Packets 113
Sole Skillet 115
Spanish Rice, Vegetable 51
Spiced Yam Hash 55
Spicy Lime Vinaigrette 22
Spicy Onions, Sweet And 58
Spicy Vegetable Omelettes 128
Spinach Chicken Salad 33
Spinach, Creamed 63
Spinach Salad, Seafood 37
Spuds, Smashed Celery 57
Steak Dinner, Italian 77
Steak Loaf, Bruschetta 67
Steak, Margarita Marinated 74
Stew, Lamb Orzo 120
Stew, Saucepan Beef 117
Stew, Saucepan Lamb 116
Stir-Fry, Pork Noodle 147
Sugar Peas, Sweet 62
Sun-Dried Tomato Cornbread 50
Sun-Dried Tomato Crostini 59
Sunny Rice Salad 26
Sweet And Spicy Onions 58
Sweet Curry Sausages 64
Sweet Lime Vinaigrette 16
Sweet 'N' Spicy Dressing 27
Sweet Potato Salad 11
Sweet Sugar Peas 62

T

Tangy Chicken Potato Bake 91
Tangy Mango Dressing 26
Tarragon Shrimp Linguine 102
Teriyaki Chicken Pizza 127

Teriyaki Tofu Pizza 12
Tex-Mex Toss 2
Tofu Frittata, Potato 13
Tofu Pizza, Teriyaki 12
Tofu Salad, Maple Miso 3
Tomato Cornbread, Sun-Dried 5
Tomato Crostini, Sun-Dried 5
Tomato Dressing 2
Tomato Salad, Grilled Beef 2
Tomatoes, Corn-Stuffed 4
Tortellini Chili Bake 6
Tortilla Bake, Chicken 9
Tuna Quiche, Curried 9

V

Vegetable Asiago Egg Muffins 13
Vegetable Kabobs, Potato 5
Vegetable Omelettes, Spicy 12
Vegetable Pearl Salad 1
Vegetable Spanish Rice 5
Vegetables, Bulgur 4
Vegetables, Curry-Glazed 4
Vegetables, Honey-Garlic Glazed 4
Vegetables, Maple-Glazed 4
Veggie Pockets, Roasted 4
Vinaigrette, see also Dressing
Citrus Balsamic 1
Honey Mustard 1
Lemon Oregano 3
Maple Syrup 3
Spicy Lime 2
Sweet Lime 1

W

Walnut Green Salad 1
Wedges, Mushroom Pasta 12
Wedges, Pesto Potato 4

Y

Yam Hash, Spiced 5

Z

Zesty Chicken Kabobs 9
Zucchini Frittata, Ribbon 14

Recipe Notes

Recipe Notes

Recipe Notes

The Company's Coming Story

Jean Paré (pronounced "jeen PAIR-ee") grew up understanding that the combination of family, friends and home cooking is the best recipe for a good life. From her mother, she learned to appreciate good cooking, while her father praised even her earliest attempts in the kitchen. When Jean left home, she took with her a love of cooking, many family recipes and an intriguing desire to read cookbooks as if they were novels!

"never share a recipe you wouldn't use yourself"

In 1963, when her four children had all reached school age, Jean volunteered to cater the 50th Anniversary of the Vermilion School of Agriculture, now Lakeland College, in Alberta, Canada. Working out of her home, Jean prepared a dinner for more than 1,000 people, which launched a flourishing catering operation that continued for over 18 years. During that time, she had countless opportunities to test new ideas with immediate feedback—resulting in empty plates and contented customers! Whether preparing cocktail sandwiches for a house party or serving a hot meal for 1,500 people, Jean Paré earned a reputation for good food, courteous service and reasonable prices.

As requests for her recipes mounted, Jean was often asked the question, "Why don't you write a cookbook?" Jean responded by teaming up with her son, Grant Lovig, in the fall of 1980 to form Company's Coming Publishing Limited. The publication of *150 Delicious Squares* on April 14, 1981 marked the debut of what would soon become one of the world's most popular cookbook series.

The company has grown since those early days when Jean worked from a spare bedroom in her home. Today, she continues to write recipes while working closely with the staff of the Recipe Factory, as the Company's Coming test kitchen is affectionately known. There she fills the role of mentor, assisting with the development of recipes people most want to use for everyday cooking and easy entertaining. Every Company's Coming recipe is *kitchen-tested* before it's approved for publication.

Jean's daughter, Gail Lovig, is responsible for marketing and distribution, leading a team that includes sales personnel located in major cities across Canada. In addition, Company's Coming cookbooks are published and distributed under licence in the United States, Australia and other world markets. Bestsellers many times over in English, Company's Coming cookbooks have also been published in French and Spanish.

Familiar and trusted in home kitchens around the world, Company's Coming cookbooks are offered in a variety of formats. Highly regarded as kitchen workbooks, the softcover Original Series, with its lay-flat plastic comb binding, is still a favourite among readers.

Jean Paré's approach to cooking has always called for *quick and easy recipes* using *everyday ingredients*. That view has served her well. The recipient of many awards, including the Queen Elizabeth Golden Jubilee medal, Jean was appointed a Member of the Order of Canada, her country's highest lifetime achievement honour.

Jean continues to gain new supporters by adhering to what she calls The Golden Rule of Cooking: *"Never share a recipe you wouldn't use yourself."* It's an approach that works—millions of times over!

160